CHASING DREAMS

in the

Boondocks:

A Golf Course Comes to Life

by Bill Haney

To Doug —
Old friends are the best —
Warmest regards,
Bill Haney
26 July 2004

CROFTON CREEK PRESS

SOUTH BOARDMAN, MICHIGAN

Text © 2004 by Bill Haney
Illustrations © 2004 Joe Simko

First Edition
10 9 8 7 6 5 4 3 2 1

Published by Crofton Creek Press
2303 Gregg Road SW
South Boardman, Michigan 49680
E-mail: publisher@croftoncreek.com
Web site: www.croftoncreek.com

FOR MARCY AND THE KIDS

Sisyphus was given to exemplary punishment: the Judges of the Dead showed him a huge block of stone and ordered him to roll it up the brow of a hill and topple it down the further slope. He has never yet succeeded in doing so. As soon as he has almost reached the summit, he is forced back by the weight of the shameless stone, which bounces to the very bottom once more, where he wearily retrieves it and must begin all over again, though sweat bathes him limbs, and a cloud of dust rises above his head.

The Greek Myth of Sisyphus

1·9·6·6

One

As we came around a curve we saw a big red barn on a small knoll. Just fifty yards farther east stood a white two-story farmhouse on the north side of Curtis Road.

I slowed the station wagon as Marcy checked the newspaper ad to compare the address. No house number in sight, but this could be the place in the listing. More likely it would be another dry run, just another summer Sunday drive in the Michigan countryside.

In six years we had looked at more than a hundred farms and vacant parcels, so I had no special enthusiasm for the ad that read:

> Fifty-five acres fifteen minutes from city of Jackson, half-hour from Ann Arbor. Two-story frame house, newly decorated. Michigan hay barn, cement block milk house, 30 by 60 foot pole barn. Five acres pure hardwoods. Thirty acres in crop. Trout stream. Gently rolling. $23,500.

This place sounded promising enough to look at, but so had dozens of others.

Beyond the buildings, those fifty-five acres lay in a patchwork quilt of light and darker green hues, here a field of pasture grass, there a tall stand of ripening corn, and farther out some unfamiliar silage crops, all this surrounding a rectangular stand of mature oak and hickory. In the waves of July afternoon heat, that dense, dark woods floated like an island on an emerald sea. Easy enough to envision a fairway sweeping up the slope, alongside the woods, then doglegging left to a green tucked into an elbow atop that distant ridge. A test for any golfer, a hole like that.

It's only a first glance, I cautioned myself, but the place shows more potential than anything we have seen in six years of scouting.

The barn was the style popular throughout the southern counties of Michigan after the Civil War, erected by returning veterans. Still, if it was indeed a century old it didn't look its age. The house, probably just as old, sported a fresh coat of white paint on its clapboard sides and its west face gleamed in the bright summer afternoon. The rest of the house hunkered in shade beneath the massive arms of three majestic elms. Marcy would be the one to decide on the acceptability of the house, but to me it sure looked livable. Then again, after the glimpse of the enticing woods and rolling fields, this could have been the Bates Motel and I would have said, Well, isn't that charming?

I eased the Olds wagon off blacktopped Curtis Road and north onto the horseshoe-shaped gravel driveway. The kids hung out the open car windows, bug-eyed at the red hay barn. We crunched slowly through the gravel, easing past the cement-block milk house and, looking to our left, saw still another outbuilding on the north side of the hay barn, this one a large, recently built pole barn. So, three nice outbuildings—very encouraging.

A large man in plaid work shirt and dungarees stood in the cool elm shade, watering a bed of freshly planted flowers from a garden hose. This would be, I guessed from my phone call responding to the newspaper ad, Daryle Heselschwerdt. I had checked him out and learned he was the area's shrewdest cattleman and wheeler-dealer trader in failed farms. He would pay cash, the story went, harvest the standing crops, auction the equipment, livestock, and furniture, spiff up the house, and sell the place for a good profit.

Sunlight glinted off the shimmering stream gushing from the hose, and Daryle, seeing us turn into the driveway, made a show of drinking that water, savoring it, advertising its cool purity. He needn't have bothered. He could have been Norman Bates himself, clutching a butcher's knife, grinning fiendishly, and still I would have walked up to him and asked if we could have a look at the place.

But we had seen several places that showed well, only to reveal fatal flaws beneath the veneer. Despite this good first impression, many things would have to pass muster with Marcy and me before we would make an offer on this fifty-five-acre farm in Grass Lake Township, Jackson County, Michigan. I had my list of deal-breakers and Marcy definitely had hers. If it came down to a tiebreaker, we both knew that Marcy, as the mother of our four small kids, held the trump card.

Marcy and I got out of the car, followed quickly by Mark, Jennifer, Patrick, and Rebecca. Mark, the old-timer of our little gang of four, had just turned six, so he and five-year-old Jenni made sure the two young ones didn't slam fingers in the car doors.

Daryle smiled bashfully as he came toward us. He was a husky six-footer, perhaps thirty-five years old, looking every bit the farmer from sunburned forehead down to his sturdy boots. Everything about him said this man is used to having it his way.

He waved toward the kids.

"Quite a little brood you got there. What about it, kids, you got names?"

With his shy smile and disarming manner, Mr. Daryle Heselschwerdt seemed—as my sources suggested would be true—in a cheerful mood for a man selling his farm.

I introduced Marcy and the kids to Daryle. He wondered how Marcy managed, having four children with the oldest only six. I told him I wondered the same thing myself.

"You saw the ad in the *Ann Arbor News*," Daryle said. "Lots of folks from the university looking for land in the country. This is only nineteen miles west of Ann Arbor—maybe thirty minutes if you poke along on the back roads instead of the highway—but some of them act like it's halfway across the state."

We had seen a car drive out the other end of the big horseshoe driveway as we drove in and for a moment I was afraid it would be just our luck to have missed out on the first really promising place we had seen in six years of sporadic shopping. So I asked if the place was still for sale. Daryle said he supposed it was, and asked if we wanted to look around.

Setting aside the thorny problem that fifty-five acres was simply not enough, the property appeared to be closer to perfect than I thought we would ever find. We had looked at so many places, at so many parcels. Many had some or most of what we needed, but always there was something major lacking. Often the something major was affordability.

We knew from the ad that this place was well below the $28,000 we had set as our absolute upper limit. The question was, did it have the other ingredients. One key requirement was enough land to build at least a very spacious nine holes if not a full eighteen. We already knew that there wasn't enough land in this parcel, so we'd have to be able to buy an adjacent piece. And the land had to be right, which meant terrain that was neither totally flat nor extremely hilly or rugged. Some trees, but not fully wooded—preferably a mixture of open land that had been farmed prudently, small stands of trees here and there, and water. That water could be a river or stream, a lake or ponds, or a spring-fed marsh. Water was vital, whatever the source.

The soil had to be good enough to sustain a decent stand of grass, but it need not be rich bottomland. Land like that would come at a premium and so we actually preferred something a notch or two below prime farming soil. But although the old white farmhouse looked decent enough from the outside, we had been through too many places to get our hopes up.

We followed Daryle through the cool shade of the stately elms and around to the front. There was a solid front porch, freshly painted with white pillars and a battleship-gray deck. A sturdy front door. We stepped inside and onto the hardwood floor of a bare room with an irregular shape that looked like it should be set up with dining room furniture at one end and a sitting area at the other.

To the right was a living room with a large picture window facing south, which meant a view of the front yard and a nice mixed woods and crop fields across Curtis Road.

Next to the living room was a stairwell with one set of stairs up to the second floor and another set down to the basement. On the north side of the stairwell was a long, narrow, rectangular room that looked like it had been a spare bedroom but could easily become a playroom or storage room.

The entire first floor had hardwood floors and they recently had been refinished. I liked them just as they were but I knew Marcy wouldn't. She strongly preferred carpeting, and there was none in the entire house. That was a negative, but not insurmountable. Maybe I could persuade her that it was actually a positive because then we could put in our own choices of carpeting—if we ever had money enough to buy it.

Marcy brightened as she walked into a big country kitchen that had been freshly remodeled. New cabinets and lots of them. The walls had just been paneled and there was a new linoleum floor covering. New ceiling tile and a bright overhead light fixture. There was plenty of counter space and it too was new. Sunlight streamed through a large, low, south window and, on the west wall and above the big country sink, a new window that gave a nice view of the woods to the northwest. Daryle said he had just installed that window, but regrettably it was set too high for Marcy and the children to be able to see out of it. Marcy smiled at the generous cupboards.

A doorway on the north wall of the kitchen opened to a laundry room, which in turn was connected to what Daryle called a mudroom where boots and heavy coats could be shed. An exterior door led out onto a small concrete-slab porch, near which we had parked the station wagon. The porch had waist-high brick walls topped with sandstone slabs. A set of eight concrete steps led down to the lawn and the steps were flanked with planters built into the porch wall. Between the back porch and the driveway, there was a small bed of iris and other perennial flowers framed off from the lawn with railroad ties.

We hadn't seen the upstairs, the basement, or the outbuildings yet, but Marcy was clearly satisfied with the first floor. I asked her what she thought of the house and she nodded, So far, so good. Marcy said if I wanted to take Mark out onto the land she'd take Jen, Pat, and Beck and look at the upstairs.

"We need to get a good sense of how the property lies out, Mr. Heselschwerdt," I said. "How far out can we go?"

"Far as you want, you don't mind getting your shoes dirty."

Mark tugged at my arm. "I'm going too, right?"

"If you come along, little fella," Daryle said, "might better stay close to your pa. Wouldn't want to lose you in the wilds."

Daryle opened a gate into a field with a lush stand of a tall silage crop I didn't recognize. Beyond that field lay a patchwork quilt of corn, pasture, and fallow fields as far as we could see, which was to a ridge just beyond and to the right of the mature stand of hardwoods about two hundred yards to the northwest. Well beyond that ridge there seemed to be a valley; some four hundred yards farther I could make out the tops of willow trees. And beyond the willow trees stood a sun-baked hill, the highest ground in sight. I doubted that hill was on this property and asked Daryle about it.

"This property goes a ways past those willows yonder. The trout stream runs through there, they call it Willow Creek. This place is fifty-five acres, more or less, and it's in the shape of a capital L, but the bottom part of the L is fatter and the vertical part shorter than an L this young fella here would draw in penmanship class." Daryle squatted down and in the loose dirt he drew a map as he talked, making X's for the house and barns and a curve for the hill. "That hill you're looking at would be on the Smedley's land. Gladys and Kent Smedley, they own fifty or so acres to the west and north of this parcel. Great view from up there."

"Is there crop growing on there? Looks a little steep for farming."

"No, that's just native grass and weeds. The story goes that old Nate Fish tried plowing that forty-fifty years ago but it's mostly blow sand and Nate gave it up for a bad idea. Which it was. And not the first or last one Nate Fish ever had."

We walked farther and Daryle stopped again.

"That hill and ridge wouldn't pay out on anything but growing grass. Nice patch of blackberries, though, partway down the hill. Old Gladys makes a great pie out of them. She's kind of the township character. Does water witching, makes black walnut cookies like to set your teeth on edge, and sees UFOs. You got a skeleton in your closet, Glad'll coax it out and set it in the front room. Got a tongue on her make a longshoreman turn red. Great old gal though. Make a good neighbor. Wouldn't be anybody trespassing you from the north, that's for sure."

We walked through a field of a cornlike crop with stalks so tall that before we had gone two hundred yards and into a shallow valley, we could no longer look back and see the house or barns.

"Look at that, Daddy. A big blue rock." Mark was pointing to a big boulder near the corner post to another field, this one planted to feed corn.

"You like big rocks, sonny?" Daryle asked, lifting Mark up onto the boulder where he could now see the horizon. I wondered where Mark got the idea the rock was blue; it looked pink to me.

"Well," Daryle said, "this would be the place for a boy who likes rocks. The glacier left some good-sized stones out there beyond the woods. I've got trip-bottoms on my five-bottom plow and I've found a few real lunkers down there a couple feet. This one here's a pebble compared with some out there."

Daryle thought about how that might sound and then went on. "Course, most of the rocks have been cleaned out over the years, so there's only a few left by now, probably. And this land is so fertile, well, you can tell that by how healthy these crops are."

Continuing north, we passed through another field and skirted a small marsh east of the woods. There was a single willow tree at the edge of the marsh. Looking back south toward the house, I already had a vague idea how that marsh and willow tree might fit into a layout.

"Spring fed," Daryle said. "If I was going to keep the place, I'd bring in a dragline crane, gouge that marsh down eight-ten feet, have me a freshwater pond right there. Nice sweet water for the livestock. See over there to the right? That's another springs. You can see the cattails, just this side of that black walnut tree there that was hit by lightning some time ago. Still alive though, lots of nuts. That's the property line on the base of the L that I was telling you about. And what would be the vertical staff of the L, that runs out there half a mile all told, toward the Smedley Hill and to the right of it."

"The Smedleys don't own that?"

"No, that'd be Ed Harrison's place. His soil's so poor you couldn't raise your voice on it. Ed Harrison, he's another story." He paused as if remembering something. "Say, that ad you saw in the newspaper? They left out that this year's crops don't go with the sale. You understand how that works, right?"

I told Daryle if we were to proceed, it was okay with us that he got to harvest the standing crops. He nodded and led us up a gentle rise and toward the woods. As we turned to head in that direction, I caught a fleeting glimpse of a slightly built figure in a faded blue denim jacket and a tan cap stepping behind a tree on Harrison's land.

"Is that one of the neighbors, Mr. Heselschwerdt?"

Daryle turned and looked where I was pointing.

"Don't see anybody. Where?"

"He was near that tree with the broken limb hanging down."

"Probably one of the Coppernoll boys. Anyhow, that stand over there holds four-point-seven acres of pure hardwood. I know the ad said five. Mostly white oak, some hickory. Could have sold the board feet off to a lumber merchant for a good price, but the woods adds something to the place."

"How old do you figure these trees are?"

"Just a guess, say sixty-seventy years old. Those big ones maybe a hundred. Most likely the hay barn and house were built with wood from the ancestors of these trees. Over there, the west edge of the woods is the property line and there's some hackberry in there. I tell you that because those berries are toxic to livestock. Would you be keeping cattle or horses?"

"No cattle, that's for sure. As for horses—"

"Got to have a pony for the young one here. How about it, Mark, is it? What would you say about a pony?"

Mark's eyes got big and a wide smile spread across his face.

"Tell you what, Mark. Your dad buys this place, I'll get you a pony of your very own. And a saddle just the right size for you. Your little brother and your two sisters would have to grow up to your size to fit into it. What'd you think of that?"

Mark's grin showed what he thought of it.

We walked to the sandy ridge and looked down at the marsh below.

"Can't get across the marsh on foot," Daryle said and spread his arm out to define the territory. "The very top of the long leg of that L-shape I mentioned continues right through the marsh and maybe another four hundred feet of firm ground the other side. You could bring in a dragline and make a pond there, throw off the spoil to the side for a land bridge to get you one side to the other."

As he talked, I was already envisioning a par three hole with a tee on the far side requiring a carry of 150 to 180 yards to a green on that low knoll just below where we stood. Still farther north and west, the Smedley property and their big hill. I turned and looked south, at the house and barn more than 600 yards away—nice rolling terrain all the way. Sure, a nice pair of long holes could run parallel there, but to do that would use up too much land and I already knew that with only fifty-five acres we didn't have enough for a full-sized nine-hole layout.

"Let's go back a different route," Daryle said, "cut through the woods on the way."

We stepped into the woods and walked into a different world. The air was cool and clean and the only sound was the soft rustling of leaves far above. The oaks, soaring seventy feet and more, swayed gently as their topmost branches bent before a wind we couldn't feel. The trunks stretched twenty to thirty feet before the first sizable limb. It was a pity the stand hadn't been cared for. Some trees were only five or six feet apart and should have been thinned decades ago.

If Daryle was right, soon after the Civil War, trees from this same stand had yielded the lumber for the frame of the house and the massive hand-hewn timbers of the barn. There were some four hundred white oak and hickory with up to three-foot-diameter trunks at chest height.

Like much of the rest of the property, the floor of the woods had been neglected, even abused by previous residents. Here, a rotted frame of a manure wagon, there the rusted skeleton of a hay baler. Little pyramids of bottles, cans, broken dishes, stacks of rotting magazines and newspapers. Mounds of used-up tractor tires, and a mean-looking tangle of barbed wire fencing embracing decayed wooden fence posts. A serene woods treated as a trash dump.

We angled through the woods and came out at the corner closest to the barns. Mark had tramped his six-year-old legs the whole way without a complaint, taking it all in, never falling behind. When we got back to the house, we went right to the outside spigot and let the hose run until the water was cold, then had long drinks of the water Daryle had been showing off when we drove in.

"Comes from two hundred feet, through bedrock," Daryle said. "They tell me old Nate Fish used to say that water is ten thousand years old."

Whatever, it was delicious.

While Daryle charmed Mark about ponies, I went to take a look at the barns. The huge door of the big red barn rolled aside easily on its hanging tracks and I stepped into the cavernous upper level, amid neatly stacked hay bales. I climbed over the bales and, from an opening in the barn's north wall for a grain conveyor boom, looked out to see how the property lay off to the north. Good—several holes could be run north or south. While it's almost impossible to build a course without some east-west holes, you keep those to a minimum so golfers aren't playing into the sun hole after hole.

But there was one major problem with this property—there just wasn't enough of it. Unless every acre is usable, fifty-five acres is not enough to build a full-sized nine holes. And seldom is every acre of any parcel usable or available. You lose land to the maintenance buildings, clubhouse, parking lot, pro shop, practice range and, in our case, the house and yard. Also, on this place, there were wetlands and trees that we wouldn't disturb. The far hills were nice but while extreme rapid changes in elevation offer dramatic scenery, they also can make a piece of land less desirable if your clientele walks instead of rides power carts. Golf car rentals provide such a big portion of revenue that more and more golf courses were actually prohibiting walkers, but that was the opposite of the kind of course we intended to build.

The big golf course developer has ways of getting around almost any natural impediments. If he wants to push the land around, modern technology has provided the means to do it. If instead your goal is to build a golf course into the land with the least possible intrusion, you find yourself losing a couple acres here, ten acres there.

A swath of perhaps five acres alongside Willow Creek was wetlands. We'd have to find a harmfree way to get across Willow Creek and the marsh to bring into play the ten acres on the north side bordering the Smedleys.

Other complications took away even more land. We would lose nearly five acres by keeping the oak and hickory stand intact. The four-acre rectangular field lying west of the barns and between the road and the woods was big enough for one hole but not for two. So, maybe that becomes the practice range. And we knew that once we got into sketching possible layouts onto paper, there would be pieces here and there that weren't actual fairways and roughs, but just in-between places you went through to get from a green to the next tee. All in all, of the original fifty-five acres, we would probably have less than twenty-five acres available for maintained golf course grasses. Well less than half enough.

The character of the land, however, fit in with our concept of a natural Scottish-style course. Ours would not be a manicured, parkland course with specimen trees framing each green, neatly sculpted white-sand bunkers, and tiers of tees banked with landscape timbers or paver blocks, and fountains billowing spray umbrellas. Our course would be no country club with flower beds, tennis courts, and swimming pools. Then too, from a maintenance standpoint, a more natural character made sense because it could be mowed completely in half the time.

So, lots of good features but the size was an insurmountable negative.

Marcy was still in the house with Jenni, Pat, and Becky. Daryle and Mark were sitting on the back-porch concrete steps and I could guess what they were talking about.

I looked off to the east, where the bordering land was fallow fields. Maybe forty acres there, nearly flat, characterless. Good investment property for someone looking for premium residential building sites but not for my idea of a golf course.

To the west of the woods, twenty acres of fields that just might be usable. But doubtful.

Due north of the base of Daryle's famous L was a twenty-acre rectangle of land that had a little bit of promise. But, judging from the look on Daryle's face when he mentioned the quixotic Mr. Harrison as lord of that manor, that land would come with bad karma. Even if Harrison's parcel were big enough, perfect, and cheap, I had a feeling that it would come with more problems than we wanted to buy into.

That left the fifty or so acres to the northwest, the Smedley property, with its hills and ridges that were extensions of the topography, with Willow Creek and its marsh meandering through the heart of it, with sandy loam hills and plateaus rising above its north and south margins. Yes, the Smedley land would be ideal. For sure we had to find out whether it was available before even considering buying the old Nate Fish fifty-five from Daryle Heselschwerdt.

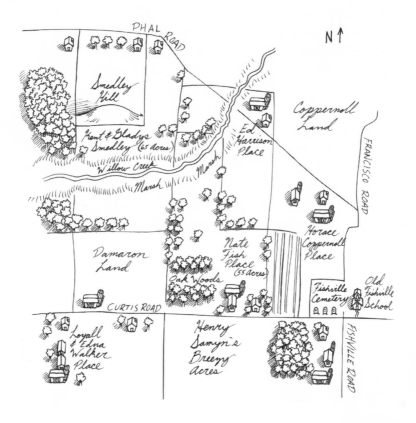

Marcy came out to see what Mark and I had learned on our walk. We had seen so much in the hour we were gone, I didn't know where to start. So I told Marcy I'd tell her about it in the car on the way back to Ann Arbor. She took me inside to show me the rest of the house.

Once up on the second level, it was quickly obvious that all the updating had been confined to the first floor of the house. The bumpy walls were plaster over lathe, clearly a long-ago do-it-yourself production—and the self who had done it was no pro. Some of the walls had been wallpapered over—the paper was yellowed, stained, and peeling. The largest bedroom was on the east end of the long rectangle, a smaller one to the west, and in between a cavernous walk-through bedroom with barn scene wallpaper. With partitions, paneling, and doors, that wide-open bedroom could be converted into a smaller third bedroom by cutting out space to make a hallway into the west bedroom. And there would still be room left over for a second full bath.

Throughout the second floor, the double-hung windows ran from the ceiling to within six inches of the floor. One nice thing about those windows was that they provided unimpeded views and probably a nice breeze, but Marcy was concerned about danger—the windows were too easily accessible to the children. The windows were of a style I had never seen before, with built-in screens that rolled up into cavities in the sill. Except that the screens had long ago crumbled to rusty dust.

Down in the basement, I saw something that was all–too familiar from my childhood: a huge furnace served by a coal stoker. It did not bring back warm memories. Well, I had the proper implement to fill that stoker because somehow, despite all the moving around, I still had the D-handle coal scoop I had used when I was a kid living in Big Beaver, Michigan.

The coal bin, furnace, and old stoker dominated nearly half the basement. Another quarter had a concrete floor and old shelves used for storing things that would get dusty and moldy until one day they were thrown away. The pump and wellhead squatted on bare earth in the other corner, nearest the stairway. The walls were Michigan fieldstone, white-washed not too long ago. A cellar door opened to concrete steps leading up to the backyard, with the opening covered with a pair of broken and rotted doors.

The basement was not a plus, but it was serviceable, and if a basement had turned out to be the nicest feature of any house, we wouldn't be making an offer anyhow.

We returned to the main floor and I saw Daryle on the front lawn, still talking with Mark about the pony of the little guy's dreams.

There was only one question left to ask Marcy.

"Well?"

"I like the kitchen, lots of cupboards. This first floor is pretty good, with the new paneling. We'd have to get lots of rugs or carpets. I'm sure there's much work we're not seeing. Wiring. Insulation. I don't know about that coal furnace. The water is real good. One bathroom won't do it. And we'd have a ton of work to do on that second floor." She paused, looked around.

Marcy looked out the windows, nodding her head. "We could live here," she said. "The house would be okay, after a lot of work. But what about the barns, the land?"

I told her the barns were very good, lots of space. We'd have to convert the milk house to locker rooms and bathrooms. The pro shop could go somewhere in the lower level of the barn, nice hand-hewn timbers, nice rustic feel. As for the land, no, there isn't enough, but there is vacant land on three sides. There might be a chance we can add what we need; we'd be crazy to buy this land before we knew that.

"So," Marcy said, "what do we do now?"

"See if he'll take a five-hundred dollar deposit."

Marcy looked at me and smiled. She knew I was already hooked. And she knew as well as I did how foolish it was to make an offer before checking for adjacent available land. But she also realized this was the best we had seen in years of looking.

"Are you going to offer him his asking price?"

"Yeah. Sure, he might take less and probably would. But on the other hand, this is the best we've seen in six years of looking. And it's several thousand less than we were expecting to have to pay. I'd hate to get haggling with him and lose it."

She nodded and handed me the checkbook. I went out to the front porch to ask Mr. Daryle Heselschwerdt how to spell his name.

"Just like it sounds," he said with a sly laugh, "except there's an E on the end," a line he had much practice with.

WE PULLED OUT OF THE DRIVEWAY and took one last lingering look. The house, the barns, the land—it was all somehow different now. We were now looking at it as a place where we would be living in just a few weeks. On land where we would build a golf course. Or at least half of one if we didn't get lucky on next-door acreage.

Instead of going back the way we had driven in, I turned east onto Curtis Road. We all wanted to see what was to be found in this new neighborhood. We wanted to see if there was a view of the new home-stead from another direction.

In a half of a mile we came to a crossroads. Near the northwest corner, a tiny long-abandoned cemetery. A sign said Fishville Road.

Hmm. Daryle had mentioned that the place we were buying had long been known as the Nate Fish place.

On the southwest corner was the farmhouse and barns for the farm that extended west and whose hardwood stand and fields faced our soon-to-be new home. There was a big weathered white sign on the peak of the barn: Breezy Acres. Henry Samyn. Kitty-corner from Mr. Henry Samyn's homestead, smack on the northeast corner, was a small, very old brick building. It was now apparently a home but had long been a one-room schoolhouse, the original Fishville School.

We turned south onto the gravel Fishville Road to see what might be seen. Crop fields. A couple frame houses. A stand of Christmas trees. More stands of Christmas trees. Dirt lanes winding between stands of Douglas fir here, Colorado blue spruce there. And a couple of low outbuildings encircling a fleet of veteran tractors and trailers. Beyond, many, many more Christmas trees. And a sign proclaiming this place, appropriately, as Christmas Tree Lane farm. Pony-drawn sleigh rides. Cut your own or we cut. Free hot chocolate, coffee. Christmas decorations. Cookies and prizes for the kids. Our kids agreed that sounded pretty good.

We continued along, over winding, hilly roads. Much of the same wherever we looked: farm fields, red barns, the occasional recent-vintage brick home probably built by a family whose wage earners worked in the city of Jackson to the west or one of the auto plants in Chelsea or Manchester to the east and south. We wandered around, pulling over to the side of the road now and then to find on Marcy's map just where we were. Some of the farms, like ones identified as one or another Coppernoll family, seemed prosperous. A couple spreads on Norvell Road sported nearly new barns and silos, with hundreds of level acres under crop and low-profile working oil wells that perhaps pumped up the modest cash flow.

Heading north now, on Norvell Road, about three miles from the Nate Fish place, we came upon the high school and soon coasted into a residential section of the village of Grass Lake. I recalled from a Michigan history book that this village was much the same as hundreds of other hamlets in Michigan whose destinies were altered by the automobile.

In the late 1800s, this was a thriving community of more than a thousand souls, energized by an infusion of money from tourists seeking health enhancement at the town's mineral waters spa. Then the mineral waters ran out and Grass Lake Village's boom times were history. At the turn of the century, the Inter-Urban electric rail line connected Grass Lake to Detroit and Jackson, many of those visitors staying over in the village before making connections on a spur line to the Wolf Lake gambling casino ten minutes to the south. But by the 1920s, the automobile drove the electric car line out of business, new roads bypassed the town, and Grass Lake village was soon the village that time forgot.

What remained was quaint. We passed through several blocks of residences and turned west onto the main drag. Several blocks of impressive century-old frame homes, most of them in tidy shape. This was The Block, where the titans of Grass Lake commerce had lived in the town's heyday as a spa.

Then, one more block and we were into the business section. A couple of gas stations, Dairy Freeze, furniture store, Braun's Pharmacy, Wolfinger's Hardware, the local variant of every town's We-Buy-Junk/ We-Sell-Antiques Shoppe, two restaurants, a few other establishments and, dominating the downtown, one very distinctive building. Made from Michigan fieldstones and executed with an architectural flair, complete with stained-glass windows above the doorway entrance, was what appeared to be a train station. In fact, as we learned from the young man filling our gas tank at the Sinclair station next door, for more than a century the eye-catching structure indeed had been a bustling train depot. Now it was the home of the number one source of information in the township: The *Grass Lake News*. We picked up a copy of the little tabloid newspaper to study it at home later.

The teenaged boy at the gas station spoke highly of the burgers and shakes at the Dairy Freeze. We took his advice, then headed back to Ann Arbor with full stomachs. The kids quieted down or went to sleep and in the rare silence Marcy and I were lost in separate thoughts.

I had timed the trip coming out and was doing it again heading back to see if it was actually nineteen miles and thirty minutes to the west edge of Ann Arbor. But to get to work every day, I'd have to loop around the city several miles to get to Bendix Aerospace Systems Division on the far northeast side. And that meant driving into the sun both ways each day. Again. It seemed we always ended up living west of where I worked.

Well, small price to pay to realize a dream, that's for sure. There were bigger questions—the quality of life in general, for the kids, for Marcy. It wasn't a problem for me—I had grown up shoveling coal into a stoker. And even that stoker was a miracle of modern technology to me. Until I was twelve, my family was without an indoor toilet and instead of a bedroom, I slept on the front porch in the warm months and on a couch or the living room floor when it was cold outside. I was in the sixth grade when my mother got a small inheritance and we went really upscale and replaced the coal stoker with a used oil burner that inserted into the existing furnace. That freed up space in the basement because we no longer needed a coal bin, so in that spot Dad built me a bedroom out of two-by-fours and Sheetrock panels faced with knotty-pine paper that looked almost like real wood.

A return to tending a coal stoker was acceptable to me. But for the whole family, this move would mean we'd be giving up the Lookout Circle house, the only new home we had ever lived in. We'd be leaving our made-to-order ranch house with the raised hearth fireplace and the genuine walnut paneling, sitting there regally on the choicest lot in the subdivision, a lot for which we had paid an extra three hundred dollars just to be under the shade of the grand old oak in the front yard. It was the only home the kids had known, with Mark now barely six, Jenni just turned five, Pat three, and Rebecca two. They had friends there, and their early childhood memories. Mark had just learned to ride his first two-wheeler and had proudly made it all the way around the block and back home again, earning his first silver dollar.

On that street, five houses down, Jenni's little girlfriend was hit in the temple by her sister's wild swing of a golf club and died. It was on that street that a gust of wind caught the front screen door, slaming it so hard it shattered, sending a shard deep into Marcy's upper arm, blood spurting out and she ignoring it as she picked up baby Patrick from the bouncy chair and saw razor-sharp fragments all around and under where he had lain but somehow found not a scratch on him.

That was the Lookout Circle house and it was perfect for our growing family in almost every way. Heck, we could sit on our own front lawn on Fourth of July evenings and watch the fireworks zooming up from the hollow beyond as if staged for our exclusive enjoyment. And walk to

Buster's Market on the corner. Or to the osteopath two blocks farther. And see the great snowy owl perched on the telephone pole on his way north in the spring, south in the fall.

So, we were giving that up. All that. And for what? To move to a century-old house with a coal stoker. A house that had been spruced up to sell, that's what. But a house that in the winter was probably drafty with cold hardwood floors and not a stitch of carpet that Marcy could walk on barefoot. One bathroom. Old wiring and plumbing, you could be sure of that. And what about that basement. A Michigan basement, he called it, a folksy name for a crypt with mostly fieldstone walls and bare dirt where sat the well pump and tank.

I looked at Marcy, who was deep in thought. I could guess what about.

The bare floors. A single bathroom with an old tub. The unfinished second floor. And those cellar steps, I saw how she looked at them. Those steps up to the backyard, topped with that rotted hatch door. That cellar door—the entire basement—an accident just biding its time. Every good rainstorm, there we'd be, I could see it now, down there bailing water. A regular bucket brigade, Marcy there ankle-deep in the quagmire, fill the bucket, hand the bucket to a kid, poor little kid pass the bucket along to a brother or sister. Fill the bucket, pass the bucket, pour the bucket out, the water streaming in through the cracks between Nate Fish's fieldstones faster than we can bail it out, but can't stop now, have to fill the bucket, reach for another in slow motion like zombies until the gaunt little waifs drop from exhaustion and we all float away, across the flooded fairways, down the sluice to Walker's Lake, through the Raisin River system, into Lake Erie, over Niagara Falls, and right out into the Atlantic Ocean.

All because I just had to build a golf course.

"This is really dumb," I said, more to myself.

"What?"

"This whole thing. Moving. Moving out to the country. To Jackson County. Moving anywhere away from the nice home we've just built. A neighborhood we like. The kids' friends and all. The neighbor friends you have there. Doctors, dentists. Close to my work. Everything. And for what? To build a golf course with whatever we gain from selling our house. And we don't even have it listed yet. And even if we also sell the Hampshire Street house we're renting out—or would be if we still had renters. For sure we'd have to sell that too. Even then, fifty-five acres isn't enough. We'd have to buy some connecting land."

"There's vacant land on three sides. There's the Smedley place that Daryle—"

"We don't know that. They hear we're building a golf course, they'll want an arm and a leg, presuming they'd sell at any price. Sure, they'll hold out, figuring land on a golf course will be worth a fortune some day. Even so, where's the money come from to buy more land? Here we put down a deposit and we have no idea if—"

"Bill, this is what you wanted to do. This is what has to be done to do it."

Silent for a time. I'm thinking, Does the world really need another golf course? Does Michigan? This state already has more golf courses open to the public than any other—incredible considering it only has a six-month season.

"I know," I said. "But now . . ."

"Look, since the first day I met you you've said you were going to build a golf course. That you'd done everything else a person could do on a golf course except actually design and build one. I've been hearing that for ten years now. And we've looked at I don't know how many places. There's been something wrong with every one of them. Not enough land. Wrong kind of land. Great land, no buildings. Great house and barns, too much money. Great house, outbuildings, and land, right price, but no water. Hey, here's a place that sounds perfect, but it happens to be in New Zealand."

"Yeah, right. This is the first place that really has what we need. That we can afford."

"And that we just wrote a five-hundred-dollar check to hold."

More silence.

"If you're going to get cold feet now," Marcy said, "what's it going to be like when the going gets tough? When—I don't know—the irrigation system breaks down? The weather turns bad and the grass won't grow?"

Silence again.

"That stuff I can handle," I said. "I'm used to cleaning up after mistakes. I can deal with not having enough money, with old, broken equipment, and with having to learn how to do things myself because I can't afford to pay to have someone else do it. That part is not what has me worried."

"Then what?"

"I don't know. I guess it's just that, this is it. All those years thinking about this, looking for just the right place. Now what it comes down to is . . . my God, the old Nate Fish farm. Not enough land. Nowhere near enough money to fix up the house, to buy equipment and supplies. Maybe we should stop the check."

Marcy shook her head. "Do you really think you'd ever be happy with yourself if you did that?"

Maybe that was what I wanted her to say. That way when it turned into a total disaster, it wouldn't be on my head alone. When it sapped every cent we had or could ever earn and left us hopelessly in debt, when the old farmhouse fell down around our ears and the parched grass curled up like a burnt leaf and died before our eyes and the nearby farmers and fair-weather friends got together and hooted at me for having such a stupid idea, and when—worst of all—the dream of building my own golf course had turned into a nightmare from which I could never awaken and never again could I fantasize about how creatively fulfilling it would be, how rich a growing-up place it would make for the kids, and maybe most of all how damn much fun it would be to design and build my own golf course, maybe then I'd have someone else to share the blame with.

So it was a relief to hear Marcy determined to press on. More determined, for sure, at this moment than I. But then another wave of doubt washed over me because with her support that meant there was indeed no turning back.

"So this is it, then?" I said. "We do it?"

"If you don't do it now," Marcy said, and I knew it was the last word that could be said on the subject, "you never will."

Two

I t was a different kind of voice than I was used to hearing on my phone at Bendix Aerospace Systems Division. Familiar somehow, but I couldn't place it. This was no scientist or engineer.

"Mr. Haney, you were wondering about those big elm trees by the house looking off color? Well, I checked it with a fellow knows his trees and he says to tell you those are American elms. So you don't need to worry about them being Dutch elms."

Daryle knew what that meant. I knew what that meant. It was only American elms that were susceptible to Dutch elm disease and not one in a thousand survived it. Those great old elms were going to die and the house would be standing there stark and barren without them. Not only that, I would have to pay to have them taken down because they were far too close to the house and, with base diameters up to four feet, way too big for me to do it. We had already agreed on the price and were set to close in one week on the place. Marcy and I were committed to following through, even allowing for the loss of the trees.

Daryle obviously was concerned I might back out. Maybe the trees gave me some leverage to work down the price. But were there more ticking bombs, Marcy and I knew little about life in rural Jackson County. We knew that people in sophisticated, affluent Ann Arbor considered Jackson County to be only a small step up from Siberia, a fit place only for farmers and blue-collar hourly workers. That was okay with us, but I wondered if there was something about the Nate Fish place I didn't know, something serious. That would be no surprise. We had looked at it only an hour or so before I was writing a check to Daryle with an E, a fellow who had done deals like this far more often than I.

But even if there was some problem, some secret we would learn only too late, the place was still worth the gamble. It was the only property we had seen in years of looking that came remotely close to meeting our requirements, not the least of which was that the price was right.

"Oh, one more thing," Daryle said, "tell little Mark, after we close on the place we'll go down to the Napoleon horse auction. There's a nice mare coming up in a few weeks. Gentle. Fit your little cowboy just fine."

THE GOING-AWAY PARTY would have been more enjoyable if we hadn't been the guests of honor.

I had gone to a lot of parties and thrown more than a few; I always had fun. But the few times Marcy and I were the center of attention, I would have rather spent the evening in a cave.

There was an awkward feeling to this gathering at first because barely two weeks ago we had stunned these good friends with the news that we were moving.

"Moving? You're moving? I can't believe it. How could this happen so fast?"

That was the response we heard again and again from our neighbors on Lookout Circle when we told them we had just closed on a farm in Jackson County, that in a week or so, we would be leaving.

Well, it was hard for us to believe it, too. We had looked at so many places for so many years, we had come to accept that we might never find the place.

It always seemed to me that it was good to feel bad about leaving a job or a neighborhood. If you liked it where you were then it meant you were leaving not just to escape a situation but to go to something new that was even better. If that was true, then it was understandable that Marcy, the kids, and I all felt miserable about leaving Ann Arbor. We were leaving a new home in a friendly neighborhood. The diverse, stimulating environment of a major university town would be replaced by downright rustic country living where you had to drive a fair piece for whatever it was you might want.

The bon voyage party was made easier because we knew we would keep seeing many of these people, including three of our closest neighbors. Wayne Wrightman would come out in a couple days to erect a rooftop antenna and install that modern miracle, our first color TV set. Chuck Wilson, registered surveyor and golfing companion, had promised to let me hold the surveyor's rod while he manned the transit for a proper survey of our new land. Tom Lyndon knew I'd definitely be calling on him for irrigation expertise and, I hoped, for a good deal some day on irrigation equipment. And Marcy would trek back for the Friday night bowling league with the neighborhood ladies and keep those friendships alive.

Yes, it was a major relief, we responded again and again, that we sold our Ann Arbor home so quickly and for $24,500—$5,000 more than we had paid to have it built three years previously. For once we were on the right side of a real estate transaction. In the same week we also sold our previous home, which we had been renting out, profiting $3,000 on that transaction. Now we were on a roll.

Once the previous mortgages and real-estate agent fees were paid off and the new down payment was made on the ten-year land contract with Daryle, we had slightly more than $5,000 left. And all we had to do was make a long list of improvements on the old Nate Fish house, buy equipment and supplies, and build a golf course. The first call on that money—and whatever other cash we could set aside from my Bendix salary and income from freelance writing—would be to make the house as pleasant and comfortable as possible.

I imagined it wouldn't be more than one winter before we'd be replacing the coal stoker gravity furnace with a forced-air oil burner, insulating the paper-thin walls, carpeting the floors, installing new windows, paneling over bumpy walls, and turning the wide-open second floor into three bedrooms and a second full bath. There would be wiring to upgrade, and plumbing. For the first time we'd be living without city water and sewers. The closest sidewalk was five miles away.

That far out in the country, the TV antenna Wayne would erect would have to have a big array on a high mast and a rotator. And while the siding had been freshly painted, I suspected the paint covered very weathered if not decaying clapboards that would one day soon need covering with new siding. The front windows stared like wide-open eyes with no lashes or brows and I supposed I'd end up putting decorative shutters all around to spruce the place up. That decaying cellar door would have to be replaced right away and for sure I'd have to run heat to the mudroom, insulate the pipes, and put up storm windows all around.

I didn't want to do the math. I didn't want to know how little that would leave to build a golf course. To even get started on the land we would have to buy a tractor, mowers, construction equipment, seed, fertilizer, and lots of materials. At some point, we'd have to convert the barn into men's and women's locker rooms, a maintenance area, and a pro shop/clubhouse.

Looking farther ahead, to a time when the course was producing money instead of draining it, the upper level of the big hay barn might house a country restaurant. When that far-off day came we could knock out some of the north wall, where the granary now stood, and put in ceiling-to-floor windows to create a great view of the course.

No way could we afford contractors for even a fraction of those projects, but there were a couple of major tasks for which we simply would have to bring in professionals. Some of the heavy lifting—building the ponds, rough grading the greens and tees—would take large equipment and skilled operators. The rest, we'd have to do ourselves.

So, what resources did we have to apply against this venture? A bit over $5,000 where ten times that wouldn't be enough.

As for human resources, there were four kids who would grow up on the place and with the place and learn while they were doing. Four kids, the eldest just turned six—all kinds of things they could do—hold the lamp, fetch the tools, dig out weeds, pick up rocks, make lemonade. Other things, too—fly kites, climb trees, tend a garden, play with a dog, run free in open spaces, brighten gloomy days. And perhaps eventually, work the pro shop counter, mow greens, drive tractors and trucks. Hit a million golf shots. Run the place.

There was Marcy, with zero experience as a handyperson, who knew little about golf and cared less. Marcy, who had never lived in the country and who had the higher priority of caring for four kids. But Marcy, who was resourceful and resilient. And more than that, a good sport.

And there was me and whatever time and juice I had left after working for the paycheck we needed now more than ever. I brought zero experience as a golf course designer, architect, operator, or construction chief. A broad but shallow golf resume: worked on golf courses one way or another since age ten as golf ball scavenger, shagger, caddie, greens mowerman, pro shop attendant, night watering man, instructor. President of the Ann Arbor Men's Golf Association and host of a radio show on golf. Well, there was one other credential: among my three scholarships at the University of Michigan was the Chick Evans from the Western Golf Association, a private scholarship program for caddies.

That meant I knew just enough to be a real danger to our financial well-being and my own dream.

There we had it. The impetuous leading the inexperienced. What more could you want, stepping up to build your own golf course?

FOR THE FIRST TIME, we had moved into a place with far more storage space than we needed—at least at first, and only if you counted the barns. By the time we unpacked dozens of boxes, set up beds, arranged and rearranged the living room furniture, and hooked up the stove, washer, and dryer, we had had enough for the day. I parked the rented truck in the pole barn. We would unload the odds and ends tomorrow morning and I would return the truck then.

We had our first dinner in our new house and got the kids bathed, vowing that building a bathroom on the upper floor was topmost on our long "to-do" list.

Once the kids were settled in, Marcy and I went outside to walk around and listen to the night. All the windows in the house were open, so we knew we could hear the children. But all we heard in the warm August darkness was thousands of crickets and frogs from the marsh—our marsh—to the north. We moved away from the spill of the bright mercury vapor lamp in the driveway between the house and the barns. When we looked up, the black sky was spangled with more stars than we had seen in our seven years in Ann Arbor. The warm air wafting from the fields was dense with the sweet aroma of ripening grain.

There it was, out there in that sultry summer darkness—the land on which the dream of a golf course would come true. Standing there, with nothing to say that was worth disturbing the sounds of the night, we wondered, What next?

WE WERE STILL SHUFFLING FURNITURE two days after the Big Move when Wayne Wrightman showed up with the used but new-to-us color TV. Taking advantage of a lull in the strong west winds, he immediately went up on the steep-sloped roof and, agile as a high-wire walker, quickly erected the tallest antenna mast I had ever seen. He strung the lead wires and the juice wires to the antenna rotator securely on heavy-duty standouts, "because with the winds you get out here you don't want to be up on this roof reconnecting them too often."

Ten minutes later the kids jumped up and down and clapped when they saw their first color television at home. Wayne painstakingly adjusted the set, explaining to Mark the technicalities of what was happening as he was "Degaussing the set so you'll get realistic color."

We had moved to the country but technology had come to us.

THERE WERE NEIGHBORS TO MEET. There was so much we needed to know, even more we were curious about. The best place to start our education about Grass Lake was right here with our neighbors on Curtis Road. First on the list would have to be the farmer who worked the land directly south across Curtis Road, on property that Daryle told us had previously long been a part of the Nate Fish farm. Daryle told us he had sold that land off separately to the farmer whose homestead was on the first intersection to the east. I remembered that was the place on the corner of Fishville Road with the big sign on the barn: Breezy Acres. Henry Samyn.

I pulled into Henry's gravel driveway and was greeted by a formidable black dog with white feet, showing a little bulldog and some other indeterminate blood lines. After checking me out, the dog padded back to a set of steps leading to a rear porch and plopped down. As I approached, the door opened and a short, powerful man of perhaps thirty-five came out. His ruddy round face was already split in a broad smile. He was wearing full overalls and a T-shirt out of which sunpinked biceps bulged. As I neared him, he thrust out his right hand, and as I took it, he looked at me narrowly to see my reaction. That hand had no fingers, but it didn't stop him from squeezing mine in a powerful grip between his thumb and palm. He nodded when he saw I had no problem touching his maimed hand.

As we talked, Henry Samyn squatted in the driveway and scooped up a handful of gravel. He poured it from palm to palm, looking up at me. He squinted his pale eyes against the bright sun and asked me was I planning to farm the place, then offered to tell me what he knew about the land. The dog came over and nuzzled Henry's arm until he got the belly stroking he was after.

"Name of Boots. First time I saw him, looked to me like he had stepped into a pail of white paint, get his feet like that. What else you gonna name the guy. You got a dog?"

I told him about Yukon, our Airedale–German shepherd mix. About our Siamese cats, Jethro and Delilah, and about the kids. And about where I worked and where we were from and where I met Marcy.

It seemed I was answering more questions from Henry than I was getting information from him.

"Henry," I said, "how are the people around here?"

He looked up at me, his eyes narrowed.

"Well, Bill, just how do you mean that?"

"I mean, what are they like? They easy to get along with? Keep to themselves? Neighborly? What? You know, how are they?"

He paused, then squinted up at me.

"Well now, how were they where you came from?"

A BIG YELLOW SCHOOL BUS pulled into the driveway and the driver got out and came to the back door. As was common in the township, the bus driver was a woman. She introduced herself to Marcy as Barbara Schroen. She said she lived on Norvell Road, "the place with the goofy pond, just south of the Phal Road."

Barb said she was giving her bus a trial run and saw the children's swing set in our side yard, under the black sweet cherry tree. So she stopped to see what customers we had for her. Marcy explained that Mark was six years old and would be starting the first grade, Jennifer would be going half days in kindergarten, Pat was a year away from school age, and Beck two years.

Before she left, Barb recommended a baby sitter, her daughter Schatze. Even though we didn't expect to be going out very often, Marcy told Barb that when we did we would take her up on the offer. A few weeks later, we did. Schatze, though, was a high school senior and already past her prime baby-sitting years, so she passed us along to a succession of freshman and sophomore girls. When the trail finally led us to Mary Joseph, we stopped.

Mary Joseph was a willowy sixteen-year-old sophomore at Grass Lake High School. We didn't know at the time that Mary was the most popular girl in high school. There was a good reason for that—she was as

29

kind, sweet, and good-natured as she was lovely. By the time she was elected Miss Congeniality, then Homecoming Queen her senior year, we had long since learned she was as loved by the rest of the village as she was by Marcy, the kids, and me.

Some day, we thought, those are just the qualities we'd like to have behind the pro shop counter.

Three

The note was printed in ink in clear black letters. I read it, re-read it, and handed it to Marcy.

The words were clear and legible:

"Conspiracy. Arson. Death. The legacy of Leoni and Grass Lake." No signature. No date. Just a simple post card addressed to "The Haneys, 13202 Curtis Road, Grass Lake, Michigan 49240."

Now what the hell was that all about? Was it a joke? If so, we didn't see the humor. Was it a threat?

The word "conspiracy" was baffling. Arson and death? Menacing words, all right, but that word "conspiracy" made no sense. How could anyone think our building a golf course was part of a conspiracy?

Neither Marcy nor I could name a single person who might have sent it.

Then we wondered if the Detroit postmark was a clue. But we couldn't draw any conclusions from that either because we knew almost nobody who lived in Detroit proper rather than the suburbs. Did someone drive all the way to Detroit just to get that postmark and confuse us?

"How about that one, Mr. Heselschwerdt?" Mark said.

He pointed to a frisky palomino pony that had just been walked into the ring. The pony pawed the dirt and tried to jerk free of the tether.

"Well, Mark, he's a cute one, all right. But he'd take an awful lot of training and even then, palominos aren't the best around little kids. Now, you'd be okay, of course, but he might not be safe for your little brother and sisters."

Mark thought about that, said he understood, and waited patiently.

Many horses and two hours later, a good-sized chestnut mare pony was brought in. She stood quietly while the auctioneer—who was Daryle's brother Dale—invited bids.

"What do you think of that one, Mark?" Daryle asked. "I know that pony. Talked to her owner. She's good and healthy. Gentle nature. Pretty good one, I'd say."

Mark vigorously nodded his approval.

The bidding went on and I wondered if Daryle was going to bid on her. I could see a couple of bidders raising their hands, calling out a "Yep" or "Ay-huh." Still Daryle hadn't said a thing, just tugged at his ear a couple times.

Mark looked anxiously at Daryle. Dale banged his gavel and shouted, "Sold!" and Mark's face sank.

"Well, Mark," Daryle said, "got you a good little pony there."

"We did?"

"Sure did. Better start thinking of a name for her. I'll bring her on over this weekend. That be okay with you?"

I KNEW THERE WAS SOMETHING FAMILIAR about the eighty-year-old white-haired woman who came to open her back porch door to me.

I told Mrs. Edna Walker I had been driving by her Honey For Sale sign for a month, meaning to stop in and buy a jar. She invited me in, said she recognized my robin's egg blue pickup truck as one that had been going past a lot lately, along with the Olds wagon she saw parked at the old Nate Fish place. She asked the names and ages of our children as she motioned for me to have a seat at the table. It was a turn-of-the-century kitchen dominated by a huge wood-burning cook stove that could heat the entire house and part of the outdoors..

"Mrs. Walker, I may be slow putting two and two together. Are you the Walkers with a produce stand at the Ann Arbor Farmer's Market? I thought I recognized you from there."

"My husband Loyall and I have been truck farming there for forty-seven years now. I tell him that's just about long enough. He says, We'll keep doing it 'til we get it right. You've seen us at the Farmer's Market?"

I told her we had lived in Ann Arbor the past six years and bought vegetables, honey, and jelly from her a few times. I remembered that sign in front of their stall—Loyall and Edna Walker, Grass Lake, Michigan. But I hadn't made the connection they were the same Walkers.

She smiled the kind of smile I would have liked my grandmother to smile at me, perhaps because I had never really known my grandmothers.

"Well, Walker is a common enough name. You know, if we were any decent kind of neighbors we would have been down long before this to welcome you. Do I hear that you're planning to build a golf course on the old Nate Fish place?"

I said that was right and told her a little about our plans. She seemed pleased to hear that we liked the area and said she reckoned that a golf course made sense on land that wasn't exactly prime for farming.

"Loyall used to shake his head over what Nate Fish and the others tried to do on that place. It's a pretty piece, that nice oak woods. You know those oaks are the next generation off the ones that produced the lumber that built your barn and ours and a few others hereabouts. Some of the wood from that stand probably found its way to Chicago and west."

I asked her how that would be.

"You know the spot back there where Willow Creek runs through at the narrowest neck in the marsh? It's only a few rods from where your land abuts Ed Harrison. Below the Smedley Hill. Well, that's where the wagons crossed in the 1820s, when so many were heading west out of Canada, New York, and the east. Many a wagon got stuck there, and more than a few oxen and horses, too. And the earliest settlers in this township are folks who just gave up and stayed here because they couldn't get any farther. Some of them, the story goes, cut into that white oak stand for lumber to repair broken wagons. Those that got through ended up settling in Illinois, Nebraska, however far they could get and stake a good claim."

She filled my coffee cup and set out a platter of cinnamon buns. The aroma filled the room and I hadn't realized how hungry I was.

Mrs. Walker—I couldn't bring myself to call her Edna as she had asked—talked until the coffee ran out, telling me what she could about the Fishes and the others who had lived in our place and nearby. I paid her for the honey and thanked her for the coffee and buns. She promised she would come down the road to meet Marcy and visit.

"I'd like to do that one day, Mr. Haney. And I do hope you have better luck on that land than the ones who lived there before you. We always assumed it started with that terrible business with Nate himself but I suppose there were things long before that. Then those two men dying in the silo from the gas fumes. Seems like every few years it was something new, something tragic. The latest that I know of was that awful accident with the young Merz boy on his go-cart. Well, just listen to me. A body would think I was saying the place was, I don't know, cursed or something."

"Mrs. Walker, you mentioned something terrible happened to Nate Fish? Could you tell me more about that?"

"Actually, no. My husband Loyall was the one who found him and Loyall's a strong man. When he said I shouldn't ask him ever again about it, I knew that was it. Let's just say it was tragic and leave it at that."

I thanked Mrs. Walker again and as I drove off, it occurred to me that the Walkers—with the possible exception of the Coppernolls, with the big farm to the northeast—might be the only people still alive who had personally known old Nate Fish. And had seen many of these tragedies, as Mrs. Walker called them, just down the road at the old Nate Fish place. Yes, hearing all that, I guess a body might wonder if the place was cursed.

It took a few months but we finally found a closing date that worked for both the Heselschwerdts and us. Daryle had insisted on taking us out for an evening's entertainment to celebrate the closing of the deal. After an all-you-can-eat southern fried chicken dinner with all the trimmings at the Chicken Shack in Jackson, we went to Daryle's favorite bowling alley.

Kay Heselschwerdt and Marcy were having a fine time, and so was I because I found a groove on lane six and every ball I rolled there somehow found the pocket. As the frames progressed, Daryle got quieter. I finally figured out that he was as serious about winning at bowling as everything else.

In the third game, Daryle started with back-to-back strikes and flashed me a big grin as he sat down.

"You know," he said, "I was ready to take fifteen hundred less for the Nate Fish place."

"I guess one of us got the better of the other, then, Daryle. Because I was prepared to pay you thirty-five hundred more."

I couldn't tell from his expression if he knew I was stretching the truth as much as he was.

I SHUFFLED THROUGH THE MAIL on the way back to the house from the mailbox. I stopped when I came to a personal letter addressed in block printing that was vaguely familiar. There was a Detroit return address.

"Marcy, take a look at this letter."

"Who's it from?"

"I don't know. Someone in Detroit. But the printing reminds me of that post card we got a couple months ago. Remember? The one about arson, conspiracy, and death?"

Marcy looked at the envelope.

"That's my sister Bevie's return address, right on the campus at Wayne State."

She opened the letter. I waited while she read it and then handed it to me. The first part of the letter talked about family news, and then Bevie described projects she was doing in her job at the Labor Archives of Detroit Public Library. In the course of her research, Beverly had come across several references to Grass Lake and Jackson County. She thought we would be interested so she had made photocopies and had set them aside for us. She would bring them to us on her next visit because she knew we would be interested in the strange and important events that had transpired here.

And, she wondered, did we get the post card she sent a couple months ago? The one that repeated the headline from an 1851 Detroit newspaper article reporting on the arson bombing of the Michigan Central Railroad depot by a conspiracy of farmers from Grass Lake and Leoni in Jackson County.

"Mystery solved," Marcy said.

It was a relief to learn that we didn't have an enemy out there threatening us. But it only whetted my appetite to learn more about the history of this place.

I THOUGHT DARYLE HESELSCHWERDT meant to be saying "sorghum" but was pronouncing it "sore-go" because maybe that was the way locals did in Jackson County. A few weeks after we moved in, listening to the farmers talking around the grain elevator in town, I learned better. The impressive crop still growing to the north of the barns on our land was indeed called sorgo, at least in Jackson County. It was a hybrid cross of cattle feed corn and sorghum. It looked very much like giant corn, the spires topping out at ten to twelve feet and the stalks flush with dark green leaves. It was grown as a "green manure" crop, harvested while still vibrant emerald and high in nutritional value for beef cattle.

Daryle also had a healthy crop of conventional feed corn nearing maturity in the five-acre field west of the barns, a field boxed in by Damaron's fallow pasture on the west, Curtis Road on the south, and our oak woods on the north. Looking at it, you could believe what farmers said about going out on a still night to hear the corn grow.

We would slip through the rows of corn and sorgo, unable to see anything but the sky above, feeling our way to a fencerow where I could climb an upright railroad tie embedded as a corner post. Perched there, I would lift up the boys to show them where we had wandered.

As a term of the sale in the land contract, the rights to the crop stayed with Daryle and he told me he would have the crop off before the weather turned. I thought he must mean the transition from summer to fall, but when September gave way to October and then November, we wondered if he would ever get around to it.

One day before Thanksgiving I saw our neighbor to the east, Horace Coppernoll, out in his field and asked him to have a look. He squeezed a kernel to test its moisture and said the crop was fine, drying slowly. Horace wondered what's the hurry. Too late to plant winter wheat now.

I told him we wanted Heselschwerdt to get the crops off so we could have a good look at the land and get a better idea what kind of a cleanup job we were facing. We were a long way from even thinking about how the course might best lay out, but it was going to take a lot of walking it before we knew it well enough and we wanted to get started. Horace stroked his grizzled chin and said he reckoned the crops would come off when they were ready. He said he hoped I had kept my day job, then went back to his own place.

A few days later, one cool November day, Daryle Heselschwerdt showed up with a big flatbed trailer carrying his 4020 series John Deere. He backed the mammoth tractor off the flatbed and asked me where I wanted him to park it for the night. He said he'd bring over his harvester and gravity boxes in the morning and start bringing in crop.

The next dawn, I heard Daryle's big diesel throbbing outside our east windows. I looked out and for the first time saw a slice of those fields freshly shorn. I went downstairs and watched the big machine creep along, inhaling a great wave of plant silage and leaving brown earth and neatly sawn-off stubble in its wake. The machine processed the crop in several steps. V-shaped prongs funneled the stalks into the vibrating knife blades, where they were severed with surgical precision two inches above the ground. At that height, the operator could take virtually all of the crop while keeping the rig safely above the ground, avoiding barbed wire, fencing, and other metal that would foul the mechanisms or damage blades. Big rocks were no prob-  lem, for the unit would simply bounce over them. But rocks that were just the right size to wedge into the V's could jam up the works.

After the stalks were cut, comblike sweepers raked the material into the maw of a grinder that quickly shredded everything into a fine mash. That pulp was passed along by conveyor into bins, or jetted through a long gooseneck periscope boom into the wheeled cribs, called gravity boxes, being towed along behind. Once one gravity box was full, it was detached and parked off to the side and an empty one was hitched on. If the operator had helpers, the boxes could be driven to a silo where the green manure was blown in to be stored until needed. Often farmers would go in together, one buying a combine, the other a corn-picker. They would share the big equipment and help each other get crops in. But not Daryle. He liked to go it alone. And he was one of the few around who could afford it.

One problem with green manure was the toxic fumes it generated in enclosed spaces. Every so often the *Jackson Citizen-Patriot* and the area weeklies carried a story of a farm worker made severely ill or even killed by inhaling the fumes while working in a silo.

With the stories of bad luck that seemed to visit our old Nate Fish place occasionally, I wasn't surprised by Mrs. Walker's story that in the 1930s, two farmhands had been asphyxiated in the glazed tile silo that once stood beside the milk house.

I thought about those farm accidents as, off and on that weekend, we watched Daryle's John Deere creep over the land like a colossal insect devouring everything green in its path. By nightfall Sunday, Daryle had the crop in. We could finally see the land on which we would build our golf course—that is, half of it, unless we could buy enough adjacent property.

"DADDY," PAT SAID, "I was going out to kick the ball and there were these two really, really old guys on the back porch."

"Did they say anything?"

"No, they just sat there being old."

On the way to the back door, I looked out the mudroom window and saw William Rollman and another white-haired man. Rollman was well known for building genuine log cabin homes, which he was still doing well past his eightieth year. I opened the door and took a closer look, but didn't recognize the man with him, who looked even older. Rollman's fingers fussed with the brim of his hat as he introduced himself and his friend Jeb and said, "Mr. Haney, I heard up to the elevator you was giving away railroad tie corner posts and fencing to anyone with the gumption to pull 'em out."

I wondered how folks at the grain elevator in town could have heard that because I never had said that to anyone, but they were right. I did intend to take the fencing down and had no further use for it. Rather than haul it to the township landfill or find a place to stash it, I'd prefer to see it go to someone who could make use of it.

"Well, yes, Mr. Rollman, we're getting rid of everything but the paddock and that pasture field where you see the chestnut mare pony and her colt."

"Nice pony."

"Daryle Heselschwerdt gave her to my son Mark. She just foaled that little colt and we were surprised when Daryle brought us the two of them. Pokey and Gumby, the kids call them. So far all we've done with her is feed them lots of oats and apples."

"Cute colt," he said. "Looks of the mare, I'd say she's eating for two again."

"Oh, I don't think that could be," I said.

"You don't, eh? Well, time will tell." Rollman looked at Jeb, nodded seriously, and looked out over the white wooden paddock fence and to the fields beyond. He seemed to be taking inventory of the fencing.

"Then too," he said, "I expect you'll be using that field yonder for part of your golf links."

Well, communication clearly was not a problem around the township and village. I started to describe how the cornfield beyond the barns would likely be a fairway for a hole that would probably run north along the woods. I stopped talking as the two men looked at each other. Jeb looked up into the sky and Rollman stroked his throat with a leathery hand. Maybe golf wasn't their game.

"Well then," Rollman said. "Best we get started."

I looked at the two old men, both now looking closer to ninety than eighty. I told them the corner posts were creosoted railroad ties and very heavy and said I'd change my clothes and give them a hand.

Jeb cleared his throat, packed a slug of tobacco in his cheek, and shook his head.

"No need," Rollman said. "Jeb and me've pulled a few miles of fence in our day."

He gestured toward the two big elms on the west side of the house.

"Real shame about those elms. They were already good size when I built this porch we're standing on. We had to chop some mighty big roots to pour the foundation and Nate Fish grumbled about it every swing of the ax, even though I was the one doing the swinging. I suppose you'll want to get those trees down before winter. One of those big limbs ices up and crashes through the roof, could ruin a night's sleep."

The biggest tree was less than fifteen feet from the house, and west, at that, the direction from which the heaviest winds came. A mammoth limb was balanced, precariously it now seemed, directly above the girls' room.

I asked Rollman if he knew anyone who did tree work at a fair price.

"Well, the Dubois boy, the one works at the newspaper in town, he's real good from what I hear. Wouldn't know how easy he is on price."

"Before you go, Mr. Rollman, I have a question. You said you built this porch for Nate Fish. Then you must know what happened to him."

He paused a long while.

"Well, what happened was, he died."

"I got that impression from Mrs. Walker, down the road. But she said what happened to him was terrible. That made me wonder."

Rollman looked at Jeb and thought a while. Jeb turned away.

"That was forty-odd years ago, maybe longer," Rollman said. "Get to be my age, memory plays tricks. No, I wouldn't want to say."

I watched the two old men walk slowly to their truck. Before they got in, they went over to a concrete slab at the side of the driveway between the house and the barn and looked at it while they talked. I had noticed the six-foot-square slab when Daryle was showing us the place and asked him about it. He told me it was the foundation for a windmill derrick that drove a corn sheller. The derrick and corn sheller had long since been removed. Most of the slab was now covered with gravel drifted from the driveway, so only a couple feet protruded an inch or so above the ground. I figured I would leave the slab there and put a railing alongside it for use as a golf bag rack.

Jeb scraped at the slab with the toe of his boot and shook his head. Then the two got in the truck and left.

While they were gone to get their tractor, I went out to the barn to get a couple of shovels. I stopped on the way and looked at the concrete slab. At one corner I could see a rust stain from where a steel anchor bolt probably had been sunk into the concrete, one of four tiedowns for the corners of the derrick frame, I assumed.

I took a last look at the elms. The three that were closest to the house would have to come down and I wouldn't risk working on any of them myself. They were all huge, all slightly leaning toward the house, and all had large limbs jutting out over the roof. I'd have to look up this Dubois fellow soon.

I went inside and changed my clothes and decided to wait in the house and watch from an upstairs window to be ready when the two frail old men needed me. I already felt sorry for William Rollman and Jeb. I could envision them digging and pulling and wrestling posts for hours. Even then, I couldn't imagine they would ever be able to get everything down and loaded before dark. Just a week earlier, Mark and Pat and I had taken three shovels to the corner posts out on the ridge beyond the woods and it seemed as though it took an hour just to get a single post extracted. And then it was so heavy I strained my back horsing it into the pickup bed and the next day Marcy was driving me to Dr. Koffeman for what he called a subluxation and I called a sore back. No, those posts had been put in to stay and there would be a lot of sweating and swearing before they were out.

I sat in a chair by the big north window just as Jeb parked the pickup truck and trailer near a corner post. He took a pair of sidecutters, a hammer, and a big screwdriver out of his overalls and set to work loosening the wire fencing, prying out the nails and putting them in a pocket. Admirable frugality. And I wouldn't have to worry about one of those nails impaling a tractor tire.

In a few minutes, Rollman chugged in on his Ford 8N tractor. I could see he had a tow bar installed between the arms of his three-point hitch and a length of logging chain coiled around the top link. He backed the tractor up to the fence post and I thought, The old guy is going to nudge the post with the tow bar, loosen it up and make the digging easier. William Rollman's ma sure didn't raise no dummies.

Then he eased down the lever controlling the rear hydraulics so the arms and the tow bar dropped to just above the ground. Now that surprised me. I had thought he would raise the arms to get more leverage higher up against the post, then back slowly against the post and push it loose. Instead, when Rollman had the tow bar tight up against the post a couple inches above the ground, Jeb took hold of the logging chain, coiled it twice around the big railroad tie at ground level, looped it onto the tow bar, and snugged the chain's hook into a link. That took maybe fifteen seconds. Jeb nodded and Rollman revved the engine a bit, raised the control lever, and up came the three-point hitch arms. And up came the chain securing the tow bar to the railroad tie. And up came the railroad tie. Up, up, and totally out of the hole that had kept it solidly half-buried for several years. To lift it free took maybe ten seconds.

In a leisurely half a minute, these two octogenarians had extracted a railroad tie corner post the like of which had taken the boys and me nearly an hour chipping into compacted earth with shovels. And they had done it without touching a hand tool; the only muscles they had used were those required to maneuver a lever and coil a chain.

Jeb steadied the heavy post with one hand. Easy for him to do because it was perfectly balanced where it was cinched to the tow bar by the logging chain. As Rollman backed the tractor near the pickup truck, he gently lowered the hydraulics and Jeb guided the post. In a few seconds the big post was nestled into the bed of the truck.

They moved along the fencerow—no hurry, no wasted motion. The longest part of the job was prying out the horseshoe-shaped nails and they could have avoided that by snipping the wires with Jeb's sidecutters, but of course that would have wasted both a few feet of fencing and perfectly reusable nails. In less than two hours, the entire fence that had confined the north field, all its smaller intermediate fence posts, and every massive railroad tie corner post was stacked neatly in the bed of the pickup truck or piled on the trailer. Then they put the aluminum swinging gate on top and cinched it down with ancient chainbinders.

They drove back up to the house and parked in the driveway and I went down to see them.

"Mr. Haney, I see you have a couple shovels here," Mr. Rollman said. "I'd like to borrow them, fill in those holes. Hate to hear one of your kiddies or ponies stepped in one and broke a leg."

IT WAS A DIFFERENT PLACE with all the fences gone except for the paddock and Pokey and Gumby's pasture. The two old men had done such a good job that from a distance there was little evidence the land had been fenced off into many separate fields.

Now instead of visualizing it in my mind, I could walk the land and get a feel for how a given hole might work, how a sequence of holes might be routed from one to the next. There was still a lot of learning to be done before we would put a pencil to paper and much, much cleansing in store before this land would support a stand of grass. But we were getting a better understanding of this place. How the wind blew over it. How the water flowed through it. How the sun fell on it. How living things might grow best in it. We were getting a sense of what this place was before man got after it. We were getting a glimmer of what the glacier had in mind.

Four

One fine fall morning, as the oak leaves that were not yet crackling underfoot still shimmered in the sunshine like burgundy wine, as flock after flock of snow geese winged southbound, their honking audible though they were barely visible so far overhead, Pat and Mark took me for a walk.

They led me to the south ridge. There we turned and looked back.

From here the oak woods seemed much smaller than its just-under-five acres and the house and barns were monopoly pieces on the horizon. The ground rose and fell in graceful sweeps and it was easy to envision a green on this very spot. Yes, a green here at the end of a long serpentine fairway, its tee more than 500 yards distant, to the east of the woods and beyond it perhaps a hundred yards or so from the barn. The fairway would swoop up to this crest in a double dogleg to end here on this south ridge. Disaster would lurk beyond, as a ball struck too boldly would fly over the green and trickle down the sharp slope to lose itself in the marsh below.

"What's over there, Daddy?" Mark asked, pointing to the west. It was a gradual continuation of the high south ridge we were standing on, widening into a broader plateau on the south and falling sharply into the marsh on its north.

"Yeah," Pat said. "And that big hill on the other side of the swamp. Who does that belong to?" Pat was pointing at the highest point around, the Smedley Hill, the crown of the ridge north of the marsh.

I told the kids that Daryle Heselschwerdt had said that both areas the boys had pointed to were one parcel of land, fifty or so acres owned by people named Smedley. From where we stood, it was tempting to imagine that land combined with this. Right away you could see how two side-by-side, out and back, par four holes would fit on the plateau. Then, you would have to find a way to get your golfers across the marsh to a green somewhere on the firm ground on the other side. Once over there, you would take those golfers up the slope to a tee high up on the Smedley Hill. What a view that would be. But that land I was fantasizing about was someone else's property and we were already in for all we could manage. A journey into frustration, laying out holes on somebody else's land.

We headed back toward the house, taking a different route this time, along the fencerow that separated our land from the Smedley plateau on the west. We cut through our oak woods and explored it on the way. To Mark and Pat, I imagined, this fifty-five acre farm must seem a very big place indeed. But spacious as it may feel to them, there was no way more than four or five holes could ever be fit into it.

A COUPLE DAYS LATER, I stopped in at the *Grass Lake News*, the first time I had been there since ordering a subscription and meeting the owners, Bob and Bobbi Mather.

The sturdy door was partway open but I knocked on it anyhow. I heard a radio playing loudly and, wondering if anyone heard, I knocked again, more loudly.

A bald man of about thirty appeared and looked at me quizzically. He wore a full beard, bushy but trimmed, and no mustache. If this was Hank Dubois, his gold-rimmed glasses made him look more like a teacher than the town's Mr. Fixit I had heard so much about. He had powerful-looking arms for his lean frame and was wearing a pressman's rubber apron and a pair of thick, ink-stained gloves.

"Delivering something?" he asked, looking over my shoulder to see if there was a delivery truck to be seen.

"No, just came by to meet a Mister Dubois. William Rollman told me Dubois does tree work and—"

He pulled off a glove and thrust out his hand.

"You're looking at Hank Dubois. And you say it like "do-boys," not the French way. Come on in. By the way, no point knocking on the door. Everyone knows it's never locked."

The press was running and its labored whirring and clattering combined with the blasting music from the radio made it almost impossible to understand what Dubois was saying. When we went inside, the noise was even louder.

"And you don't have problems," I shouted, "with people coming in at night?"

"To steal what? Old newspapers? Lead ingots for the Linotype machine? Everybody knows there's nothing of real value here. We do keep the darkroom secure but that's so kids don't get into the chemicals."

I asked if we could turn the radio down a little so I could hear him better.

"Only got two settings, loud and off. Fix that one of these days. I guess it is a little on the loud side. I'm about done with this run—press will be off in a minute. Have a seat."

The closest seat of the two in the room was an oak desk chair on rollers. It was pushed up to the keyboard of the Linotype machine. It reminded me of the chairs at the *Michigan Daily*, the University of Michigan student newspaper, where without ever having to bother to get to your feet you could zip from the night editor's horseshoe desk to the teletype machine with one good push and if you really got your feet into it, you could roll halfway down the long main aisle to the five-cent Coke machine. I sat down and looked at the keyboard.

"You probably know better," Dubois yelled over his shoulder, "but don't get close to the pot."

I did know better than to touch the small cauldron of molten lead hanging just inches from my left knee. That was the metal from which the slugs of type were cast, then once used, were dumped back in to be re-melted and used again, over and over.

The press wound down and now it was possible to hear, despite the tinny throbbing of ad jingle music from the radio. Dubois suggested we step outside to talk where it was even quieter. We leaned up against a railing outside the quaint old railroad station.

"How many work here?"

"At the *News*? Bob Mather—he's the owner—and me. Bobbi—that's Bob's wife—she reviews books for the *Detroit Free Press* and she's a real good writer, so once in a while when the spirit moves her, she'll write a feature or an editorial to aggravate the populace. Otherwise, Bob just kind of edits copy from press releases, minutes of meetings. Bob sells ads, sets type, runs the business. I run the equipment, take pictures, do the dark-room stuff."

"I guess that keeps you pretty busy."

"Not so's you'd notice it. We do custom printing to bring in revenue. Fliers, posters, invitations. You name it. Could even do golf score cards."

"I hear you also do trees."

"That's on my own time. So, you want those dead elms down?"

"You know the ones?" I asked, "at the old Nate Fish place on Curtis Road, east of Norvell Road?"

"Ought to. Helped the Merz boys build a tree house in that biggest elm outside the kitchen window. I was born just east of that place, half mile the other side of Fishville Road, down past the cemetery and Henry Samyn's Breezy Acres. Everybody else calls your house the Nate Fish place—it was always the Merz place to me. When I was a kid I slept overnight there quite a few times. Kind of like a barracks up on that second floor. Helped slap up that barnyard wallpaper. Played hide and seek in the barn, hung tire swings in that oak woods. Fished the trout stream out back."

"You think those elms need to come down?"

"Oh, they're going to come down, all right. Only question is whether someone takes them down or you wait for Mother Nature to do it at a time of her choosing."

I asked him what kind of money we were talking about.

"Lots of heat left in that wood," Hank said. "I burn wood so the logs are worth something to me, means I can give you a lower price."

"I'm all for that. How low?"

He looked up to the sky, scratched his throat beneath his beard, and said, "Well, those trees, they lean toward the house. That means I have to do it one of two ways. One, I get up there on the house and into the tree with ladders and take off those overhanging limbs a chunk at a time. Then I work down the main trunk, taking a few feet at a time. Hate doing that. Takes forever. Means I spend a lot of time working with ropes to secure the branches so they don't get away from me, fall through your roof."

"That doesn't sound like a whole lot of fun. What's option two?"

"Option two is I bring over my big truck with the cable and winch. Then I get up in the tree as high as I can and it's still solid wood. There I tie up the business end of the cable. Then I get down and start my directional cut with my chain saw. Take a wedge out so the narrow edge exactly faces just the direction I want to drop it. Big as the base of that tree is, I'll have to use the five-foot two-man saw."

"What happens if you've figured it wrong and you've got a tree going in the wrong direction with a cable connecting it to your winch and truck?"

He looked at me as if he couldn't believe what I had said.

"That's why you figure it out right to begin with. You want it to be real boring. No surprises."

"This is starting to sound like a big operation."

"Not really. A little tricky but I've done a whole lot tougher. It gets easier once you've done it a few times. First couple, you sweat a little hoping you've figured the drop right. See, once that tree starts down, there's no changing its mind, that's where it's going to fall. Gravity. That big one outside the kitchen window, we're looking at eighty foot of tree and the way I figure to drop it, it'll just about miss your 300-hundred gasoline tank and paddock fence but not by more than a foot or two."

"You sure do remember that house and yard pretty well."

"Partly that, but I've been eyeballing it as I drive past to visit my folks. Figured a guy building a golf course on that farm would know enough to take down those trees before someone got hurt."

Hank Dubois hadn't done any work for me yet, but I was already convinced the man knew what he was doing, that he studied a problem, developed a plan, then executed it methodically. That was bound to come with a price tag.

"Drop them, cord them up, clean up the brush," he said, "one hundred seventy-five total for the lot. Now, if you want me just to fell them and you'll cord and clean up, then—"

"When can you start?"

THE MORE I LOOKED AT THE TREES, the sorrier I was to lose them but the happier I was that someone with experience would be taking them down. I watched Hank study the biggest tree, the one closest to the house. He measured its shadow, looked at the position of the sun, then paced off from the base of the tree to the gasoline tank near the paddock fence.

On the way past me, he said, more to himself, "Going to be tight."

I stayed out of the way, making mental notes. In the coming years, I would be doing a lot of tree work myself and while I had put in a few hours with a chain saw, I had much to learn. Felling a tree out in the open was a lot easier than having to drop it with a margin of error of no more than a couple of degrees.

Hank positioned the truck to give him an angle that would avoid the mercury vapor lamp pole and the telephone lines on the south side of the drop area and the fence and gasoline tank on the north. He left the truck running while he played out enough cable to reach to the tree. Hank's stepson Mike scrabbled up the tree with a rope connected to the cable, hauled the cable up, and fastened it around the main trunk about thirty feet above the ground.

They made the first cut belt-high with the two-man saw. They cut for a few seconds at a time, stopping frequently so Hank could check the angle and the depth. Once he was satisfied with the first incision, they made a second pass on an angle from about four inches higher to loosen a wedge a third of the way into the trunk. Then Hank took a smaller chain saw and finished slicing the wedge free. He knocked the wedge out with a sledge hammer and then went around to the other side of the tree and began to cut through toward the open notch on the other side. He cut only partway, then shut off his saw and walked quickly to the truck. He set the truck engine on a fast idle, reached up to the winch, and hit a button. Slowly the winch began to take up the slack in the cable. When it had drawn fully tight, the top branches of the big tree shuddered. Hank stopped the winch, returned to the tree, and restarted his chain saw.

As Hank cut deeper into the undercut notch, I heard the first splintering cracks of the tree shifting away from the house and in the direction Hank was trying to drop it. He shut off his saw, carrying it with him as he jogged to the truck. He hit the winch button again and the tree began to tip, pistol-like cracks splitting the air. It tilted, paused, then rushed to the ground with a breath-taking whomp and crashed with a thud that shook the earth. The topmost branch barely grazed the gasoline tank and paddock fence. Broken branches rebounded off the driveway and rained down for several seconds.

The tree now lay on precisely the line Hank Dubois had calculated. I heard cheering and clapping from inside the house.

"One hundred and twenty-seven," Hank announced after counting the rings a second time. "That tree stood there every day since the year 1839."

EARLY THE NEXT MORNING Hank and Mary showed up with their four kids. The first huge tree with its mammoth branches took the most time but once the Dubois team got into a rhythm it went fast. By midafternoon, the remaining three trees were down, corded, and hauled off. Hank, Mary Jane, and their four kids had worked more than thirty people-hours for $175 and many cords of firewood.

When they had gone, Marcy and our kids walked around with me to look at the place from different angles. We walked out a ways onto the land, then turned to see how much different the skyline looked.

Bereft of the trees that had crowned it for a century, the house looked barren and forlorn. Nate Fish wouldn't have been happy about it and neither were we. But there was no sense agonizing over it.

"Daddy," Pat said, "how come we cut down those nice trees? I wanted you to build us a tree house in the big one."

"I know, Pat. I liked them too, but they had lived their full life and then they died. We had to take them down or some stormy day they might have come crashing into the house."

"We can plant other trees," Mark said.

"And we will," I said. "Hundreds of them."

DECIDING ON WHICH TRACTOR TO BUY was turning out to be tough. We now had less than $5,000 to fix the house, buy equipment, build a golf course, and turn some old barns into work space, clubhouse, and pro shop. And we were going to spend half of that on a tractor and somehow do everything else with the remaining half? Well, maybe we could buy it on time. What's another monthly payment?

The only tractors I had much experience with were the Ford 8N models Bill Catto ran at Sylvan Glen, in Big Beaver, where I worked as a teenager. I hadn't been in an 8N tractor seat since I was sixteen but that didn't stop me from yearning for one.

The 8N was a legendary workhorse, the first ones built in 1947 when American industry had not yet fully perfected built-in obsolescence. Building ultra-durable tractors proved to be bad business for Ford. The old tractors refused to die and frugal farmers didn't throw money at new models just to get a shiny paint job. It took a lot of abuse to put such a basic and simple machine as an 8N out of commission. Many used ones that had been given up on by naive or lazy owners and sold for a hundred dollars for spare parts were exhumed by savvy handymen, patched up, and made fit for years of service. Every farmer had a story about an 8N bought for $200, repaired for $50, run hard for ten years, and sold for $1,200.

But much as I admired the 8N, we could not overspend for a twenty-year-old tractor that had none of the features we needed. Especially not when we could buy a new John Deere or Ford 2000 for less than $2,700 and have the security of a warranty in case we got a lemon.

Henry Samyn ran only John Deere on his place and was baffled that I would even think of any other brand. Henry made a lot of good points. There was no Case dealer nearby. The International Harvester dealer in Grass Lake had folded years ago and Dunkel Brothers Ford was another nineteen miles away in Brooklyn, almost to Lenawee County. That left exactly one tractor dealership nearby—Boley Brothers John Deere in Napoleon. More important to Henry, though, were a tractor's capabilities.

Henry pointed out that the John Deere had live power to the rear power takeoff shaft and that was essential for powering many implements used for farming. It also had a tractor's equivalent of an automatic trans-mission.

I told Henry those were two features we didn't really need around a golf course and in fact didn't want because those were things that could go wrong and be expensive to repair if they did. And those two items pushed the price of the Deere up more than $400 higher than the same-size Ford 2000. For that money, I could get the rear tires loaded with ballast, put weights on the front tires, and buy a brand-new agricultural disk, an essential piece of equipment for fitting down the land.

Henry heard my reasoning but wouldn't back down: the higher quality and better materials in the John Deere made it a better value—enough said. A week later when a big flatbed delivered the Ford 2000, Henry watched from up on his tractor just across Curtis Road. As he made a turn, he stopped, looked, then shook his head and drove away.

Marcy and the kids came out of the house to have a look at what we had just spent more than half of our $5,000 budget on, or more precisely, had just committed to that much on a time-payment plan. Whereas John Deere tractors were a bright green with yellow accents, Ford colors were a strong blue with white trim. With its fire-engine-red grading blade already mounted on the rear three-point hitch, the 2000 looked good just sitting there—or at least patriotic.

"Can we go for a ride, Dad?" Mark asked, for himself and the other kids.

"Yeah, Dad," Pat said. "Teach us how to drive it."

"Driving tractor is a few years off yet for you, Pat," I said. "We'll see about a ride later."

They all walked around and looked at the tractor from every angle as I climbed onto the seat and started it up. The kids wanted to know about every lever, what every dial meant, whether it could back up, how fast it would go.

"What's this thing sticking in the back for?" Mark shouted over the idling engine.

"That's called a swinging drawbar. See, what we do is put this big steel pin in there and that lets us hook up something we can pull behind. Like a trailer or that old stoneboat I bought at the auction so you guys can pick up rocks for the next year or two."

"Or a toboggan?" Pat yelled.

"Yeah," Jenni said, "a sled or a toboggan!"

"Sure, a toboggan. But only when there's plenty of snow so we don't tear up the grass. Another thing we can pull is called a harrow, which is like a big comb that we'll use to smooth out the soil after we've floated it down with the disk."

"What's a disk?"

I pointed toward the barn at the implement we had offloaded separately.

"That rig over there with all those sharp slicers on it that you kids can't go anywhere near. That, we don't pull. We mount it to the tractor with what's called a three-point hitch—that's the arms that red grading blade is attached to. That lets us lift it up and lower to however deep or shallow we want to go. Look, I'll show you."

I lowered the rear hydraulics and took off the grading blade. Then I backed the tractor around to line up the arms of the three-point hitch with the connecting rods on the disk. Once they were lined up, I hopped off and hooked it up. That sure brought back old times from my days at Sylvan Glen, although I had spent many more hours mowing greens there with a walk-behind mower than I did on tractors, a cushy job by comparison. I moved the lever that controlled the rear hydraulics and the three-point hitch went up, raising the big heavy disk easily off the ground.

I pointed to the rear of the tractor where a big metal cap protruded four inches, a protective cover for the power takeoff shaft. I reached down and took off the cap and described how the PTO drives rear-mounted equipment like large rotary mowers to do tasks it would take hours to do by hand.

"One thing Daddy didn't show us," Marcy said, "is whatever that is that's mounted on the fender. How about that, Daddy?"

"Oh, that."

"Yes, oh that," Marcy said, and gave me what my mother used to call "the family look," an expression that says, Let's see you talk your way out of this one, buster.

"Well, that's a radio."

"A radio on a tractor?" Mark said.

"Yeah, tractors don't have radios," Jen said.

"Well, you see," I said, "if Mommy is out there mowing away hour after hour, she's going to get awfully bored."

Marcy eyed me again.

"And Mommy's going to want to know how the Detroit Tigers are doing. See, the Tigers had a pretty good team this year and they've got a good chance to win the pennant next year so Mommy sure wouldn't want to miss all that excitement when she's out there all day on the tractor."

"And then," Marcy said, "there's University of Michigan football in the fall I just couldn't bear to miss."

"If Mommy's out there on the tractor all day," Jen said, "who's going to watch us?"

"Don't pay any attention to your father, kids," Marcy said. "I'll be right here with you guys. He's the one who'll be riding around on his fancy new tractor, listening to ball games."

I could live with that.

A FEW WEEKS LATER, I saw Hank Dubois at the *News* and mentioned the lesson I had gotten from William Rollman and Jeb in extracting fence posts.

"That fencing was only a couple years old," Hank said. "Ron Merz paid top dollar to put that in, not long before he sold out to Heselschwerdt. And those aluminum farm gates, everybody's looking to buy one of them used. Hope you got what all that was worth."

Hank went back to adjusting the Linotype machine, then when I didn't say anything he looked up at me, tapped a big wrench against his open hand and shook his head. "You've got so much money you can afford to give valuable stuff away? I told you, let me know when you're getting rid of something. We'll take it down to my place, put a sign on it. I do that all the time. Lots of traffic on Norvell Road. I could put a sign on my garbage, people would buy it."

What Hank was saying was essentially the same thing he had said a while earlier when I gave Henry Samyn the corn crib and the 1956 Chevy station wagon I had bought earlier for $65. And he said it when he heard I gave away the old weathered barn boards to a friend in Ann Arbor who was remodeling his family room with a rustic motif. He said it when he looked in the barn and saw I was letting a couple of Ann Arbor friends store their boats in the barn over the winter at no charge. He had even said it when I offered to pay him for a chain saw blade he broke when he was cutting down our dead elms.

For a man who didn't talk much, Hank Dubois said a lot of things worth thinking about. He had a point, all right, but I thought I did too, and I explained it to him.

"I know I could get some money out of those things, Hank. But there's such a thing as opportunity costs."

"Which means what?"

"Everything comes with a cost. The time it would take me to sell that stuff is valuable itself. When there's already not enough hours in the day, that time is worth more than what I'd get selling those things. I don't have enough time as it is to get the place in shape for a golf course, to build a pro shop and restrooms and a maintenance area in the barn, let alone to turn that house into something livable and do my job at Bendix."

Hank hadn't been convinced before and he wasn't now.

"But I told you," Hank said, "you don't have to bother with it. We could move the stuff down to my place and—"

"And transfer the bother to you? Then it's you going out and talking with every guy who stops to have a look, haggle over price. You don't have time any more than I do."

Hank wiped the grease off his hands with his red bandanna and sat down at the Linotype keyboard to test it out.

"All I'm saying, Bill, the time may come you'll wish you had the few hundred dollars you'd have got for the stuff you gave away."

"Hey, Hank, I appreciate your concern but in five years when we're turning people away and looking for more land for another nine holes, what's a few hundred dollars then. Right?"

"Well, then it won't bother you to hear that Mr. Rollman sold that fencing you gave him. Says he got a hundred ten dollars for it."

Hmm. I guess Mr. William Rollman didn't fall off the melon truck yesterday.

Hank turned back to the Linotype keyboard and tapped out enough letters to make a couple of hot slugs that zipped and clattered through the elaborate maze of channels and clanked to a stop in the tray beside him. He plucked them out with his thick calloused fingers and handed them to me.

"Careful, they're still a little hot."

It took me a few seconds because I hadn't read the backwards type of Linotype slugs since my days at the *Michigan Daily*. But I finally figured it out. The first slug read: The quick brown fox jumped lightly. The second slug read: First you have to get that far.

I WAS FILLING THE GAS TANK on the ancient E-3 Co-op tractor I had found for $120 when a black Lincoln pulled slowly into the driveway. The big sedan with the darkened windows was towing a small enclosed trailer and as the driver eased along the gravel circular drive, he lowered his window and peered at me through dark sunglasses.

The car had Illinois license plates. The trailer looked to be custom made, with two separate compartments separated with heavy metal screening, perhaps for transporting animals. The driver got out of the car slowly, stretching an apparently stiff back, and looked around. He was a large man of forty or so, wearing a dark suit that looked as though it would be uncomfortable if he wore it on the drive from Illinois.

"Well, let's have a look at those shepherds. Where you keep them?"

I told the man I didn't have any shepherds.

He said he drove up from Chicago to buy two German shepherds. He looked around again, scowling. "You're Loyall Walker, aren't you? Guy I talked to on the phone about the two security dogs."

I told him he had driven past the Walker place. In the distance, the Walkers' shepherds were barking, yapping, howling as it seemed they always did. I had no idea how many dogs the Walkers had back there, in kennels behind their south barn, but there had to be quite a few.

The man drove off and I watched as he pulled into the Walkers' driveway. Edna came out to meet him and they walked together toward the dog kennel.

When I told Marcy about the visitor from Chicago she said there had been two or three previous such visits. We wondered what was so special about the Walkers' German shepherds that people would drive over from Chicago for them.

Five

I had just finished editing a film I had written and produced at Bendix for NASA on how the astronauts would deploy the Apollo Lunar Surface Experiments Package (ALSEP) on the moon. The film was part of my responsibilities as configuration manager on ALSEP, the most satisfying of the dozen or so military and space projects I had been involved with.

Ten years earlier—actually two years before NASA was created—my first assignment in the military-space industry had been to edit the parts manual for the Saturn booster rocket engine. That had been at a summer job at Rocketdyne Division of North American Aviation and it was a kick for me, an English major, to have a tiny role in mankind's journey into space. That assignment also brought me a secret clearance and paved the way for subsequent jobs at Chrysler Missile Division, Lockheed Aircraft, and Bendix Aerospace Systems Division.

But over time, our kids got older and the Cold War turned frigid and the arms race heated up and making a living in the war trade became intolerable. Finally I couldn't face working on yet another proposal for submarine-launched multiple-warhead missiles or tactical fighter aircraft or satellite-killing satellites. I told the company I wanted to work only on space programs with, one hoped, peaceful missions. Bendix management accepted that, but understandably they didn't like it. I knew I had limited my prospects in the defense-space business. So I was intrigued when I got a phone call with an unexpected opportunity to do a freelance editorial assignment on something that had nothing to do with either a military or a space program.

The call was from Govert van den Bosch and the offer was to shape and edit a book by a world-renowned economist. I had known Van at Bendix before he became head of administration for the University of Michigan's Institute for Social Research, a pre-eminent laboratory staffed with leading scholars in economics, political science, group dynamics, psychology, and other social science disciplines.

One of the institute's most prestigious scholars, Dr. George Katona, needed an editor to pull together a long-overdue book. Would you be interested, Van asked, in working on it freelance?

I told him my first priority was to build a golf course on property we had just moved to and I needed all my spare time to do that. So there were only two things that would entice me to do a freelance assignment: money and more money. In truth, beyond the opportunity to make some extra cash, I welcomed the chance to get a break from the engineering and hard science world I had been working in for eight years, a milieu in which I got along well but always felt the outsider. And well I might have felt that way because with my liberal arts education, that's exactly what I was.

As Van described the job, it sounded straightforward. Read a previous book or two by Dr. Katona to get familiar with his writing voice; next, meet the great doctor himself and win his confidence. Then organize the project and create a schedule for it. Finally, edit and prepare the manuscript for publication as a book. I hadn't done a project of that exact nature before, but I had done similar things many times. I was eager to begin.

But first, Van said, even to do this one-time freelance project, I had to "run a bit of a gauntlet." I had to meet and be approved by the director of the institute, the eminent scholar Angus Campbell.

From the moment I first heard that name, I loved it—Angus Campbell. Hearing it, I would envision Alec Guinness in a somber, black-and-white film about a craggy old Scot who was trying to save his ailing golf course while his eyes smoldered with some inner torment we would learn of only in the last reel.

But this Angus Campbell was not a bit like Alec Guinness. He was taller, even more slender, and slick bald. But he had the same intense eyes and angular features as the actor and the moment he entered the room, you felt you were in the presence of someone special. Indeed, Dr. Angus Campbell was the real engine that drove his Institute for Social Research to a pinnacle as the foremost university-based social science research organization in the world.

Professor Campbell, I learned quickly, was that unique scholar held in the highest esteem by colleagues, the academic community, government officials, and client sponsors. Yet he was also a dynamic speaker and gifted writer who could communicate in powerful, clear terms to readers with only a modest education. While many of Angus's fellow scholars disdained the masses, Angus was one of a very few truly brilliant scientists and scholars who cared about making his research findings accessible to virtually all audiences. He believed that since much of the institute's research was funded by taxpayers, it was only right that those regular citizens also be told in plain language what was learned at think tanks they paid for.

"What this place needs," he told me, "is someone who doesn't know the taboos, who doesn't bow before all our precious sacred cows. Perhaps that is something you and I shall discuss one day."

First, though, there was the matter of the Katona opus.

We agreed on a $1,000 fee and Angus took me to meet the resident tyrant to a generation of economics students.

The esteemed Dr. George Katona was out of central casting as the rumpled academician. The gruff old curmudgeon took no prisoners, suffered fools neither gladly nor otherwise, and ate smart-alecky graduate students for lunch.

In answer to his question, I replied that, no, I was afraid I had read only one of his opuses, *The Mass Consumption Society*, but not his other seminal works. No, not even *The Powerful Consumer*.

Dr. Katona regarded me as if I were some lower life form that had slithered into his presence. He reached behind him to his book shelf and plopped one, two, three books in front of me, waved his hand as if brushing away a pesky gnat, and turned his back to me as if I had never been there. We were off and reading.

Weeks later, when I would reshape or—horrors!—prune shards of the prose I excised from Katona each week, he would light up a cigarette, expel a great cloud of gray smoke, and fume at me, "Now, Beeell, now look here." That was all. He would not go on to tell me what to look at or where "here" was. He would just tap my offensive editing with a nicotine-stained index finger, shake his head, and puff. Finally he would purse his lips, nod reluctantly and almost imperceptibly, and go on to the next patch of my blue penciling. And again widen his eyes and say, "Now, Beeell, now look here."

Those first sessions with George Katona were uncomfortable. He could terrorize anyone and I was no exception. But there was a difference: the honorable Professor Katona did not hold my future in his tobacco-tanned hands. He was not the chair of my doctoral committee. He could not choose to either grant or deny me tenure on the faculty. The only power he held was to fire me from a freelance project, the income from which I fortunately did not need desperately for survival.

Though overdue on not one but two books, George remained resolute. "The work will be done when the work is done," he would say, even to Angus Campbell. "We write for the ages." All other attempts having failed to extract the manuscript from Dr. Katona, I was the last great hope. Angus knew that. So did George. And so did I. So when, that autumn, George and I wrestled over my axing of the final excessive caveat and he signed off on my work, an impression had been made.

And that, I thought, was the end of it—until Angus called me with the surprising news that George was delighted with our collaboration. Angus felt that anyone who could delight the irascible Professor Katona would be a substantial asset to the institute.

Angus invited me to lunch and went straight to it. Would I join the staff of the Survey Research Center of the Institute for Social Research—a faculty appointment, he called it—with a mandate to bring the research findings of the center and the institute to all of its relevant audiences? He wanted to see that the institute's research product would continue to be made available in the appropriate forms—monographs, journal articles, working papers, books—to the scholarly and academic communities. But he wanted the knowledge learned by this august institution conveyed to the widest possible audiences, including the audience so long disregarded if not held in contempt by many of his colleagues—the general public.

"Faculty appointment" did not mean I would have teaching obligations, but rather that Angus's status-sensitive colleagues would cooperate with me because they would see me as a bit more of an equal, even though I held no Ph.D. in a social science.

Specifically, Angus hoped I would dynamite past-due book manuscripts from the grasp of his fellow social scientists, perhaps assist in arranging publication of those works with scholarly houses or university presses, edit or co-author or personally write articles both for journals and for more popular publications, work with him on the feasibility of a nationally syndicated column on insights from the world of the social sciences. And more.

I told Angus that seemed an ambitious agenda, but do-able. However, he should know that Marcy, my children, and I had just embarked on a perhaps too-ambitious project ourselves, moving from Ann Arbor to the countryside of Jackson County to build a golf course.

Angus smiled. "My father had a saying when I complained he was piling too much work on me, 'When you want a job done, give it to a busy man.'"

"Well," I responded. "Did it work on you?"

"Every time," he said.

And so it would, I expected, on me.

Six

On the Friday after Thanksgiving, for maybe the fiftieth time in the three months since we moved in, I took a notepad and a pen and went out to pace off some distances. As I crested the ridge beyond the oak woods, I saw a figure in a blue jacket and a tan cap step behind a tree in the fence line between our land and Harrison's. When I looked again, he was gone. I remembered seeing a fleeting figure in about the same place the day we first saw the Nate Fish farm.

I now had many of the key measurements memorized but as I stepped off distances I checked the new numbers against my previous figures. One day I would have to measure yardages very accurately to be sure the distances printed in the scorecard were correct. But for now, just to get a rough idea, it was sufficient to pace it off. As I walked beside the barbed wire fence separating our property from Harrison's, I studied his fields closely and came to the same conclusion I had every time previously. Harrison's land was usable, but only barely. It would be our last resort.

The twenty acres due east of our house was available, I had learned, but it too was without character and at $500 per acre, that land was far out of our reach. Part of that inflated price was because that parcel fronted on Curtis Road, as did another twenty-acre parcel due west of the woods, carrying an identical premium for road frontage.

As I got to the top of the ridge overlooking Willow Creek and its marsh, I turned to the west and looked again longingly at the Smedley land and then farther off and to the northwest, at the Smedley Hill. And for the first time, I saw someone there, someone on the Smedley property. The person was perhaps four hundred yards away but I could see an apron blowing in the wind, a short, squat woman facing me. She raised an arm and I couldn't tell if she was simply waving or motioning for me to come over. Well, there was no way to walk directly over there. That would have to wait until we had a land bridge to the other side. I waved back tentatively, jogged back to the house, and got into the pickup truck.

Five minutes later, I drove into the Smedleys' driveway, just as the figure I had seen on the hill stepped out of the farm lane and into the side yard. I walked over to meet the woman I assumed was Gladys Smedley. She was stocky as a high-school linebacker but her sure-of-herself swagger came off as more of a sassy waddle. She stopped a few feet away to size me up, so I did the same right back at her. Shiny round face, gold-rimmed eyeglasses, brown hair going to gray and done up in a bun. Wearing a faded long dress mostly covered by an apron with two bulging front pockets. One pocket held a tall glass, which she now extracted and took a sip from as she looked me over. Then from another pocket she took a pack of Pall Malls and scratched a kitchen match to flame with her fingernail.

"About time you got here," she said. "Starting to think I was going to have one of those snooty Ann Arbor types for a neighbor." She came closer and squinted suspiciously up at me for a moment, then walked right on past me and toward the house, me trailing behind. She wheeled around. "I truly hope you're not one of those goddamn sissy gentlemen farmers. Show me those palms. By God, the feller has calluses. Heard you work at Bendix at some desk job, but there might be hope for you yet. You already know I'm Gladys Smedley. What do we call you?"

She motioned toward a couple of metal chairs pulled up to an ash pit at the end of the driveway where a fire smoldered. I sat while she filled her apron with small sticks of wood from a cord stacked against the garage.

"I keep that fire going pretty much spring up to Thanksgiving Day. Warms the bones in the spring and fall and keeps the damn mosquitoes down in the summer. Course if Kent would put up a decent martin house for us instead of making them all winter long for the whole blamed county, we might have our own martins and a few less skeeters. They say each adult martin eats ten thousand mosquitoes a day. Ha! Believe that, I got this bridge I'll sell you. What're you drinking?"

I looked again at the glass tucked into Gladys's apron front pocket that she somehow managed to carry around without spilling. I told her whatever she was having was fine with me.

"No, you don't, sonny, you're not finding out that easy what I'm sipping all day. Now make up your mind. Beer? High ball? Wine? Soda pop?"

I poked at the fire and had it going good by the time Gladys came back with a beer for me, the safest call. She wanted to know just exactly what it was that I did at this Bendix place. "Only thing I know about Bendix," she said, "is years back they made a damn fine washing machine. Wouldn't I like to have one of them now, better than the junk they fob off on you nowadays. A whole damn economy built on buy the next thing."

I looked up and saw the moon was low in the sky so I called her attention to it as I explained about the project I was working on called ALSEP, the Apollo Lunar Surface Experiments Package. I had been on ALSEP since its first days; it would be deployed on the lunar surface in three or four years by Apollo 14.

I told Gladys I was neither a scientist nor an engineer, just an English major with a secret clearance who went bad. I told her that I really was working out of my element and that I was thinking seriously of changing jobs, of leaving Bendix after seven years there for a job at the University of Michigan.

"Just as well. It's not as if everything is so ducky here on Earth we gotta piss away taxpayer dollars to put a few toys on the moon. I swear, been downhill in Washington since Harry Truman told 'em all go to hell. That man had the right idea. Can you tell me in words a simple soul like me can understand just what we can possibly learn on the moon that's worth all that money?"

I admitted that when I started on the project I was skeptical that the equipment would ever get built and if it did—given the government's track record for canceling programs for whatever reasons—that it would make it to the moon. I guessed that if President Kennedy's goal of putting a man on the moon by the end of the decade of the sixties was achieved, there was a good chance that Congress would pull the plug on funding future programs.

Gladys was as good a listener as she was a talker and although she stared into the fire while I talked, she listened carefully enough to throw in a sharp comment every so often. So I explained what little I knew about advances that might flow from the space program—in medicine, materials, propulsion systems, new power sources. I told her the speculations about what might be learned about the sun, our solar system, and even about the Earth from those instruments the astronauts would set out on the lunar surface.

I expected some stiff arguments or at least just peevish close-mindedness from Gladys. But once I had exhausted what little I knew that might interest her, she just sat there, nodding, sipping, poking the fire. Saying nothing.

The smoke from the fire had already caused me to move my chair two or three times while I talked. Now it was coming at me again.

"Following you. Does that to some people."

"What?"

"The smoke," Gladys barked. "There's people the smoke just follows, no matter where they sit, how often they move, the smoke follows 'em."

"You really believe that?"

"Haven't seen me move since I sat down, have you? And you've moved, what, three-four times. That's not evidence enough? I guess if I can believe that maybe your space program isn't just a colossal boondoggle after all, you can believe the smoke follows you when you see it with your own eyes, for the great Chrissake."

I WAS HAVING TROUBLE getting used to a party-line phone and kept picking it up for my neighbors' calls, but this one—two longs and one short—was for me.

"Mr. Haney, my name is Bill Newcomb. I hear you're building a golf course."

"That's right. Mind if I ask where you heard about it?"

There was a pause. "Several people have mentioned it. If it's supposed to be confidential—"

"No, not at all. Just curious. Where are you calling from?"

"Ann Arbor. Actually, a lot of people around here know about it. You had that Saturday morning radio show on golf and you were head of the Ann Arbor Men's Golf Association, so word has gotten around."

"I guess it has. We've barely started out here."

"So I'm not too late then?"

"For what, Mr. Newcomb?"

"Call me, Bill, please. To take on the design for you. As you may know, I'm associated with Joe Dye. I'm sure you're familiar with his firm and the great courses he's done. I'll have a credit on the one we're finishing right now and then I'd be available to take on yours."

"Well, Mr. Newcomb, I truly do appreciate your interest and your offer. But I really don't need a designer, thanks."

"Uh huh. Somebody mentioned you were planning on designing it yourself."

"That's right."

"Not to be impertinent, Mr. Haney, but have you ever designed a golf course before?"

"No, I have not."

"You'll have a lot tied up in that place. And you're not worried about making mistakes?"

"Actually, Mr. Newcomb, that's why I'm designing it myself."

"You expect to make mistakes and yet you're still going to design it yourself?"

"That's correct. For sure there will be mistakes. But they'll be my mistakes. If I'm going to have to live with mistakes, I'd rather they were of my very own making."

"So you're going to invest good money in building a course, maybe go into heavy debt, but if it doesn't pan out because the design isn't good, you can handle that because you don't have a problem living with your own mistakes."

"Maybe it's because I've had so much practice at it."

MARCY AND I TALKED about Angus Campbell's offer. It was time to make a decision.

We both knew very well that my strong opposition to the Vietnam War had made me one of a tiny clutch of three doves amongst a great flock of hawks at Bendix. And while I felt as patriotic as any of them, it was increasingly uncomfortable to hold a secret clearance and work inside a defense industry whose principles I did not endorse. Marcy understood and supported me when I said my first priority was to change my own mission in my "day job," and that it was a nice bonus to contemplate helping Angus Campbell achieve goals with more positive and lasting implications for society.

So, just four months after we moved to Grass Lake to build the golf course, and just weeks after I completed the Katona book ahead of schedule, I owed Angus Campbell an answer.

Even if he hadn't been so persuasive, it was an easy sell. More money would have been nice, but I was content to take basically the same $13,300-a-year salary to move into a fresh working environment. Bendix had been very good to me and I had many friends there, but the ALSEP project would be wrapped up in a year or so. After that there would be no clear prospect of a meaningful role on another NASA program and Bendix management knew I would no longer work on military projects.

There were other attractions to taking the university position. I looked for greater satisfaction handling the products of social science research than I had found in my eight-year immersion in the cold pragmatics of science and engineering. I'd have the customary and generous faculty perks, including inexpensive tickets to a rich offering of cultural and athletic events.

While visiting the institute on the freelance assignment, I could see that the work environment was relaxed to the point of being sedate. That was both good and bad. And very enticingly, there would be five weeks of vacation and a full-year sabbatical every seventh year—quite desirable for someone building a golf course on the side. Angus went over this with me, then said, "To be candid, one of your most desirable assets is that you're not a social scientist or a scholar. It seems to me that you like getting things done. And we have much here that is worth doing, worth communicating, and frankly it isn't happening quickly enough and well enough to suit me."

When Angus laid all that out, there might have been another possible response, but only one presented itself to me.

I told Angus I had to give Bendix ample notice, wrap up the ALSEP film and some other items, and would start in five weeks, the last week of December.

IN LESS THAN FIVE MONTHS, our lives had changed dramatically and irrevocably. Marcy and I assumed (and hoped) the change would be for the better. In the early summer of 1966 we had been comfortable in our new house in an Ann Arbor neighborhood we greatly liked. The kids had friends on our quiet street and in school. I had the job at Bendix, a Fortune Top 50 company where I had seven years of equity, a great boss, a good reputation, an exciting role on significant space exploration projects, and a decent salary and great employee benefits. And, probably I had something else, the seven-year itch.

So much had changed in those five months. In July we had first seen the Grass Lake property and had given Daryle Heselschwerdt a $500 earnest money deposit. In the first week of August we had closed on the deal. In the third week of August, we had moved into bucolic Grass Lake Township in comparatively depressed Jackson County.

We had exchanged the comforts of a new and modern home for a hundred-year-old house that was about to devour buckets of money, gallons of sweat, more than a few drops of blood. And, oh yes, there were these acres of ill-used land that may or may not submit to becoming a golf course and even if they did, we had somehow to find another forty or fifty adjacent acres; if not, we'd have something new under the sun: a four-and-a-half-hole golf course.

GLADYS SMEDLEY SHOUTED INTO THE PHONE that she had a jar of her end-of-the-garden relish with my name on it.

When I got to the Smedleys' house, Gladys was standing in the driveway giving animated directions to a pleasant-looking elderly man whose husky six-foot frame dwarfed her. He ran his craggy fingers through his thinning white hair as he listened patiently to Gladys, something he apparently had a great deal of practice doing.

"Mr. Haney, shake hands with the lord of the manor, Byron Kent Smedley. Let's get out of the way right now why I don't call him by his first name. Imagine him out there in the fields working—and don't you know that would take a good imagination—and I have to call him in. Now, can you hear me bellowing 'Byyyy-ronnnn. Byyyy-ronn?' No way can you get any edge to 'Byron,' name's just too damn soft and sophisticated for a lug can't get the printer's ink out from under his fingernails. Why, he'd never hear the end of it from that wiseacre Horace Coppernoll, me hollering 'Byyyy-ronnnn.' Now, 'Kent,' there's a name you can snap right off sharp and clean and they by God know what you mean."

I glanced over at Kent, who just harrumphed and shook his head. He stuck out a big, gnarled paw and fixed me with a pair of pale blue eyes that had already seen too much of this world.

"Kent, Mr. Haney's trying to get the lay of the land before he starts building that country club of his. Now, I know it never crossed his mind he's about to make all his neighbors into property paupers once his fancy golf links is in and our assessed evaluation goes clear through the damned clouds. So, just to show him there's no hard feelings, you take him on out to our big hill, let him see how nice his place looks from up on just about the highest point in the county."

Kent was already underway, shuffling hunched over, with short quick steps and I wondered if that was because of his years of lugging eighty-pound chases of Linotype for the old presses they still ran at the *Citizen-Patriot* in Jackson. I asked him how long he had been at the *Cit-Pat*.

"Too long by half," he said, in a rumbling baritone, made the more gravelly by decades of his and Gladys's tobacco fumes.

We tramped through the fallow field of meadow grasses stretching from the Smedley's backyard, a field rising gently for three hundred yards to the crown of Smedley Hill. From there it appeared that most of the Smedley's property north of the Willow Creek marsh was on a ridge twenty to thirty feet higher than any land on our side. The hill fell away more gradually down to the marsh than I had expected.

Near a bend in Willow Creek was a small knoll of perhaps two acres, possibly the patch where Gladys had said she once raised a fine stand of hay. On the south side of the creek and the marsh we shared in common was our ridge, paralleling the spine of high ground on which we stood. The marsh was broader and more lush as it stretched west into the Smedley property, fed by hundreds of fresh springs charged perpetually by rainwater percolating down through the sand and gravel strata.

"I've stood out here at dusk," Kent said, "and watched your mercury vapor light come on. And in the winter, that red barn of yours stands out real sharp. Looks like a Christmas card painting. Your house looks a little bare with those big old elms gone."

The tiny house and barns did look very nice from here, a good half mile away. I already had a few ill-formed ideas for golf holes, and I couldn't resist visualizing how a pair of par fours would fit beautifully on that far ridge of Smedley's that flattened into a plateau and, looking the other way, how you could shape a par three to carry completely over water, from one side of the marsh to the other. The challenge, however, would be not to place a great hole here or there but instead to route nine holes in the most effective, satisfying sequence, building to a crescendo while making the best possible use of the land overall.

Kent pointed to the southwest, at a little stand of maples and lilacs halfway down the hill. "Few months ago I picked a good gallon of blackberries right there and Glad put them up for the winter. Always figured Nate Fish or one of his kin must have planted them, maybe fifty-sixty years ago. Glad just yesterday made as fine a blackberry pie as I ever tasted. She might have a slice left for you when we get back. But if you're up for a little walk, I'll show you the woods on our west boundary. With the leaves down, you can see quite well."

"You mean you own farther on over to the west?"

He waved an arm and we started toward the fifteen acres of mixed woods, running from the oaks and hickories on the crest, down through the quaking aspen, into the black willows, hackberries, and blue beech down at the edge of the marsh where the wetfoot varieties thrive. We picked our way diagonally down the sandy ridge, through varieties of trees that gradually changed every fifteen to twenty feet of elevation.

"We started out with just the house and its fifteen acres, then added this forty," Kent said. "Nobody ever made a dime farming it since long before Nate Fish tried growing popcorn here back in the teens. Imagine that? I'm no farmer but even I would know better than try to row crop the blow sand on those hills and ridges."

Kent stopped and looked at a fine specimen of a sassafras tree, its few remaining crimson leaves shimmering with an iridescent sheen in the late afternoon sun.

"It's lain fallow these fifty years since," Kent said. "Foolish thing we bought it. It is about as useless as a piece of land as I've ever seen. But we got it for next to nothing and Glad wouldn't have it any other way. Starting right after our honeymoon we'd walk out here of an evening. We'd just come out the back door and off into our own field and next thing you knew we were standing up there on the big hill, looking at the view. And Glad would get real quiet, not a common condition for her, as I'm sure you have observed. 'Peaceful,' she'd say. 'Real peaceful.'"

Kent stooped to pick up a crisp, withered sassafras leaf. It took him a few seconds to straighten up and he winced a bit. He held out the oddly shaped leaf to me, tracing its three lobes with a finger.

"No two sassafras trees alike, same as with snowflakes. See how this one is shaped almost like a human hand wearing a mitten, that lobe there like the thumb sticking out."

He tucked the leaf in his shirt pocket and pointed partway up the hill.

"Those walks in the evening were special to Glad. I could tell she was worrying that someone would buy this forty before we did. And yet she knew we couldn't afford it. I was chasing type then at the *Cit-Pat*, before I got promoted onto press. She's worrying somebody buys it and next thing they've ripped out the berry patches, scared away the sandhill cranes."

We walked to the knoll and beyond it to a field Kent said would be lush with wild blueberries and strawberries in season.

"Strawberries run real small," Kent said, "but Glad always says there's just so much flavor per berry, no matter the size. You take those big ones from California, look so good in the store? Like a chunk of balsa wood dyed red for all the flavor you get. Still, you have to have a real taste for berries when you're paying taxes on forty acres just so you can pick five dollars' worth. Well, it makes Glad happy, it's good enough for me."

We both took a last look around. This forty or so acres was about as perfect as it could be for our purposes. But I knew there was no way we could afford it and it was obvious how dear it was to the Smedleys.

Kent started up the hill, then stopped partway up to catch his breath. He looked at me, squinted and said, "I believe we've got something you want, Mr. Haney."

I just looked at him.

"That slice of blackberry pie I promised you. Maybe Glad has a scoop of vanilla ice cream to go with it, too."

Seven

The snow stung my face and coated my glasses as I looked back and tried to see our car. I could barely make out the glow of the headlights and the flashing emergency lights as they pulsated through the snowdrift. The winds ripped across the open fields, dumping a fresh and deeper blanket on the crusted two-foot layer already on the ground. One good thing—there was plenty of gas in the tank and Marcy would keep the kids calm until I got help.

We were less than five miles from home but it was midnight and we were stuck in the biggest blizzard in memory.

The tops of the fence posts barely poked above the snow, just enough that I might be able to see where the intersection would be. It took much longer to get there than I had thought when I shoved my way out of the car where it was half buried on Francisco Road, but finally I found it—the east-west line of fence posts. I turned west, directly into the biting storm, heading for where I remembered the closest house must be, perhaps three hundred yards away on Grass Lake Road. The only illumination now was the distant barn light at Judd's farm. I looked in that direction only a few seconds before my glasses caked with snow, then I bowed my head and followed the line of the fence posts. The next time I looked up, I saw a yellow glow through windows in the house.

I had been slogging through the drifts for maybe twenty minutes and I had gone at most a quarter of a mile. Now the drifts in places were up to my chest and I could make headway only by turning sideways to reduce the resistance of my body against the ever-deepening snow.

My breath came in deep gasps; the frigid air bit deep into my lungs. Despite the cold, my back was damp with sweat. The pant leg pulled out of my right boot and it filled up quickly with snow that melted against my skin, then began to freeze. I remembered that feeling too well from childhood days.

Maybe fifty yards before me now, the Judd place came and went through white billows, ragged yellow shafts spilling out from windows.

There should be a mudroom around the back, the way there now visible in the surreal blue-white glow of the barn's mercury vapor lamp. No bell. I knocked. No answer. I banged on the door. Soon I heard steps and a muffled voice, "Now just what damn fool would be out on a night like—"

And the door opened. I had met Charlie Judd at a high-school basketball game. But with my frozen beard and the snow covering every inch of my clothes, he didn't recognize me. My glasses fogged in the warmer air and I took them off. I could barely see Charlie but could tell he was looking over my shoulder for the headlights from a car, truck, tractor, some kind of vehicle. He would see only the trenches I had carved in the snowdrifts. I stood in the mudroom, wiping my glasses on my shirttail, the only dry part of my clothes, and between gasps told Charlie we were stuck in a drift a quarter mile east. He shook his head and started putting on heavy winter clothes.

We threw a scoop shovel and thirty-odd feet of three-eighths-inch logging chain into the bucket of Charlie's front-end loader. In less than twenty minutes we were riding several feet above the drifts in the heated cab of his king-size John Deere. On the way to the car, I tried to visualize the underside of the Olds wagon, wondering where we could hook the chain to the frame.

Marcy had the dome light on and although the windows of the Olds were steamed up, I could see the kids moving around, jumping up and down, celebrating the coming rescue.

I got out, grabbed the shovel, and started to scrape away a path to the car. Judd yelled something that the wind carried away, then he waved an arm for me to move aside. He chomped his front-end bucket into the chest-high drift where the front end of the Olds was impaled. He dumped the snow downwind and in four or five big bites had his bucket scraping the first bare pavement we had seen in the fifty miles since we left the Christmas gathering at Marcy's folks' house more than two hours earlier.

The car was now free enough that we could crawl out of the big drift but that only got us as far as another drift and yet another. Still we could not get enough traction on our own. So we hooked up the chain to the undercarriage of the Olds and Charlie towed us off Francisco Road and to the intersection with Grass Lake Road, then to his driveway, and finally another two hundred yards beyond. Now we could head west straight into the wind on Grass Lake Road, where the layered snow was only eight to ten inches deep.

I got out, unhooked the chain and dropped it into Charlie's front-end loader bucket. I gave Charlie a twenty-dollar bill—all the money I had—and told him I owed him a big favor. He grunted and shook his head.

We now had less than four miles to go. One more doubtful drift in a valley on Fishville Road a mile from home but I kept the speed up and we blasted through it. Less than a mile now, maybe close enough for me to walk home and get a tractor if we got stuck again.

We passed the Coppernoll place and the Fishville cemetery and then made out the glow of the mercury vapor lamp on Henry Samyn's Breezy Acres barn. If this was as far as we could get, I'd offer Henry a choice between towing us home with his John Deere or taking us in. But as I started the turn onto Curtis Road we saw that the surface was in better shape than what we'd just come off of. As we turned onto where I guessed the blacktop would be, for the first time I felt we had a chance. When I pulled into our driveway and took my hands off the steering wheel, they felt like rusted claws—white-knuckle driving was a cliché for good reason.

The kids were too wired to go right to sleep so Marcy made popcorn and hot chocolate and they played with Pat's Hot Wheels game. I could hear them in there, laughing at Cocoa the cat going crazy trying to catch the little cars as they whizzed through the chutes and around the curves. I sat at the kitchen table, my head stuck in a little tent Marcy rigged up so I could inhale steam to ease the wheezing in my frostbitten lungs. It was a nice feeling, sitting there at the kitchen table, drifting, as I breathed the warm menthol vapors, hearing the kids' voices from a long way off, remembering that feeling from a long time ago. Breathing deep, drifting . . .

It's too cold to skate any more. It's not snowing so much but the wind is still blowing so hard. The gusts throw ice needles against my cheeks. Everybody has gone home. It's no fun anymore skating alone.

My legs hurt. I wish I had ankle supports. My feet are so tired from trying to stay up on the blades. I take off my skates and put on my frozen boots and tie the skate laces so I can loop the skates around my neck. Now my fingers are like icicles. I lose one mitten as I crawl up the creek bank and plow through the deep drifts toward home, a half-mile away. I'll come back when the snow melts and look for the mitten.

By the time I get to Rochester Road, I'm gulping cold air that hurts with every breath. Too tired to make it home. I'll go to Haney's Oil Well. My Dad will be there by now—it's afternoon so he'll be home from his night shift job at the creamery and working on cars at his service station. I can warm up by the big stove and rest.

He's welding something and has his big welding mask on. I watch the beautiful blue light for a few seconds, then look away because I know if my father sees me looking at it he'll say again, "You want to go blind? Just keep looking at a welding torch without a mask, we'll be fitting you up with one of those leader dogs. Then it's no more baseball, no more books for you. Just the blackest darkness you can imagine. And don't think I'm going to nursemaid you. Un-uhh, your own damn fault you're blind and don't say I didn't warn you."

So I turn away and instead look at the reflection of the blue flame in the front window and watch the red globs of melted metal that bounce and roll on the floor. The golden sparks fly all over like a million shooting stars. I see a brown dog run across the road so I know I haven't gone blind yet but my chest feels tingly inside and makes funny noises.

Dad finishes his job and shuts off the torch. He flips up his mask and sees me there, warming my hands by the pot-bellied stove. He fishes in his overalls and pulls out his Old Golds. He lights one up and says to me, "First man says, 'A man went fishing and caught three fish. When he got home he had five.'

"Second man says, 'How could that be?'

"First man says, 'He caught three bluegill and when he got home he had three bluegill and two smelt.'"

I know it is time to laugh so I do.

Dad says, "Now you tell it, Billy."

I tell it exactly the way Dad told it and he doesn't laugh or even smile.

"What did I do wrong?" I ask.

"You had it fine right up to the end. Then you should say, "He had three bluegill and two of them smelt."

I think about it.

"But Dad—"

"You want to make people laugh or not?"

"Make 'em laugh."

"All right then. Now sit there and be quiet and wait for the next person comes in. Then you get up and let him sit on that chair and you tell him the way I told you to. Watch 'em laugh."

I wait. In a while, Paddy Patterson comes in and sits on the chair. He takes out his pouch of Red Man and puts a wad of tobacco in his mouth. He chews a while and talks to my Dad about how cold it is outside for brass monkeys and nuns. Then he leans over to spit a long brown stream at the coffee can next to the pot-bellied stove that once I got too close to and scorched my new winter Mackinaw, the first real wool winter coat I ever had and from then on it smelled funny. Paddy misses the can and hits the hot leg of the stove and it sizzles and steam comes up.

"Paddy—"

"It's Mr. Patterson to you, squirt," Dad says.

"Mr. Patterson, a man went fishing."

Paddy Patterson looks at me and smiles. He is the shortest man in all of Big Beaver and even more Irish than my Dad. He has bright blue eyes, a nose that is red all the time, and white bushy eyebrows. "The most patriotic face in town," he'd say when the other men made fun of him or called him one of Santa's elves. Paddy is the only man in town who is shorter than my mother, who always says she is exactly five feet one inch tall, but is really at least two inches shorter than that. Dad reminds her of that almost every time they argue.

Paddy likes to go for walks, even if it is real hot or raining or cold, but people are always stopping their car and trying to coax him to get in. They say it is weather unfit for man nor beast. Then Paddy comes to my Dad's gas station and tells him people just won't leave him alone to finish his walk. Lots of people like to come to Haney's Oil Well because you can buy True Blue Sunoco, best gasoline money can buy and even the best is not good enough for your engine if you don't change your oil regularly.

"Okay, Billy, a man went fishing. Orchard Lake, I suppose?"

"Yes, Mr. Patterson. A man went fishing in Orchard Lake. He caught three fish and when he got home, he had five."

Paddy squints at me.

"Now wait a minute. He caught three fish, you say? And when he got home there were five. There must be a catch there. How could three fish turn into five, Billy?"

Now I had him. "Because he caught three bluegill . . ." and I look at my father, who has his hand over his mouth, trying not to laugh before I say the punch line. "And two of them smelt."

Paddy stares at me.

"Get it, Mr. Patterson?"

Paddy seems confused. My father turns away, laughing into his hand, so I know at least my father gets it.

"Billy," Paddy says, "that would still be only three fish. See, he caught three bluegill and even if two of them smelled bad, then he's still got only three fish."

"No, Mr. Patterson, that's not the way it goes. Listen, I'll do it again. But you have to listen really close this time, okay?"

Paddy Patterson leans forward and looks at me while I tell it again. When I'm done, he just shakes his head and looks at my Dad, who is laughing so hard snot comes out of his nose and he coughs and his face gets all red. So I know that maybe what they say about Mr. Patterson being just a dumb mick is right because my father is half as Irish as Mr. Patterson and he sure got it.

He is still laughing about it when he comes home for dinner and tells *my mother and she just says, "Ray, why must you tease the boy like that? Just leave the boy alone."*

Mom doesn't know Dad isn't teasing me. He's just teaching me how to tell a story the way he does, making people laugh.

WHEN I WALKED INTO GLADYS'S KITCHEN to hand her the Christmas card I hadn't gotten into the mail on time, the table was laden with jar after jar of her legendary end-of-the-garden relish and a dozen or more Ball canning jars of peaches. Kent sat there quietly, wiping off jars, writing on labels. Gladys handed me a box with several jars of relish and peaches and a small bag of what looked to be bits of nuts.

"Don't know what those are, do you? Well, those are black walnuts. Mind, I didn't say English walnuts that by comparison yield about as much flavor as a good chaw on a fence post. No sir, these here are black walnuts and what you do, grind them up real fine but, mind you, only when you're ready to use them. Otherwise you keep them stored in the fridge, they last forever."

"Gladys, that's sweet of you. This will be real—"

"Don't give me sweet. Give me three dollars. You don't figure I do these for my health, do you? And that's a bargain 'cause I'm just getting rid of the excess from Kent always gathering ten times what we ever could use. Scoops 'em up by the bushel, then he empties them out on the driveway. Runs over them with the car to bust off the outer husk. Brings 'em in to me and that's when the real work begins. Those shells are hard as a bullet."

Gladys rapped an unshelled nut on the table for emphasis.

"Anyhow, when your missus goes to bake cookies or maybe those little crescent doo-dads, what she does, just sprinkles a quarter teaspoon into the dough for a good-sized batch and mixes it in good. Now I know that doesn't seem like much, but these black walnuts are some kind of potent—not like some people who will remain nameless. Now, where's my three dollars?"

Out of the corner of my eye I could see Kent shake his head, snort, and turn away.

1.9.6.7

Eight

The Alberta Clipper picked up moisture as it roared across Lake Michigan and by noon when it hit Jackson County it had already swollen into the second severe storm of the winter. By midafternoon, the layer of ice on the windows of my office in Ann Arbor was crusted with snow. By nightfall the slippery streets were deserted and there was no way I could negotiate nineteen snowdrifted miles to Grass Lake. I carried four hundred pounds of ballast on the deck of the pickup truck to improve traction, but no rear-wheel-drive pickup truck without tire chains could be controlled on such slick, snow-packed roads.

I called Marcy to tell her I would spend the night in Ann Arbor with friends. I had filled the coal stoker hamper that morning, but with the frigid temperatures and bitter winds, she would have to keep it topped up and shear pins handy. Replacing a shear pin got your arms covered with coal dust but was simple enough to do after the first time, as Marcy had already learned.

While I had a restless night's sleep in Ann Arbor, I kept thinking of Marcy and the kids making their first solitary stand in the old Nate Fish house against a full-bodied blizzard. Winter storms sweep out of the northwest in Jackson County and our barns were too far from the house to provide a windbreak. As Marcy made dinner, she could feel the west walls shudder against the gales. Bad news: no elms to break the wind. Good news: no elms to crash through the roof.

After dinner, Marcy let Yukon, our Airedale–German shepherd mix, out for a run and as the evening wore on, she began to wonder why he hadn't come right back in such weather. Maybe he had curled up in the barn to ride out the storm.

Marcy got the kids into bed and was catching up on some paperwork when, at ten o'clock, the phone rang. Two longs and one short. Our ring. She answered the phone but no one responded. Minutes later, the phone rang again. Still no one on the other end of the line. She started to wonder what was going on. It was her first night home alone in a heavy winter storm, without me and without the big, gruff dog, but with four kids asleep in a house trembling under blast after blast.

The phone rang a third time, and still no one spoke. Then a fourth. This was ominous. Marcy looked outside and, in the bright wash of the mercury vapor light, saw nothing but a thick blanket of snow, getting deeper by the minute. No cars had passed for some time on Curtis Road. And no sign of Yukon.

The phone rang a fifth time. Marcy let it ring several times, then picked it up suspiciously. She clicked it two or three times to break the connection, then heard, "Mrs. Haney! Don't hang up."

It was a woman's voice, one she had heard before but now couldn't place.

"Mrs. Haney, I have to work tomorrow and I can't get any sleep with that dog of yours."

The voice was only faintly familiar and it took Marcy some time to register. It was Esther Samyn, Henry's wife. They had been over one evening and while I had talked with Esther several times, Marcy scarcely knew her. Esther proceeded to tell Marcy that Yukon was scratching at their door, whining, and barking to be let in. Marcy would just have to come down and get him so she could get some sleep.

"I'm very sorry about that, Esther, but I don't see how I can do that. Bill couldn't make it home from Ann Arbor so he's staying there. I'm home by myself with the children. I can't leave them alone. And I don't even know if I could make it there in the car, with the snow so deep in the road. No cars have gone down the road in hours."

Esther told Marcy that one way or another she simply had to get down there right away and get that dog. And she hung up.

Marcy went upstairs and told Mark she was going to have to go out for a few minutes but would be right back. Did he understand? Yes, he did.

It took Marcy some time to get the snow cleared off the station wagon. She let it warm up, then gingerly backed it away from the house. Only by memory could she tell where the driveway was. She crept toward the road, knowing that if she didn't have the car lined up properly, the wheels would drop down into the culvert and there would be no getting out without being towed.

Marcy inched out to where she thought the road must be, and

finally saw depressions in the snow that she hoped were the drainage ditches on either side of the road. She kept the car in low gear the entire half a mile to the Samyn's driveway. The barn light above Henry's Breezy Acres sign gave enough light for her to pick out the driveway and as she turned in, Yukon bounded toward her. She opened the door and he scrambled over her and into the passenger seat, his long, flapping tongue licking her, his fur matted with snow.

Marcy followed her own tire tracks home. She told Mark she was back, go back to sleep. And she gratefully curled up on the couch, Yukon already snoring at her feet.

THAT FIRST WINTER, it seemed as if every time I was away on a business trip, a major storm would hit. And there would be Marcy in that creaky, drafty old house with four little kids and a coal furnace fed by a stoker that sawed off so many shear pins we had taken to keeping a box of ten-penny nails right next to it and using those instead. The nails were much softer metal than the actual shear pins and would snap off whenever the worm gear that fed the coal into the furnace from the stoker bin encountered a too-large or too-hard lump of coal. Then you'd hear the higher-pitched whine that meant the shaft was running free.

As I drove the fifty slip-sliding miles from Detroit Metro Airport, where my plane from Washington, D.C., had delivered me three hours late from my trip, I wondered how Marcy had fared in this latest storm. I came in through the mudroom, kicked off my boots, and set down my suitcase and briefcase.

Marcy fixed me a cup of coffee and we sat at the kitchen table.

"Things have been okay here," she said. "Broke several shear pins but it only took a minute to put new ones in. Didn't you say there was a way we could replace that old stoker with an oil burner insert?"

"That will be a priority, you can bet we—"

"There goes another one," Marcy said, and I took my coffee cup and went down to the basement to put in a new nail in the stoker shaft.

Musty old basement. Three of the walls were Michigan fieldstones, set in mortar; the fourth was poured concrete. When it was built a hundred years before, the floor had been left in dirt, but later a concrete floor had been poured, covering all but a small area where the well shaft had been drilled and the pump and tank sat. And a good thing too, because after a heavy rain, when the water gushed down the cellar steps, you could broom it off onto the dirt, which was four inches lower than the concrete floor, and unless it had been a real gully-washer, the water would percolate down through the dirt. "A setup like that," Gladys told me, "they call a 'Michigan basement,' as good as a sump pump and doesn't draw a watt."

Over in one corner, I had the slates for the disassembled pool table raised up on blocks, just in case we had a major flood. Against another wall, the shelves were filled with kids' toys and stuff still unpacked from the move. Stuff. We had boxes and boxes of stuff. Some of them hadn't been unpacked since two moves ago. But you never knew. No sooner did you toss out or give away stuff than you needed it. Marcy and I agreed that just after you disposed of it, count on it, you'd need that stuff. That was the nature of stuff.

The north wall was dominated by the big old furnace. The previous occupants, Hank Dubois told me, kept the house toasty by burning wood thinned from the woods. "Sure, you can burn nugget coal, if you want to spend the money," Hank said, "but with all that free fuel out there, you might better burn wood. Warms you three times—when you cut it, when you load it in, and when you burn it. Can't hardly beat that."

I had no doubt Hank was right. And I hoped some day to have the time to do just that. It was a nice prospect, being outdoors while getting winter exercise, cutting and splitting wood, then getting free home heating. But if that day ever came for me, it would be long after we had a house remodeled and a golf course built.

In a town with nicknames such as Motown, City of Wheels, Motor City, and Car Capital, an event called the Detroit Auto Show was about the biggest deal of all.

The moguls of Ford, Chrysler, and General Motors knew it wasn't truly the largest and best such event in the world, that it trailed well behind Paris, Frankfurt, and a few other venues for that distinction. Still, virtually the entire economy of the state of Michigan was based on the automobile business. If you didn't make cars, you worked at a place that owed its existence to the automobile. It might be a company that provided parts or services to one of the Big Three, or you might wait table at a restaurant, take tickets at a movie theater, pump gas at a service station, or handle laundry at a dry cleaner's that would be out of business five minutes after an auto plant decamped from Flint or Hamtramck to the Sun Belt.

In 1959, several hundred recently laid-off auto workers—calling themselves the Fifty-Niners—said the hell with it and moved lock, stock, and entire family to Alaska. A few years later, fed up with the feast-but-too-often-famine life on the assembly lines, another exodus departed for Texas, leaving a sign on the chainlink fence surrounding an abandoned GM plant on Clark Avenue: "Will the last one out of Detroit please turn out the lights."

But Detroit had seen bad times before, had heard the death knell for the internal combustion engine so often it knew the notes by heart. Good times or bad, the Detroit Auto Show went on and hundreds of thousands came from the suburbs, and from villages like Grass Lake, to see the shape of the new Detroit sheet metal. From all over the state and the Midwest they came to gawk at the futuristic concept cars, these sleek specimens with all the gizmos, these gleaming beauties with their 400-horsepower hearts.

Whether the nameplate said Le Sabre or Edsel, once these vehicles were transmogrified from concept car to production model, they had run the bloody gauntlet past legions of bean counters and efficiency experts. By the time they limped into the showroom, the once-leading-edge concept cars were seldom recognizable as those Auto Show dream machines the young bucks had salivated over four years ago.

Eventually the bottom-line-minded accountants manage to wrestle the creation from the hands of the designers and craftsmen—the "car guys" whose only crime is that they want to build great, beautiful, exciting cars. Then a frightening Jekyll-Hyde transformation takes place. Now it is the bean counters' turn. Off goes this gadget. Away with this strip of chrome. Replace that engine with those smaller ones we have stored by the tens of thousands at a railside warehouse in Ypsilanti.

The car guys sneered with contempt at the MBAs and lawyers running their business. If we keep doing this, they warned, one day the

European and Asian manufacturers will be eating our lunch.

But for now, they still came in droves to the Detroit Auto Show.

And as we settled into the Grass Lake farm and set about making it habitable, we were glad they did. Glad because the moment the Auto Show ended, the booths were cleared out, the drapes were taken down, and the carpet was taken up. This was carpet that had lain under a display carousel on which had rotated a new automobile, with at most only a high-heeled model and a pitchman touching a shoe to it. This was carpet that had never been trodden by a single spectator. And, best of all, this was carpet that could be had, first-come, first-sold, for exactly $1 a yard.

We checked daily with La Mar Carpet Suppliers to find out when they would have the Auto Show carpet rolled up and back at their huge warehouse. Finally we got the word and backed up our spacious Olds Scenic Cruiser station wagon to their loading dock.

The La Mar folks weren't about to quibble over a yard here or there. They had thousands of yards to move and hundreds of buyers already lining up for it. There was no such thing as examining depth of pile, comparing textures, eyeballing backing, holding the carpet under incandescent as well as fluorescent lighting to see how well it matched with the sample cloth you clipped from the back of the sofa. No, this was your basic quick-cash, quick-carry business.

Yes, we could pick the rolls we wanted. No, we couldn't unroll the carpets one at a time and pick the best. Sorry to hurry you mister, but . . .

Roll upon roll upon roll of carpet was stacked in towering pyramids. You could have any color you wanted, as long as it was vibrant yellow, traffic light green, fire engine red, or royal blue. Well, yellow was out of the question. The more green the better on the fairways but not inside the house. The red would be kind of fun for the kids' bedrooms and not bad for the upstairs hall and what the heck, while we're at it, why not just do the entire upstairs in it? Wouldn't want to have red throughout the house, so let's do the first floor in a different color. What about, oh, say, blue?

Approximate yardage was written on a tag on each roll. We needed a tad over 150 yards. Figure in tax and $3 for gasoline and add another $5 for fast-food lunch and we'd have the whole place under carpet for $163 and change.

Hard to tell from the edge of the rolls but this one here looks like it has never been walked on. Forget that one—spotted with oil and grease stains. We'll take this one, that one, those two there, this roll here, and if there's room throw that one in the back of that Olds wagon, too. Oh? We have to do the throwing in? Well, for a buck a yard . . .

As we wedged in the last of the rolls, I marveled that barely one day after this very carpet was beneath the wheels of a Lincoln or Buick, it was here on the warehouse loading dock. And within two more days it would bedeck the floors of the former Nate Fish homestead. Brand-new carpet. Almost. Buck a yard. Cash and carry. What a country.

The kids nestled into crevices between the rolls where a couple of them would be asleep before we were out of Detroit's city limits. As we pulled out of the parking lot, I heard the tailpipe scrape, a warning to avoid potholes, which on Michigan roads would be a challenge for the next sixty miles.

Now I had to find a deal on carpet edging strips and carpet tacks. And hope that my back held out until I had this 150 yards of carpet covering those nice hardwood floors I'd probably never see again.

A week later, it was down to Hillsdale for a similar deal on real-wood paneling that had been damaged in shipment. A long drive, but $1.50 a panel made it shorter.

THE WINTER OF 1966–67 was developing into one of discovery. What we were discovering was that it took a lot of work to bring a century-old house up to the level of a fixer-upper.

Before finishing the upstairs, we tore down an ancient unused chimney so we could put the hallway to the kids' bedrooms where we wanted it. That unleashed billows of ancient soot and dust. Once the residue of decades of wood and coal fires was cleaned up, we laid carpet, put up partitions and paneling, replaced nonfunctioning and broken windows, slapped on paint, hung wallpaper, and installed doors. And we pledged that come warm weather we would install a used fuel oil insert burner in the big old furnace to replace the coal stoker.

The wiring was vintage Nate Fish and so wire by wire, outlet by outlet, fixture by fixture, that was replaced. But that still left us with an ages-old, tiny 60-amp fuse box serving the entire house and barn. Under the tutelage of Marcy's father and Pop, his registered electrician friend, I put separate 100-amp circuit-breaker service boxes in both the house and the main barn.

The kitchen wasn't working quite right because it needed central counter space. When I saw an ad for a used dishwasher "Like New— Works Great" for $50, it seemed like a good idea to put that in the middle of the big country kitchen and build a large counter over and around it. After $60 for parts to get the "works great" dishwasher oper-ating, $50 for plumbing costs, and $40 for materials to build the casing and countertop, we had made the kitchen functional.

I thought we had knocked off just about all of the crucial items until one sub-zero morning Pat woke me to "come see the fountain in the laundry room."

Somewhere behind the washing machine, the hot-water pipe had split in the night, creating a geyser. That explained why for hours we had heard the water pump coming on.

In the bitter cold, the walls, windows, ceiling, and floor were coated with a glittering layer of ice. Actually, it was kind of pretty. I shut off the main water supply at the pump and tore into the rapidly decomposing Sheetrock wall to find the kinked and split copper pipe. It was uninsulated and exposed to the outside wall under the laundry room floor.

That was one of those domino jobs: you had to fix one thing to get at the next thing to repair another thing. But before being sucked inescapably into the vortex of plumbing repair, it seemed prudent to have a professional do the rough plumbing for the new full bath on the second floor. The result—a quick improvement in quality of life for the entire family.

We had been in the place less than six months, a house that was "ready to move right into" that summer day when we first saw it. Now, our first winter almost over, it was finally a comfortable dwelling inside. And we had made it so for less than $1,500. But now we had less than $3,000 in the bank. And a monthly tractor payment on top of the land contract check to Daryle.

Nine

During our first winter on the farm, Gladys Smedley gave me plenty of homework. In late March of 1967, I drove over to return her orange crate overflowing with old copies of Organic Gardening & Farming, a sheaf of yellowed pamphlets, and a bundle of well-thumbed almanacs.

The weather was still cool but there she sat by the fire pit at the end of the driveway. Gladys told me to set the box next to her and motioned me to get wood from the nearby pile. She looked tired and I thought her color was a little off but I knew better than to ask her how she felt. I tossed a few sticks on the fire and poked it to flame.

"Gladys, I ordered the seeds you recommended. I've got them started in the house under lights and—"

"See those castor bean plants?" she asked, pointing to a photograph in one of the magazines. "Not those, those—the tall plants there at the end of the snap bean rows and there again by the tomatoes. Well, they emit a chemical that keeps the aphids and other sap-sucking insects away from your garden. But I better never catch you growing them in your garden."

I asked why.

"Because the beans are poisonous, that's why. And they're pretty things, pretty enough that little kids think they're good enough to eat. You've got enough on your mind without your rushing a kid to the emergency to get his stomach pumped."

I'd have to remember that, all right.

Gladys seemed pensive for a time, then jabbed a finger toward me..

"See," she said. "You did it again."

"Did what, Gladys?"

"Third time you've moved your chair since you sat down. Smoke's following you again. How many times you seen me move?"

"Well, now that you mention it—"

"Damn right, none. Some the smoke follows, some it doesn't. You, it follows."

I hadn't disputed that the first time Gladys lectured me about it and

I didn't again. What I did was, I moved the chair. There was no breeze and soon the smoke curved away from me and went straight up.

Gladys and I talked about vegetables, about which melons did best in what kind of soil. About the many splendors of compost. About the pros and cons of topping your tomato plants so the nutri-ents would go to the fruit instead of forming new stems and leaves. About how to cut an X on the stump of a cauliflower root after you harvest the head and that stump will grow four little cabbages the size of golf balls. As Gladys talked, almost imperceptibly the column of smoke began to drift and twist slowly but surely toward her. It had to be but a momentary aberration. Surely any moment it would shift again, toward me or away from us both or straight up in the air, anywhere but at Gladys. It wouldn't dare.

But it did. She sat there, puffing her Pall Mall, now engulfed not only in its smoke but also in the acrid blue-gray fumes of the wood fire. She continued to lecture me on how to check the sex of a zucchini to tell a bitter one from a tasty one.

"Maybe you should think about quitting smoking, Gladys."

"Oh, ain't you the smarty-pants."

"What?"

"Don't you 'what' me, Mr. Wise Guy. I can sniff that out a mile away. Had thirty years practice with that Kent."

"Gladys, I don't know what you're talking about."

"The hell. The smoke is what I'm talking about. And you know whose fault it is, don't you?"

"No, I don't. Whose?"

"Yours. Who else? Never had a problem with the smoke before. Not once. Sat by this fire a thousand times before you ever showed up. Now here you come and you've got the smoke so screwed up it doesn't know which way to go."

And she got up and ground out her cigarette in the gravel and stomped into the house.

Less than a minute later she appeared at the back door.

"You just going to sit there screwing up the smoke even worse or you coming in to get to it with me?"

"Get to what?"

But she was already back in the kitchen.

I went in and sat at the kitchen table, wondering what was coming next.

"Well, let's hear it," she said.

"Hear what, Gladys?"

"Now are we going to just spar around with foreplay here or are we going to get right at it?"

I wasn't quite sure what Gladys had in mind getting at, but my palms began to sweat.

"Gladys, I'm not sure—"

"You're not sure? Then, mister, just what the hell did you have Kent tramping all over our back forty last fall, him with a bad back and you've got him down there amongst the blue beech where God knows it's a miracle he could ever make it back up the hill. And you're not sure? Well, tell me this, are you sure you want to build a golf course?"

"Yes, I'm sure. That's why we bought the old Fish place and—"

"And you made it no secret that fifty-five acres wasn't nowhere near enough. Every time you look at that forty of mine and Kent's—abutting as it does your place—why, you about drool. Now you're going to tell me you're not sure you want to buy that forty from us?"

Either I was transparent or Gladys Smedley was a sharp observer. Probably both.

"Well, you're right, Gladys. About everything."

"I'd say, 'as usual,' but I don't want to come off the braggart. My lord, doesn't take a string of fancy letters after your name to figure that one out, does it? Well, then. How much you offering?"

"I really haven't gone so far as to fix on a figure, Gladys. I didn't know whether or not you and Kent would be willing to sell."

"Of course we'll sell it to you. Provided the price is right, that is. What the hell we going to do with that forty? Back thirty years ago I pulled a damned good crop of hay off that one little knoll by the creek. You know, I witched a well down there with my plum branch. Like to tore it right out of my hands when I hit the spot. You could drive in a casing and have you an artesian well. Anyhow, where were we?"

"You were saying you weren't using the forty and—"

"Yes, from time to time I make jam and pies from those berries, but no, we've got no real use for it. Wouldn't be all bad having a golf course right out there off your backyard. Long as it's far enough away I don't have golf balls rattling off my roof. Now let's hear that price."

"All I can say is, from what I hear, vacant landlocked parcels hereabouts have been going for a hundred an acre and—"

"A hundred an acre! You've spent too much time in those ivory towers in Ann Arbor you think a hundred an acre is the right price for that land."

"I didn't finish, Gladys. I said that's what people have been paying for some. But that land of yours is—"

"Sure as hell is not worth any hundred. Poor blow sand on those hills, marsh either side of the Willow Creek. Boggy down where the berries grow. Man'd be a fool to pay any hundred the acre. You'll give us eighty-five and not a cent less."

What could I say?

"You just going to sit there with your mouth open or we going to drink on it?"

Marcy was as stunned to hear about the deal for the Smedley land as I had been when Gladys told me the way it was going to be. Then I told her there was one other thing.

"I thought so," Marcy said. "What's the catch?"

"How we pay for it."

"Oh, that detail. Now that you mention it, how do we pay for it? With the expenses fixing up the house, the monthly land contract and tractor payments, and what we've set aside for equipment, we're about at the limit. At least until we've increased the value of the place enough to get new financing. So where do we get the money for the Smedleys?"

I told Marcy we would get it from the Smedleys. They would sell to us with nothing down and hold a ten-year, 6 percent land contract.

Or longer if we needed it, and we could pay it off earlier if we decided to.

Left unsaid was how likely it was that the course would ever make serious money. But now there was one thing we did know: with the Smedley parcel we would have enough land to build a sprawling nine-hole golf course.

That night after dinner, I told the kids the big news: we got more land. Now we were going to be able to build the golf course. They wanted to know what's for dessert.

THE NEXT DAY I GOT A PHONE CALL from Kent Smedley.

"Bill, I hope this is a good time. You and I need to have a little talk."

One of life's immutable laws I had learned long since: When your boss or your wife says, We need to have a little talk, you are not going to enjoy what you hear next.

Kent was neither boss nor wife to me, but from the subdued tone of his voice as well as the actual words, I felt in my gut I was not going to like what he had to tell me.

In the five minutes it took me to drive to the Smedleys' house, I convinced myself that it was all over, we would not get the Smedley forty. I could imagine the seemingly mild-mannered Kent listening to Gladys's account of the deal she had made without his participation or approval. Him rising up like an outraged bear, slamming his great catcher's mitt of an ink-stained fist on the table, roaring that it would be only over his dead body that some city slicker sweet-talked his naive little Gladys out of that priceless property and for a paltry eighty-five dollars an acre? Outrageous! I'll have that Haney by the throat and open a new orifice or two for him!

As I got out of the pickup truck and walked to the back door, all seemed quiet inside. The thought flashed—deadly quiet. Then, with relief, I heard Gladys's voice. Thank God Kent hadn't taken out his wrath on his poor Glad. As least not yet. Maybe he was saving her for dessert, after he had devoured me.

Gladys met me at the door.

"I've got some straightening up to do in that firetrap of a garage," she said. "You two boys go ahead and have your talk."

I had thought my heart had already sunk to bedrock, but with

Gladys fleeing the scene of the impending crime, my spirits plummeted to new depths. Kent motioned to a chair by the kitchen table. I sat and wondered how I was going to tell Marcy and the kids. Here it was just one day after celebrating the highest moment we had enjoyed since the move, knowing for the first time that we would have the land we needed to build our golf course. And now—

"You're probably wondering why I called you here," Kent said.

God, another of those bone-chilling clichés you hear in a bad movie and never expect to have directed at you in real life. Why don't I just say I'm sorry, it was all my fault, Kent, don't blame Gladys. Just put me out of my misery quickly please, but spare poor Gladys, she meant well but she's innocent, innocent do you hear me—

I nodded.

"About selling you the forty. There's something Glad didn't mention to you. Something important. It may be that she assumed you would know better. And maybe you do, so I hope you won't be insulted when I bring it up."

Was it the money? The terms? Or maybe they didn't really own the land free and clear and Kent was going to tell me I had to assume their debt in addition. Whatever, so far Kent was talking calmly, his massive hands resting on the table and not clenched around my neck. So far.

"There would have to be conditions. Important conditions."

Ah, conditions.

"Now, Glad has already committed to an arrangement with you and so there's no question about that. Unless you have changed your mind, it's a done deal, just as you and Glad agreed."

I wanted to jump up, kiss his balding pate. But what of these conditions? Could there be a deal-breaker there?

Kent said it was important that I understood about the berries. The blackberry patch on the south slope. The wild blueberries and strawberries in the low ground east of the knoll. Could I design the course to avoid tearing up those berry patches?

I assured him that the blackberries, being on a severe slope, would be off track of any fairway. And I'd be sure to bypass the strawberry field too.

Kent smiled. "It's not that we would have picking rights to the berries. It's just that we wouldn't want to see them destroyed." Then he looked stern again. There was more.

The Smedleys were equally concerned for nesting sandhill cranes in the adjacent property owned by the Grass Lake Rifle Association. The Association didn't allow any hunting there and just used a few acres for sighting-in their guns, so there were many ducks, herons, red-tailed hawks, Canada geese, and even a sandhill crane rookery on their land.

"They fly over to our forty—that would be your new forty," Kent said, "and make false nests sometimes to lure fox and other predators away. While I think of it, I've been saying forty acres but after looking at it, I presume you'll want to get to the top of the big hill, is that correct?"

I had not dared to ask for what Kent was now offering. "That would be ideal. That way we could put a tee up there that would command a view of everything below. Yes, that would be perfect."

"You're visualizing where we stood last fall before we started down the hill? All right, then, we'll tack that slice onto the square forty, bring the whole parcel to forty-five acres in all, more or less."

I told Kent that was more than we could have hoped for. And as for the birds and animals, we would do nothing to affect the wildlife in a negative way. Also, we wouldn't touch the marsh except to elaborate Willow Creek into ponds in two or three places. And all we would do there would be to excavate material and build land bridges alongside the ponds and that will give us crossovers to the north side and the big hill, and back.

Kent nodded. "Ducks and herons would like those ponds. Glad would like that. You know, she comes on with tough talk and wants the world to think she says flat out whatever is on her mind. And most of the time she does. But there are things that are close to her that she doesn't want it known how much she cares about them."

"Like the berries and the birds," I said.

"Yes, like the berries and the birds." Kent let out a long sigh. "I'd like to believe you know what you're doing, Mr. Haney. You haven't asked my opinion but if you did I'd have to tell you I think you're crazy. Not that the idea of a golf course on this land is a bad one. Actually, that's the best use I can think of for land that's been so abused. But the way you're proposing to do it? Un-uhh. I never heard of anyone building a golf course alone and without a big checkbook."

I explained to Kent that I wasn't really alone because I have a very resourceful wife and four eager kids. Kent agreed the children could do worse than grow up in the country, helping to build something with their own hands, but he doubted how much they and an over-burdened wife would actually be able to do.

"And you with a full-time job," he said. "You'll be forever getting this done . . . if you ever do."

I told Kent we'd get it done because we would have to get the money flowing back in the other direction. "But I've got no illusions about how long it might take," I said. "I'm figuring three, maybe four years. But we're going to do it our way or not at all."

"And what does that mean, your way?"

"It means totally by ourselves. No partners. Nobody else's money invested. It means an ecologically defensible golf course. No harmful chemicals. No country club pretensions. Just an authentic, natural course that fits so comfortably into the land it looks like it has always been there. And with as many or more birds and animals as before."

"That's ambitious enough," Kent said. "Anything else?"

"Now that you mention it, maybe a place where here and there a golfer can stop along the way and pluck an apple or pick a handful of berries."

PAT WAS BOUNCING A TENNIS BALL against the back porch steps when I got home from work and pulled into the driveway. I sat in the car a while and watched him. Pock, and the ball would come zinging back to him and he'd snag it in the webbing of his glove. Pock. Snag. Pock. Snag. Again and again. Four years old, a tiny glove barely big enough to handle a tennis ball and he could play against the stoop all day and the stoop would wear out before he would.

I got out of the car and Pat wheeled and fired his heater at me. It hit me in the chest and I snagged it before it hit the ground.

"Good hands, Dad, good hands."

We started up the steps, Pat with his baseball glove on his catching hand, dragging my briefcase in his right.

"Mom's hurt," he said.

"Hurt? How?"

"Where Pokey kicked her. Pokey kicked her real hard. Mom is mad at Pokey. She said some bad words to her."

It was quiet in the house. No one in the kitchen or the living room.

"Pat, where's your mother and the kids?"

"Somewhere. Maybe upstairs."

I yelled for Marcy, then Mark and Jen.

No answer.

I hurried up the stairs, calling for Marcy and the kids.

"In here, Dad." It was Jen's voice, coming from the girls' room down the hall.

When I went past the boys' room, Mark was lying on his bed, reading, as usual. That was a good sign.

"Jen, where's your mother?"

"I'm right here," Marcy said, her voice coming from behind the door. "What's the matter?"

"Pat said you were hurt. Pokey kicked you?"

"You bet she did. And she did a real good job of it. See?"

Marcy pulled her slacks down, exposing huge, purplish-yellow bruises high on both thighs.

"Wow, that hurts just looking at it."

"You ought to see it from this side. It's just a good thing she got me on the meat and not right on a bone or kneecap."

I went to the window and looked out into the paddock. Pokey was munching contentedly on the grass. Her colt Gumby was nearby. Pokey looked awfully big—maybe William Rollman was right and she had another foal in her.

"How did it happen?"

"We haven't been riding her enough," Marcy said. "Daryle said we had to work with her regularly to keep her gentle. So Mark and I saddled her up and that went okay. Then we brought her over to the fence and I climbed up on the fence to get on her from there. I don't know what happened, she moved or something as I was mounting her, and wham! she jumped forward and I slipped backward and she kicked up both rear feet and that was it."

I looked at the bruises, getting more florid before my eyes. I looked at wide-eyed Jen and at Marcy. She was hurting, angry, and determined.

"We can't risk it, you know," Marcy said. "If that had been one of the kids—"

"Say no more. I agree completely. We'll find a good home for her and Gumby." And, I thought, for the young one still inside her.

A week later, it was a good news–bad news day for the kids. The good news was they got to meet an astronaut, just at the time NASA's space program was making astronauts into rock-star celebrities. The bad news was, the astronaut was visiting our farm to take away their ponies.

Actually Ron Reddick was not an official NASA astronaut. I knew him from when I worked at Bendix, where he played the role of "astronaut subject." He was a Bendix engineer whose assignment was to learn how to handle the experiments for the Apollo Lunar Surface Experiments Package I had worked on for years. Wearing a cumbersome space suit and plodding in ankle-deep dusty fly ash to simulate a possible lunar surface condition, Reddick would unpack and deploy each instrument, learning techniques and tricks he would then teach the astronauts scheduled to travel to the moon on Apollo 14 in 1971.

Before I left Bendix, I had talked with Reddick while he was taking a break from his hot, dusty work. He mentioned then that he too lived in the country. I remembered that and when I phoned him and told him I was looking for someone with land who wanted a free pony, he put in a quick claim.

He knew far more than I did about loading a horse into a trailer, so I stayed out of the way with the kids and watched. Reddick tied hobbles connecting each front leg to a rear leg so Pokey couldn't dance around. With that, and a handful of apples, he had her quickly and safely into the trailer. Gumby needed no encouragement to follow along after his mother.

Marcy and I were concerned about how the kids would take this—only a few months ago Daryle had delivered the ponies. But as Reddick drove off and Pokey's tail flicked what seemed a good-bye out the trailer's open rear gate, the kids waved and there were no tears. They seemed to understand that, as Marcy explained to them, Pokey needed much more attention than we could give her. That it was just not fair to her and too dangerous for our family to have her here. She was going to a home where the Daddy knew a lot about horses and would work with her every day and where little Gumby could be taught early.

The next day, the boys and I took down the paddock fence. With it, the last remnant of a working farm disappeared from Nate Fish's fields.

A few days later I came out of the barn just as a pickup truck was driving away.

"Was that Daryle I saw driving out a while ago?" I asked Marcy. "I wasn't expecting him."

"Yes," Marcy said. "He didn't come to see you. He brought something for Mark. Mark, show your daddy what Mr. Heselschwerdt gave you."

Mark held up the small portable radio he had been pressing against his ear.

"Mr. Heselschwerdt said he was sorry we had to give away my pony. He said this radio was for me."

Ten

When the snow melted in April and the land was bare for the first time in almost five months, I was curious what our spread looked like from other vantage points.

I didn't know whether my neighbors would object to my entering their property without permission, so one day when I saw Horace Coppernoll on his tractor, working his highest and driest field to the east of our place, I waved and got his attention. He didn't look happy about being stopped and so I apologized right away and the crusty Horace softened—as much as he ever softened. I asked him if I could come onto his place and have a look at our land. Horace shook his head and snorted as if he couldn't believe what I had said. He went back and shut off the big diesel engine and motioned for me to follow him.

"Horace, I was wondering, do you know what happened to Nate Fish, used to live on my place?"

Horace squinted at me and thought about it.

"I was just a youngster when Nate died. People didn't want to talk about that for some reason. Some kind of strange illness, or maybe a bad accident. I used to ask the old-timers—never got a straight answer. Nope, I guess I never really knew. He's buried over there in the little cemetery, the one hidden in those weeds on the corner of Fishville and Phal Roads across from Henry Samyn's place. You could see his tombstone there if it hasn't been knocked over or carted off."

We walked east, then north up a slight rise. Looking back, our place—the white house, big red barn, and oak woods—stood out boldly against the western horizon. The sunbaked south ridge, with its light loamy sand hills rising above the marsh, was like a golden crown. From here you could see how sharply the ridge dropped off some twenty-five or more feet to the marsh. Willow Creek was clearly visible, a fresh trout stream meandering through Horace's land, across a small slice of Harrison's, and then through more than a half mile of what was now our land, including the Smedley parcel we had just acquired.

Along the stream side, the great twisted limbs of the black willow trees groped skyward as the gnarled roots forever clutched the saturated earth. Beyond the willows to the north stretched more marsh before the land rose gradually, then abruptly to another ridge of hills. That would be one of our biggest challenges: to tie the firm high ground on the south rim of the marsh to Smedley Hill and the usable land on the north. And to do it without disturbing the marsh and its wildlife. Easy enough to make it scenic and golfable, but to do it so that it looked like the golf holes belonged there, well, that was something else again.

"Dozens of live springs in that marsh," Horace said. "I have a few on my land, but nothing like that. A farmer wants only so much land lost to marsh and old Nate Fish sure had his share and somebody else's besides. This place of yours is really a poor spread of land for farming, but I suppose you knew that before you bought."

He walked a few yards and pointed toward the biggest black willow tree.

"Anyhow, a few years back I noticed a gathering pool of water alongside the stretch of Willow Creek that runs through my north sixty. Now, I was certain that water wasn't there just a day or two before. Hadn't rained a drop, so something's going on. That piece of ground is low but it's rich and tillable and I had a nice patch of beans started down there. And now, damn it, this rising water was about to drown

them out. Said to myself, What the hell is going on?"

Horace walked a few yards farther and pointed off to the north, to another cluster of trees north of Phal Road.

"See that patch of trembling aspen? Well, the creek comes through my place up there, then feeds through a corner of Harrison's land, then on into your place. Now, with no rain in some time the only way there could be water in my bean field is if someone has dammed up the creek downstream. I come and talk with Ron Merz—he owned your place then—and I ask him about it. He claims he hadn't done anything like that on his place but he tells me the water flow coming in on him from that trout stream, why, it's diminished, all right. So I tramps onto Harrison's land and no sooner I set foot on it, out he comes, stomping and arms flailing away like he does. Damn banty rooster."

From the couple glimpses I had seen of an elusive man near our common property line, I had begun to suspect it might be Harrison himself, watching me from his land. And from hearing Gladys's stories about him, I could picture Harrison taking out after Horace.

"Sure enough, the crazy coot had thrown timbers and stumps and what-all into the narrowest neck of Willow Creek on his land just this side of your property line. Clogged it up pretty good and had him a fair-sized lake in that backed-up water.

"So I say, 'Ed, just what the hell do you think you're doing?'"

"'Doing?' he says, 'Making me a lake, is what I'm doing. Man can do what he pleases on his own property. We call that the American Way.'

"'No, Ed, we call that illegal,' I says, 'when it affects the water flow of the man upstream or downstream from you, illegal is what we call it, Ed. And not very smart in the bargain.'

"'Well, how's that?' he goes. 'I'm fixing to have myself a trout pond here where I can offer my clientele a guaranteed trout, three dollars the fish. How's what I'm doing make any nevermind to you?'

"So I look at Harrison, not believing what I'm hearing. Can the man really not know? 'Gravity, Ed. They call it gravity. You give it a chance, water's going to run downhill, every time. You put up this dam, it cuts down the water flow into the Merz place and the law won't let you do that if Ron Merz don't like it. Now that's up to Merz whether he likes it or not. But your little lake here is backing right up onto my bean field. And that's up to me. And I say that dam is coming out of there. Right sudden.'

"Well, Harrison went stomping around and around in these little circles, like a rabid skunk when its brain is gone dead, not knowing what the hell to do or say. Finally he sputters, 'Saying I agree to take it out—just saying I do, mind you—how'm I supposed to get that dam out of there?'

"'That's down to your account, Ed,' I said. 'You put it in there, you get it out.'"

Horace pointed at the spot on Harrison's land where the incident apparently took place.

"So Harrison got him a sack of ammonium sulfate fertilizer, pours in a couple gallons of fuel oil, laces in a dynamite cap. Stretches a wire from that to a car battery. Like you'd rig up in your marsh to blow a waterfowl hole—you know, a pocket of water to attract the ducks and such. Later in the afternoon that same day, I hear this deep 'whomp' and I know he set that sucker off. By evening, just like pulling the plug on your bathtub, my bean field is drying out. "

Horace shook his head and laughed softly.

"That Harrison, always something," Horace said. "Hell fire,

Harrison grumbles about his bad luck. He wouldn't know bad luck if it came up and bit him on the hinder. Nate Fish could have told him a thing or three about bad luck."

"I guess Nate wasn't a very lucky guy, from what people say," I said.

"Huh, I'm told Nate would say, 'What a man needs is half as much free advice, twice as much good weather, and three times as much good luck.'"

As Mark and Pat combed out one rock after another and tossed them into the stoneboat, I looked back toward the house and barns, some 250 yards away. One fact was obvious. The course had to start and finish near the house and barns; not right next to the buildings, but within 100 to 200 yards. That was because we simply couldn't afford to build separate buildings for a clubhouse, pro shop, and bathrooms. There was no other option—we had to use the big hay barn for those facilities. And because the top level of that barn wouldn't be usable without considerable work on the leaky roof and walls, we were limited to the lower level and probably the concrete-block milk house, as well.

But that was okay. We had more than enough decisions to make already, so we were grateful that there was really no other option.

The three barns were attached to each other. The hundred-year-old red hay barn dominated, facing Curtis Road, just fifty feet to the south. The barn's top level perched on a small hill sculpted to create an earthen ramp leading up to a pair of fourteen-foot-high barn doors. The doors were mounted on hanging rollers running recessed in an overhead track. The layout was set up long ago so that horses could draw trailers of hay bales from ground level up the slope and into the barn. There farm hands would stash a winter's supply of hay for cattle feed. The bales would reach some twenty feet high, up past rafters that had been hand hewn from trees in the nearby oak and hickory stand and fastened with big wooden pegs.

Inside the barn against the north wall was a fully enclosed granary for storing oats, rye, and cracked corn.

The lower level of the barn had walls of field rocks and mortar. The massive beams supporting the floor of the upper level were even larger hand-hewn oak timbers, also joined with wooden pegs instead of nails. The floor was poured concrete with channels recessed eight inches deep by a foot wide that signified this had indeed been a dairy farm. The cows would munch on their feed at one end and drop manure into these channels at the other. There were special broad, flat shovels that fit neatly into the floor channels to scoop the manure out. Those channels would have to be filled and the entire floor covered.

We would need as much as two-thirds of this ground-level interior for dry storage of fertilizer, seed, and other supplies and for a maintenance workshop. It was not only solid and safe down here, it was downright cozy. With a little tightening up we would be able to work on equipment in the winter with a space heater to get the temperature at least into the forties.

That left the east one-third of the ground level of the hay barn for the pro shop. Set up there, the pro shop would give immediate access to the restrooms and be at the northeast corner, which meant it would face the house on the east and the golf course on the north. There were now solid walls on both those sides. We'd need to put the door into the pro shop right at the outside corner. That meant I would have to take out the existing barn boards, so while I was at it, I might as well build entirely new walls. Then I could install very large picture windows to bring in light and give the expansive views we wanted of the course.

Setting up the maintenance and storage areas would come first, and soon. It would be a couple years, at least, before we'd tackle the pro shop and the bathrooms.

On the ground level, the hay barn connected at its northwest corner to the southeast corner of the pole barn. Constructed of creosoted lumber and sheet metal siding, the pole barn had a sheet-metal roof. It was closed in on three sides, and open on the east, facing the house. At thirty by sixty feet, there was plenty of room to house the equipment we'd need: greens mowers; a triplex riding mower for tees, aprons, and approaches; rotary and reel-type hand mowers for collars and severe slopes; a big Brush Hog rotary chopper driven by the tractor PTO; aerators, sprayers, and spreaders. We'd need two or three tractors and perhaps another truck and once we got them, they would be parked there. So far we owned only the Ford tractor, an ancient E-3 Co-op tractor, a tilling disk, grading blade, and a tractor-mounted rotary chopper; the rest we would have to find at auctions, through ads, or just putting out the word that we were looking for used equipment.

The cement-block milk house was a tight, dry building. It was tucked up flush to the east wall of the hay barn at the ground level with a doorway into the barn's lower level. We toyed briefly with dressing the milk house up and using it for the pro shop. But instead we decided to create separate men's and women's changing rooms by building a wall out of paneling and two-by-fours dividing the milk house. Golfers could change clothes there and have sanitary facilities. That would require plumbing and a separate septic tank and drain field or dry well.

We had already corrected another negative—the entire barn had shared electrical service from the ancient and woefully inadequate 60-amp service box in the house. A marvel they had run milk-processing equipment and everything else off that tiny electrical service. We had learned to always keep a flashlight and plenty of fuses handy until we upgraded that.

There was now one new factor to consider in designing the course. We had added further to our land holdings—and our burgeoning debt—by taking out a land contract with our neighbor to the west. The Damarons sold us ten acres west of the oak woods. The price of $500 an acre was far more than we could afford, but we knew it would give us new options in course design and perhaps be valuable one day for home sites. So in one early design, I toyed with placing a long par four skirting the woods to give access to the Smedley parcel. But I soon discarded that notion because it meant giving up land that might be used for a practice range and—a new problem—it would make the nine-hole layout too spread out to maintain efficiently.

Because we were committed to not invading the oak woods, there was really only one good way to get golfers out onto the spacious parts of the land and then back in again on the final hole. We had to run a fairway north more or less alongside the woods, then turn it left, or north by northwest. That would have to be a long hole, probably a par five, so that when golfers reached the green, they would be in the very heart of the course, at the place we found ourselves calling the south ridge. That was the eight-acre hole I had many times visualized and reluctantly abandoned. But now, with the Smedley land, that majestic hole was feasible. Because you don't want to have your first hole be long and tough, it would be best if we could make that hole number three.

Then golfers could play a pair of holes, out and back, on the big plateau that Kent Smedley said had lain fallow since Nate Fish had grown popcorn there in 1915. If there was enough room on that plateau for side-by-side par fours, say numbers four and five, that would bring the golfers back again to the center of the course, not far from number three green. For maintenance and irrigation it would be good to have two greens and their adjacent tees reasonably close.

Yes, the layout of the first five holes was falling into place.

Next, high on the crest of the south ridge and facing north, we could place elevated tees for number six. That hole would feature a dramatic carry across a pond excavated from the wetlands. To build a green down in the hollow beyond the marsh would require clearing out a lot of hawthorns and scrub growth—could be a great golf hole. From there, golfers would walk up to the crest of the Smedley Hill. And there they would tee off for number seven, another dramatic downhill hole traversing the slope back downhill, skirting the blackberry patch, and finishing at a green on the knoll where Gladys Smedley once grew a fine crop of hay.

Now we had to bring the golfers across the marsh and back to the clubhouse. So to get to number eight tee would require a walk beside the wild strawberry patch. This one was a natural—a par three hole that would bring the golfers back over another pond to a green on the sandy knoll not far from the property line with Harrison.

The finishing hole was obvious. To reach the final tee, golfers would walk up the hill from eight green to the south ridge. There they would find the tee box for number nine, with its fairway running parallel to number three. And that would bring them back near the clubhouse.

I had toyed with several other sequences, but as Mark, Pat, and I filled the stoneboat once more, this was the layout that ran through my mind again and again.

We dumped the rocks in a crevasse gouged by years of water erosion and swung by the woods to load the pickup truck with old rusty fencing and wire for yet another trip to the township landfill. Before I got back into the truck, I stopped and took yet another look for the design sketch I was eager to put on paper that night. Yes, that was the

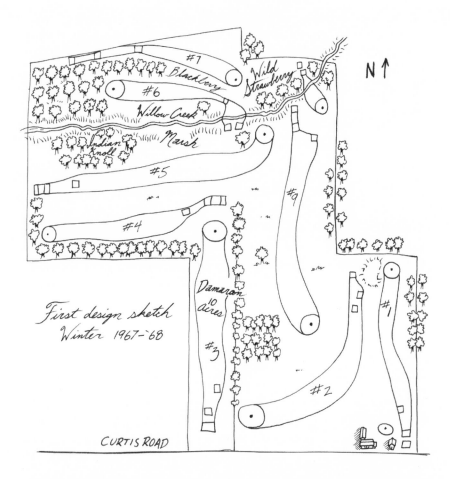

First design sketch
Winter 1967-'68

CURTIS ROAD

N ↑

only way it could be. Numbers three and nine had to parallel each other to get the golfers out into the heart of the course and back again.

All that remained was where to locate numbers one and two. But that too was now obvious. We'd have to start with a short par four and a par three in the land to the east and north of the house and barns—there simply wasn't room enough for anything bigger. And that was good—two fairly easy opening holes to get golfers warmed up.

In a couple of places we'd have to watch the angles and where we placed the tees so we didn't have golfers hitting into adjacent fairways. But it was feasible. And in my imagination, at least, it played well.

The kids asked what I was looking at. I told them I was trying to figure out how to build a golf course into Nate Fish's old popcorn farm.

Eleven

But Professor, the idea is, it's a name people get a kick out of saying."

It was perhaps my fifth futile rebuttal tack. I was no closer to convincing Professor Carlton Wells that the name I had chosen for the golf course made sense, as dreadful as it sounded to him.

"William. You are suggesting that people enjoy saying 'The Boondocks?' Really? What people?"

Carlton was as determined to challenge me on the name we had chosen for the golf course as he had been relentless with me fifteen years earlier on matters of grammar.

"I can't imagine someone in polite society using that expression," he said, "let alone enjoying the using of it. I should think they would be repelled at the prospect of playing a golf course with such a name."

"That's the point, Professor Wells. Anybody turned off by the name wouldn't play an unmanicured country course like this anyhow. They'd be playing Barton Hills or Washtenaw or some other country club."

"And who then will be playing your course?"

"Farmers. Blue-collar workers. Regular people from the little towns around here. Kids who get turned off by pretentious names. And folks who play golf for the enjoyment of the game itself, not to be seen at the club, to schmooze with a business prospect."

Carlton took a grip on the six-iron he used as a walking stick when tramping on the land with me. He found what he was looking for—a nasty dandelion plant. He took that effortless, classic swing that had made him state amateur champion in the 1920s; the clubhead neatly chopped the weed off at the roots, which was precisely what he wanted to do with the name we had chosen for the golf course.

"I cannot abide an unplucked weed," he said. "And another thing I cannot abide is an inappropriate name. With all due respect, William, that is precisely what you are proposing. Why would you inflict such a disparaging name on the only golf course you will ever build? This is the only golf course you plan to build, I trust?"

"That's the promise I made to Marcy."

"Then good for Marcella. But why on earth would you put such a name on your only golf course? Why not Willow Creek, for example? A perfectly apt name for a golf course with Willow Creek running through it. Eminently appropriate and evocative. Or The Oaks. Or Sandhill Marsh. My goodness, there are dozens, literally dozens of obvious, relevant names."

"That's part of the reason right there," I said. "There are courses all around with names like that, some with exactly those names, Willow Creek, for example. I know of at least four of them."

Carlton was determined, insisting that "boondocks" is not even a legitimate word but merely a slang expression of recent origin, used primarily by American soldiers to describe a thoroughly unpleasant wasteland. "The connotation is a miserable, bug-infested swamp of southeast Asia. Now I ask you, is that what you want people to think of when they hear the name of your golf course?"

"I don't think that's what comes to mind for most people, Professor. They think of a place that's off the beaten path. Like the outback in Australia. And that's what we're trying to convey, a place away from the hustle and bustle. I can't tell you how many people have said the same thing when they've come out for their first visit."

"And what is that?"

"'Boy, you're really out here in the boondocks,' they say. And it works with local people, describing a place out of the ordinary. So it seems like a natural to me. Besides, I've never heard of another golf course called The Boondocks, have you?"

"A lesson there, perhaps?"

The good Professor Wells was relentless. He rattled off scores of traditional, completely justifiable names. They all lacked the one quality I thought would make the course memorable, cause it to resonate with people: the relevant unexpected. He was persistent; I was unyielding. The Boondocks it would remain.

I HAD HEARD THE SCREAMING from down the road twice before. Both times I headed inside to get to the phone to call the sheriff, but before I got to the house the screaming stopped. I decided I must be wrong, it couldn't have been a person, it must have been an animal. Raccoons screech and wail during mating, maybe that's what it was.

Still, what if someone was in trouble—a child being beaten, a woman being attacked—and I didn't do anything? Then again, how stupid would I look, calling in an alarm and it turns out to be an animal or maybe kids at play? I phoned Henry Samyn. He hadn't heard anything. The Walkers should know—the sound had come from just past their place. But no one answered the phone. I went back to work, uneasily deciding it must have been some animal.

That evening, I went over the Smedleys' to pick up yet another jar of Gladys's end-of-the-garden relish. She came out on the stoop to meet me, wiping her hands on her threadbare apron. I wondered if she had made the apron that way, out of grain sacks, with two big baggy pockets in the front, one to hold a red pack of Pall Malls, the other a tall juice glass with a little sip of whatever in case she was going to be away from the kitchen table for more than five minutes.

Just as Gladys invited me in, I heard the scream, echoing through the hollow.

"There! Gladys, you hear that?"

"Have to be stone deaf to miss it. Damn fools."

Another scream verging on a howl.

"But what is it? Sounds like a woman being attacked."

"Which is exactly what I thought a couple years ago when I called it in the first time. That brought a deputy sheriff out here, sirens blaring, lights flashing. A woman being raped over there on Curtis Road, I told 'em, at the abandoned place half mile or so west of where you live, just down from the Walkers and Damarons."

"Was it? A woman being attacked? What?"

"Goddamn gooney birds is what it is. Don't know who's the crazier, those people or their damned so-called pets."

"Who are you talking about, Gladys?"

"It's those renters—probably squatters more likely—staying in that old ramshackle place where your Curtis Road bends just before it dead-ends at Norvell. Drove over there in the police car with the deputy sheriff, pulled into the driveway, and up struts this mangy peacock, tail feathers all spread, cock of the walk, all right. Just then he cuts loose with that scream of his. Deputy looks at me and says, 'You can sign a complaint if you want, but I'll tell you right now, the judge will throw it out. People living in the country got a right to their pets, so long as they keep them on their own property.' I'm just sure that lazy deputy'd be so understanding it was his wife's eardrums they was caterwauling into."

Gladys turned and opened the screen door, shooing an invisible fly away. "You want that jar of relish or not? Don't know why I slave over that garden, only to give away what comes out of it, what with this upset stomach all the time."

"Gladys, you already gave us several jars."

"That was months ago. They'll be all gone by now. Your kiddies need lots of that roughage. Keeps 'em regular. Now get in here before all the flies escape."

It was a standing joke that it was Gladys's garden. All Gladys did was order the seeds, hand Kent a planting plan, and then badger him into preparing the plot, planting, weeding, watering, and tending until it was harvest time. Then Gladys would waddle out and tell Kent how to pick each tomato, green pepper, or acorn squash. She'd remind him every year that "those castor beans are poisonous. I only put them in to keep the bugs off my vegetables. Now, Kent, you pick those castor beans and dig a deep hole and bury them before some child goes sick over 'em. Should have pulled those plants out like I told you before they set fruit."

Gladys made one other major contribution to her garden. Every March she would sit by the fireplace, calendar turned to April and May. Colored pens and crayons in hand, she would pore over the charts in Organic Gardening and Farming, searching for the most propitious day and hour for planting each vegetable. She'd pin up the calendar to the corkboard by the refrigerator, then stand back and admire her work. There, to be seen from across the kitchen, were the big X's she had made on certain days with a fat brown crayon.

When I asked her, she said, "Brown X—Day of the rot. Any seed put into soil on that day—take your big red beefsteak tomato that might look juicy and healthy—then you turn it over and what do you see?"

I had no idea what I would see but I was confident I was about to learn.

"Ugly brown spot, big as a quarter on the outside and when you cut into it, why, the whole dang thing is just rotted through. Day of the Rot. That's your brown X right there and you never, I mean never, plant above-ground vegetables that day. Now, these double red bars you see on these other dates? Well, now, those are the especially bad times for just your vine crops, your peas, say."

"What do the yellow marks mean?" I was getting in the spirit of it.

"The yellow. If you was to have pole beans and such, never would you plant those seeds on the Day of the Parch. Peanuts, they do their business below ground and sweet potatoes, they'd be okay, too. Were you to put in peas or pole beans though, don't you know those vines would look vigorous, and the blossoms would come and the pods would start, but then, pffft, like that, they'd dry out. You could water 'til you sucked your well dry and those pods would be as brittle as chitlins and not bean one or pea one inside a one of them. That's the yellow."

With that, to illustrate her point, Gladys drew another emphatic double red line through an otherwise fine-looking day in the long-past month of May, in a week that had already been blighted twice with the big brown X condemning Tuesday and Friday with the Day of the Rot.

"Here," she said and thrust a copy of a magazine at me. The cover trumpeted that inside was the Solitary, One-and-Only, Original Spring Planting Guide Which Alone Will Ensure Bounty From Your Garden.

"The bible," Gladys said. "This is why I can pull bushels of vegetables off my little patch. And every one perfect, except when Kent gets an attack of the lazies and don't water proper or lets the weeds get ahead of him. You live by the charts in this magazine, you'll never want for a healthy garden again."

"Gladys, I had no idea."

"Well then just what have you been doing? What, may I ask, is your planting theory? Do you plant by the weather and the soil temperature?"

"Yes, isn't that—"

"With no mind to the moon and planets?"

I sensed I'd regret admitting it, but I did. I always started seedlings in the house in March, under lights. Then let the soil warm up and waited for a nice day, usually early May.

"And I've had pretty good luck over the years because—"

She cut me off with a snort and lit a Pall Mall.

"And dumb luck is just what it is. There are things you don't trifle with, young man. Planting seed or setting out seedlings when you don't know what the moon and planets say about it is just pounding good money down into the ground. I sure do hope you're going to be more careful when time comes to seed in your golfing links."

"Well, Gladys, I'm always open to learning—"

"Maybe you and me better have a little talk about this fancy grass seed of yours and how and when it gets committed to the earth. You're going to be careless about it, you just might end up harvesting a nice crop of dust. Not at all sure I want to associate with someone throws his money away like that. What makes this golf course grass so special, anyhow? A good stand of timothy or clover's not good enough for 'em?"

So I told Gladys a bit about grass. As I talked, I was surprised at how much I seemed to know. I went on and on, impressing myself more every minute.

"Now wait a minute, sonny boy. You're telling me that you're sowing rye seed as a nursery crop for other kinds of grass?"

I explained to Gladys that you needed to have different grasses for different parts of the golf course. The fairways had to be a mixture of blues and fescues because they had different periods of dormancy. They also germinated at different rates and if they sprouted and then there was a prolonged dry spell, much of the crop would die. So as insurance, I was planting annual rye grain the first year to set down roots and hold the topsoil. Then I would seed into that with perennial rye grass seed as well as blue and fescue. The annual rye grain would live one season and die but would provide a shield for the grasses and give them a toehold for their roots. The rye grain would sprout quickly, be able to withstand heat and drought and that would give the blues and fescues a chance to get started. Then, over time, as we mowed lower and lower, the blues and fescues would take over and dominate the perennial rye grass.

"I've seen these tournaments Kent's had on the television where after they've hit their long shots, they're puttering or whatever the hell they call it to roll the ball into the hole. Now, that grass looks different, cut real short and a different shade of color. What's that all about?"

I described to Gladys how bent grass is different, how it is mowed with special mowers and lowered one sixty-fourth of an inch at a time until it's only an eighth of an inch and even shorter on tournament courses. How it must have lots of water, but not too much. And the water has to percolate through the root zone not too fast, not too slow. I told her about the many kinds of diseases and fungus problems it's susceptible to. And how tricky it is getting it started because the seeds are so small.

"One way to think about it is rye grain seed runs about thirty thousand to a pound. Rye grass is ten times that small. Blues and fescues are ten times that and more, maybe three to four million seeds in a pound. With bent grass you have eight million seeds in every pound."

"Like fine grains of sand."

"Finer than that. You grab a big handful of it, you're holding maybe a million bits of life and it's like dust or powder. You don't plant it on a windy day, that's for sure. When we get to that point—which won't be for maybe two years—we'll mix the bent seed with sharp sand. We'll plant it at dawn before the wind comes up, then cover it quickly with oat straw as a mulch. We water it down so the straw makes a blanket that holds the seed there until it germinates. And hope we don't get a rainstorm that carries it all away before it catches."

Gladys shook her head and tapped a cigarette against the back of her hand. She lit it and blew out a big puff.

"My, my. All that bother just so a bunch of fat, rich men can wear silly clothes and chase after a little ball with a club."

I HAD SEEN THE BIG DIESEL-POWERED CRANE behind the Bassill's house for more than a week, dredging out a pond. It didn't seem like a very bright idea to me, digging a pond for swimming in that kind of soil, but Bob Bassill was determined to have it done, so he had brought in Larry Briggs, the best dragline crane operator in several counties.

We hadn't planned on doing the golf course pond work until the next year but this was too good an opportunity to pass by. We had heard from several people that there were few pond diggers in the area and they were booked up far in advance. More than that, Larry Briggs was the virtuoso of crane work. He had put in many years on the Mississippi canals and when he returned to Michigan he was able to pick and choose his jobs and name his price. He had the highest rates in the area but was reputed to be so good and so fast, you would end up with a better job for less money.

I told Mary Bassill we wanted to talk with Briggs about moving his rig two miles to our place when he finished their pond. Mary, who could be very persuasive, went even further and talked Briggs into changing his schedule so he could do ours.

Two days later, Briggs walked out with me to size up the job. I had several ideas about where we'd like to have ponds. Two or three locations were more or less targets of opportunity—a pond or two up front was essential to provide water to the front four greens. But their precise locations weren't important and I could design those holes after we located springs we could tap.

Farther out, on the back of the property, toward the Smedley Hill, a couple locations were very specific and absolutely crucial. For hole number six, we had to cut one pond into the marsh, at a right angle to Willow Creek, creating a clear-water pond spanning from one side of the marsh to the other. In the process, the spoil—the material we dug out—would form the foundation of a land bridge so golfers could get to the north side, where they would play to a green at the base of Smedley Hill. Then the golfers would walk up to the top of Smedley Hill for one of the finest views around as they played hole number seven, across and down the hill to a low-lying green.

From that green they would walk past the wild strawberry field to number eight tee. That hole would have no fairway at all, because in front of its tee we would carve another large pond out of the marsh which would extend all the way to a green on a knoll not far from Harrison's property line. We needed that pond at number eight not only for scenic value but also to get the spoil to create another land bridge alongside to bring the golfers back to the south side. We would have to lay large metal or concrete tubes under the land bridges to carry Willow Creek and bring year-round fresh water into and through both number six and eight ponds.

So we needed a minimum of four ponds. While Briggs worked on the first ones, I would scout the land to see if there might be another one or two spots where we would need water and where there might be springs that could be opened up. If so, I could tweak the design to work this in.

We were lucky to have found a pro like Briggs working so close to our place. We knew we could neither count on nor afford a second round of pond work so we needed to get everything done while he was here. Because we had not yet arranged for funds for any pond work, I quickly made a visit to Dave Findlay, branch manager at the Grass Lake Bank, to talk refinancing.

"If you're going to have a golf course," Dave said, "you have to have grass. That means water. When you compare the cost of a fixed underground sprinkler system with your idea of several ponds and small surface pumps, you're way ahead as far as being cost-effective. Running those pumps and moving pipe around is going to take a lot more time and work, but I'm not telling you anything you don't already know. Tell you what—we'll pay off your land contract with Daryle Heselschwerdt, write you a new fifteen-year mortgage with an additional three thousand dollars in your account, which we'll add to the mortgage. Your payment will be about the same but for a longer term and you'll have a little more cash to work with."

Sure sounded good to me.

On the way home, I wondered what I would have done if the bank had turned us down. Obviously they considered our project a good risk or they wouldn't be underwriting it. My dependable stable income from the university and an employment record with never a day's interruption helped inspire their confidence. But we were skating close to the edge. I had no concerns about being out of work, although I was very aware that I had to stay healthy to build this golf course. For one thing, we could never afford to pay to have it built by others if I was out of commission, but more important, that wasn't the way we wanted to do it. I knew I couldn't bear to sit around and watch others build the only course I would probably ever design. And we wanted the kids to have the satisfaction of having helped build it.

Now that we had money for the ponds, I had to reach an agreement with Briggs to be sure we kept within that amount. I showed him what we had in mind and asked him for an estimate.

"You can pay me whichever way it suits you, Mr. Haney," Briggs said. "We can do it by the hour, at seventeen dollars per. Or by the job. Now, if you decide to go by the job, I'll size it up and give you a figure and that'll be the cost, no matter if it takes me one day or ten days. Now, doing it that way, I have to protect myself against trouble. Because you almost always run into something you didn't expect. On the other hand, if I don't have problems, you'd have been better off having me on hourly. Your choice. I will tell you that most folks find once we've finished it up and computed it both ways, they were better off had they gone the hourly. But like I say, your choice."

"Larry, is the meter running if you have an equipment breakdown?"

"That's about the only thing I don't nick you for. I break a cable, need to weld a plate on my bucket pan, that's on me. Otherwise, the clock starts the minute I back my rig off the trailer and it keeps on ticking 'til I load her back on. Give you an example. We'll do these two ponds up front here first. Piece of cake, both of 'em. Way you staked it out, I've got a quarter acre of digging by seven to nine feet deep, give or take. Right out in the open like that, knock them off in, say, ten-twelve hours each."

That would mean I would be getting ponds for about $200 apiece. More than that, I'd have Briggs save off the good topsoil to the side, the peat in another pile, and the marl and subsoil separately. That way I could screen the topsoil and the peat to blend them with sharp sand to make the right mixture to build the greens. So in a way, the value of the soil and peat could be deducted from the cost, making the ponds an even better bargain.

"We get those easy ones up front done," Briggs said, "we move out back to the marsh. Now just to avoid bad surprises, I'll warn you right now that when I'm moving to a new site, you'll see turtles streaking past me. My top speed over land is one-half mile an hour, so you're paying me fifteen-twenty dollars just to get to the next site. You might ask why I don't load the rig back on the trailer. Reason is, it takes me longer than that to reload onto the trailer. What's more important, with this going to be a golf course, I wouldn't want to chance a loaded truck on those hills, being so sandy and severe. Make one hell of a mess."

I wondered how many times Larry Briggs had given this short course to clients in his thirty-five years of dragline work.

"Anything else I should know, Mr. Briggs?"

"Some folks like to watch as I work. That's fine. You're paying for it, get to see it. But it won't look pretty while I'm going at it. Some diggers, they finish up a job in the evening, then quit for the day. Not me. Always like to finish at a setting about mid-day, then move to the new site, take a few bites, see what we've got under there. Then it works around in my head overnight and I make better progress the next day. So every day when I shut her down, I leave what looks like a real fine mess. I tell you this so you won't be muttering to yourself, What the hell am I paying this guy for, tearing up my place like that."

We took the hourly rate. With good luck, we could bring in four ponds for $900 to $1,000. On top of that it would cost $300 for the steel tubes that would carry Willow Creek under the land bridges Briggs would build in rough form with the spoil he dredged out of the marsh as he made the ponds. Henry Samyn said he would take a truck to Charlotte to pick up the tubes and Briggs would use his crane to set them in place in the creekbeds.

For $1,200, we would have ponds that would add scenic value, enhance the quality of the course, and provide constant fresh water for our greens. Our only ongoing expense for irrigation would be the gasoline used to power the pumps that would be stationed by each pond.

THE FIRST TWO PONDS went even easier than Briggs had speculated. We called the first pond the Willow Pond because a thirty-foot black willow dominated its southwest corner. That pond would be about fifty yards in front of where I planned number nine green. Looking down on it from the ridge made for an attractive tableau to finish the round—until you dunked a ball in the water.

The other pond on the front side we called simply number one pond because it was positioned just left of where we would locate the first green. It was excavated from a marshy area that extended across the property line and into Harrison's land. I had Briggs bail most of that spoil to the east side to build up a foundation for number one green. That would make a more inviting target and would give us the option of different pin placements that would either diminish the pond as a hazard or, if we put the pin far to the left, bring the pond into play. Some of the rest of the spoil we heaped to the west of the pond as a foundation for a championship tee box that would make the par three second hole a challenging, slightly uphill 210 yards.

As Briggs was finishing the second of the front two ponds, Marcy and the kids and I walked out one evening to have a look. In our year here, we had gotten used to the terrain, to the gentle uninterrupted sweeps of land we would see many times a day from the house. Now we had two great craters gouged out with impressive pyramids of earth drying alongside. One mound near each pond was good topsoil Briggs had carefully skimmed off and saved to the side. The rest was marl and muck, smelling of rotted organic matter. Once this material dried I would spread and disk it into sandier soils.

So far, there was not much water in the ponds, but Briggs assured us that as he dug he had opened several live springs—they would charge the ponds and in a few days the water would be up to the brim.

Pat wanted to know if there would be fish in the ponds. I told him there weren't any right now but we would go fishing and bring back a pail full of fish to stock the ponds.

"Can we have goldfish?"

"I don't think goldfish would be happy in these ponds, Pat. Maybe bluegill and largemouth bass would do better."

"Yeah, let's put in bigmouth fish. Then there's lots of room to get the hook in when we want to catch them again."

As the crane creeped toward the site for the Willow Creek ponds, we winced as the huge cleats on the bulldozer-like tracks pressed six inches to a foot into the earth and left paths it would take some work and a few weeks' time to heal.

When Briggs got to the first setup near Willow Creek marsh, he puzzled over the stakes I had driven in to outline the boundaries of the pond as I envisioned it. As we stood on the plateau overlooking the area, he asked why we didn't have him build just one big pond, right in the middle of the marsh. I told him we needed two ponds because we had to have two different holes and two land bridges—one to get the golfers to the north side, one to get them back.

Briggs nodded. "You care where I place the tubes to carry the creek through? I'd like to move that stream bed so it flows in at the north end and out farther south a couple hundred feet. That way the water will be moving constantly and you won't get so much algae and weeds."

I told Briggs that was the kind of thing I wanted him to suggest because he knew what made for a better pond.

"Well, I don't know a thing about golf," Briggs said. "But I know about water flow. I'd rather see one great big pond instead of two smaller ones, but if that's the way it has to be, that's the way we'll do it."

We did need to do it that way but I was careful not to inhibit a man who was considered an artist with his machine. I got an inkling earlier how particular he was about his work when he explained to me why he used only a type of crane called a dragline instead of a rigid-arm style.

"I have a forty-foot boom on my rig," he said, "and by using a dragline instead of the rigid-arm crane, I can fling my bucket out another ten-fifteen feet. Might not sound like much, but that means I can dig a bigger radius before moving my pads."

Briggs had a wide-body truck bring in the pads so they were there when he started on the ponds in the marsh. The pads were mammoth timber rafts weighing a couple tons each; Briggs had to use them when working in marshes. He had a big hook welded onto his bailing bucket and we watched, fascinated at his deft touch, as he manipulated that hook into a big steel ring mounted on the pad. Then, one at time, he dragged the pads out onto the marsh, walked his rig onto a pad, then reached around behind, picked up another pad, and placed it ahead of the last. That way he could march slowly and safely into boggy places where otherwise he would immediately sink.

As I watched Briggs tiptoe his rig into the marsh and begin carving the pond for number eight, I thought about what his work was costing and what it represented. Seventeen dollars an hour was a lot of money, but it was justified in light of the years Briggs had spent learning his craft and the amount he must have tied up in his equipment. It seemed a bargain, to get these important ponds—water sources, hazards, and visual enhancements—for a small percentage of what our entire investment would be to construct the course.

But there was another value we hadn't considered in bringing in Larry Briggs to dig our ponds. Entertainment. There was more work to do than there was time to do it but this was a one-time experience for Marcy, the kids, and me. So we would sometimes sit there on the south ridge and watch the crane artist transform the landscape.

THIS NARROW NECK IN A MARSH that stretched for miles alongside of Willow Creek was, according to Horace Coppernoll and Edna Walker, the very spot that the pioneers had crossed on the way to Chicago and the West. Where Briggs was parked now was where I had slogged in with chest waders to set a stake. As I drove in the stake, I struck a piece of metal. I pulled it out of the ooze and looked at it. A bracket. A very old, rusted bracket with shards of rotted wood protruding from bolts that had fastened it to some structure or other. I tossed it up on dry ground.

It looked like it might once have been part of an old farm implement he perhaps could identify, so a few days later I showed the old bracket to Horace Coppernoll.

"Yeah, I've seen that kind of bracket before," Horace said. "An old-timer. And judging from where you found it, I'd say that bracket once held up the ribs of a wagon. See, hold it this way and you can see how it clamped onto a rib here and at this spot onto the floor plate. I'd guess that's what these pieces of wood were from, the floor of the wagon."

Horace guessed that the bracket came from a covered wagon.

"Where you've got Briggs digging into your marsh, that's the narrowest place across the wetlands. During dry spells that go on for a few years, as they've been known to do around here, that narrow neck of the marsh dries right up. Saw it that way maybe twenty years ago for three-four years. So the wagons going west from Detroit to Iowa, Nebraska, wherever, that was where they crossed Willow Creek. Old Nate Fish, he reckoned that made the place a historic site."

I looked at the rusted bracket.

"When would that have been, Horace? The wagons going through?"

"Would have been in the 1820s, maybe into the '30s. Before the T-rail tracks were laid down. Some of 'em, though, that old marsh sucked their big old wagon right down. It's the next thing to quicksand in there, you know. Then they'd unhitch their animals and unload what they could.

They'd carry their possessions over to the dry ground on the north side where those little wild strawberries grow. There they'd wait for the next wagon come along. They'd hitch up their own horses or oxen on long ropes to help the new fellers across. Helping out while earning a favor, too. Then if there was room, they'd load on their goods and hitch a ride themselves."

I had heard from Edna Walker that was where some of the founding fathers of Grass Lake came from. A few that lost their wagons decided it wasn't meant to be that they got farther west. They still had their furniture and tools and there was plenty of timber around so they built houses on what became Phal Road or Fishville Road. Among those who stayed were Nate Fish's grandparents, now buried in the tiny Fishville cemetery at the corner of Phal Road and Fishville Road.

Horace handed me back the bracket and got an impish look in his eye.

"But Gladys Smedley told me you're one of those academics over at the university in Ann Arbor so no doubt you already know everything there is to know about that."

The couple times I had spoken with Horace previously, he had punctuated his local history lessons with a barb about my straight job at the university. He'd call me "professor" or "Dr. Haney" although more than once I had explained to him that I was not a teacher and told him what I actually did at the institute. He had wrinkled up his nose at the words "social research." He snorted and said, "Sounds subversive. Hope you're not running with those liberals pushing one-world government."

I took the covered wagon bracket home and nailed it up above my workbench in the lower level of the barn, alongside the horseshoes, rusted hoe heads, and other remnants of the days when Nate Fish raised popcorn on these acres and wagons lumbered their way to Chicago.

I went back out and watched Larry Briggs fling his bucket far out into the marsh and thought about the covered wagon bracket and wondering what other secrets were buried in this land.

Twelve

When my brother Dick retired from the Air Force as a lieutenant colonel after twenty-five years in military service, he was still only forty-three years old and ready to start another career or two. His last tour of duty was at the Pentagon, and Dick's family was comfortable in Silver Spring, Maryland, so they stayed there while Dick looked for the right situation. For brother Dick, the right situation meant a job where there were problems he could fix with a little hard work and a lot of ingenuity, where he could motivate and leverage people, and where he had enough freedom that he could get out onto a golf course a couple times a week.

Soon he had a management job at a large coal and oil distributor, and was in charge of a fleet of more than a hundred big delivery trucks.

Dick always thought there was a better way to do things, so he studied the routings for each driver. He saw they were criss-crossing each other on the roads, spending more time in transit from one side of the District of Columbia to the other than they were actually delivering product. So he reconfigured all the routes and soon the company was delivering more coal and oil in less time at lower costs. Then he studied the service records and saw that the company was holding on to old trucks too long and paying high repair costs, only to surplus the vehicles a year later. Dick computed the best time to dispose of each type of vehicle and what model new truck to replace it with.

It was just a short step, then, for Dick to identify which one of these surplus trucks would be the most useful to a brother building a golf course on a thin budget.

"Thought you could use a dump truck out there so I earmarked one if you're interested," Dick said in a phone call in June 1967.

I had told him we had a crane operator dredging the ponds and that we planned to start shaping out several tees and greens in the spring of '68. Much of the cost of sand, dirt, gravel, and other bulk materials was in the delivery. We had sources for those materials nearby, including some on our own land, so a dump truck would save us a lot of money, which was a good thing because that was something we didn't have a surplus of.

But wouldn't any kind of a truck that was in running condition be too expensive? It wasn't as though we had budgeted for this. In fact, we had just assumed we couldn't afford a dump truck.

"This fall I'll be writing off five of our fuel delivery rigs," he said. "They're Ford F-700's and one especially is still nice and solid. I know a guy who will replace the oil tank with a dump bed and a hoist for a fair price. But it might take him a couple months before he can get to it."

"Sounds great, brother, but I don't think I could handle even a fair price for an F-700 with a dump rig."

"Is four hundred and twenty-five dollars too rich for your blood?"

I hesitated. "You mean for him to take off the tank and install the dump bed?"

"No. Four and a quarter, total. Truck, dump bed, hoist. But that includes sandblasting the frame and a new paint job. I have a guy likes to do that for not much more than the cost of the paint. How's forest green with black trim sound?"

Dick also "knew a guy" who had a Worthington G-5 Lo-Boy golf course tractor to sell. It had dual rear wheels, front-end hydraulics and a jumbo snow blade for clearing driveways. The man was going out of that business because of lack of snow and an excess of slow-paying customers—he'd take $300 for the tractor and blade and throw in a full set of tire chains. Dick knew yet another guy nearby who had a crane and could pick up the tractor and deposit it in the dump bed so I could bring it back at the same time.

The G-5 was legendary among golf course maintenance men, a tractor that was specifically designed for golf course work. With its low center of gravity, you were riding with your butt about two feet above the ground. You could maneuver under tree branches and through tight spots around tees and greens that you wouldn't want to get near with a full-size tractor with heavy-cleated agricultural tires. And it would be all but impossible to tip it over. With its straight four-cylinder Fireball engine it would have enough power to tow a three-unit gang of fairway mowers, even up our steepest hills.

You could never find a tractor like that for sale at a golf course because maintenance supervisors ran them until the engines died, then they re-bored the block and installed new cylinders, pistons, rings, and rods. When they were done, they had an engine with more horsepower than when it came out of the factory. As far as anyone knew, these tractors would run forever. A Worthington G-5 would do work for me that would cost more than $3,000 in a new tractor.

The more I thought about it, the more indispensable this G-5 tractor became. Here was a piece of equipment that a few minutes ago I had never thought about and now I just didn't see how I could do without it.

I often accused my photographer friend Doug Truax about being that way about cameras and their accessories. He seemed to have dozens of cam-

eras and thousands of dollars' worth of flashes and motor drives and light bars and light-reflecting umbrellas and interchangeable lenses and filters but there was always something he didn't have and couldn't do without. The next new gadget to come out, he had to have it. I told Doug he had a disease seldom fatal but expensive to treat: equipmentitis. Now, as I contemplated the utter impossibility of life without an F-700 Ford dump truck and an ancient Worthington G-5 tractor, I had to wonder if Doug's disease had mutated and infected me.

By any standards, to get that much equipment for less than several thousand dollars was a bargain. Still, even $725—plus airfare to D.C. to pick up the equipment—was far more than we had budgeted. Then again, any amount was more than we had budgeted, so that would mean another trip to the bank, unless I could raise the money some other way. I took an inventory of our assets. That didn't take long.

There really wasn't anything left to turn into cash—except for two precious possessions I would keep forever. No, there had to be another way. I just couldn't part with the pool table and the sitar. The pool table was stored in the basement, well above the flood line, I hoped. It had traumatized Marcy helping me carry the two heavy slate slabs down the cellar steps, she and Mark on one end, fearing any moment they would lose their grip and the slate would fall and shatter. The table remained stashed in the basement in the same disassembled state it had been in since we took it apart and moved it from Ann Arbor. The sitar rested mutely in its handmade box, undoubtedly awaiting some three o'clock in the morning when I would caress it lovingly and draw out of it the single pure note I had thus far mastered.

Perhaps the sale of these two precious items would fetch the $725 for the dump truck and G-5 tractor, but to sell them I'd have to advertise and then put up with people coming by all hours of the day and night. They'd probably want me to set up the pool table and run a rack or two of nine ball, just to show them the rails were lively and the slate solid and true. And anyone interested in the sitar would surely want to hear a raga on it and while I was confident in the single note I had perfected, I was several notes and a lot of technique shy of a raga. Yes, any time spent in showing the pool table and sitar would be valuable time drained away from my job, renovation of the house, construction in the barn, and work on the land.

The pool table and sitar would stay—the money for the dump truck and G-5 tractor would have to come from freelance editing, selling a short story or article, or somewhere else. But it was too good a deal to turn down, so I told brother Dick, yes, thanks much, let me know when the truck will be ready.

I WAS IN THE MAINTENANCE SHOP when I heard the throaty grumble of Larry Briggs's pickup truck. I looked out to see him heading out for his last half day of dredging. His crane was set up at the base of Smedley Hill, carving out what the kids had already dubbed the crescent pond.

While digging number six crossover pond nearby, Briggs had noticed a spring seeping just below Gladys's blackberry patch on the south face of the sandy Smedley Hill, about a third of the way up. He asked me if I realized that the seepage from that spring would create a perpetual wet spot across number six fairway. He could fix that by dredging a pond on the other side of the fairway, at the base of the hill. That pond would absorb the runoff from the spring, keeping the fairway drier. That was something I never would have foreseen. A catch-basin pond in that location did something else—it added a further scenic and strategic dimension to what we knew would be the toughest and most talked-about hole on the course.

The job Briggs had done on the first five digs exceeded our expectations. Although he would have scoffed to hear it, he had added a creative flair to each of the ponds. Number one pond had a nice kidney-shaped contour to it, embracing the back and left side of the green. To number six pond he gave an hourglass shape. Number eight pond was similar but swelling larger toward the green, which gave the hole a nice symmetry in relation to the surrounding terrain. The egg-shaped Willow Pond in front of number nine, the first one he dug, already had a design feature—the black willow tree—and didn't need further sculpting. The dig in the marsh below number four green had not been a pond but merely a channel to bring water from Willow Creek as close as possible to firm ground so we could station a pump to irrigate four green and five tee from that source.

And the sixth and last dig was the crescent pond he would finish up today.

Briggs had been keeping a running total of his hours, as we had, and advised me each day of how we stood. With today's work, our bill would be slightly more than $1,800. That included two three-foot-diameter

galvanized tubes twenty feet long to carry Willow Creek beneath and through the land bridges and a third smaller tube at a second location on the number six land bridge to carry accumulated spring water into that pond. We were far over our original budget—getting to be familiar territory—but also had gotten two more ponds.

I walked out to watch Briggs finish up and to invite him in for lunch, where I would write him a check.

As I got near the south ridge, I noticed it was strangely quiet. For weeks we had been hearing the big diesel engine on his crane all the way to the house, a half mile away. I had started down the slope to cross over on the drying pile of spoil that would soon become a land bridge when I heard a noise behind me. I turned and saw Briggs's truck behind a small stand of trees where on sunny days he would park it in the shade. As I got close to the truck, I stopped and stared. Briggs' legs and boots jutted out from underneath the truck—and they weren't moving.

Something instantly flashed through my mind, something Mary Bassill had said. She had told me that Briggs mentioned having had heart problems. I tried to imagine what had happened. Maybe he had a heart attack just as he was getting out of his truck, then somehow unconsciously rolled under it. Or maybe he had gotten out of the truck, left it out of gear, and it had rolled over him. Whatever. Something had happened.

After pausing at the initial shock, I ran toward him. How was I going to get help—if he was still alive? I was a half mile from the house and had walked out. I'd have to run back and—

"Goddamn, son-of-a-bitching peckerwad." The voice came from under the truck, angry but strong. Just then the legs thrashed and I heard a metallic clanking.

"Larry," I shouted. "You okay?"

I heard a thud come from under the truck.

"Larry? Are you all right?"

He shinnied out from under the truck, a pair of wirecutters in one hand, rubbing his forehead with his other hand.

"Yeah. No, damn it. You scared the hell out of me when you yelled and I raised up and banged my head on the oil pan. Hurts like a sonabitch."

"Damn, Larry, I'm sorry about that. Gee, it's swelling up already. You're going to have one big goose egg."

"You ought to feel it from this side. Jesus H. Christ. What were you shouting about, anyhow?"

"I saw you there under the truck, not moving. What would you think? What's going on anyhow?"

He reached under the truck and came out with a tangled mass of rusted barbed wire.

"Goddamn stuff was wound all around the driveshaft. Had to cut it off a coil at a time with these sidecutters." He got up, threw down the jumbled ball of barbed wire and brushed the dirt off his pants and shirt. "My own damn fault, not watching where I was going. You got a cigarette?"

"I don't smoke anymore."

"Neither do I, I guess. Wife took mine away."

I picked up the barbed wire and put it on the deck of his truck. "I've been cleaning up junk like that since we moved in. They just tossed rolled-up old barbed wire anywhere near a fencerow, then the weeds grew up and you can't tell it's there."

"Tell me about it," he grumbled. "Like goddamn land mines. Well, my own carelessness. That hour's on me. I'll still have this wrapped up by noon or soon after. Then we can bring the trailer in from the north side, coming in from Phal Road, and load up. That'll save tracking all the way back up to your house. I'm just moving across the road to scratch out a pond for your neighbor Henry Samyn."

"When you're ready, Larry, drive your truck back up to the house. We'll have a sandwich and something cold and I'll write you your check. We don't like to keep a man waiting for his money."

"That'd be nice. Appreciate that. See you about one o'clock. Provided I don't locate another few yards of your barbed wire."

MARK STARED AT THE BASKETBALL-SIZE ROCK he and his brother and sister had just rolled into the stoneboat, and muttered something. I asked him what he said.

"I said, 'Why couldn't we start with something easy, like a tennis court.'"

"Or a bowling alley," Jen said.

"Or a baseball field," Patrick added.

"No," Mark continued. "Not us. We had to start right out and build a golf course."

And that we did. We were indeed building a real-in-life, full-sized, red-blooded, championship-length golf course. Carved out of the thornapple trees and scrub growth of one hundred rolling acres of Michigan's Jackson County, nineteen miles west of Ann Arbor, and as far as the kids—and maybe the golfing population—were concerned, a million miles from anywhere.

The stone Mark had been wrestling with was half again too heavy for his seven-year-old arms. He and his six-year-old sister, Jennifer, and four-year-old brother, Pat, had already pried out, hefted, and grumbled over so many rocks that they had developed categories and sometimes names for them: That's a puttystone. Look at this pockety one. This one's the third-heaviest kind. Here's the cousin of the big blue rock. And every once in a while they would come across a treasure, like an arrowhead, or a fossil of an 85-million-year-old horn coral.

It wasn't all forced labor. There were rides on the stoneboat and in the trailer, towed behind the tractor. There were even rides up on the tractor itself, on Dad's lap with tiny hands helping steer, or standing with both feet on the foot plate and both hands clutching the fender as Dad hooked a finger in a tiny belt loop. There were trips to the township landfill in the pickup truck and impromptu stops at the Dairy Freeze. There were ball games of every type—basketball against the outside barn wall and, once I got the floodlights up, inside the cavernous red barn when it was cold or rainy. Catching fungoes and learning how to hit the cutoff man on the relay. Climbing the Jungle Gym and the sweet cherry tree. Squirting the tent worms off the catalpa tree with a hose. Touch football with even little Becky darting away from defenders like a waterbug and Pat and Mark learning to sell a fake on a hook-and-go pattern.

There was playing with kittens from the Siamese litters and puppies from the springer spaniels. There were the strays fed until their owners showed up. Counting fireflies and gazing for shooting stars. Music and books and games. There was the wonder of the garden—

planting seeds indoors, seeing them sprout, transplanting seedlings into the ground, checking every day to be the first to see a blossom, then a tiny tomato or cuke, finally harvesting and eating what you had grown and then if you struck a bumper crop, opening up a veggie stand along the road to sell the bounty.

Even though they had barely started in school, it didn't appear that studies would ever be seriously challenging for any of the four. They were so curious, their questions endless, their appetites for answers insatiable. The younger three had to deal at school with being in the wake of Mark, whose biggest threat was boredom. Marcy found ways to feed those appetites so their minds would stay alert and inquisitive. While we worked together out on the land, I played word games with them, taught them the million songs my mother had taught me from her own childhood and others I had memorized or made up over the years.

With their labors on the land, there was not an ounce of fat on the four of them. And even less lard between the ears.

It didn't take long into a conversation in the village to hear yet another story about Ed Harrison. In the ten months since we moved to the farm, I had knocked on his door three or four times to introduce myself but never got an answer. Then one day as I backed out of his driveway, I got a glimpse of someone ducking into the old barn behind the house, a slightly built person wearing a blue denim jacket and a tan cap. It was only a brief look, but I immediately thought of the person I had seen several times near the Harrison fence line and I remembered Horace Coppernoll's stories about our neighbor. Whoever it was obviously didn't want to be seen or see me, so I left.

I thought I knew where I might go to solve this little mystery.

When I described to Gladys the elusive man and the previous fleeting sightings, she sat there in her chair by the end-of-the-driveway fire pit, pursed her lips, and tapped a cigarette on the chair arm. She sat stone silent, her lips tightening with each faster, harder tap until the cigarette broke in half. She tossed it into the fire and took out another one. She was heated up enough that this one she could have lit without a match.

"Just one regret when Kent and I sold you that forty-five acres," she said. "I only wished we could have sold off all our land that bordered on

Ol' Flannelmouth's. Then again, you've got enough fronting him as it is and I wouldn't wish all that misery on anyone."

Gladys told me there was a long history between the Smedleys and Ed Harrison, the man she referred to as "Ol' Flannelmouth . . . Sir Beetle-Brain . . . Crazyhorse . . ." and anything else she could think of to avoid speaking his name. There had been random skirmishes long before what she called The Come-to-Jesus Confrontation.

One day many years ago Harrison showed up on Gladys's doorstep with a thick sheaf of paper he claimed was "conclusive evidence" of his claim. The material apparently included a deed, a property abstract description, and a land survey. Those papers—stamped with an official seal and "legal to a T," he insisted—proved he owned the entirety of Grass Lake Township, including the property Gladys and Kent Smedley had been living on for more than thirty years.

"Haven't said anything before now just out of being neighborly," Harrison said, according to Gladys, "and with my various holdings it's not as though I need it. But for reasons I'm not disclosing, I've decided to put an airport in here and being that this here house would be in the path of my runway, you need to clear out by tomorrow because come Monday I'm bulldozing this place down."

The way Gladys told it, as she and I sat staring into the glowing coals of the fire pit, that was the last time Ed Harrison would ever by God dare shove a bunch of papers in her face. She sat there a while, eyes narrowed at me, sipping whatever it was she had in that glass.

"Well, Gladys, what'd you do?"

"What'd I do? Now just what the hell do you think I did? I grabbed ahold of his goddamn priceless documents. Lucky for him it wasn't his scrawny neck. Already knew what those papers was but I looked anyhow. Sure enough, damn fool had the same basic paperwork as exists for every parcel of land in the whole township. The only difference being that Harrison didn't have the amendments and filings that showed how the land had been parceled up and sold off over the years.

"Well, he grabbed for that passel of worthless paper, but I was too quick for him. Rolled it up and whacked him about the head and shoulders with it until he backed off my porch. Still can see those weird eyes of his a-bugging out. I just kept flailing on him until the old fool fell over backwards, and there he laid in the gravel, not ten feet from where you sit. He's gawking at me and sputtering. I tossed his priceless papers on top of him and they blew all around, him scurrying to gather them up.

"Don't you know, sight of that got me to laughing and that set him off on a burst of profanity that he must have thought was going to shock me until I come right back at him with some choice ones of my own. He brushes himself off, like with that dingy denim jacket must be the only one he owns you could tell the difference. He waggles a bony finger at me, vows I'll regret the day I dealt rudely with Ed Harrison. He makes a big show of limping back to his old beat-up truck, putting on that I've hurt his back and he's gonna sue me."

Gladys fell silent, then went into the kitchen to refresh her drink. I guessed that must be all of the story. She sat down in her chair and fired up another Pall Mall, smoking it halfway down before I finally had to ask if that was the end of it.

"With Ol' Flannelmouth, there's never an end. I figured I needed to take a little walk, clear my head of all that nonsense, so I walked back to the big hill that's yours now. Stood there and took in the view of the Nate Fish place, well, now it's going to be The Boondocks or whatever damn fool name you're going to call it. Stood there and smoked a cigarette. Just about cooled down when I hear a tractor engine coughing and sputtering up by the house. I hustled these old bones right back here and damned if right over there, there's a pile of dirt blocking my driveway."

She poked angrily at the fire with a long stick and worked up a storm of sparks.

"And there was Sir Beetle-Brain. Up there astride that one-lung John Deere that someone gave up on as junk and he towed it home and threatened it into running. And what's he doing now? Got my driveway blocked off with a pile of dirt he scraped off from that worthless little corner of his what abuts onto my property and he's been trying to sell it to us for twenty years at a price like there's gold buried there.

"Next thing you know, like that's not enough, he's pushing up another big pile of dirt right in the middle of Phal Road. Can you believe it? This goes on for fifteen, twenty minutes. Here come cars, trucks, and even Barb Schroen's school bus can't get through. Horns beeping, people getting out and looking at me like 'What's the crazy old coot up to now?' And I go with my hands raised up, like 'Don't ask me.'

"Then his tractor quits on him, just dies right in the middle of the road. Him, sitting there like the damn fool he is, crosses his arms and won't move. He glares at me and I give it right back at him. But do I say a word? Ha! Finally he has to look away—nobody outglares Gladys Smedley."

She gave me a taste of that Gladys glare and I was a true believer.

"Well, then. The cars back off, Barb jockeys her school bus 'til it can turn around, goes back the other way, the cars behind. Gets real quiet. So now it's just me and Crazyhorse. Me glaring, him studying his dirty fingernails.

"Finally here comes the deputy sheriff and right behind him is Hank Dubois to take pictures for the *Grass Lake News*.

"Now, you might have thought that would put the fear into Ol' Flannelmouth. But he turns to me, smiles that rotten-tooth smile like to make me flat-out puke, and you know what he says?"

I had no idea and even if I had I sure wasn't about to take a guess and run the risk of being right.

"The grinning fool says, 'You old bag, you just played right into my hands.'

"What he could possibly mean by that," Gladys said, "I have no slight clue. Then he reaches in his coat pocket and for an instant there I did truly wonder if Loony was going for a pistol. But no, out comes that worthless deed and survey description I had just whacked him on that dumb head with.

"'Here you go, Sheriff,' he says. 'This here'll straighten things out once and for all.'"

"Then the danged idiot gives those papers to the deputy, telling him how it proves that him—the buffoon of Jackson County—owns the whole of Grass Lake Township, including my place and the Coppernolls and the Walkers and the old Nate Fish place, and even the very road we were all standing on. The whole township! And that's why he blocked it up, says Harrison, because it's his land and he's tired of people driving on his road and even though the county paid to put it in, he had never given permission and he was tired of everybody driving on it. Just tired of it.

"Well, when it comes to brain power, that deputy himself was a few warm days shy of ripe. But even though he'd had a dose or two of Harrison before this, he simply could not believe what he was seeing and hearing. That deputy didn't say a word, just went back to his car and got on the two-way radio to the station. While he's gone, Harrison is just grinning there like his defective deed is the ace of trump and they're going to coronate him king of the township right on the spot.

"Oh, the look on his face when the County Road boys show up with a road grader and push that pile and Harrison's old wreck of a tractor right back in the ditch where it belongs, him fussing and yelling so wild it takes the deputy and some besides to throttle him down.

"Then—if you can believe it, because I know I wouldn't if it hadn't happened to me—couple months later when he's in court fighting the ticket he got for obstructing the road, what's he do? He calls me for a witness, a witness for his defense! Most damn fun I ever did have in a courtroom."

Gladys tossed her cigarette into the fire and stared a long while at the embers.

"That was in the fall, don't know how many years back. Doesn't matter. That winter, the first big snow we got drifted over so deep, couldn't none of us on the Phal Road get out for two days. Just like those couple blizzards last winter. Of course with that miser Kent we don't have a tractor to plow out and the Coppernolls are away visiting relatives, so here we sit, snowbound and not a Pall Mall in the place. Then I hear this chug-chug-chug and I say to myself, Oh, no, what's he up to now. And there's Crazyhorse out there. And what's he doing? Clearing our driveway all the way from the road to right here at this fire pit, just as smooth and nice as a baby's bottom. Did everyone else, too, on the Phal Road, from the Fishville Road right up to the Norvell Road. The old fool didn't say a word, just did ours and everybody's and then went back to his place."

Gladys shook her head and stared into space.

"Kent said maybe Ol' Flannelmouth was mellowing, but I know better. He was just waiting, all that time just waiting to do something nice 'cause he knew how much that would piss me off."

IT SOUNDED LIKE A GOOD IDEA when my brother Bob made the offer. It was to be the old win-win-win proposition.

Bob and wife Sue would send their fifteen-year-old son Matt to spend the summer with us. Matt was not a farm boy—the family lived in pleasant suburban Yorba Linda, California—but he was a fine athlete, in great condition and, Bob assured us, was delighted at the prospect of living on a farm for the summer and helping clean up and prepare the land for a golf course. A win, then, for Matt. By the time the summer was over, he'd know how to drive a tractor, a truck, how to do some things around a farm, and have a great tan. And a win for Bob and Sue in that it introduced their oldest son to a healthy outdoors environment and a new experience. A win for Marcy and me because there was no expectation of compensation.

When days later my sister Madeline called and put forth her sec-ond-oldest son Tim for the same deal, we felt doubly blessed.

Marcy and I were apparently the only ones concerned about being perceived as slave drivers, so we made it clear that we didn't have money to pay the kids what they would be worth.

Not an issue, we were told. The kids see this as a chance to get away from home into a different environment and do some things that should be as much fun as they are useful. Besides, we were told emphat-ically, the boys really, really want to do this.

The first few weeks went well enough. The boys got along together and were quiet around Marcy and me. Either in the evenings, or before I went into work at the institute, I'd talk over tasks with them and usu-ally when I got home the chores were done.

Weeks passed. The boys' tans deepened.

Henry Samyn asked me where the two boys came from and I told him.

"Then they'll be going back to their homes when school starts," Henry said.

"Yes, sometime in August, I imagine."

"Hmm. Not until then?" And Henry squinted at me, then turned away.

"Henry. What?"

"Best I don't say anything."

"Too late for that. Come on, Henry, what is it?"

Henry shook his head and walked around in that little circle the way he does. He kneeled down and with his left hand, the one with the fingers, he scooped up a handful of gravel and fooled with the pebbles. He looked up at me with that round sad face, shaking his head, uneasy about something.

"Bill, you ever heard the expression, 'One boy, all boys; two boys, half a boy; three boys, no boys.' Ever heard that?"

"No, that's the first time I heard that one, Henry." But that was really all he had to say and I knew at once why he was bringing it up.

"I just hate seeing 'em taking advantage of you, knowing how much you and Marcy are putting into this place, what it means to you. And hey, they're good kids. It's that they're . . . well, they're just kids, is all."

Henry threw the gravel down and scratched Boots' belly.

"What are you saying, Henry?"

"Shoot, Bill. Not their fault they're not farm kids. They didn't grow up knowing second nature what's done and not done on a place. One of 'em, you'd get all kinds of work. But you take any kid, not just town kids like Matt and Tim, give 'im a tractor, a truck, and trust 'im while you're gone, doesn't take a genius to figure out what's going to happen."

"And what's that, Henry? Help me out on this."

"Well, damn it, I've been biting my tongue 'til it bleeds. See, you're at work at the university, Marcy's at the store with the kids. Well then, Matt and Tim are tearing over hell's half acre on your land, one on the tractor tearing up one side, the other on the truck doing wheelies around him. Playing tag or whatever, pushing those rigs to the limit. A wonder one of 'im hasn't gotten hurt or smashed up your equipment, one."

Henry stood up and shook his head.

"I don't know. Maybe I shouldna said anything, dammit. I sure did my share of screwing around when I was that age. But I stopped short of busting up a man's equipment or almost killing myself."

"Henry, if something had happened, and you hadn't said anything, you wouldn't be happy with yourself. No way I could know about it otherwise. Now I do. Now it's on me. I'll take care of it. And thanks."

THE NEXT TWO DAYS, I thought about how to get it in front of the boys without putting Henry in a bad light. Henry knew they would be gone in a few weeks and he'd likely never see them again, but still, if I could avoid it, I didn't want them to leave resenting him. Also, I had to confront them without them thinking Marcy or one of our kids had told on them.

Driving home from my Ann Arbor office, I decided I would go out in the fields with the boys after dinner and see if we came across spinouts or gouges they had left from tearing around. That would be a way to open up the subject. Then we could talk about it.

The kids hurried to finish dinner because it was Becky's third birthday, July third, and they were eager for cake and ice cream and maybe a drive to see some Fourth of July fireworks. But first there were presents for Beck to open. Matt and Tim were especially quiet. I wondered if they just thought our little birthday party was too corny to sit in on so I told them they didn't have to stick around if they didn't want to; they could have their cake and ice cream later. They looked like they had just gotten a pardon from the governor and were out the door.

After the party, I changed into my work clothes and went out to look for the boys. I saw them leaning against the barn, talking. As I approached, they fell silent and looked at the ground.

"All right, guys. Who's going to tell me whatever it is?"

"Uncle Bill," Matt said. "It wasn't really Tim's fault—"

"But it wasn't Matt's, either," Tim jumped in. "It was just one of those things that happen."

"What 'things that happen?' Is somebody going to tell me what you guys did or am I supposed to guess?"

They kept glancing toward the pole barn. I looked over and noticed that the tractor and truck were both parked much farther inside than usual, back where it was dark. I started over that way, the boys following. In a few steps I could see there was something wrong with the disk. It was still mounted on the three-point hitch on the rear of the Ford 2000 tractor, but clearly something was out of kilter.

I went up and looked at it more closely. The axle of the right rear section had been severely bent backward.

"We tried to straighten it," Tim said. "But boy, that steel is really strong, you know?"

I had bought that disk brand new for $330 at Dunkel Brothers.

The tractor and the disk were the only two pieces of new farm equipment I had ever purchased. We would go over each land again and again from every direction, smoothing out the remnants of years of deep moldboard plowing. The disk was the perfect implement for scalping down the crown furrows and floating the soil from the crowns over a few yards to fill in the troughs called dead furrows. That had to be done on every individual land here to erase the inevitable washboard appearance of fields that had been farmed for years. We also used the disk to wipe out the last vestiges of fencerow ridges that ran helter-skelter, dividing up the spread into a pasture here, row crops there, and the paddock up by the barn. The disk was an essential tool for restoring the whole spread to its original contours.

Only after countless hours of disking would we work each land repeatedly with a spring-tooth harrow to comb it even smoother. Then we would drag it with the tine-tooth harrow to make it finer still. All that was preparatory to rolling, fertilizing, and seeding. No matter how many steps you went through, to get smooth fairways you had to start out with a good job with your disk.

And now, somehow, that crucial piece of equipment had been damaged. It wasn't ruined—three of its four sections hadn't been hurt—but it would be out of commission until we could either straighten or replace the axle of the one bent section. I wondered if we could do that without cracking the housing and ruining the bearings.

What I couldn't figure out was, how did this happen? I had hit buried boulders with that disk, hit them so hard I'd bounce up from the tractor seat and the disk was so sturdy it barely caused a discernible ding in one of the blades. So, it had taken a very powerful blow to bend that shaft.

"The way it happened, Uncle Bill," Tim said, "Matt was turning, see, and here I come across like this. Out there by the woods? With a load of old fence posts and rocks in the pickup and I guess I don't see him and he doesn't see me and then—wham!"

I went to have a better look at the front end of the pickup, which had been pulled even farther into the dark recesses of the pole barn. There was just enough light to see that the right front fender had tried, at considerable speed, to occupy a position already held by another solid object. The headlight was smashed, the fender caved in, the bumper bent. I took

a closer look. Until the front of the truck was repaired, it would seem that it was looking at you with one eye closed, a half-frown on its down-turned lip. Under the broken headlamp, there were dark blue flecks of paint ground into the robin's egg blue of the truck's paint job.

I took a closer look at the damaged disk. Two of the blades had robin's egg blue streaks of paint on their serrated edges.

"Matt. Tim. I'm just guessing now, but I'd say this was something that could never have happened if the truck and the tractor hadn't been operating too close to each other. Or am I wrong?"

Two heads, shaking no.

I remembered Henry's comment about boys racing around on the wide-open land playing vehicular tag.

"Looks as though two boys were tooling around, seeing how close they could come and somebody misjudged. Is that about it?"

Two heads, nodding yes.

"I'll let you guys work out where we go from here. Let me know when you figure it out, okay?"

I WAS LOADING A TANGLE of rusted barbed wire and rotted fence posts into the back of the pickup truck when Ed Harrison stepped over the rickety wire fence between his property and ours and approached. I stood up and stuck out my hand, about to introduce myself. Harrison stood directly in front of me, ignored my hand, and looked far up into the sky.

"I've decided I'd be willing to sell to you after all," he said.

I didn't know what he meant by "after all" because we had never discussed the subject and in fact had never spoken before that moment. I let that pass and asked him his price.

"Six hundred twenty-five the acre," he said.

"Well, that's somewhat more than what I take to be the market in this area, Mr. Harrison."

"I'll think over your offer and get back to you," he said. And he turned and walked quickly away.

What offer? I was baffled and wondered what he thought I had said.

A week later, he came up to me again.

"On that price, with the frontage and all, that would average out to $1750 an acre. That's for the whole parcel, the twenty acres south of Phal Road and fronting this here property you're calling yours."

"Well, Mr. Harrison, even the $625 you mentioned last week is a lot more than I'd be prepared to pay and we've recently bought adjacent land anyhow so—"

For the first time he looked at me, his eyes wide and wild.

"Most likely what I'll do with that land, donate it for a hospital site. They're looking for land and that comes with a tax writeoff, you know. Ambulances, sirens, and all. That or rent it out to a guy wants to dump his junk cars there. You don't buy it, fine with me. Don't be saying I never gave you first shot at it."

And he was gone.

Thirteen

In August, as we completed our first year in the old Nate Fish place, Matt went back to California and Tim to Livonia. The damage to the truck and disk was never mentioned again and I considered it an even wash for their labors on the land. The boys had high school facing them and the next time they saw our place it would be, we hoped, a golf course and vastly different than it was in the summer of 1967 when they had a hand in the early phases of conversion.

It had taken all spring and summer but by mid-August we had the junk cleaned out of the oak woods and had the front thirty-five acres fit down for fairways, a practice range, and the lawns around the house and barns. With Matt and Tim gone, Mark and Pat again took turns riding on the tractor with me as we went over the land. And we went over it again and again and again, in every direction, first with the disk, then the spring-tooth harrow, and finally the tine-tooth harrow. For the last pass over the ground before seeding, I set the tines to leave shallow grooves for the grass seed.

Finally, one year almost to the day since we moved to the farm, all traces of farming were erased on the front thirty-five acres. Getting the land prepared for seeding had taken far more time than it would take to do the actual planting. Now I could start spreading two tons of 20-20-20 fertilizer bought at $55 the ton at the Grass Lake Elevator. Once that was on, it would be time to drive to Maumee, Ohio, to pick up the seed and begin planting.

As I swept around the pole barn on my first pass over the practice range, I saw Henry Samyn waving at me from his field across the road. I hoped it wasn't something that would take too long because the forecast was for two more clear days, then showers continuing for several days. I had to get that fertilizer on and the rye grain in and germinated as a nurse crop to hold the soil for the mixture of fairway grasses going in next. And I was renting the spreader on day rate.

I hopped off the tractor and detached the harrow. I shifted into road gear and swung the tractor out onto the road. Even though the road was flat and straight at that place and the visibility good, I slowed as I pulled onto the pavement. I always paused at that place now, ever since Hank Dubois told me that the Merz boy had been killed at that spot. Hank said the young boy was playing in the road on a low-riding go-cart and the pickup-truck driver saw him too late. I had pulled out of that driveway countless times since Hank told me that and on each occasion I thought of the Merz boy, the youngest of several brothers who had slept in the same room my own two boys now occupied.

Henry Samyn was waiting for me, standing on the shoulder of the road, looking at something out in his field. I could see our dog, big, gangly Yukon, and Henry's black mixed-breed Boots romping around out there, tugging away at something. There was a powerful aroma wafting from the field and I wondered if Henry had spread manure, although it didn't smell exactly like that. It smelled worse.

"Like to make your eyes water, hey, Bill? Guy who pumps out septic tanks, I let him dump it on my fields once in a while. Saves him the time and cost of running it to an authorized treatment site. I let it dry out, then disk it in. Wherever I do that, adds quite a few bushels to my corn yield."

I shook my head and Henry laughed. "Say, reason I waved you over, can you keep Yukon tied up a couple hours 'til I get this done? Every few minutes he and Boots get to fighting, and it always seems to be right out in front of where I'm working. I'm on and off this tractor so often breaking 'em up I can't get a damn thing done."

Yukon was a carefree sort who rarely paid attention to me or anyone else, so I was surprised that when I whistled and shouted for him, he actually came to me. He licked my hand and thumped his strong, unbobbed tail against my leg.

"Man, does he stink," I said. "I'll have to hose him down good and let him sleep in the barn for a few days."

I started to take off my belt and was going to slip it through Yukon's collar as a leash. He couldn't be trusted to follow along behind the tractor. Before I could get the belt in his collar ring, Yukon saw something that Boots had in his jaws that he wanted and in an instant they were at it. And this time they weren't playing. This was serious snarling and deep-throated growling, ears laid back, fur up, and teeth not only bared but snapping viciously. One moment big Yukon was on top, going for Boots' throat, and the next Boots was up and gnashing at Yukon's flanks.

"Hey, there!" Henry yelled. "Damn it, one of them's going to get hurt."

Each dog had its teeth sunken into a leg of the other dog and, in one big ball, they rolled up against my legs. Without thinking, I reached for Yukon's collar.

"Bill, keep your hand out of there or—"

But it was too late. Yukon had instinctively gone after what he coded as a new threat and his jaws clamped down savagely on my right wrist. There was a flicker of recognition in his eyes and he tore away, his teeth still buried in my wrist. I jerked my arm up and for a split second could feel Yukon's eighty pounds coming up with it. Then he let go.

Henry got ahold of Boots as Yukon skulked away and lay down by my tractor.

"Looks like he nipped you there, Bill." I moved the few steps toward Henry and held out my wrist. It was the first time I had ever seen one of my own bones. "Yeah, you might better get home, have Marcy dress that up 'fore it festers. Want me to run you back?"

The deepest gash was at the top of the wrist, an inch or so above the big knob of the wrist bone. That was where I had briefly glimpsed the bone and the severed ends of some gristly things I guessed would be tendons or ligaments . . . or maybe I was just imagining that. I turned my arm over. The wounds on the bottom side of the wrist were just deep punctures, no tearing. For a few seconds there was almost no blood and it was obvious no major artery or vein had been cut. There was a little pain, but I had felt worse many times from thornapple thorns, hitting my thumb with a hammer, and a dozen other accidents. Mostly I felt stupid for having gotten between two fighting dogs and irritated that I was going to lose a little time treating the wounds. If the cuts got infected, that would slow me down just when I had grass seed to get in.

I looked at Henry as he looked at the gash. Here I was standing beside a man who had lost all the fingers from one hand and he didn't let it stop him from doing just about anything. The slit in my wrist was looking pretty trivial.

I still had to get Yukon home. As I moved toward him, he lay there passively, giving no sign he was aware of what had just happened.

By now there was a thin stream of blood trailing down my hand and running off the tips of my fingers and Yukon licked at it as I slipped my belt into his collar.

"You sure you don't want me to run you back to your place, Bill?"

"No, Henry, I've got to get Yukon home and tied up. I'm thinking, What if he did that to one of the kids? Just on instinct, but with those jaws . . . I'll come back later and pick up the tractor."

It was less than a quarter of a mile and by the time I reached our place, the bleeding had slowed to a trickle and my fingers were stuck together from the congealed blood. I was walking in the gravel on the shoulder of the road and was about to step through the drainage ditch and onto our front lawn when I heard a car behind me. It stopped near our mailbox and I saw someone roll down the passenger seat window. A young man leaned out. "Excuse me, sir. Do you live here?"

I tied Yukon to the mailbox post with my belt and walked over to the car.

"Yes, I do. Can I help you?"

"Yes. No, not really. It's just that . . . I used to live here."

"Right here? In this house? Then you must be one of the Merz boys."

"Yeah, I am. It's where I grew up. Then after . . . after a while we moved. I just wanted to show these guys."

I had a sudden sense of how this young man must have felt—himself just a boy when it happened—when his younger brother lay dead in the road, if Hank had described it accurately, only a few feet from where he now was.

"You're Mr. Haney, the guy building the golf course here, then."

"Right." I could see there were three more teenagers in the back seat. They and the driver all craned forward to have a look at their friend's house.

"You guys want to come in, have a look? We might have some lemonade. Or I can make a pot of coffee."

"No, no. That's all right. But mister . . ." And he pointed at my arm. "Your hand. Your hand is covered with blood."

I had forgotten about the small wounds. They didn't hurt at all, just a dull throb and a numbness. I was thinking about the pain this young man and his family must have felt, how that had to have cast a black cloud over that house for them from that day forward. And so, maybe to lighten the moment for myself more than for them, I said, "By golly, you're right. Guess I better go in and put a Band-Aid on it."

As one, all the kids in the car leaned forward, looked at my hand, at my face, to see if I was for real. I don't know what they thought, whether this guy with the bloody hand was one tough dude or a real horse's ass.

"Well, Mr. Haney, thanks anyhow for inviting us in. I just wanted to show my friends where I used to live."

They drove off, slowly, quietly. No squealing tires, no roaring engine. I didn't know if the driver was aware of what had happened there some years earlier, if young Merz had told him about the go-cart, about the driver who didn't react in time, about his brother. I looked at my wrist. The back of the hand above the fourth and fifth fingers had no feeling and it seemed likely there was some sensory nerve damage there but the fingers wiggled and seemed as strong as ever. It was an injury so small, so insignificant, so puny.

My doctor insisted that both dogs be tied up for ten days to be observed for possible rabies. I told him there was no reason to believe either dog was rabid but he held firm, saying rabid skunks and raccoons had been reported in the area and the consequences were too serious to take any chances. It wasn't just that I might have to have shots, there was the safety of the kids to think about. I told the doctor I was sure it was Yukon and not Boots who had bitten me but he said, "When it's two dogs in a fight and one clamps on your arm, you can never be that sure."

Henry was not happy about having to tie Boots up. I couldn't blame him. That dog went everywhere with Henry, keeping him company when he made runs to Maumee for fertilizer or seed, riding shotgun in the big spreader truck when Henry was doing a paid trick applying lime. Boots would sit nearby while Henry worked on his equipment, maybe even sleep at the foot of his bed. Now poor Boots had to do a week in isolation, tethered to a rope. I was sorry I had told the doctor and sorry again I had told Henry that's what the doctor insisted the regulations required.

Yukon was another story.

As big as our place was—now 110 acres including the 10-acre parcel to the west bought from Roy Damaron—it couldn't contain him. He was a roamer and sometimes I'd get a call that he was seen more than a mile away. Henry had told me about another wide-ranging dog that had terrorized a flock of sheep and their young lambs. He hadn't attacked any but he chased them so aggressively that the terrified lambs bounded away frantically on their stiff legs and suffered fatal internal injuries.

I didn't want to hear that Yukon was responsible for hurting livestock or somebody's pet. Or tearing up someone's garden. I didn't want to pick up his body off the roadside if he got hit. I had already buried too many unwanted pets that city people had gotten tired of and dropped off on their Sunday ride in the country. But most of all, I didn't want him around the kids. Thank goodness Marcy agreed. And she pointed out that it didn't have to be a vicious attack on his part—he was so big and frisky that he could hurt a child seriously just being high-spirited. There was no other way. Yukon had to go.

SOMEHOW WE'D FIND A PLACE for Yukon, but that would have to wait until the rabies tests came back negative. Before that, we had planting to do. First I would have to spread fertilizer and the rye grain seed. The spreader I had rented would apply fertilizer and seed at the same time but it was too big for my Ford tractor, so Horace Coppernoll loaned me one of his big John Deeres. I didn't know until I climbed into the seat that it was a hand-clutch tractor, and I hoped my injured hand wouldn't be a problem. But as I tried it out around Horace's barn, the big hand-clutch lever was easy to operate even with a couple numb fingers. Horace opened a fence and waved me through a field where I could connect with my land instead of driving around on the roads.

Another bonus with this tall tractor was the great view it gave of the place.

I lifted Mark up to show him and to see if we could find a job for him helping spread the grass seed. He had already calculated the total number of seeds we would be sowing. I took his word that it was somewhere in the trillions.

Mark learned quickly how to manipulate the controls to open and close the spreader chutes and actuate the fan that spread the seeds and fertilizer granules in a twenty-foot arc behind us. Covering that wide a strip with every pass, we made great time. After one full day and part of a second, we had put in over half a ton of rye grain seed and the two tons of fertilizer.

Now that we had our nurse crop committed to the earth, we had to get a mixture of Kentucky bluegrasses and creeping red fescue in before the rye grain germinated.

THE OPTIMUM WEATHER WINDOW for grass planting was closing rapidly so we had to get the fairway seed in now or lose a growing season. I borrowed Hank Dubois's stake truck and Mark, Pat, and I drove to Maumee to pick up one and a half tons of fairway seed mixture.

As soon as we got back, I loaded the spreader hampers and started over the land. The weather was hot and dry with rain still two or three days away. If we got the entire thirty-five acres fully seeded, then got a nice steady rain, we could expect germination within a week.

By evening the next day, we had the front half of The Boondocks planted. Now it was up to the weather. All we could do was wait.

"WHEN, DAD, WHEN?"

The rain came and it was a good one, soft, steady, and long. The next day a new front moved in and it was clear, sunny, and hot. Perfect germination weather.

Mark went out every morning. And several times during the day. And in the evening after supper. He was determined to be the first to spot tiny green spears poking up.

The fifth morning after sowing, Mark ran in and announced. "We've got grass!"

Indeed, we did.

Even from the back porch you could see it, here and there, in the lowest spots, the slightest pale green sheen. Mark rounded up Marcy and the kids and we went out for a closer look. Most of the color was from the rye grain but here and there, when we got down on our hands and knees, were the tiny fine spears of fescue and blue.

Pat wanted to know why all the spouts looked the same color.

Why wasn't the bluegrass blue and the red fescue red? I explained that all the grass would be green in one shade or another, but that once the grass was mature, he would see the differences that gave the grasses their descriptive names. The bluegrass—not really blue—would be darker and richer than the rye grass or the meadow grasses in the pasture fields nearby. But the red fescue would actually have red runners flat against the ground and the blades would be more of a medium green.

"When do we get to mow it?" Mark asked.

"That won't be for a few weeks yet. And it will depend on when it rains and how much."

AFTER TWO WEEKS PASSED and there was no sign of any illness in Yukon, I called the Animal Shelter in Ann Arbor and described the dog to them. The next day they called back and said they had an elderly couple who needed a mature dog that was big and scary-looking with a loud bark but actually had a friendly disposition. They had several acres, all fenced in. They had recently lost their watchdog and didn't want to start over with a puppy. That sounded like a list of specifications written with Yukon in mind.

I told the kids Yukon had gone to a home where he would be happier and why that was necessary, but that yes, we would get a new dog. Only this time it would be a breed I was familiar with, one I knew would be friendly and safe and the right size for them. Our next dog would be a liver-and-white springer spaniel puppy. And they could help name him.

Fourteen

It got very quiet around the place in September. Mark started the second grade, Jen the first. Pat and Beck were still at home to help fetch tools, play with the kittens, hold the flashlight, toss whatever ball was handy.

I had saved the last of my vacation days at the university to be sure I could be home to mow when the grass was ready. While waiting for the grass to fill out and strengthen enough for mowing, I overhauled the used Jacobsen fairway mowers I cannibalized from a five-unit gang and a three-unit gang scrapped by Ann Arbor Country Club and the University of Michigan Blue Course. Then I borrowed a grinder and lapping machine and worked over the old units until I had the bed knives and reels surgically sharp. It took Walt Bauer's good counsel and some Rube Goldberg rigging to fit all these disparate units together and it yielded an almost psychedelic conglomeration of orange, green, yellow, red, and blue paint jobs, but now I had a seven-unit gang that would mow a fifteen-foot swath.

I checked the grass every day, eager to mow but concerned about running over it before it was ready. Finally it was time. I hooked up the fairway mowers for their inaugural run.

My first pass was too slow and tentative. I saw quickly that the mowers cut more evenly when I kept up speed. By the third pass I was pleased with how well the mowers worked, but it was obvious that the two outboard units were set higher than the other five. I looped back up toward the barn and parked in the old paddock area. I shut off the tractor and got down to fetch the tools to adjust the outboard units.

"The new-mown hay sends all its fragrance," Marcy called out from the back porch.

Indeed the aroma from the first mowing on our golf course was sweet.

THE NEXT DAY, I finished the first complete mowing of the front thirty-five acres. Mark and Jen were in school but Pat was nearby, dribbling a basketball when I grabbed his hand and took him up to the house. I reached inside the mudroom door and grabbed my golf bag and a shag bag of golf balls.

"Are we going to play golf, Daddy?"

"Not actually play golf-course golf, Pat. But we are going to hit some shots."

"But how can we play golf without the poles with flags on them so we know where to aim?"

"What we're going to do is just hit some shots, right off the grass or bare dirt if we have to. That will help us see how our layout of the holes is working. And that way we'll know where to put our own flag-sticks."

"You mean like on the big drawing you made? With the pictures of where the holes will go?"

I told Pat that some things look good when drawn on paper, but then when you go out onto the land, they don't work so well. "That's what we have to find out. And I need your help to do it. Are you up for that?"

"Sure. Let's go!"

"And while we're out there, I'll show you how to swing. Then, if you think you're going to like golf, I'll cut down some clubs to fit you. That way you can practice when I'm not around. But you can't ever swing a club if other kids are nearby. Can I trust you to do that?"

"You bet! I want to get good at golf."

So little Pat and I tramped from place to place, spraying golf balls in every direction. Pat wanted to be the one in charge of picking up the balls. I thought that was a fine idea. We'd split up the work—I'd hit the balls, he would chase them down.

It was too early to tell what kind of a golfer Pat would be, but it was already clear he would make a fine caddie. At least he was getting an early start. I watched him scour the young fairways, holding up each ball he found, as precious a find to him as a nugget of gold. Yes, he was getting a very early start.

I was much older than Pat when I was introduced to golf. I was almost ten years old when, in 1946, I first stepped on a golf course to caddie for two of my brothers just home from the War. Four years later, my caddie days were over because I had been promoted into the pro shop hierarchy as assistant to the caddie master at Red Run Golf Club.

It's a name I've heard before. Horton Smith is a very special name in golf history, that's what Assistant Pro Tom Talkington says. The tall man with the wavy blond hair is the same Horton Smith who won the first Masters Golf Tournament in 1934, Mr. Talkington says. That means he deserves to have a special caddie.

It's exciting to get to caddie for Mr. Horton Smith, even though I left the caddie ranks a year ago when I was thirteen and am now on the pro shop staff. Sort of. I don't actually work in the pro shop. My assigned post is the cream-colored stucco caddie shack far enough away that noisy caddies won't bother golfers.

One of the club-cleaner boys will watch the caddie shack for me, Mr. Talkington says. That has never happened before, so I know that caddying for this great golfer is something very special.

I didn't mind caddying again after being promoted. Sure, my official title is assistant caddie master, the lowest rung on the ladder, but I'm on salary and bonus. Even Dad is hourly at the Creamery. My salary is five dollars a day, six days a week, off on Mondays, which is the day they let the caddies play the course and members aren't allowed. And I get a bonus at the end of the year if the caddie shack takes in a certain amount in sales.

Mr. Talkington is right. Every shot Horton Smith hits is perfect. Every putt either goes in or burns the lip and stops inches away. It's a treat to get out in the sun after day after day inside the dark caddie shack.

But the next day, that's where I am again, on my tall stool behind the counter.

My boss is Marshall Benjamin, the caddie master as well as my football and basketball coach, first at Big Beaver junior high and now in my freshman year at Troy High School. Two years ago I helped Mr. Benjamin get started in golf—I loaned him my golf clubs and then caddied for him at the public course, Sylvan Glen. I never imagined that two years later he would turn around and hire me. I would "hold down the fort," he says, down at the caddie shack. That way he can stay up at the pro shop and soak up more about the game. "And pick up inside tips on smart investments from the members," Mr. Benjamin once whispered to me.

My place of business, the stucco caddie shack, has one pale light bulb and a broken toilet. The only furniture is my tall stool behind the counter and a big picnic table in the middle of the room. The table is supposed to be for caddies to eat their lunch on but almost always it's used for card games I'm supposed to break up. There's an old refrigerator and a little oven for heating hot dogs and sandwiches.

I sit most of the day on my stool behind a counter. Underneath it is where I store boxes of candy bars and potato chips. On top of the counter I keep the caddies' cards in neat stacks. The smallest stack is for the captain caddies. These are not just boys, they're grown men who started caddying before I was born, or so they tell me. They get the best "loops." That meant they get the car dealers or the pro athletes from the Detroit Tigers, Lions, and Red Wings. Like Paul "Dizzy" Trout and Gordie Howe.

The captain caddies come in after five hours in the hot sun and take over the picnic table. The one who draws the lowest card has to go to the market for beer, even though I tell them they're not supposed to have beer here and they say, Shut up, kid, or you want a fat lip? After fifteen minutes of five-card stud, one of them gathers up a pile of dollar bills and a few fives and the other three captain caddies throw their cards down and cuss, then bum cigarettes from the guy who won and go home broke.

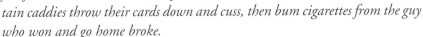

A bigger pile of cards is for the "A" caddies. These kids have been around for three or four years and they know it all. They know that Aubrey Flood is nick-named "Flat-rate" Flood for good reason. They know that if you get in a foursome with Mrs. Knupp, you get on the other side of the green when she kneels on one knee to line up a putt and you get a free show. They know that Bob Babbish is a great golfer but you better get out of the line of fire if he misses a three-foot putt.

Everybody knows that Big Tom Draper carries a pocket full of dimes to mark his ball on the green and if you stand nearby, he'll toss you the dime after he puts his ball back down. And most of all, they know how to make life miserable for the "B" and "C" caddies. They make them hand over their candy bar, sometimes even their whole brown bag lunch. And they challenge them into pitching pennies against the wall, losing on purpose to con them into moving up to nickels, then quarters. Once it gets to quarters, it's brutal. The "B's" and "C's" come into the shack with long looks on their faces, unfolding the dollar bill they've hidden in a shoe, asking for quarters to try to win back the money they just lost.

The "B's" get the loops the captains and "A's" don't want. There are more than two hundred and fifty golfers playing at Red Run on a normal summer day, but the top caddies get to carry double, and loop in the morning and again in the afternoon. So, many of the lower-rank caddies sit on the rail in the shade of the elm trees or mess around hour after hour, day after day, and never get a loop. I know how that feels because that's the way it was for me when I was eleven and starting my career.

Now things are different. Now I'm part of the pro shop staff, almost. In a world where even the club cleaner is higher than a caddie, I have arrived.

But just arriving at the course is a challenge almost every day. Red Run Golf Club is at the edge of the city of Royal Oak at 12 Mile Road and Rochester Road. I live in Big Beaver, a village just north of 16 Mile Road, a block off Rochester Road, and every day it's an adventure to cover that four miles and arrive at my caddie shack by 7 a.m. The first three days in my new job I took my bike. That went great. The road was flat almost all the way and I could make the four miles in twenty-five minutes. I figured if I did that all summer that bike ride would make up for not caddying any more and help build up my legs for football.

Then, on the fourth day, a caddie borrowed my bike to go to the restaurant over on Main Street. He promised he'd be back in fifteen minutes. I never saw that bike again, which is what I get for trusting a "B" caddie in the first place.

Next I hitchhiked. That went good for three days—until my father heard about it. So then I started taking the Martin Line bus, but that was a nickel, which is enough to buy a Snickers or a Pepsi. Spending a dime every day all summer long would mean you were out seven dollars and thirty cents, just for riding a bus four miles twice a day. Then I thought of the perfect solution. Mr. Harold McGrann was a boarder at the house next door where my friends Carol Stehl and Beverly Solem lived. Mr. McGrann drove right by Red Run every morning at exactly 7 a.m. I knew that because I had seen him go right on past me in the days I still had my bicycle. So I asked Beverly if she thought he'd let me ride with him.

Beverly said she knew that Mr. McGrann likes his privacy and doesn't like kids much. And he's fussy about his car. She said she knew he'd say no but she'd ask him anyhow.

I was not very hopeful about my chances. But then Beverly called to me over the back fence, "I asked my mom to ask him. He says if you're ready *when he leaves at 6:45 sharp tomorrow morning you can have a ride, but don't be thinking it's going to be a regular thing."*

I knew if I was real nice to Mr. McGrann and showed him what good company I was, he'd want me to ride with him every day, both ways. There was a lot I could do with that seven dollars and thirty cents I'd be saving.

Next morning I was up before 6 a.m. I burned the bacon, just the way I liked it so there was no chewy fat left, just all crispness. While it was draining on a paper towel, I smeared Miracle Whip on both slices of bread. Then I squashed it down nice and flat, the way it tasted best. I wrapped the sandwich in waxed paper and stuffed it into a brown lunch bag.

At 6:30 I was standing beside Mr. McGrann's shiny maroon 1947 Mercury. If he looked out early, he'd see how punctual I was. He didn't look very happy when he came out, and didn't answer when I said, " Good morning, Mr. McGrann. And a delightful morning it is, don't you agree?" He just tossed his own lunch bag on the seat, started the engine, and motioned for me to get in.

He still hadn't said anything by the time we got to 15 Mile Road and so I figured he was waiting for me to start the conversation.

"President Truman sure has his work cut out for him with that 80th Congress, doesn't he, Mr. McGrann?"

My father was a union steward and so I knew about politics. The only trouble was that we were Democrats, and if there were any others anywhere in Big Beaver, I never met them. Still, my comment about President Truman couldn't have offended Mr. McGrann, even though my father had said all our neighbors had been for Dewey. But maybe Mr. McGrann couldn't even stand the sound of President Truman's name because he never replied. In fact, he never said another word until he pulled over onto the gravel shoulder, next to the entrance to Red Run Golf Club.

"Out," he said.

I grabbed the brown lunch bag and got out.

"Thanks very much, Mr. McGrann. See you this afternoon at 4:30. I greatly appreciate—"

But my words were smothered in a cloud of dust. Mr. McGrann was sure in a hurry to get to work.

At noon, I closed the door for my fifteen-minute lunch break. I groped among the ice chunks floating in the pop cooler and found the coldest bottle of Pepsi. I put a nickel in the till because otherwise Mr. Benjamin's books wouldn't balance. Then I dug into the brown lunch bag. Strange. There were now two sandwiches, instead of one. And an apple. And a banana. And a little plastic box with three chocolate chip cookies. How could this be? Had my mother somehow sneaked out of bed when I wasn't looking and replaced my bacon sandwich with two ham and cheese sandwiches, then got back in bed and pretended she was asleep as I looked in on her before I left the house? That wouldn't be like her. It was a mystery. And it was the best brown bag lunch I ever had.

That afternoon I was there beside the road right on time, waiting for Mr. McGrann to pick me up. His maroon Mercury came along but then it roared right past me. Mr. McGrann just stared straight ahead with his jaw sticking out, so it's no wonder he didn't see me.

When I got home, Beverly Solem was sitting on my front steps. That was unusual.

"Billy, you got me in real trouble with our boarder. He said you tried to poison him and it was my fault, too."

"There was this one mistake, Beverly. See, we accidentally swapped lunches and— "

"What did you do with Mr. McGrann's lunch, Billy?"

Girls ask the dumbest questions. "I ate it, of course. And he had mine to eat, so it evened out. See, it was just a honest mistake. If he hadn't put his lunch bag right next to mine—"

"Well, he didn't eat yours. He took one little bite and spit it out. Said he shouldn't have expected anything more from the cretin son of a goddamn Democrat."

BROTHER DICK CALLED IN MID-SEPTEMBER to ask how the grass was growing. He said, Oh, the dump bed has been installed on the Ford F-700 truck and the paint is drying. And the Worthington G-5 tractor and grading blade were all set. I could pick up my equipment by mid-October. The weather should be perfect then to fly into Washington, D.C., and drive back through the fall colors in Pennsylvania and Ohio.

A few days later, I was musing about how I would use the dump truck and the G-5 when I saw Henry Samyn walking across his field toward me. He wiped his forehead with a bandanna as he crossed the road, smiling like he had done something stupid, the way I'd smile when I came to tell him I had gotten the tractor stuck again and needed a pull.

"Did it again," Henry said. "Ran her dry."

We got a five-gallon can out of the barn and walked around the rear of the house to the cellar doors, so as not to risk dripping fuel oil onto the fancy dollar-a-yard carpet upstairs. The new cellar doors I had installed looked good, nice dark green paint job. Henry didn't notice.

"Bill, when you going to get you a diesel?" Henry asked. "I hate dipping into your fuel oil every time I run out."

We headed down the steps to the basement to fill his can from our three-hundred-gallon tank. I was glad I had gotten a reconditioned oil burner installed and had gotten rid of the massive unpredictable coal stoker and the messy coal bin. That left plenty of room in the basement for the oil tank and additional storage space besides.

"Every time, Henry? Couldn't be more than twice because we've only had the oil burner a few weeks. Anyhow, I thought I might be getting a diesel engine in a dump truck my brother's fixing up for me but turns out it's a regular gasoline engine. That works out better anyhow because that way I don't need two three-hundred-gallon tanks with different fuel."

Henry was curious about the new truck my brother was arranging for me; we talked about it as we walked out to where his tractor had stalled out. I told him it was many miles from being a new truck, but I knew my brother would have it in nice shape. I told Henry the truck would be there for him to use, too. I was glad for the chance to share equipment with him.

"You're driving that rig back all alone? From the East Coast? What happens you get tired, want to get some sleep?"

"It's only twelve hours' driving or so. Unless I run into traffic or weather. I'll just drive straight through."

Henry got up on his tractor and I handed up the fuel and a funnel.

"Could do that, I suppose. Unless you run into trouble. You know, that F-700 engine is known to be a little cranky at times, 'til you get used to it. Drove a few of them. Know 'em pretty well."

I finally figured it out and said, "You're right, that wouldn't be a whole lot of fun, stranded on the Pennsylvania Turnpike in a strange rig. Henry, don't suppose there's any way I could talk you into coming along, riding shotgun, is there?"

Henry handed down the empty can and fired up his diesel before he climbed down and answered.

"Well now, Bill, I don't know. Depends. How we gonna get there?"

"Have to fly, wouldn't we?"

"One of those jets? Can't say as I've ever been in one of those."

"But you've flown in propeller planes?"

"Can't say as I've ever been in one of those, either. Suppose we'd be in one makes those contrails you see way up there?"

He took out a rag and wiped a drop of fuel oil off a hood that he somehow always kept sparkling.

"I'd say that was likely, Henry. I'd probably want to go week after next. Would that work for you?

"Yeah, I guess that'd work. I get these fields buttoned down, I'll tag along, seeing as you're picking up the tab."

THERE WOULD BE NO GREENS or tees until next year but the early October weather was nice and the fairway grass was filling in well, so I continued to test the layout. This time Mark went along to help shag balls and pace off distances.

I was satisfied that holes one and two did what opening holes should do—get the golfers off to an easy start without either boring or intimidating them. Then I moved over to number three and, after hitting a few dozen shots from various locations, was pleased the long double-dogleg par five was shaping up to be a fine golf hole. It was a short walk from the location where we would build three green over to the spot where I was thinking of locating the tees for number nine. From those tees the golfer would play back up toward the house and barns. I didn't want the Willow Pond to come into play on the tee shot and I wanted the water to be well short of the green so that the final strokes would be testing but not too exacting. I hit twenty or so drives from the spots where I expected to build the tees and when I walked up the fairway, I could see that the hole was working the way I had intended, except that I decided to push the green another ten yards away from the pond.

I realized that as the design concepts became reality, I would need to keep going out on the land and hit shots and then go back to the drawing board for adjustments. And I would have to keep doing that, over and over and over, until I got it right.

"I'VE THOUGHT ON IT A GOOD BIT," Gladys said, "and for the life of me I still cannot understand why in God's name anybody would want to build themself a golf course with all that fussing and sweating and money and risk, then along comes a bug or bad weather and like that, you're out of business. Why would someone want to do such a thing? Can you answer me that?"

I searched for an answer clever enough, or profound enough, or funny enough. I couldn't find one, because the truth was, if there was an answer, I didn't know it.

"For the challenge?" I offered meekly. "For the satisfaction of doing it? Gladys, I don't know about other people, but for me it's just always been something I knew I had to do. Ever since I was a kid ten years old and I was caddying for my brothers when they came home after the War. Ever since I heard one golfer after another say that someday he was going to build a course and I found myself saying the same thing. In fact, I said it so often I felt I was on the hook with myself to actually do it. So, years later, when Marcy and I started going out, I would tell her about it. Maybe it ended up that I had to do it mostly because I just could not not do it. Especially since Marcy knew all along and supported it, so . . ."

Gladys reached over and patted the back of my hand.

"Just what I thought, honey. You haven't got a clue."

Fifteen

We cruised in above the Potomac for our landing at Washington National. Henry Samyn had a good view of Arlington Cemetery out the right side window, then, as we banked, a quick look at the Capitol and the Washington Monument out the left.

At the rental car office, people were grumbling that traffic was tied up around the Capitol. Despite that we headed into the District, to Dick's office at Griffith Consumers. To give Henry a look at the landmarks, I took the Memorial Bridge and drove past the Lincoln Memorial and the Washington Monument. When we turned onto Pennsylvania Avenue and drove past the White House, there seemed to be exceptionally large crowds for a weekday in mid-October.

"What'd you suppose all those pickets and signs are about?" Henry asked.

"Judging from the beards and the beads," I said, "it's not farmers protesting low wheat prices. I hadn't connected until just now what's going on today. It's an anti–Vietnam War demonstration."

"These long-haired hippies don't know how lucky they are," Henry said. "Living in a free country. The Soviet Union, they'd get their heads busted and their butts shipped off to Siberia just thinking about protesting against the war."

"That's the way it all started, Henry," I said.

"The way what started?"

"This country. Two hundred years ago, with citizens protesting against the government."

"Well, hell, Bill. That was a little different now, wasn't it?"

It was quiet for a while and soon we were out of the heavy congestion and headed toward New York Avenue to look for the place my brother worked.

"Yes sir, you better believe that was different," Henry said. "Who wouldn't protest, getting bossed around by Englishmen."

We meandered around until we found New York Avenue. In a few minutes we spotted the big sign identifying Griffith Consumers, the coal and oil delivery company where my brother worked. Tucked into a corner in the cluster of buildings was the main office and, as we pulled in, my brother came out and saw us. In less than five minutes, Henry and Dick were old pals sharing stories.

Dick took us into a wing of the sprawling plant that hadn't been used for years. We went down a dark hallway, turned a corner into a well-lit area, and there we saw it, gleaming in its new paint job of forest green and glossy black.

"Damn, Dick," Henry said. "Your boys sure do good work. Looks like it just came off the assembly line."

"You wouldn't guess that one topped two hundred thousand miles a long time ago," Dick said. "But I had it overhauled and the dump bed is like new. Oughta give you a lot of good service, brother."

I climbed up into the cab and had a look.

The cracked upholstery and well-worn foot pedals showed that the F-700 was indeed a seasoned veteran, but when I started the engine it hummed smoothly. The lights, horn, turn signals, everything worked fine.

"Have a look inside that dump bed," Dick said.

I got out of the cab and stood on the running board and peered over into the bed. Dick already had the fire-engine-red Worthington G-5 tractor tucked in place, along with a huge yellow snow blade that was actually oversized for the tractor.

"Had to take off the outboard right rear wheel to fit it in there," Dick said. "That center of gravity's so low you couldn't roll that thing over if you tried. Knowing you, you'll try."

Henry climbed up and had a look. "Umm, that is tight," he said. "You could slip a dollar bill in the space left over. But not a two."

Although it was a close fit side to side, there was still room in front of the tractor. Dick saw me looking at that space. He walked over to a darkened work bay across the room.

"Come on over here and I'll show you what we're going to put in there right now to make a full, balanced load."

There was a large coil of rubber hose and a big gasoline-powered engine mounted to a large pump.

"That hose is inch and a half inside diameter," Dick said. "Not exactly standard, but you can get adapters at a good plumbing supply shop."

Henry hefted a coil of the hose and looked at it.

"That's real rubber. Heavy but nice and supple."

Dick went to move the bulky Marlowe pump to give us a look at the eight-horsepower Wisconsin engine that powered it.

"You guys want to give me a hand with this?" Dick said.

"Let me check," Henry said, holding up both hands and waggling the fingerless one so Dick couldn't miss his meaning. "Yep, by God, still got one good one left."

We skidded the pump and engine and lined it up with the overhead winch rail-mounted from the ceiling. Henry hooked a chain into the big lifting eyebolt mounted on the engine block and Dick ran the controls to lift the pump and engine rig and deposit it into the truck bed. Henry tied a rope to secure the coiled-up rubber hose and Dick hoisted that into the space between the tractor and the pump, where it would provide a cushion between the two. We now had a snug load that wouldn't shift.

Dick and I took the stairs and Henry drove the truck down the ramp. He parked it in front and met Dick and me at the office where I gave Dick a check for $725 for a truck, tractor, blade, pump, and hose that would have cost me many times that on the open market, if indeed I could get it at all. Dick handed me the title and the bills of sale. Everything had gone so well we were ahead of schedule. I wondered if Henry might want to drive around the District and see some of the monuments, but when Dick had another suggestion, Henry broke into a big grin.

"I know you have to dump the rental car off yet, but you may want to do that tomorrow morning," Dick said. "You might want to keep the rental car to use it tonight. Eileen has your room set up at our place in Silver Spring, so after rush hour tomorrow morning it's only a half hour into the district to register the title transfer. And just a few blocks from there you can drop the rental car."

"Sounds fine with me," I said. "But why do we need the rental car tonight?"

"Well, Eileen will have dinner ready for us about six. Then there's some sights you'll have to check out in Baltimore. East Baltimore Street is kind of a tough section but just the place for a couple of country boys to see sights you might not encounter in the cornfields of Michigan."

After dinner Dick gave us a Baltimore city map and a key to his front door "just in case you happen to get back after eleven o'clock."

HENRY AND I WORKED our way up one side of East Baltimore Street, stopping just long enough for a short beer or a quick look in a dozen sleazy bars, lounges, or clubs. We were partway down the other side when Henry met Ginger. Here was Henry, a squat and powerful five-foot-six with a perpetual sunburn and pale blue eyes almost invisible under bushy blond eyebrows squeezed down against the sun, even at night. And there was Ginger, well over six feet in spike heels, topped by a beehive of auburn hair the size of a bushel basket, breasts spilling out in every direction from a red sequined top, and a black leather mini skirt taut as a banjo string under which could be found, she proclaimed, "nothing but me, lots and lots of me." Around the neck of the sunburned, blond Henry, the fleshy, deeply tanned arm of Ginger, heavy with bracelets, glistened with an almost metallic sheen.

The bartender gave a jerk of his head and Ginger disengaged herself from Henry long enough to take her turn slithering up and down the shiny pole on the bar above us.

"This one's different, Bill."

"Different how?"

"You can't see it? She's not one of them easy women, like those others. She's only working here to make enough to pay for an operation for her mother."

"Really?"

"Oh, yeah. She even told me how to handle it when the bartender asks for our order. See, if I ask her what she wants, she has to say, 'A split of champagne.' And that sets you back twenty bucks right now. So she tells me, when the bartender asks, you just say 'The lady will have a shell of beer, same as I'm having.' Then you're in for only three dollars."

Ginger was on the other side of the runway now. She looked over her shoulder, gave Henry a big smile, and mouthed something that looked like 'Hi, Tommy.'

"Who's Tommy," I said.

"Shhh, she's talking to me," Henry said. "That's how you do it, a place like this. For the Chrissake, you don't give 'em your real name."

I said to Henry, "If you don't buy her champagne, then she won't get as much of a commission—if that's what they call it. And maybe she'll get in trouble with the bartender for letting you in on how it works."

"My point exactly," Henry said. "That shows she's different. More like us. Well, like me, anyhow. We've got that—what's the word?—rapport."

Ginger worked the customers and came full circle on the stage above and back in front to us, a fan of dollar bills tucked in her bra and a couple of fives in the band of her tiny skirt. She smiled at Henry and bent over backwards in a move that Henry said, "would have my vertebras going off like popcorn." Then his eyes bulged. He turned to me and said, "By damn, I thought she was kidding when she said that about nothing under that little skirt but big old her. You ever see such a thing?"

Henry drew a few looks as he took out his red bandanna and mopped his forehead.

I went to the men's room and when I got back, Ginger had Henry all but smothered in her bosoms. The bartender was looking discreetly the other way.

I could barely hear Henry's muffled voice. "Hey, now. I thought you said you were only dancing here for money for your mother's operation."

"I did say that, Tommy boy," Ginger said. "Do that mean a girl can't enjoy it? Right there, Tommy. Umm, you are the sweet one. Now, let's see what you got going down there for little Ginger."

I called the bartender over and was about to order another beer when Henry let out a yowl that jerked the bartender upright. He glared at Henry, and the dancers and customers looked to see what was happening. Henry pulled out of Ginger's grasp and twisted away from her, clutching his crotch.

"Jeez-O, Ginger, why'd you go and do that? Son-a-bitch, that hurts."

The slender dancer gyrating on the bar above us leaned over and smiled at Henry. "Honey boy, that's just Ginger's way of showing affection."

"Hell of a way to show it," Henry shot over his shoulder as he headed for the door, waving to me to follow.

Ginger folded her arms across her chest, which took some doing, and loomed over me. "What's with that boy? He got some kind of a problem?"

I eased around Ginger and toward the door.

"War wound," I said.

HENRY WAS STILL SQUIRMING and looking pained the next morning as we left the District office where I filed the change in registration of the truck. Henry wanted to get the feel of the truck before we got out onto the highways so he drove and I sat in the passenger seat. I figured if he wanted to talk about the going-away squeeze from Ginger, he would without me asking, so I just watched the throngs out around the Capitol. Thousands of people out there, enjoying the sunny and cool October day, happy citizens out enjoying a visit to their nation's capital.

"Bill, you smell something? Take a look at that temperature gauge. Yep, she's running hot, all right."

The engine coughed and sputtered, then smoothed out as Henry shifted out of gear and coasted.

"Must be a stuck thermostat," Henry said. "Two-dollar part and it causes more damn headaches. We'll let her idle back. Good thing this happened before we got on the highway. We'll find a parts store or I'll just pull over and we'll take the damn thing out, run her wide open."

Now we were passing the White House and could see that this was not just normal visitor traffic. The farther we went, the more police cars and mounted police. Anxious parents kept their children close by as they watched the growing tension between demonstrators and police.

I looked at the temperature gauge. "Still running hot."

"Yeah, I'll shut the engine off, coast a ways and let her cool."

With the truck now coasting quietly, engine off, as Henry tried to cool the overheated engine, we could hear the chants of the demonstrators and orders being shouted through a bullhorn: "Demonstrators, back up, disperse, or you will be forcibly removed and arrested."

Another block and the streets were lined with military vehicles. Hundreds upon hundreds of National Guardsmen lined in cordons on both sides of the street. Men in battle fatigues or camouflage posted at each intersection, vigorously directing traffic, shouting, "Keep moving, keep moving!"

A bearded young man hanging from a statue exhorted the crowd. A ring of kneeling guardsmen watched intently, rifles pointing up in the air.

"Henry, this does not feel good. Look at those guns. It's like they're expecting a war."

"Yeah. We're getting the hell out of here." And Henry reached for the ignition switch to restart the engine.

We were smack in front of the Washington Monument when we heard the explosion. Acrid smoke stung our eyes and the roar from our freshly blown muffler was deafening. But I didn't know what had happened.

"Get that dump truck out of here! Now!" We heard the bullhorn as if through layers of cotton. "You, green and black Ford truck. Move it!"

I looked out the window, expecting to see every rifle in the world pointed at us. The demonstrator hanging on the statue waved wildly as his crowd scattered. The guardsmen with the guns seemed confused, scared, waiting for an order, glancing at us, then at the officer with the bullhorn.

"Move that goddamn truck! Now!"

Henry downshifted and the roar from our blown muffler raised an octave as we rumbled away.

Henry turned at the first cross street, then turned again, and in less than a minute we were away from it. He pulled over to the curb and shut the engine off.

"Can you believe that," he said. "When I shut the engine off to let it cool, there were unexploded fumes in the manifold so when I turned the key back on and the fumes hit that hot muffler—blam!"

"Henry, did you see those guardsmen? Those guns?"

"I was busy but I'll take your word for it."

"Now I know how a deer feels," I said. "Frozen in the headlights, poachers sighted in on him."

We sat there a long while. When the engine was cool we found a gas station and got directions to a parts store. In less than an hour, we had a new thermostat in and a new muffler on, and were headed toward Michigan.

THE TRUCK PURRED QUIETLY along the Pennsylvania highway, the needle of the temperature gauge holding steady in the normal range.

We pulled into a truck stop and over dessert I mentioned to Henry that he wasn't squirming around like he had been since Ginger had told him to turn his head to the right and cough.

"Hey, you're right." He felt down there and smiled. "Thought she had cracked that nut for good. Guess that action at the Capitol got my adrenalin flowing and flushed her out good for me." He sipped his coffee and smiled. "That Ginger, she was something, huh?"

1·9·6·8

Sixteen

Hank Dubois and I were in the maintenance area of the barn, grateful to be working inside on the gray, messy days of March. While we waited for the snow cover to melt so we could see how the grass wintered, we were busy getting equipment ready for what we hoped would be lots of mowing in a few weeks. We both looked up when someone rolled aside the big door and came in. With his dark clothes and sunglasses, I thought I could guess what he was after.

"You looking for German shepherds?" I asked him.

He pointed a finger at me and worked his thumb like the hammer of a pistol. "Bingo. Where you keeping them?"

"I don't. You want the Walkers. Back about a quarter mile, toward Norvell Road, the way you came in. Other side of the road."

He looked around the room, at the equipment, engines, and stacks of fertilizer bags and barrels of grass seed.

For some reason, he walked over and tapped Hank on the shoulder and said to him, "What kind of farming you do here?" Perhaps he thought that Hank, with his bushy beard and well-worn Caterpillar baseball cap, looked more the farmer than I.

Hank gave the man a long, cold look before answering.

"Not farming." He pointed a wrench at me. "He's building a golf course. The Walker place is the next one down."

Hank turned his back on the man and went back to his work. The man stared at Hank's back for a while. He turned to go and before he slid the door shut he said, "Bright idea, building a country club out here in the boondocks. I can just see these hicks beating your door down for tee times."

I looked out the window and watched his big black sedan, towing a trailer, pull out of the driveway.

"Well, at least he got the name of the place right," I said.

Hank snorted and shook his head and we worked in silence for a while. Then he said, "Chicago tough guys. Really like to play the role."

"How do you know he's from Chicago? Sounded like a Bronx accent to me."

"Most of them are from Chicago, the ones after Walker's shep-herds."

"Hank, I don't know what you're talking about."

He looked up and frowned. "You really don't know what they're getting from Loyall Walker? They've been coming here since I was in grade school, when my folks lived down past Fishville Road. Every once in a while, they'd get lost and pull into my folks' driveway and ask directions to the Walkers. I got curious and one day I got on my bike and pedaled up here. Parked the bike in what's now your woods and sneaked back through the tall weeds along the creek bank. Couldn't see or hear much from there so I crawled through the culvert under the road, then down below the bank of the drainage ditch that runs back to Walker's Lake. Creeped over to where I could see Loyall and this fella load two of the meanest dogs you ever saw into one of those special trailers they use."

I remembered the three or four times cars had pulled into our driveway pulling trailers like that. We had given directions to the driv-ers, sending them down the road to the Walkers.

"I was so curious," Hank said. "I had to get closer to hear what they were talking about. So I inched up, heart thumping away. I just knew any minute they'd see me, set those dogs on me. Then this guy pulls out this big wad and peels off one twenty after another and hands them to old Loyall Walker. God, Loyall was old then, he must be over eighty by now.

"Anyhow, Loyall hands the man a pair of these huge black leather gloves with long sleeves about up to your elbow and a mesh onion bag full of cans of dog food. Then he tells him the dogs are trained, just like the man asked. They'll eat only this food and only from him when he's wearing these gloves. Otherwise they'll starve before they'll take food from anybody else. That's to keep them from eating something some-one has poisoned. And they'll attack anyone comes in through a door or a window unless they see those gloves poke through first."

I was trying to visualize this. Kindly old Loyall and Edna Walker raising attack dogs for Chicago gangsters. And running this business for decades out of their rustic old farm.

I LOOKED AT THE DESIGN and saw that it was good.

At least it was as good as I could do and I was prepared to live with it. As we awaited spring of 1968 and the appearance, we hoped, of acres and acres of healthy grass, it was not too late to make changes in the design. But after a critical, even harsh, look at it on paper and then tramping around in the order the holes would play, there was no way I could improve it.

I had played enough golf courses fashioned by the big-name designers and had listened to more than enough television commentators gush about them to develop a cynicism that bordered on hostility. Those big operators were so proud of how much earth they had moved, how they had subdued nature to complete their conquest of the land.

Marcy listened patiently to those rants, to my orations on philosophy of golf course design, and always had the same response.

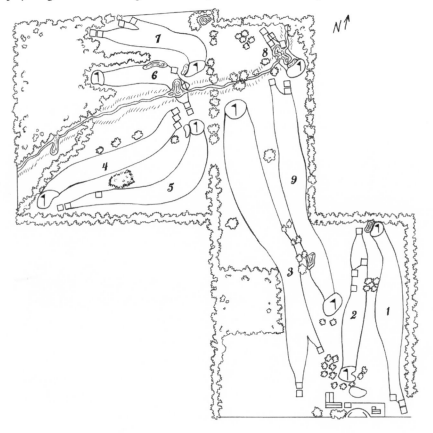

"You're a snob," she said. "You look down on people who don't share your views about the sanctity of the land, about golf course design and construction."

She was right. And I was amazed she couldn't see that my snobbishness was a superior snobbishness, in some cosmic sense, to the snobbishness of the golf course designer elite.

There could never be a statistic on it, but it would be a fair guess that most golf courses are designed either on airplanes or in air-conditioned offices. Big-name designers/architects and even bigger-name pros have legions of eager proteges fashioning computer models for courses that exist only in their imaginations. When a big commission for the next lavish golf-casino-resort complex comes through the door, those esoteric designs are brought forth and somewhere an unsuspecting spread of land will soon be transformed to match that fantasy.

In Hawaii, lava is ground up and then sculpted with lumbering earth graders into a sequence of undulating par fours, serpentine par fives snaking through the lush foliage, and par threes where the tee is perched on a huge mound that wasn't there last week to produce a breathtaking sheer drop to an inviting inverted-saucer green far below. There is generally only one direction on these modern meldings of grass and commerce: downhill. Downhill from a spectacular overlook to a green guarded by a manmade lake with fountains and waterfalls or perched on the rim of a bluff with an ocean crashing into the rocks below. And there are powerful economic reasons for that. Golfers don't like to slog along fighting gravity, knocking a ball uphill. A course such as that, golfers grumble about to other golfers. Word gets around; open tee times sprout like untreated crabgrass.

Then too, if a designer built a course into a spread of land instead of forcing an artificial composition onto the place, what you would have is a golf course with its own unique ebbs and flows, with personality quirks—in other words, a natural golf course. On such a course a golfer could walk the entire round and indeed would want to walk, the better to experience the place. It has worked well for the Scots for several centuries. But—when golfers walk, there goes the revenue lost from not having a mandatory golf cart policy.

So, on modern American courses, especially resort courses, most of the holes play downhill from tee to green. That means the golfer has to be routed over a fair piece of real estate and uphill again and again to reach yet another scenic overlook. Those long traverses from a green to the next tee require quicker and easier transport than hoofing it. Otherwise, many golfers no longer used to actually walking a course would be unable to make the trek, and if they could would be so depleted and disgusted by the eighteenth hole they would never return. And golf course operators would see the desired target four-hour round degenerate into five- and six-hour rounds, meaning that fewer golfers could play. At greens fees costing several days pay for a foursome at top-line resort courses, slow play is an economic disaster.

So, a course designed to pay homage to the idiosyncrasies of a piece of land is unthinkable to the bankrollers, and therefore to the designers and architects they employ.

I had thought about these things when I made the first crude sketches for the design of The Boondocks. About the cookie-cutter designer courses as well as the courses that reflected my own prejudice patterns. About the courses I admired that restored a piece of land that had been abused by decades of bad farming or rapacious mining. Courses that instead of being built on prime farmland or in an ecologically sensitive area or in a place spiritually sacred to Native Americans were instead sited on once-ugly used-up open pit mines and landfills. Although tens of thousands of golf courses have been built since the beginning of the twentieth century, any thoughtful list of the greatest fifty golf courses of the world would still contain many of the same names from the nineteenth century and earlier.

Our objective with The Boondocks continued to be a modest one: to design and build the most fitting course possible on this rundown Nate Fish farm. And to do it with the least possible disturbance to this land. We wanted to produce here a links that fit so comfortably into the place that it would feel as if it had always been there. To play or just to look at such a layout would feel right. If we did it right, when we were finished, the shape of the land would be much as it had been ten thousand years ago, as it was left by a glacier that inched along, recontoured the earth, and deposited what it had carried with it.

In our countless treks over this place, we had come to understand what this land was before man got at it. Before Nate Fish tried to grow popcorn on its loamy sand hills. Before a succession of farmers before and after Nate inflicted careless row cropping that let the winds blow and rains wash thousand-year-old topsoil down into the marsh. Before later residents used the eroded ravines as dumping grounds for bottles, cans, broken dishes, worn-out stoves and washing machines, coils of rusted barbed wire, rotted manure spreader beds, and unidentifiable fragments of used-up farm implements. Before the rolling hills had been parceled off every which way, with endless strands of barbed wire and a patchwork of whatever fencing could be spliced together to keep whatever out and whatever in. And everywhere, the rocks. Pebbles the size of marbles. Rocks as big as a baseball, a basketball, a breadbox. Stones the size of steamer trunks and boulders the size of a Volkswagen and many times heavier.

We exhumed the junk from the washed-out crevices and took it to the township landfill for proper burial. We rolled many of the stones back into the bowels of the earth, where they had resided before countless deep moldboard plowings gouged them to the surface, leaving them exposed and bare when the topsoil blew away. Now with our basic design in hand, we looked for ways to use the biggest of the boulders as design features.

Those days, when the thornapple trees were their most vicious, when we pried up a stone only to find two bigger boulders beneath it, when we choked and coughed in the hot, dusty air, we thought maybe those other golfers were the lucky ones after all, those millions who have said they would build a course but never actually undertook to do it. Those folks are more fortunate in many ways than they can know. But in other ways not so lucky, for they also have missed an experience that would have changed their lives. Perhaps for the better. Perhaps not. But changed, certainly.

And not only their own lives, but scores of lives around them— their families, friends, and people they never met until they began the project. The kids who would come to the place to wade the creek for lost balls, to caddy, to work the greens, to hang around and learn a game, and maybe a life. The golfers, who would praise or cuss the place, depending on a chance bounce into or away from a pond, a putt that hung on the lip or just toppled in to save a par, tie a match, or win a beer. All that, they would miss. All that, one day we would remember. And all we had to do was get there.

GASOLINE DELIVERED to the three-hundred-gallon tank for off-road use was 25¢ a gallon—but you could claim a refund on the state tax paid for off-road use. Farm fertilizer was $55 a ton—that is, if you bought the high potency stuff, 20-20-20. If you could make do with 10-10-10, you could get it for $45 the ton. Used mowing equipment could be found cheap at the area golf courses, if you got your bid in first, accepted it as is, took it apart, loaded it yourself, trucked it off, and didn't come back to complain when it didn't work because you should have expected that in the first place.

With prices like that, if you had a steady job paying $1,100 a month, low needs for personal comforts, a supportive wife and kids, and were willing to work sixteen hours a day, you could begin to build a golf course. But you couldn't finish it unless you had the help of others who had been there, done that. Chief among that cast of supporting characters are head greenskeepers and equipment gurus at nearby courses. I already had my mechanical wizard in Hank Dubois. As we segued into the turf-growing phase of the project I was grateful that I knew a legendary magician with turf grasses and golf course equipment, Walt Bauer.

Walt had been in charge of course maintenance at several area courses in his sixty-some years. He was now performing his wonders at a place recently renamed Ann Arbor Country Club. That course had changed its name from Loch Alpine Golf Course to attract the not-quite-made-it-yet set who couldn't pony up the stiffer ante or survive the social gauntlet at the well-established Barton Hills or Washtenaw Country Clubs at the outskirts of Ann Arbor.

Walt and the other old-timers still called it Loch Alpine because that's what it had been for forty years and they, as I, liked the sound of it better. Loch Alpine was typical of many courses in Michigan and hundreds throughout the country—it had been built in the Roaring Twenties when money was easy and even the rich man's game seemed within reach of blue collars. Many courses built in those days were done with the same recipe: take a piece of bottomland that lay alongside a year-round stream and gouge out heaps of the rich loam. Let that dry out while scooping sand and gravel from a nearby glaciated hill, set up a huge screen and a conveyor belt, and put some men to work processing material. Work it into a profile of layers that would drain water at just the right rate, not percolate through so fast the green would burn out on windy, hot days, nor so slow as to pond the water and promote root rot and fungus diseases in wet, cool weather.

Beneath all this, a network of drain tile was positioned. On top of the tile grid, layers of gravel of varying sizes, then sharp sand. The sand must have grains with angular edges, not like the common round-grained sugar sand that would set up like clay and impede the gradual trickle-down of water into the gravel and then the drain tiles below. And topping it off, the growing medium, a mixture of loam and sharp sand.

But at Loch Alpine, like many low-lying courses, you were left with fairways that were impossible to maintain. The peat was so spongy that walking across those fairways was like walking on a trampoline. Because peat froze and heaved in winter, springtime would find those low fairways full of hillocks, bumps, crevices, and pockets. Fairway mowers would pass right over these depressions and there the grass would grow long, lush, and thick. A ball could trickle into one of those pockets and be impossible to find, right there in the middle of the fair-way.

Yet just a hundred yards away would loom a gravelly hill, or a stand of trees with roots snaking an inch or two above the ground.

On such a course, equipment was constantly being battered and broken. You could work hours grinding the flyknives, or reels, of a seven-unit gang of fairway mowers. When they left the maintenance barn they would be perfectly true and razor sharp, but one pass through a gravelly ridge, one ill-advised sweep too close to a tree and its hidden roots, and you could hear a reel screaming in protest as the flyknife rat-a-tat-tatted its new ding against the bed knife. The faster you went, the higher the whine, the greater the damage. Or worse, you might look at the swath just mowed and see a streak of unmowed grass, telltale evidence that an entire chunk had been amputated from a bedknife and now that unit would have to be disassembled and a new bedknife installed. That would lay up the whole seven-unit gang for God knows how long, and there you have half a fairway mowed and a golf league ready to tee off in less than an hour.

On such a course, a Walt Bauer is the single most crucial employee. Not that the head greenskeeper is recognized and compensated accordingly. The pro can call in sick and assistants can take over without a beat missed. The chef or head cook has a capable sub. One of the greens crew can fail to show and someone else can mow his greens or rake his traps. But the head greenskeeper is the orchestra leader without whom there is no rhapsody in green. He has to know it all. He has to do it all, if need be. When he has trod that land a few thousand times over decades, he knows literally every square foot of its 160 or so acres. He knows which tees to pamper, and which can be ignored in a pinch without fatal cost. He knows what kind and how much treatment to apply to which greens and when. Without so much as looking, he can smell the difference in the funguses—dollar spot, brown patch, and red thread. He knows the dangers when the humidity and temperature meld above ninety day after day.

He knows every gear in every unit. How to fix that little thingamajig on the pressure sprayer when it plugs up halfway through a tank of ammonium sulfate. And most of all, he knows how to keep aged junk equipment purring, cutting, spewing, rolling, verticutting, coring, and the hundred other things each has to do to provide bluegrass fairways and bent-grass greens and white sand bunkers that four hundred golfers a day can drive across and tromp over and take totally for granted.

Men like Walt Bauer are mentors. No one could ever learn by himself, through trial and error, everything that must be known to build and maintain a golf course. Without the grizzled old veterans to train, teach, coach, demonstrate, explain, and yes—sympathize and encourage—no one could ever build a golf course on his own.

The kids had never had a puppy. Yukon was already full grown when he was given to us. I was relieved that it hadn't really been traumatic for them when we had to find Yukon a new home. They liked the clumsy old galoot but he was never a cuddly dog and we hadn't had him long enough to form many good-time memories.

But somehow the place did seem incomplete without a dog, so the only question was how soon could we find the right puppy. The choice of breed was the easy part. We didn't want another big dog like the Airedale–German shepherd mix. No matter how friendly, that was just too much dog around the little kids. We didn't want a tiny one either. We wanted a medium-sized friendly dog that was comfortable inside or out and could roam the land with us without tiring. That matched up perfectly with Marcy's personal preference and mine for a springer spaniel.

When I brought home the liver-and-white pup, the instant choice for a name was Rusty. The kids not only got to watch Rusty grow to adulthood, the next year they also saw him become a sire himself. Tom Lyndon, our friend from Ann Arbor and our irrigation consultant, had a black-and-white female named Pepper and soon the kids were playing with five tiny puppies. Tom got the pick of the litter along with two other puppies. We took two liver-and-white males. We gave one to Joe Smith, the overseer of the township landfill, who brightened every time we came in with a load because he could pet Rusty for a few minutes while we offloaded. Joe had a very bad heart and his outlook was not good so it seemed the right thing to do to give him the big male of the litter. We kept the frisky little liver-and-white with a blaze of white on his liver-colored back and the kids named him Blazer.

That same year two of our three sealpoint Siamese cats, Delilah and Samson, got together to produce the first of their three litters of kittens. We gave purebred Siamese kittens to relatives, friends, the Mathers at the *Grass Lake News*, people at the institute, and workmen who helped us, until we ran out of homes. Then we got Delilah spayed and settled down with two dogs and three cats.

Seventeen

T he sound of air escaping from a punctured tire, whether on a car, a bicycle, or a kid's toy, was not new to me. A tire goes flat, you take it off, extract the tube, hot-patch it, put it back together, and go on with your life while waiting for the next hiss. And there is always a next hiss.

I had lived all my life, it seemed, with the imminent expectation of the next flat tire. During World War II, when I was a little kid, when we'd saved enough gasoline ration stamps, we would visit relatives in Piqua, Ohio, or Gillette, New Jersey. New rubber was reserved for the war effort and so, like most everyone else, we drove on "tires so worn you can see the air through them," Dad said.

That was the reality, and to cope with it you carried a couple spare "baloneys," an extra inner tube, a patching kit, and a pack of kitchen matches to heat the adhesive. You also factored in two or three stops along the way. One memorable day we made it the entire 210 miles to Piqua without a flat, "but that only means we'll probably have five on the way back," Dad said. As usual, he had exaggerated. It was only three.

It was much the same with my first several cars. Tire technology had improved by then but the economic climate had not. You simply ran tires until they were slick bald, then you swapped them for four-dollar recaps, did a lot of praying, and kept your bumper jack lubricated and your tire-changing irons handy.

No surprise then, that my last job the summer I was fourteen turned out to be the week that lasted forever at Carkner Studebaker in Birmingham. There I had one assignment: changing factory-installed blackwalls for the more fashionable wide white sidewalls preferred by the gentry of Birmingham. I did that ten hours a day one week in August for 50¢ an hour—and glad to get it. And I vowed never again to change another tire. At least I never changed another tire on a Studebaker.

More than fifteen years later I had climbed a few rungs up the economic ladder and had the safety of a family to consider. I still could not afford a new car, but I was able to buy new tires. Yet I could not escape the scourge of skinned knuckles and blood blisters on the ball of my thumb for now it was tires on kids' bikes, on a myriad of trailers, wagons, and miscellaneous maintenance machinery. Everywhere I looked yet another pneumatic bladder was threatening to leak.

I reconciled myself to a lifetime of flat tires. Trying to gain perspective, I reckoned that being cursed with a chronic case of flat tires is preferable to a plague of bad transmissions, a high-mortality disease with which I had also been infected but which was currently in remission. Now, with four children and a responsible-sounding position in social science research, I deluded myself that I had become an easygoing chap, able to take the worst that life could dish out and not become flustered or irritable. Marcy had a different opinion. But at least I had become almost stoic about fixing flats.

Then, it happened. I ran into the ultimate enemy of the pneumatic tire: the hawthorn tree, known to farmers by the name usually spoken with venom—the thornapple bush.

When you hop off the tractor to adjust the mowers, and you shut off the engine to save fuel, and you hear that telltale hiss, that is not a nice moment. But bad as it is, the hiss is infinitely preferable to the whizz. For what the whizz signals is escaping liquid from a big tractor tire. There is a reason one hears a whizz instead of a hiss—what is exiting from that big ag tire is not air, but water. And not just any old H_2O but water that has been loaded with chloride.

There was a reason I had not known about loaded tires before I was thirty. I had grown up in farm country but not in a farming family. By hanging around farm kids and occasionally helping school pal Lawrence Smith, whose father owned Big Beaver Feed & Grain deliver chicken scratch and animal feed I learned the lingo and got comfortable around barns, farm equipment, and tools. The problem was I got too adept at faking familiarity with farm things, so my friends figured I knew more than I did and didn't tell me about anything.

I certainly never learned anything useful from my father, a terrific mechanic by every account including his own, who was more interested in ridiculing me for not knowing something than he was in explaining or demonstrating anything. Once I was hanging around Dad's Sunoco service station and he sent me home five times for a wrecking bar. Each time that I returned with what I thought he wanted, he would say, "I reckon that's a bar, but it's not a wrecking bar. Now go back and get the right one. You'll know it when you see it."

He wouldn't describe it further, just that I'd know it when I saw it. After the third or fourth trip, I might have seen it, but I never knew it. On the fifth return, I showed him what I had brought, certain this time that I was totally wrong because what I held out to him was a tool I had always heard him and others call a crowbar. "Well, you finally got it right. But it's too late now. I made do without it. Now take it home and put it back where you found it."

He was teaching me something all right, but I doubt that he understood what.

It only made it worse that he was patient and good-natured when teaching other kids in the neighborhood the things I wanted to learn from him. The War took those years away from my three brothers and brother-in-law, as well as nearly all of the village's men between ages eighteen and forty, so if you didn't learn about those things from your father, usually you just didn't learn at all.

So the way I knew my tires were loaded was because I had paid $20 extra for loading each tire at Dunkel Brothers Ford Tractor in Napoleon, Michigan, when they were readying my new Ford 2000. I took Don Dunkel's advice and had them loaded because, as he put it, "When you're pulling a plow, or a disk, or any kind of load, you need every last ounce of traction you can borrow. Without that weight for ballast, you'll just sit there and spin. Another thing—even on level going when pulling your gang mowers, you'll bounce so damn much you'll rattle your spine and be spending half your time on the chiropractor's table." Aha. So the water was for weight and the chloride was to keep the water from freezing in the winter. Clever, these farmers.

It became apparent quickly that Don Dunkel was right. You simply couldn't begin to work without loaded tires. But Mr. Dunkel didn't tell me that you got something else along with loaded tires: problems. Chiefly, how do you change a tire, loaded or not, when the tractor is already perched precipitously on the side of a hill and you are alone? Especially when the combination of tire, rim, and wheel weighs the best part a hundred pounds when the tire is flat and empty, and weighs a couple hundred pounds more when it has been repaired, reloaded, and is ready to re-mount. How do you do it? When you're doing it alone and almost invariably with an unsafe jack and the wrong tools, you do it very carefully and with lots of swearing.

Fortunately, this is something at which you get better over time. Unfortunately, it is something at which I got much better than I ever wished to. We stopped counting after the fifteenth puncture. Even at that number, thanks to thornapple bushes, my tires had whizzed away $300. Yes, every time one of those vicious thorns pierced a tire, I looked into loading those babies myself. No, there is no way. Then you factor in the time it takes to get the wheel off, load it into the bed of the pickup, and drive it to Napoleon to get it patched and reloaded. Even more costly is the lost use of the tractor, which is a minimum of four hours, and, if it's a weekend or hunting season, as much as three days.

WE WERE NOT CALLOUS about the fate of live things that occupied the land before we came here. We cut very few trees. We tenderly transplanted huge decades-old spreading yews that were smack in the middle of where we wanted to route number four and five fairways and were delighted that we never lost a one. I made creative concessions, as promised to Kent Smedley, to bend number seven fairway away from Gladys's wild blackberry patch. Mark and Marcy talked me into sparing and then rehabilitating a couple of gnarled apple trees that had been shattered by lightning and gone unpruned for forty or more years.

With perhaps two exceptions, we revered life. One exception for which I make no apologies is moles. Industrious marvels, yes. Tolerable when tunneling through a bent-grass green, no. The second exception is thornapple trees. They were a stubborn and stalwart opponent and we acknowledged that. But so high were the stakes and so great would be their unchecked power over us that there could be no compromise. After the fifth flat tire, we knew we had to make our stand. A botanist would call these trees Crataegus mollis or by their deceptively placid common name, downy hawthorn. But to us there was nothing soft or downy about them; they were vicious thornapples. It was either them or us.

Clearly this would be a long battle, and a bloody one with heavy casualties. Such was my respect for my opponent that I would bring my tractor no closer than thirty feet from its trunk. Then I would crawl under its lowest limbs to amputate branches festooned with hundreds of long, piercing needles, merely to gain access to the trunk. Once past the outer defenses, I would wrap a logging chain around the base of the trunk. I learned quickly that no matter how careful I was, I would come away with bloody forehead and punctured hands. So after the first foray, I went into battle wearing a sturdy hat and leather gloves, and with deliberate caution.

With the chain secured to the tree at one end and the tractor's tow bar at the other, I would exert a steady draw to extract the tree, roots and all. There the tree would lie on its side, seemingly so harmless that—for a brief moment only—I would rebuke myself for having done this. I would swear that at the moment of extraction from the earth where it had grown these many decades, there had been an exhalation, a gentle swirl of air as the roots pulled free, as if the tree had surrendered one last gasp of oxygen, a sound satisfyingly reminiscent of the whizz of a punctured tire and pleasing to my ears.

There came a time, in the spring of 1968, when we had uprooted the final thornapple tree and I proclaimed to Marcy that the war had been won. She looked at me and shook her head. Three times that morning she had stepped on thorns that punctured her rubber-soled tennis shoes and pierced her skin. Little did I know that even after death these monsters could wreak such havoc. It was my fault, because before I learned better, I had dragged the trees to one of the several burn piles we maintained on the place. There I would delight as they writhed in flame, giving way in their final moments to inert and placid ash. Reveling in that sense of triumph as the final thornapple was reduced to embers, I jumped off the tractor, turned off the engine, and began coiling the logging chains. And then I heard it. The sound I had thought never to hear again. It was coming from my left rear tire and no mistaking it. It was . . . the whizz. Instinctively, stupidly, I put my finger over the jet of chloride-laden water as if to force it back into the inner tube. And there, still impaled in the wound, was the culprit. The ultimate piercing machine: a three-inch thorn.

I looked down at the puddle already spreading on the ground and there, in the grass, was another and another. A thorn here, a thorn there. Thorns, it seemed, everywhere. I realized too late how cavalier I had been in disposing of the fallen warriors, and I was to pay for my carelessness in casualties long into the future. All the routes to the burn piles were strewn with thorns that had broken off along the way, only to lie there patiently, timeless as a nail. Waiting. A hundred thorns, a thousand, waiting, just waiting until a tire passed over, tilted them to the perfect angle of attack, then poof—or rather, whizz—and I would be reminded yet again who are the real victors and who are the vanquished when one wages war with a life form that was ancient long before mankind trod the earth. Perhaps, I thought at that moment, if in the Garden of Eden the tree had actually been a thornapple, all this never would have happened.

IT WAS JUST BEFORE MIDNIGHT of June 25 when the winds came up. The first gusts were from due west and the barns deflected the blasts so they hit the windows and wall of the girls' room in waves.

"The whole house is shaking," Marcy said as she got out of bed and went to check on the kids.

The house shuddered under the pummeling but surely it had stood up against worse than this in its hundred years. Surely. We went back to an uneasy sleep.

About two in the morning it seemed the storm had passed. Then, after three, the window panes on the north wall of the house began to vibrate like tuning forks—a front from the northeast was now dominating. I got up to look and in the flashes of almost continuous lightning, watched the rain slash horizontally across the fairways. A sheet of water covered the old paddock area and a ribbon of white water overflowed the culverts and raced through the grass waterway across fairways number one, two, and nine. Rainwater ponds glistened in the depression in front of where we would build number one green and in the valley below the oak woods. More lightning flashes. The Willow Pond and number one pond would soon overflow their banks. Water rushed and pooled where we had never seen water before.

I went down to the basement, fearing the worst. But the basement was bone dry—my new cellar doors had performed beautifully. I went back to bed, wondering what daylight would bring.

The next morning, Marcy and the kids and I ventured out apprehensively to see how the land handled the massive storm and to look for damage.

The grass waterway carrying runoff from Coppernoll's fields and through our place had passed its first test. A river now ran along the bed of the waterway, carrying hundreds of gallons a minute through our property and to Walker's Lake a half mile to the south across Curtis Road. At the height of the storm, the rushing water had carved small trenches alongside three of the four concrete culvert tubes we had installed at the junction of the waterway and the middle of each of the front four fairways. But those minor washouts would be easily fixed with a few wheelbarrow loads of soil and a pound of grass seed, and this had been the storm of the decade.

Judging from this severe test, we could see that the front four holes of our course would be playable within a half hour after the heaviest storm. Our decision was vindicated not to bury tile and drainage pipes and instead to grade the land with grass waterways.

The kids splashed through the casual water puddles and Marcy and I walked past the oak woods and along three fairway to the south ridge to see how the back half of the course had fared. Most of the land bought from the Smedleys would be high and dry, but we knew there would be a couple of problem spots. Number six green and some of its fairway would always be wet longer, in part because they were so low-lying, and also because the thick woods into which number six green was nestled was open only on the east and it was rare to have wind from that direction. Water would also stand a bit longer in the valleys in front of greens three and five in the cooler months. And golfers might occasionally get their spikes wet on the path along the wild strawberry patch between seven green and eight tee.

The big question was how did the berms hold up, the land-bridge crossovers at number six and eight ponds?

We came up over the south ridge and stood on the high plateau we now called the Crossroads because so much action was located there: three green, four blue tee, five green, and the back tees for number six. We looked down to where we had always seen a great expanse of waist-high marsh grasses. The marsh couldn't be seen.

The entire five-acre span between the land bridges for numbers six and eight was now a lake.

The water lapped up against the wall of number six land bridge to within a foot of its flat top. We started down the slope to have a closer look, Mark and Pat racing down ahead of us.

"Look!" Mark yelled. "A whirlpool."

The land bridge was acting as a dike, holding at bay the temporary lake that had formed from the torrential rainfall and the runoff from the high sandy slopes on either side. When Larry Briggs excavated number six pond and built the land bridge alongside it, we had installed two galvanized steel tubes—one with a five-foot diameter, the other a two-footer—at normal water level, one near each end of the land bridge. The large tube carried Willow Creek; the smaller one handled the gathered water from the many springs bubbling up from the marsh, charged by the rain falling on the sandy higher ridges. But this new high-water level was far above normal. It had crested high above the tube intake, backing up the water and creating the lake. As the water tried to rush through the two pipes, it built up tremendous suction forming a powerful whirlpool as the water was inhaled through the two tubes and jetted out into six pond on the other side.

The ground above and around the small tube remained solid. But thirty yards farther up the land bridge, the picture was not so good. There the torrents had carved a new channel alongside the big tube. We had lost maybe twenty yards of material. That would take some fixing but it was certainly not catastrophic.

"It could have been a lot worse," Marcy said, as we walked back to the house with the kids.

"That's for sure," I agreed. "Storms like that don't happen very often. If the land can drain that quickly, that's one problem we won't have to deal with."

IT TOOK TWO DAYS for the lake created by the storm runoff to drain and return the marsh to its normal level. We collected chunks of broken concrete and rocks—no shortage of those—and dumped them alongside the big tube. That dammed off the great gash that had been carved in by the rushing stream and channeled Willow Creek back where it belonged, through the tube and into number six pond. I mounted the grading blade onto the Ford 2000 and pushed a few yards of soil into the breach, on top of the concrete-and-rock dam we had built. I let the repair patch settle a couple days, then pushed another load of dirt onto it and crowned it to allow for further inevitable settling.

In less than a week we had the land bridge firmed up and reseeded. The Boondocks had taken a major blast of weather and was none the worse for it.

WITH THIS HEAVY EARLY SUMMER STORM, we had now experienced almost two full years of weather on the place. Each winter had seen a heavy snow cover, then a January thaw that extended to the first of February and brought two inches of rain. Late winter and early spring was cool and wet and that was a good test for how well the fairways could handle water. No matter how long or hard it rained, the high fairways, tees, and greens would drain quickly and because the sandy soils percolated moisture so well, 95 percent of the course would be playable fifteen to twenty minutes after the heaviest storm.

All in all, The Boondocks would never have to close for the day because it was too wet to play. Too much water would not be a problem. But until we had a satisfactory irrigation system in place, getting enough water to the right places at the right time would always be a concern.

I KNEW BETTER THAN TO HIRE a contractor based only on a newspaper ad. Even when you have a recommendation from someone who is happy with the contractor's work, you still don't know for sure what you're getting. But this one sounded promising. "Jennings & Negus Construction and 'Dozer Work. We Do It All. No Job Too Small." Really, what it sounded was cheap.

The moment Al Jennings and Lynn Negus drove into the driveway to size up the job, I was sure I had made a mistake. Just before the small man behind the steering wheel turned off the ignition, the enormous man in the passenger's seat reached out a massive, fleshy left arm and tossed an empty beer can backwards and into the bed of the beat-up old Dodge pickup truck. It was a practiced motion. The can landed softly on a deep layer of empties that covered the truck deck.

The big guy had trouble getting out of the truck and I wondered if it was because he had too much to drink. Then I saw he had to pivot to maneuver the massive gut that hung over his belt. His head was large, even for his big body, and he had heavy jowls that tugged on his lower eyelids, exposing permanently bloodshot eyes. With his sun-bleached blond hair and his pale blue eyes, it was no wonder his face, neck, and arms were peeling from sunburn. The man's handshake was surprisingly weak and I wondered if it was because he was wary of hurting someone with hands that looked as if they could fell a charging Longhorn. After introducing himself as Lynn Negus, he reached into a cooler on the floor of the cab and popped the top on another can of beer.

I was so focused on this great bear of a man that I ignored the lean and wiry fellow who got out from behind the steering wheel and now stood alongside me. He had hunched shoulders, a gray pallor, and a sad, tired face that made him look ten years older than his probable fifty years.

"Mr. Haney, I'm Al Jennings." He took me by the arm and led me a few yards away and whispered, "I hope you don't get the wrong idea about Lynn here. He's got this, well, condition. His doctor tells him to force liquids. With his diabetes, he can't touch those soft drinks."

I glanced at the mound of empty cans in the back of the truck. Lynn sure was heeding his doctor's advice and forcing those liquids.

Lynn took out a pack of Camels from a rolled-up sleeve of his tentlike T-shirt and lit one as he shuffled toward the Willow Pond. He could see that the pond was still ringed with the big donut of spoil that Briggs had excavated.

"Confidentially, Mr. Haney," Jennings whispered, as we followed in Lynn's wake, "years back I was a bad influence on Lynn. That's a cross I must bear. Lynn's a good man and he never touched a drop until he started hanging with me. I was into all kinds of behavior those days and he started drinking just to try and keep me out of trouble. When I committed my life to Christ five years ago, I thought Lynn would give up the drink too. I've been working on him and I won't give up until I save that tender soul I put in jeopardy."

I didn't know about Lynn's soul, but carrying at least a hundred extra pounds, downing a case of beer a day, and torching who knows how many unfiltered Camels sure couldn't be doing his body much good. I was working on exit lines, trying to figure out a way to get these guys out of here without hurting their feelings when Lynn waved a hefty arm at us.

"And you needn't worry," Al said, in hushed tones, taking me further into the conspiracy, "about him being unable to handle equipment because of his drinking. He can drink all day and it never has the slightest effect on him. But let me assure you, we have a strict policy that he never touches a drop while he's operating equipment. And despite his size, he's like a surgeon with that 'dozer blade."

Al and I joined Lynn by the Willow Pond, where Lynn asked what kind of work I had in mind. When I told him we were building a golf course, the two looked at each other and brightened.

"Always wanted to have a hand building a golf course, didn't we, Al?" Lynn growled. "Suppose you'd be wanting this topsoil moved out to your green lands, and this peat saved out. This marl, we can just blade that down, blend it into the natural contour of the place."

Al pointed at the other nearby pond, next to where we would build number one green. "Same thing over there. All that organic material will give you a nice rich stand of grass wherever we fan it out. Well, that'll be easy enough. What else we got?"

I wondered if Lynn could make it up the slope to the south ridge and asked Al about it. "Do him good. It'll remind him how much strain he's putting on his heart."

Lynn stopped twice on the way up, the second time to light a cigarette.

From the Crossroads atop the south ridge, I pointed out the layout of the course, where the greens and tees would be positioned.

"Mr. Haney, you say you're not using that field yonder as part of the course?" Al asked, pointing to a triangle of land a few hundred feet south of what would become number four fairway. "Okay then, Lynn, we can borrow fill from over there to the south, along that fencerow. We'll bring in the TD-10 'dozer to do the bigger work and maybe a TD-6 or a little Cat where the quarters are tighter."

The two of them walked around, pointing, talking over which equipment they would use where.

"Oh, Mr. Haney," Al said. "I meant to ask you. That Ford dump truck in your pole barn? Is that running? If it is, I'll bring in one of our backhoes and leave it here for you. I've got a spare International rigged out with a hoe and loader. Then you can load material into your dump truck, move it around wherever you want, on your own time. Might find it handy. Keeps you from paying us for work you can do just as well yourself."

Well, now. They would leave a tractor with a backhoe and front-end loader I could use myself? I could never have dreamed of that.

Lynn pointed toward the hollow to the west. "What about that boulder? You don't want that in the middle of your fairway. Big as a four-door sedan. I'll take the big Cat and just push that sucker right down into the marsh for you."

"Well, we have to move it, all right," I said. "But I'd like to set it in the rough between these back-to-back par four holes. See, number four goes west from here about four hundred yards and number five parallels it, coming back and ending at a green right below where we're standing."

"Yeah," Al said. "Sort of a natural design element. That'd look nice there. Your golfers are coming up over that far ridge and there's that big old boulder kind of like a lighthouse warning you away."

I turned and pointed to number six pond. Larry Briggs had done a nice job carving it out of the marsh, putting an hourglass shape on it so it wasn't just a plain oval. Running alongside it was the now fully healed land bridge, the roadway to the firm ground on the north side of the wetlands.

"The idea here," I said, "is we would have the championship-length tee right about where we're standing. Then there'd be the regular men's tee we'd carve out of the face of the slope about halfway down toward the pond. What happens is, the golfers hit their shots from these tees across the water to a fairway on the other side. Then they walk across that land bridge alongside the pond. Now, once they're across, that's where we have a different kind of job."

"Like what?" Al asked.

"We need to clear out a lot of scrub growth, then push it into a burn pile. Lots of thornapple spikes, so that's a better job for your Caterpillar treads than my tractor tires. We'll be clearing a fairway for about a hundred fifty yards into that stand of mixed woods, just left of that sassafras tree. Then you'll grade that with a gradual fall toward the marsh so it will surface drain that way."

"Does that sassafras tree go?" Lynn asked.

"Oh no, that tree stays. Glad you asked, because I should have told you we've designed the course so we're not taking out any mature desirable trees. You have any doubts, I'd want you to ask me first."

Al rubbed his grizzled chin as he looked across the pond. "They can hit the ball all that way in the air? What you think of that, Lynn? That'd be the best part of two hundred yards. My, my. Well, while we're at it we can do some fine-tuning on the run-ups to your land bridges. I see you've already got a couple tubes in place, carrying the stream through."

"That far fairway might be a little tricky," Lynn said. "Looks pretty low. Might need to truck in some fill here and there. Okay, while we've got the equipment over on the north side there, what else?"

I explained that we had the same situation a few hundred yards to the east, coming back over number eight pond and its land bridge. There we would have to shape out number eight green by skinning off the top of a knoll until we got it down to a big almost-flat putting surface. And there were two more greens—numbers six and seven—and a couple tees to rough out that they couldn't see from here but that would be pretty simple.

Neither man said much all the way back to the house. I realized that they had gotten into the spirit of the task and I found myself hoping they would give me an estimate we could afford.

"Way we work, Mr. Haney," Al said, "is we estimate it out, give you a list describing what we'd do, how many hours we calculate is involved. My wife types that up so it comes out nice and neat. Then, if that sounds good to you, that's what you're in for. If we're wrong on the low side, that's down to us and we're good for it regardless how long it takes. Other hand, if we can wrap it up sooner, price stays what we quoted."

Lynn snorted and dug another beer from his cooler. "Like we've ever finished a job in less hours than you figured."

"Lynn thinks I'm too optimistic," Al said. "He's probably right. But this one seems pretty straightforward, I don't see how we can run into trouble."

I resisted mentioning that old Nate Fish and a few others could tell him you don't have to run into trouble on this place; just stand there and it will come find you.

Eighteen

Bob Mather told me that Hank Dubois had once retrieved from a trash barrel an old Nikon camera Bob had thrown away after the Nikon repair center had returned it as unfixable. Hank started to take it apart but was stymied because it required a special tool that only a camera repair shop would have. The next day, Bob found Hank hunched over the workbench and looked over his shoulder. He saw that Hank had taken the camera totally apart and was now apparently reassembling it.

"It was this little gizmo here," Hank said, holding up a tiny part. "It's no wonder the Nikon folks said it couldn't be repaired. It would have taken them more time than the camera's really worth."

"So they were right? Now that you've gone to all that trouble you're going to junk it?"

"Heck, no. I already made the new part out of a piece from that old eight-track tape player. We'll be shooting film with this sucker in half an hour or so."

And they were. Bob had already bought a new camera, so he gave Hank the salvaged Nikon.

Hank Dubois already had worked the same magic for us many times on distressed Boondocks equipment. He played down his abilities as a master Mr. Fixit, saying most people give up on things without ever really digging into them. He figured once something was broken, what've you got to lose? Might just as well start taking things apart, never know what you might find in there.

WHEN I OPENED THE MAIL a few days later, there was the estimate from Jennings & Negus Construction. I could see what Lynn meant about Al Jennings always coming in low-ball. They proposed to:

- blade down the spoil from all six ponds, smoothing out the excess material alongside numbers six and eight ponds on the land-bridge ramps
- build up foundations and create the basic contours for all greens and tees
- clear the brush for number six fairway
- bring in two or three bulldozers and two tractors mounted with backhoes and front-end loaders to do the work, leaving one for my use
- relocate whatever boulders we needed to move
- and, something they suggested, they would push over any unwanted tree stumps.

To do all that, they estimated ninety hours of work at $15 an hour. Regardless, they would commit to do the described work for $1,350. And they would start within two days after we agreed on the deal.

I called them that night. The next day they started bringing in equipment.

SITTING BEHIND the controls of the massive TD-10 bulldozer, Lynn Negus looked like a sumo wrestler doing needlepoint. He knew just how to tickle the complex levers and controls to fan material smoothly under his blade, to feather the spoil from the ponds out onto the fairways.

Although he had no experience with golf course construction and no understanding of the game, Lynn quickly understood that tees had to be flat with gently sloped shoulders for ease of mowing and that greens had to be pitched slightly to receive shots but with no low spots where water could settle. Once he was comfortable with those basic requirements, he worked confidently and productively.

Golf courses built with big budgets would have greens with elaborate tiling systems topped with layers of gravel of varying sizes, sand, and finally, as the top layer, a perfect blend of a screened growing medium without a pebble or impurity. We couldn't afford that. We would situate our greens where the natural profile beneath them would provide proper drainage.

While Lynn roughed out the foundations for the greens, I screened and blended top soil and sharp sand to make the top layer into which we would plant the bent grass. Al Jennings had followed through on his promise to leave a tractor with a front-end loader and a backhoe and I got facile enough with the controls to quickly scrape up and pour a bucket-load of sand, then a bucketload of dirt onto a coarse wire mesh screen I had rigged up to filter out most of the debris.

Then I ran the first-pass screened dirt through a finer-mesh screen until I had material blended and cleaned enough for a green. Using the front-end loader bucket, I scooped that material up and deposited it in the bed of the Ford F-700 dump truck. Once we had the foundation of a green ready, I dumped the top layer dirt in place, truckload after truckload, and the handwork began.

Marcy, the kids, and I did most of this slow grunt work—with some grumbling but stoic good nature, finding ways to make a game of any task. But anyone who stopped by while we were at it also got conscripted. Our goal was to have Negus build up and shape the foundations of all the greens and tees over the next three to four weeks. We were shooting to get the front four greens in yet this year and the rest next year. We wanted to have one to two full years' growth on all the greens by the time we opened the course to the public.

The practice putting green was an easy choice to be first to seed in. For one thing, it was closest to the house—about thirty yards—and so we could walk out the back door and be working on it in a minute. Also, we could reach it with a hundred feet of hose. And, not least, it was, after all, a practice green. Much less serious to make a mistake on that green than on one of the nine.

There is nothing glamorous about preparing a green. It is drudgery, plain and simple. Rake and smooth out. Pick up debris. Rake some more. Roll it out with the little two-foot roller borrowed from Walt Bauer and expose tiny hillocks and depressions you never knew were there. So, rake and smooth again. Over and over. Roll it again. Rake to relieve the compaction. Roll to re-smooth it. Then do it all again. And again. Until finally it just couldn't get any cleaner, any smoother.

For some of that work, little kids are better than adults. They have a shorter distance to bend to pick up the little piles of pebbles and rubble.

With the practice green ready for seeding, we split up into two crews to prepare greens one and two. Marcy took on number two green, Jen beside her, both on hands and knees. They scraped up the piles of tiny stones and dirt clods we had raked up the day before in the final smoothing of the green before seeding. Five-year-old Pat and four-year-old Beck squatted ten yards away on the approach, digging out broadleaf weeds and prying up stones with old screwdrivers. They tossed the stones into buckets and then trudged over and emptied the buckets into the bed of the truck. It was something they probably saw themselves doing in their dreams. Rusty lay on the rear collar of the green, seemingly dozing but on guard against whatever.

Mark and I worked on the approach and shoulders for number one green, spreading oat straw as a mulch for the Windsor bluegrass we had just planted. With the tractor radio on at high volume, I couldn't hear the kids but I imagined they would be singing made-up songs about what they were going to buy with the 25¢ an hour they were earning. Pat would work enthusiastically for a while, imagining the new baseball glove or football he would buy with his earnings. A minute later he would wander off, looking for a ball to kick or throw or be racing out to the oak woods with Blazer.

It was a gem of a late August day, the kind of weather that would be perfect for the upcoming World Series. Normally that was not relevant in Michigan but in 1968, for the first time in twenty-three years, it looked like the "fall classic" would be held in Detroit. The Tigers were far in front in the American League and closing in on a confrontation with the dominating Bob Gibson and the heavily favored St. Louis Cardinals. With the irrepressible Denny McLain, crafty Mickey Lolich, and the great Al Kaline, the Detroit boys were setting new standards in coming from behind, winning game after game in the last innings, a new hero every day.

The Detroit professional teams had disappointed Marcy so many times she had written them off as a bad emotional investment, but now even she was paying attention. The boys and I hankered to be inside watching the game, but there were precious few hours left to finish our work. So we contented ourselves listening to the melodious baritone play-by-play of announcer Ernie Harwell, echoing like a sultry southern breeze over the acres in stereo from the radios on the tractor by number one green and the pickup truck parked alongside number two green. When the game got tense, we did most of our talking between innings. After six innings, the Tigers trailed by a run.

"This stuff is really itchy," Mark said. "Dad, are you sure this mulch really will help?"

Mark tossed the oat straw downwind so it wouldn't blow back in his face. He was doing it like an old pro, letting the breeze fan out the straw so it settled evenly on the new seedbed.

I reminded Mark that the mulch would do a lot of things. It holds the moisture in to keep the seedlings from drying out and dying right after they germinate. It shields out the intense rays at mid-day and, if you have to start a patch late in the year, it keeps your seedbed from getting too cold at night and slowing down growth. It reduces loss from erosion, whether wind or rain, especially on the slopes. I explained that if you get a heavy rainstorm before you have a root structure established and don't have a mulch layer, you can lose an entire seeding.

Mark acted like he had heard all this before. Which he had.

The Tigers got a run in the seventh and tied the score.

"Dad, how much more of this hay do we have to spread?"

"Couple more bales. And it's not hay, it's straw."

"What's the difference?"

"If you look at a bale of each side by side, you'd see a lot of difference. Hay has food value and that's why animals eat it. It's kind of gray and green and brown. Straw is bright yellow, like gold, and it doesn't have any food value. It's what's called the chaff, the part of the plant that's left over after the farmers have taken the grain off. We could use hay, but straw is better, especially oat straw, because it doesn't mat down as much and it doesn't contain the seed heads and weed seeds you get with hay."

"And we want our greens to have just pure grass, right?"

"Right."

Mark had that far-off look and I could tell he was figuring it out, why all this should be so.

We worked as we listened to the eighth inning. Neither team scored. Still tied.

"A blanket," he said.

"What?"

"The straw. It's like a blanket. It keeps the new grass warm at night but if the sun is too bright during the day, then it shades it from getting sunburned."

"Well, yeah. And that's especially important if we have to seed a green late."

"What would be late?"

"August is the best time to sow grass seed, which is why we're going to seed the first four greens over the next few days. Some people think spring is the time, but late summer is when Nature herself does her seeding, so that's when we should do it. Late August in Michigan generally means short hot days and long cooler nights. And the August rains are usually more dependable and softer than we get in July."

"But what happens if we don't plant a green in August? Do we have to wait another whole year, until the next August?"

"No, we'd probably still plant in September, but it's riskier if we do it then. That late, we'd have to hope for good weather."

"Like the same heat and rain we would have gotten in August, right?"

"Exactly."

"Well, Dad, it's obvious what we have to do then."

I smiled. Mark was so sure, so serious, so much older than his years.

"And what's that, Mark?"

"We either have to plant our greens in August, like we're supposed to do, or—"

"Or what?"

"We have to be lucky and have September and October be more like August."

The Tigers fell behind in the top of the ninth but got their leadoff batter on in the bottom half.

"C'mon, Mark. Hop on the tractor. We're going back to the house."

"But we're not done yet."

"I know, but we have to eat anyhow so we might as well watch the end of the game while we're doing it."

As we came up alongside number two green, I could see that Jen, Pat, and Becky had all deserted Marcy. Probably in the house having lunch, watching the game. Marcy was alone on the green, scraping a small pile of debris onto the scoop shovel.

"Marcy, let's take a break."

"Not yet. I'm going to finish this green first."

"Aw, come on. I'll make sandwiches and we'll watch the rest of the game. Tigers have a rally going."

"I've got Ernie on the radio," Marcy said. "That's good enough for me. I'm not leaving this green until there's not a single pebble in sight."

"You sound determined."

"You damn well better believe it."

The Tigers did it again. I stepped out to the back porch to shout the news to Marcy, but she had already heard Ernie call it on the radio. She waved me off and bent down to scoop up another pile.

PREPARATION OF THE SEEDBEDS had taken many more hours than would the next step, the actual sowing of seed. But spreading the seed was far and away the trickiest and most difficult operation. It began that night with measuring and blending expensive Penncross bent seed with sharp sand. That had to be done because it was all but impossible to calibrate a drop spreader precisely enough to apply the bent-grass seed by itself, especially if there was even a breath of wind.

Before daybreak the next morning, I stood beside the practice putting green with the seed-sand mixture loaded in the spreader. I had about forty-five minutes to get the seed on before the morning winds came up. That was plenty of time to cover the 3,500-square-foot green, as long as no problems developed. I made the first pass and wondered if any seed at all had come out—it was impossible to see it drop from the bottom of the spreader. I got down on my hands and knees to look. With seeds this small, the tiniest rotation of the adjustment knob made a huge difference in how much seed was dropped. I looked at the tracks made by the wheels of the spreader to compare the unseeded soil with the strip I had just passed over. The tiny seeds were very difficult to see, but there they were, already nestling between grains of sand and soil.

I finished going east and west and then made a checkerboard by going north and south. And just to be sure I had total and uniform coverage, I went on the diagonals until I had used up all the seed-sand mixture. By then the sun had risen and the breeze was up.

Mark showed up to help me spread ten bales of oat straw. Once we had the entire surface mulched with its shiny yellow straw blanket, Mark turned on the spigot by the porch and I used a fine-mist hand nozzle to wet down the straw. The wind was brisk now, but the dampened straw quickly knitted together, and it would take a strong gust to disturb it. I sat a Rain Bird sprinkler at one end of the green and hooked it up, tuning the nozzle to make a soft mist. It put out a ridiculously puny sprinkle for a golf green, but it was a start.

Mark and I backed off and had a look. The practice putting green was in. Four pounds of pure bent-grass seed. Twenty dollars. Thirty-two million seeds planted, by Mark's calculations. Only nine more greens to go.

First you get the good news: The appraiser says the property is worth more than you owe so yes, you can refinance the place. That means you are now free to toss and turn at night while your bankers sleep secure in the knowledge that once they foreclose and boot you out, they have a solid asset on their books.

For a few fleeting days—perhaps only hours—there is a feeling if not of prosperity, at least of an easing of financial pressure. Of course there is the matter of that larger monthly payment for many more years at a higher interest rate. But those numbers will seem trivial when the golf course is well established and the cash flow is more than an intermittent trickle. And this destiny is all but certain, we were told, by no less an authority than the National Golf Foundation. One day the golf explosion will have us breaking long-drive records on the moon in one-sixth gravity. Closer to home, real estate mavens promise that any day now we'll see that long-awaited materialization of a Golden Corridor ten miles either side of Highway I-94 from Detroit to Chicago. Grass Lake and The Boondocks Golf Course will be happily right in the midst of it when this Garden of Eden bears fruit. Sure.

Marcy and I knew going in that this was not a project we were going to overwhelm with money. But we did feel we had a chance to bring it off by living on the premises, watching every dime, doing the work ourselves, and mortgaging the place to the hilt.

This would not take a major attitude shift—we had been frugal from the first day of our marriage and indeed from long before. Marcy had worked as a teenager and was a careful money manager. I had had a job every day of my life since I was in fifth grade, getting my first bank account the same year.

My first regular job came at age ten, helping Mike the janitor at Big Beaver School, at 25¢ an hour with a big bump to 35¢ in the second of my four years of afterschool work for Mike. From the janitor's helper job, to caddying, mowing lawns, setting pins at the bowling alley, and picking fruit, I always had a few dollars in a savings account and a couple in my wallet. That made me—until I learned better—the neighborhood's designated soft touch. It was an expensive lesson to learn that money is much easier to hand out than it is to get repaid.

I never had much cash in my pocket but until I went to college I wasn't used to being broke. Then again, I wasn't prepared to be the provider for a family of six before I turned twenty-nine while at the same time trying to save enough to make a down payment on land for a golf course, make payments on a home, a rental house, and a car—and do this on a salary of a thousand dollars or so a month.

When we began to build the golf course, suddenly our previous financial condition looked positively rosy by comparison. We had entered dangerous waters—spending money we had not yet earned. And unless we had several seasons of good growing weather, a resurgent local economy, robust good health, and lots of luck, it would be some time before we had the money to repay debts already incurred, let alone handle new ones.

Ironically, at the Institute for Social Research I was editing and publishing material on the growing national scourge of credit card use. I was writing copy about the incredible pressure on families "living in the future" by spending money they had not yet earned. I was cautioning readers about the tempting call of the Sirens who would lure the over-leveraged onto the shoals of financial ruin. And at the same time I was enrolling my family as card-carrying members in that great American institution: debt.

As the notes mounted at the Grass Lake Bank, as we added to our account with the O.M. Scott Company for yet another shipment of fertilizer and seed, as we learned how pliable and addictive these little plastic credit cards could be, we looked back with nostalgia on those halcyon days in Marietta, Georgia, where we had traveled on our honeymoon to an exciting new life in the Peach State.

We arrived there in hundred-degree heat and comparable humidity on July 3, 1959, a week after we were married at Our Lady of LaSalette Roman Catholic Church in Berkley, Michigan. I had left a job I liked at Bendix Aerospace Systems Division in Ann Arbor—my first of three tours of duty at Bendix—for a $15-a-week raise to become a technical writer at Lockheed Aircraft, headquartered in the old Bell Bomber plant in Marietta, Georgia, said to be the largest single building under one roof east of the Mississippi.

Not infrequently, on the last day before payday at Lockheed, Marcy would round up the Pepsi bottles to cash them in for enough to buy her a pack of Winstons or me a pack of Pall Malls. We had different priorities then. But once we got my college student loan paid off and the transmission paid for on the maroon-and-cream 1950 Buick Special, my salary of $135 a week was enough to pay the $78 per month rent and live in comparative comfort.

Marcy wanted to work, to make use of her degree in social work, and she applied for and was offered a position as a caseworker. The glow of that great news lasted one day. The next day we learned that Marcy was pregnant. She did the honorable thing: advised the organization of her condition. They thanked her and did the perhaps not honorable but practical and expected thing: withdrew the offer.

Marcy's next job came four kids and ten years later at The Boondocks and it was the most merciless kind of on-the-job training. Although Marcy had no formal education in business, she soon learned it all: the bookkeeping, the endless government red tape, payroll, taxes.

But she never learned to mint money. And neither could I. So the refinanced mortgage, nourished with regular doses of new needs, grew and grew.

FORTUNATELY, SOMETHING ELSE was growing rapidly: the Penncross bent grass on the first four greens of The Boondocks Golf Course.

Many times we wondered if it was worth it—the thousands of

hours, the aching backs, the sunburned skin from the legendary steamy Michigan summers, the fussing with a barely adequate, cobbled-together watering system. But all that melted away as we tenderly peeled off the oat straw and saw the terrific catch we had gotten. Slowly, over a period of several days, we stripped the protective mulch from the first four greens. For a while golden straw threads could still be seen amongst the millions of bent-grass plants setting their roots deep into the soil. Then one day the greens had filled out to a solid blue-green luster and had grown enough blade that it was time to mow.

We brushed the greens tenderly with a coarse bristle broom to make the grass blades stand up like a GI's military brush cut. I set the greens mower bed knife at half an inch and mowed each green criss-cross and checkerboard to keep the grass from forming a grain flowing in one direction. Every week until winter I would lower the blades one sixty-fourth of an inch until we were mowing at five-sixteenths of an inch, at which the grass would rest over the winter.

Come November, we would hope for a nice natural blanket of snow to protect the greens from drying out under the sub-zero winds of January and February.

"BILL, I'M GOING TO ASK YOU A QUESTION," Gladys said. "How come you do all these things?"

"What things, Gladys?"

"You've got a full-time job. You're working on books on the side, yours and other people's. You and Marcy have four little kids, which, my lord, is getting onto a full-time job for most people if you do it right. You're writing articles for our little newspaper and God knows what else. And now you're building a golf course. Isn't that a couple brainwaves short of good sense?"

I wanted to think about that one a while, but Gladys wouldn't have it. I told her maybe it comes from being a child of the Depression. We didn't know we were poor, but I did know that if a man didn't have a job, that meant trouble.

She nodded. "You got that right. I remember those days all too well. That reminds me of something some would-be genius once wrote, 'I do not know what man was put on earth for, but it surely wasn't to have a job.' Well, that fellow has the right to say that—just as soon as he has the know-how and the gumption to cut the tree to get the pulp to make the paper on which he writes his brainstorms. Anyone who spouts such tripe first has to come up with the means to feed the world's hungry and put roofs over peoples' heads. But there's got to be more than that in your case. Come on, now. Out with it."

I told Gladys that Marcy had taken more psychology courses than I had and she says it's because of my father.

"What the hell's he got to do with it? You told me he died when you were fifteen. Not coming back after you as a ghost, is he?"

"Maybe he is. He was like an old man when I was born. Tired, yo-yo weight problem, sick a lot. Didn't have time or energy for a frisky little boy. My sister was his pet. So I did everything I could to get his attention. Had jobs since I was ten. Played every sport the school offered. Got straight A's. Debate team. Class president. Did absolutely everything and still he paid me no attention. Marcy says that's what I'm doing, still trying to get his approval. Maybe he is coming after me as a ghost."

Gladys sipped her drink and lit another Pall Mall.

"Might be something to that, after all. But if you know that, going forward you don't have to be a prisoner of it, do you?"

"I don't know about that. I guess the way I look at it now, I figure to be dead a whole lot longer than I'll be alive. If I don't waste any time while I'm still breathing, I can pack two-three lifetimes into one. So far it's working okay."

"Oh yeah, it's working just fine. Keep this up, you'll blow out a blood vessel or have an accident out there on the land. Yes sir, at this rate, with luck you may even see thirty-five."

Nineteen

I t was a dark and stormy night. Suddenly, a shot rang out."
I had always wanted to write that lead and never thought I would
get the chance. Then Bob Mather asked me if I wanted to make
a deal that would enable me to write every cliché in the how-to-
be-a-hack-sportswriter book while serving the community, promoting
the golf course, seeing lots of high-school football and basketball games
free, and finding inner peace. Well, everything but the inner peace
part.

"You know sports about as well as anybody around here," Bob
said. "Which, come to think of it, is not saying a lot. More to the
point, knowing sports is not typically a prerequisite to write sports for
a weekly newspaper with a circulation of twelve hundred, and a faithful
readership of my wife and me and a couple of retired folks who read our
articles when they run out of ketchup bottle labels."

"A pitch like that, a man would be a fool to turn it down," I
said.

"No, actually, judging from the letters I get and what we hear, just
about everybody in town reads the *News*. For a lot of them, not much
else to do and they don't want to miss out on anything juicy. And they
do love their sports. That's where you come in."

"Bob, no question there's fewer things I'd rather do on a Friday
evening than be at a high-school football game. Smell of leaves burning, cider and doughnuts, off-key band, parents screaming at the coach
to put their kid in, cute cheerleaders jumping around, all that. But I can
do that for fifty cents, don't need a press pass."

"True, but when you're part of the journalism fraternity you get a
press card to lay on your dashboard and that entitles you to free parking."

"Bob, maybe you haven't noticed, but there are no parking meters
in Grass Lake. All parking is free parking."

"Well, there's that. But you also get to stand right there on the
sidelines at the games and everybody's nice to you because they think
you might put their kid's name in the paper. Which, by the way, is not

a bad idea. But for you, there are other good reasons."

It was obvious Bob Mather had thought this out and was about to tell me why my covering high-school sports for the *Grass Lake News* was a great deal for The Boondocks.

"You need to have printing done—scorecards, posters, fliers, what not. Display ads, too, whatever. We'll set up a nice quarter-pager with a distinctive typeface, your logo, whatever copy you want and run it every issue from, say, March through the end of the season. Option B, we could pay you maybe ten bucks a column but I'd hate to see you holding your breath waiting for a paycheck."

"I think I'll take the barter deal." And I did.

If I had been able to pick any four years to cover Grass Lake High School football and basketball in the entire twentieth century, it would have been 1968–71. It was one of those magical eras that come to a small-town school maybe once a century, if they're lucky. The kids had talent, leadership, desire, and—typical of Midwest rural towns—toughness and pride. Most of the town turned out for home games and sometimes more than a hundred would travel to away games, occasionally outnumbering the home team rooters. Virtually every game was well played, many were exciting, and most were victories for the Warriors of Grass Lake.

The more the teams won, the more people wanted to read about them and the more Bob Mather would ask me to write. It helped that real hard news happened only a few times a year and so there wasn't much competition for the news hole. Bob figured if people really wanted new news, they could get it from the *Jackson Citizen-Patriot*, the *Ann Arbor News*, or the radio or television. He didn't see the *Grass Lake News* as being in competition with those media. He knew that his readership counted on his paper to find out where and when the next farm auction was, whether Doc Chappel had finally brought another vet into his practice to treat large animals, and what was on special at Wolfinger's Hardware. His readers wanted the important hard facts, like how much they were getting at the Grass Lake Elevator for nugget coal or a ton of 10-10-10 fertilizer, and if a bombshell had been dropped concerning the students' dress code at the last meeting of the school board or the village council.

And, perhaps most important, how the Grass Lake Warriors were doing.

If the football team was dominating opponents or the basketball quintet was torching the nets, everything else was pushed to the inside pages and the town feasted on an orgy of florid copy on the Warriors' latest battle.

It also helped that traditional rival Hudson had not lost a gridiron game to anyone in more than eight years and the most-repeated expression in the township those golden years for the Warriors was, "This is going to be the year we knock off those arrogant asses from Hudson."

The Hudson streak was not merely a record in Michigan—it was the longest unbeaten skein in the United States. Several times, Grass Lake had been on the verge of breaking that string, only to lose the lead and the game in the final minutes.

As I covered the high school's major sports, I got to know many of the kids. Some of them would come to me with questions about writing, about what classes to take to be ready for college. Some wanted to know how to get started in golf. A few came with requests for me to be the official photographer at their wedding—"eat for nothing and we'll pay for the film." And sometimes they approached me or Marcy with more serious concerns.

After the games, I would go directly to the old train depot to write my story. No matter the hour, it seemed there was some kind of a job churning on the ear-splitting old press or Hank Dubois was banging away on it to get it to work.

Printing presses like that had cost hundreds of thousands of dollars new and now they were totally obsolete. Oh, they still worked fine, often cranking out thousands of crisp impressions for thousands of hours. But they required trained and conscientious operators and took up huge quantities of ever-more-expensive space. They did what they did very well, but feeding off their huge rolls of newsprint or book text stock, they were limited in the trim sizes they could handle economically. Compared with sophisticated new photo-offset presses, the big, old letterpresses were slower and prone to breakdowns. They took longer to set up, generated heat, and didn't like high humidity.

For a few years—actually decades for book manufacturers—the rear guard champions of letterpress held off the invasion. Joining up with the old-timer press operators were the old-line editors and publishing house executives who called themselves "serious book publishers." The strongest resisters were perhaps the senior production managers at the university presses and small specialty book houses. Many of these men had never worked at another job. Some of them bragged they never read books, just created beautiful ones. They loved to put their own personal linen tester—a small, powerful magnifying glass with a crisp, fixed focus—on a sheet produced by a letterpress and then invite you to compare the clarity of the printing with the same text run off an offset press.

For a while, they had a point. There was a difference in quality. But by the early 1970s there was so little discernible difference that few publishers could afford the premium cost of doing it the classical way. Fewer still were willing to endure the longer delivery schedules to produce a book that only the occasional reader could know or appreciate was manufactured by true craftsmen the old-fashioned way. Then, finally, not even the sharpest-eyed veteran printers with their most powerful linen testers could tell the difference. When that day dawned, the great old letterpresses, stalwart servants so many years, became dinosaurs.

Except in the eyes of Hank Dubois.

Bob Mather had pleaded with Hank for years, "Take that damned antique out of here and bury it." He was tired of cursing as Hank worked his magic to coax another edition out of their ancient letterpress. Hank had installed that old beast years ago and it was out of service more than it was working.

Hank agreed it would make good sense to haul the old monster out and install an inexpensive compact photo-offset press. Still, any new expense was more than Publisher Bob Mather could afford. I knew Hank Dubois had another motive; he felt that if they converted to an offset press, they would have been defeated by technology.

So Hank did the obvious thing: he scoured the state until he found a working letterpress in west Michigan that was being scrapped and was free for the hauling it away. Hank rented a large truck and a fork-loader to handle the multi-ton sections. Then, by himself, he took the press apart, loaded it, trucked it to Grass Lake, and set it up quickly enough that the *Grass Lake News* never missed its weekly issue.

The Mathers hadn't exactly gotten into step with modern technology, but with the resourcefulness and mechanical genius of Hank Dubois, they were still publishing their weekly newspaper and the odd custom-printing job.

It was the same with the grand old Linotype machines. Even when new, these machines, which plinked out one character at a time, looked like something exhumed from the Jurassic period. They were notoriously cumbersome and each had its own idiosyncrasies. There was the molten pot of lead from which the individual slugs of type were cast, a letter at a time, and probably no single piece of typesetting equipment ever invented had more distinctive sounds than a Linotype with an experienced operator at the keyboard. The machine would hum, click, clatter, whiz, rattle, buzz, and clank as the operator struck a key to impress a single letter onto a slug of hot lead. After doing its job, that little metal letter would zing through a maze of channels and slots and, through an intricate series of coded notches, somehow find its way back to its own nest of sibling letters—usually. And the slug of hot metal with a whole line of words on it would course through another labyrinth and finally into a tray of other slugs of type that together made up the story.

There were dozens of things that could and did go wrong with a Linotype machine. Each ailment had its own distinctive sound. Hank Dubois could be standing right alongside a letterpress machine running at full speed and sounding like a freight train, yet he could hear from across the room a ping or buzz or clunk from the Linotype machine that signaled trouble. Sometimes it would require a simple adjustment; other times he would have to diagnose the ailment, make a tool to heal it, and occasionally make a tool to make the repair tool. In Grass Lake, the story went that if Hank Dubois can't fix it, it ain't broken.

Hank had kept Bob Mather's old Linotype spitting out its slugs of hot metal for years. There were new high-quality "cold type" composition machines on the market, compact, fast, and versatile, but Bob was content sitting in his wheeled chair in front of the machine, cigarette dangling from his lips, squinting one eye against the smoke, seldom needing to glance at the keyboard anyhow. I would sit across the room at an ancient typewriter, writing the story of the game just completed. As I finished a sheet, Bob would grab it before it hit the floor and would hammer out inch after column inch, sometimes laughing, sometimes snorting at my copy. Then he would come over, stand beside me, hold his hand out, and say, "Come on, Haney, you're slowing down. I'm setting this stuff faster than you can write it."

Which was true.

As I TRAMPED THROUGH ACRES of gold and crimson leaves, pacing distances, I couldn't get the image out of my mind. Those wagons 150 years ago, headed west, crossing Willow Creek, getting mired down in the marsh right where Larry Briggs had dug number eight pond. And then there were those clippings Marcy's sister Beverly had sent, the stories about the Great Railroad Conspiracy War and Trial of the 1840s and '50s. Our quiet little corner of Jackson County had been the scene of some fascinating events. William Rollman, Edna Walker, Gladys Smedley, Horace Coppernoll, and others had told me stories about "the old days." Who knows what else might have happened on this land?

A few days later, instead of having lunch in the institute's cafeteria or going to a restaurant, I left my office to walk around campus. The year 1967 had marked a milestone for the University of Michigan and twelve months later people were sick of still seeing the word "sesquicentennial" on kiosks and old banners around the campus and city. The university traced its origins to 1817. The celebration of 150 years provided an opportunity for the most aggressive fundraising in the school's history. And it set people to thinking about how life had been in southeastern Michigan a century and a half ago.

Well, what had life been like then? I could actually get a glimpse over lunch hour because I was within sight of two of the best repositories of that information, the university's Michigan Historical Collections and the Graduate Library's Rare Book Room.

Anyone who has delved into history knows that a faint spark of curiosity can quickly become a burning obsession.

All I wanted to do was read some accounts of what life was like in Jackson County in the first half of the previous century. What was the story behind that yellowed clipping from Marcy's sister Beverly, that business about "arson, conspiracy, and death?"

It was surprisingly easy to get quick answers on the basic facts. I had never heard in Michigan history class about the turmoil in the state in the mid-1800s, but these events were big news throughout the entire nation when they were happening. Historians asserted that these occurrences triggered major reforms in the nation's railroad law and changed American history.

Terse and unsatisfying accounts by Michigan historians led me to their sources. And those sources drew me back further in time to contemporary newspaper articles on the events as they happened.

The basic facts were agreed to by all sides: The Michigan Central Railroad had changed its policies and stopped paying farmers along the right-of-way for livestock killed. MCRR executives claimed that farmers were actually feeding their unhealthy cows, pigs, and sheep on the railroad tracks, just so the trains would kill livestock and the farmers could collect payment without having the bother of taking livestock to market. The railroad, out of patience with complaints from the farmers, further reduced payments for killed livestock, cut the fees paid farmers for fuel wood, and stopped giving free passage on the trains to farm families. Tempers heated. Trains were stoned, then shot at, and finally derailed into swamps. The climax was the arson bombing of the six-month-old MCRR depot in Detroit. The Detroit newspapers, of which there were several dozen at the time, saw the violence as the handiwork of outlaw farmers of Jackson County. At the center of the cauldron was Grass Lake.

The farmers, for their part, blamed the railroad, eastern financiers, and thugs hired by the railroad for these acts—their motive was to frame innocent country people and cheat them out of their legal rights and their land. The accused leader of the renegade band was none other than Abel Fitch, the head of the Democratic Party of Michigan. The lead defense counsel was William Seward, governor of New York, who would later run against Abraham Lincoln for the Republican nomination for president, would become Lincoln's secretary of state, and would gain enduring fame by negotiating loans from Europe to rebuild the Union after the Civil War. But, most famously, Seward's "folly" was to buy the Alaskan Territories from Russia.

The Detroit newspaper accounts were not models of objectivity. When more than one hundred deputies converged on the little hamlets of Jackson County in the dark of night of April 19, 1851, and arrested more than fifty men, the *Detroit Free Press* reported:

> More arrests were made yesterday in Jackson County, of men impli-cated with the incendiaries arrested a few days since. They are now in jail in this city. It is understood that arrangements are being made for the arrest of the balance of the county.

My first lunch-hour visits to the Historical Collections only further whetted my appetite. I began asking people around Grass Lake what they knew about these events. Only a handful of people had ever heard of them, but I found three octogenarians whose ancestors had been involved. One connection led to another and soon I had in my hands original mate-rials that historians had never seen—unpublished diaries, journals, and letters recounting in the participants' own words their version of what had happened and why.

I read the handwritten letters of Abel Fitch, the accused ringleader, to his wife, including his first, written upon being incarcerated in the notorious Detroit jail where inmates frequently died of disease or "myste-rious happenings":

> I being a captain they placed me in front, of course, and we made quite an imposing appearance giving the Detroit folks a good oppor-tunity to take a fair view of us . . . must have been a great satisfaction to the RR folks.

There was no turning back now. I had to find out for myself what had happened during those days. And I already knew that whatever I learned was worth at least an article raising the awareness of Michigan citizens about one of the most important events in the state's history.

I asked Marcy if she remembered the clippings her sister Beverly sent right after we moved in. She did, and I told her that for the last few weeks I had spent lunch hours at the Michigan Historical Collections reading about some fascinating events.

"And?" she asked.

"And nothing. I'm just intrigued with it. Amazed that something so important has been all but lost to posterity. People ought to know about this."

"Maybe I'm obtuse, but why?"

"Because it happened right here, and it changed everything."

Marcy looked up at me and sighed.

"And you're going to research it and write a book about it."

"I never said that. I'm just intrigued by it. I just want to find out what really happened, as best I can."

"And then write a book about it."

"I'm not saying that."

"How long have I known you? You don't have to say it. Well, it's not as though you have anything else on your plate."

HANK DUBOIS AND I HAD GONE IN TOGETHER on a welder but Hank had it tied up over at his dad's place, so I took the cracked fairway mower frame into town to Norman Brown's shop.

We were lifting the heavy frame back onto the deck of my pickup truck and I got my fingers pinched. I jerked them out before any real damage was done but had a nice blood blister on the base of my thumb.

"Thought for a minute there," Norman said, "you were going to be a matched pair with your neighbor. You do know how Henry Samyn lost his fingers, don't you?"

"Actually, no. I assumed it was an accident at the machine shop where he used to work."

"Well, the way I heard it, Henry was chopping corn and the chopper got stuck on some barbed wire. Story went that Henry left the rig running as he went to yank the wire out. The wire coiled around his wrist, pulled his hand in and wham! there went two fingers."

"Two? That story doesn't hold, Norman. Henry lost all four fingers on that hand, kept the thumb. How'd he lose the other two?"

"Well, after Henry put in a claim, the insurance adjuster came out and wanted to know how it happened. So Henry started up the rig to show him. When it came to the barbed wire part, Henry reached in to show him and said, 'Damn! There goes the other two.'"

"Norman, that's an imaginative story but I have a suggestion."

"What's that?"

"It might be a good idea not to have that get back to Henry Samyn. He's got a good sense of humor but I doubt it's that good."

"Did you see this ad?" Marcy asked. "A Mrs. Johnson on Francisco Road is giving away maple tree saplings. Free for the digging, it says. It might be worth you and the boys driving over and having a look."

We were there in ten minutes, bushel baskets, burlap bags, and a shovel in the bed of the pickup. When we pulled in, a tiny, ageless lady fashioned out of cowhide and bailing wire came off her porch and down to see what we were all about.

"Who might you be?" she said.

I introduced myself and my two helpers, Mark and Pat. I showed her the ad in the paper for free trees, you dig.

"That's me, all right. I'm Miz Johnson. Not 'Mrs.,' just 'Miz,' short and tidy, like me. Grab your stuff and let's get at it."

Miz Johnson led us through her backyard and past a chicken coop. She had a serious limp but that didn't slow her as she marched us around a barn and into a fallow field dominated by a huge sugar maple tree. There had once been a garden here, fenced to keep the deer out, but it looked as if it hadn't been used for four or five years. Now the abandoned vegetable patch was covered with hundreds of young maple trees and saplings, from two to eight feet tall.

"Weather's cool enough," Miz Johnson said, "to where you can bare-root 'em. Don't need to take a root ball or nothing, just bare-root 'em. I'll get you some water, douse those burlap sacks, keep the roots moist."

"How many can we take, Miz Johnson?"

"How many you want? Take whatever, don't matter to me. You look at the yards all up and down the Francisco Road you'll see the daughters of this big old grandma here. I figure she was planted in 1840, a variety not common in these parts. More thousands of young ones come off her than I want to count. State won't let me sell 'em without they do inspection, certification, all that red-tape crap. So I give 'em away whoever wants 'em. Been doing it since Chester died, Lord have mercy. He used to say the hell with it, took a dollar the dozen and if the tree police wanted to try and stop him, just bring it on. That was sixteen years ago he passed."

She went off toward the house and when she came back she was carrying a milk pail part full of water in each hand.

"Know why I do this, young fellers?" she said to Mark and Pat, as she set down the two pails of water. "Well, I'll tell you. You never carry a single pail and you know how come? Because it gets you all lopsided is why. You're going out to milk the cow in the morning and pull a half of a pail out of her you don't walk back to the house with just that one pail. No sir, you fill a second pail with just that same amount of water, carry it in the other hand. That way you're balanced." She took a hard look at me. "Yep, that way you're balanced like a Libra, just like your daddy here."

"Miz Johnson," I said, "how did you know I'm a Libra?"

"Don't matter how. I know these things. Know how I got this bum leg? I'll tell you how I got this bum leg."

She pointed off to the distance, at what I couldn't tell.

"That little hill there? Coming back in for lunch after I'm combing rocks while Chester is disking that field all morning. He's driving, I'm riding on the old Farmall, standing on the footplate alongside him. As usual, Chester's hungry so he's going too fast, hits a bump, and there I go. Ninety-six pounds was all I weighed then but I was a looker, I could show you a picture. This all happens in maybe two seconds. I'm up in the air and I know if I fall backwards, that disk would do me like a block of sliced cheese. So I just grab for whatever I can get a borrow on—Chester's shoulder, a fender, any damn thing."

I looked at the boys. They were wide-eyed.

"Wouldn't you know it, my fingers latch onto one of those big tread cleats of the tire. Course it's still going around maybe ten miles the hour 'cause Chester—he was never known for being quick—is just catching on and hasn't hit the brakes yet. This next part, he and I dispute. He claims I'd have been thrown clear and not hurt at all, had I just let loose that tire cleat. Easy for him to say, I tell him. I'd rather get pulled under that wheel and get my hip and leg crushed than get tossed like a rag doll under that disk.

"This whole left side went right under the wheel but Chester got her stopped, me under the tire and not two feet short of going under that disk. Did this shoulder too, the same time, but that healed up, more'n I can say for my lower half. Here boys, keep those roots out of the sun. Cover 'em up with that wet-down burlap and plant 'em soon's you get home. You're the fella building the golf course on the old Nate Fish place, eh?"

It took some talking to get Miz Johnson to take five dollars, not for the trees, of course, but to go against the cost of her ad in the *Grass Lake News*.

WE PLANTED MIZ JOHNSON'S sugar maple saplings in the rough between numbers one and two fairways. And in the rough between three and nine. And behind nine green. And in the rough by the big boulder in the crook of the dogleg on number five. And in the side lawn near the flagpole where we could see them every day. And everywhere else it seemed a sugar maple might want to grow.

Those trees would want a lot of watering during dry spells, but that would drive their roots down deep to where they could hold out against just about anything. And they would survive because they came from good stock.

1·9·6·9

Twenty

When given the chance, as Horace Coppernoll would say, water will run downhill.

That is why greens are built up, so that water will not pond on them. They are built up from several feet below the nearby ground level and then built up above that terrain. Bent and Bermuda and other exotic grasses need water—lots of it and at the right time—to stay alive. But there is a limit. These grasses are not wetfoot species and they will rot and die if left standing in the wet too long. So the water must percolate through them in a tolerable amount of time, being available long enough for the plant to take a drink, then seeping through into the sand and gravel layers below, into a herringbone network of drainage pipes and out and away to a collection point or into the natural water table.

When nature doesn't provide that water by precipitation when it is needed—which is usually—the golf course operator must supplement it. And therein lies one of the greatest challenges of the golf course architect and a major continuing challenge for the greenskeeper. For those on a short shoestring budget taking on what is often a multimillion-dollar project, it is monumental.

At its most elemental, a golf course is a byproduct of several problem solutions, one of the most important of which is figuring out and coping with the way water wants to flow and wind wants to blow and sun wants to shine on a piece of land.

This is why resort "stadium" courses and many Arizona desert courses are such abominations. They are fascinating in a way a freak show may be fascinating. They are technological triumphs, eye-catching examples of mankind winning a battle against nature. But even though nature will suffer considerable damage, it will eventually win the war. The idea of building and sustaining a golf course by tapping untold millions of gallons of the most precious commodity in an arid environment is, on the face of it, preposterous and to many, obscene.

On The Boondocks, we planned to install an underground sprinkler system once we had been open to the public three or four years, when presumably there would be enough income to pay for it. Until then, such an expense was unthinkable. And with the nice rainfall pattern we had observed from 1966 through 1968, we were confident that a much more modest system would be adequate. We knew that Michigan weather is fickle at best, so the system we would put in place had to be capable of getting water to the greens when they needed it, and for the tees once the greens had been served. As for the fairways and roughs, well, we would do what most small farmers do—hope for congenial weather.

So we had assembled a collection of small pumps, pipes, hoses, and sprinklers that cumulatively would provide a water source for each green. The water would come from either a spring-fed pond or Willow Creek, or a channel bringing water from the creek closer to a green. The water did not necessarily have to come into play for golfers. In fact, because many golfers get apoplectic at the sight of a water hazard they actually have to hit a shot over, our design hadn't overdone it. We would have water hazards on four of the nine holes, but by moving tee placements and pin placements, we could greatly diminish the threat. There were only two holes where a golfer playing from the regular tees would have to fly a shot completely over water.

With such an irrigation system, we would avoid—at least in these early years—the big expense of a single massive pump driven by a large electric motor located in a central pump house. Instead we would have several small or medium-sized pumps, one at each water source, and one moderately large-capacity system located centrally, each gasoline-powered. We would postpone thousands of dollars of cost involved in bringing electrical lines to those locations.

But as spring warmed in 1969, we already had learned that there were several problems with such a system. Among the negatives, the gasoline engines are noisier than electric motors. Nothing we could do about that but keep the mufflers in good shape and try to run the engines mostly at night. Gas tanks on the smaller engines are likewise small. That means they have to be refilled every four to five hours, which is a problem in a drought if they have to be operated virtually around the clock. Small portable four-horsepower Briggs & Stratton or Tecumseh engines, of the kind we needed two to four of, are notoriously finicky. The smallest particle of dirt hangs up the carburetor float and starves out the little engine.

Each of the pumps had an intake pipe which was thrust down into the water source some six to twelve feet. There was a screen on the end of the pipe to block debris from being drawn in and fouling the impeller blades, which could destroy the pump. Once a pump caught prime and blew out all air in the line and was drawing pure water, the impellers forced it through an outlet to which we connected lengths of pipe and hose running anywhere from a couple hundred to more than a thousand feet.

The small pumps used three-quarters to one-inch hose and drove two Rain Bird impulse sprinklers. That meant we could irrigate an entire green and its collars, apron, and approach in two placements.

One of our other mini-systems was the freebie from brother Dick, an eight-horsepower Wisconsin driving a big Marlowe pump; that pushed a lot of water for us. And we had a nine-horsepower Gorman-Rupp system bought from a failed blueberry farm. That system could drive a dozen good-sized sprinklers and cover two or three greens and several tees at once.

In late summer of 1968, we had started buying these used pumps and accessories one at a time. Set up alongside a water source, each of the smallest pumps would get water to the more distant greens. But when that water had to be pushed uphill, it would arrive at the green with only enough pressure to drive one or two sprinklers at a time. What we needed was a large-capacity pump that would serve as the heart of our overall irrigation system. Since we weren't going to have electric power, what we needed was a high-capacity portable pump mounted on a small trailer and driven by the power takeoff shaft of a tractor. We knew that such a system could, by itself, generate enough pumping capacity to irrigate a good third or more of our greens and tees, provided we had enough pipe, hoses, and sprinklers to attach to it.

Once we found an affordable used PTO pump and irrigation pipes, we would set that system up at a central location where we could draw water out of the trout stream or one of its connected ponds. From there we could push water in several directions at once and cover three or four greens and tees. The problem with a PTO system is that it ties up a tractor, just sitting there at a fast idle, hour after hour, driving the pump's power shaft. But I had already bought an ancient Canadian-made E-3 Co-op tractor whose sole assignment would be to serve as just such a power source for a PTO pump.

And we knew where to go to locate such a pump.

Tom Lyndon, a neighbor from our Ann Arbor days, worked at his family's business, Michigan Irrigation Service. I told Tom what we had in mind and in a couple weeks he called and asked me to meet him at their Ann Arbor warehouse.

Tom took me through the setup he felt would serve us best on our tight budget. He showed me used aluminum pipes that would be the arteries of the system, snaking out from the pump, branching off wherever we needed to take water in a different direction. These three-inch-diameter pipes were thirty feet long with rubber gaskets in a throat at one end that would slip into the next pipe, where a spring-loaded latch would seize down on it to make it watertight.

The pipes were light enough for one person to handle. Each pipe had a tap drilled so you could screw in a one-inch pipe nipple and attach a hose or a sprinkler head every thirty feet. At the very end of the run, Tom said, you would have an end cap to fit into the last pipe so all your water would be channeled through the hoses and not just come gushing out the end.

This is a portable system, Tom explained, that can be quickly dismantled and moved.

How quickly, I wondered.

Depends on how many sections of pipe and how many lengths of hose and sprinklers you have strung out. Depends on how far away you're moving it. Could be a few minutes, could be an hour. If you're not moving the pump, and all you're doing is breaking up the pipe and restringing it, you're up and going again in fifteen minutes. Moving the pump, setting up the intake pipe, and re-priming takes the longest. And it also depends on how you're moving the system.

Hmmm. Hadn't thought about that. How do you move 1,200 feet of pipe? That's forty of these thirty-foot lengths of aluminum pipe.

Couple ways, Tom said, and keep in mind it's not often you're moving them all. You'd want to keep fifteen or twenty lengths at each of two major locations. As for moving them—one, you could set up a trailer with a kind of cradle at either end so the pipes would nest into it and not roll off when you went sidehill. Pull the trailer with either a tractor or a truck. Two, you could make a rack that would go on the top of your pickup truck and carry the pipe up there. Either way is good because you sure don't want to be walking from place to place, carrying one or two lengths of pipe at a time. Take forever.

When I told Hank Dubois what we were doing, he had the solution right away. We drove to the nearby town of Michigan Center to Hank's favorite junkyard.

"Pull around there behind that shed," Hank said. "Yep, still there. Let's see what he's asking for it."

"For what?"

"That pile of iron."

"That looks like old bed frames," I said. "What are we going to do with old bed frames?"

"Older the better. One thing, older are heavier-gauge metal. Two, they're cheaper. Besides, they only used to be bed frames—tomorrow that's the rack for your irrigation pipe."

In less than three hours we turned that $8 worth of bed iron into one damn sturdy truck-mounted irrigation pipe rack. It was then that I finally learned what those slots are for on the sides of the beds of pickup trucks. You stick the vertical sections of iron in there and they become the uprights on which the top part of the rack will sit. That extends the rack bed up above the roof of the truck, and you leave those verticals protruding up six inches past the horizontal bars and crossbeams so the pipe won't roll off to the sides when you're on a slope. Because the irrigation pipes are thirty feet long, you also have to weld additional uprights out beyond the front bumper for support and to distribute the load. When the pipe is loaded, it will jut out only a few feet front and back.

You learn quickly that if you leave the doors open on the cab, you can step up onto the running board and hoist a section of pipe up and onto the bed with ease. Of course, as Marcy pointed out, you learn right quick where to grab the pipe so you have it balanced just right, as if you are a high-wire walker grasping a balancing pole. The kids discovered that although one section of pipe was too heavy and cumbersome for them to handle alone, with a kid taking each end, they could manage it.

Since planting the first four greens in August and September of 1968, we had been keeping numbers one and nine watered from the Willow Pond and number one pond, using two of the little Wayne pumps. The practice green was only one hose section from the back porch of the house and beyond that, number two green was another 150 feet, so for them we tapped into a spigot at the rear of the house. Adequate, but only barely.

Marcy, the kids, and I had long anticipated the day we would see a dozen or more sprinklers under pressure from a single system set up at the Willow Pond. That would happen in a few hours because Tom Lyndon had just arrived with what the kids had already dubbed "the big system."

Tom parked his truck by the Willow Pond and everybody began stringing sections of pipe in two lines—one toward number one green, and one toward number two green. Tom showed us how easily the sections snap together and how to put one of the custom-made T-connectors between sections, so we could run a branch of pipe at a right angle off the main trunk and throttle down to a smaller diameter pipe and hose wherever we wanted to.

We took the one-inch plugs out of several pipe sections and screwed one-inch nipples into the taps. Then we fastened hoses to the nipples and connected sprinklers to the hoses. We did that in one branch to number one green, and in a second and longer line heading toward the house with branches to nine green and two green, ending with two sprinklers at the practice green. We had new Rain Bird sprinklers and several old surplus spinning sprinklers from Walt

Bauer ready to serve our four greens and adjacent tees and approaches.

As Tom finished hooking up the intake pipe, I connected the drive shaft of the pump to the power takeoff shaft of the tractor.

Mark announced that he and Marcy and the other kids had nineteen sprinklers connected and asked whether this pump could operate that many.

"Let's find out," Tom said.

I started up the tractor and shifted the PTO into gear.

The shaft began spinning but nothing was happening.

"Rev it up," Tom shouted. "It hasn't caught prime yet. Goose it."

I brought it up to 1,000 RPM, then 1,500.

The intake pipe shuddered and the pump began to throb. In a few seconds, all up and down the pipelines, the sections vibrated as the water rushed through. One sprinkler sprang into action, then two, three. Suddenly, about six or seven sections toward number one green, a great jet of water spurted skyward, as two sections of pipe burst apart.

"Shut it down, Bill," Tom yelled.

I shut off the tractor and all of us walked to where the pipes had come apart. The force of the water had blown a big rubber gasket out and it lay there in a pool of water. The sections that had been loosely connected were now a couple of feet apart.

"Cheap lesson," Tom said. "But I'll show you why you have to be careful to always snap these sections together tight. See, now we have to disconnect and reconnect each section of this run one at a time. Eventually you'll get so good at doing this you'll be able to do it in the dark."

Marcy and the kids checked the rest of the lines to make sure there were no more loose connections. In a few minutes we had the system fully reconnected—tightly, this time. I started the tractor and slipped the PTO into gear. I could see the wide eyes of the kids and realized I was holding my breath, just like they were.

This time we could see one sprinkler after another begin to whirl as the air blew through the lines ahead of a column of water. Suddenly, like a row of flowers exploding into bloom instantaneously, great plumes of water arced from the sprinklers. The late afternoon sun glinted off the spray and set little rainbows to glimmering in the canopy of mist above each green.

The tractor engine hummed. The pump whirred steadily. The pipes throbbed gently as the water rushed through. The air was still and we could hear the staccato click-click-click of the spring-loaded impulse arms of each of the nineteen sprinklers.

We stood there and drank it all in. It was the single most satisfying, most beautiful sight we had seen on our land. At that moment, under the thrust of one power source and a single pump, with nineteen sprinklers pulsating on the four completed greens and their companion tees, the place no longer looked like a failed farm. It looked like a golf course.

Driving the back way into town, I saw an old roller in the field behind Livermore's barn on Wolf Lake Road. I had first noticed that roller at least two years before and had seen it dozens of times since. It was always in exactly the same spot so it didn't appear to be getting much use. I often wished we had a six-footer like that when we seeded the first four greens instead of the little two-footer I had borrowed from Walt Bauer. Still, we had six more greens to put in and a wider roller sure would save a lot of time.

The well-kept Livermore farm was one of the most prosperous in the township. A sign hanging from a post beside the driveway proclaimed that this was a centennial farm—one hundred years in the same family. The sign was always freshly stained, its proclamation touched up in bright red, green, and gold paint. The story was that John Livermore's great-great-grandfather Bartholomew had bought the land in 1842 from an Ottawa Indian tribe. The place almost was forfeited for taxes in 1852 when Black Bart, as the press nicknamed him, was among the more than fifty men arrested for and charged with major crimes against the railroad. The prosecutors said that Black Bart was one of Abel Fitch's ringleaders, helping to lead the notorious band of Jackson County farmers who took on the entire establishment of the state of Michigan.

I had continued to immerse myself in the archives of the Michigan Historical Collections and learned about this little band of farmers (or gang of outlaws, as the Detroit newspapers called them) who challenged the might of the Michigan Central Railroad, Detroit industrialists, Boston bankers, Detroit politicians, and the press. Their long-running, bitter vendetta had many names, including The Great

Railroad Conspiracy War and the Detroit-Leoni War. Local legend had it that Black Bart Livermore was indeed a key figure.

Almost obscured by waist-high weeds, the roller looked as though it had been there since the days of old Black Bart. But Hank Dubois said that John Livermore had bought a new roller and towed it behind his tine-tooth harrow as John worked the beanfield alongside Wolf Lake Road. Hank thought John could be convinced to part with the old roller.

As I got out of the pickup truck, John's big black-and-tan came up, addressed me with a couple of throaty barks, sniffed my boots, and licked my hand. John came out of the milk house, wiping his hands on a rag. He was big and bony with a face brown and smooth as an acorn. Unmanageable shocks of sun-bleached hair jutted out from under the green-and-yellow John Deere baseball cap that was all-but-required apparel in Jackson County. I had met Big John only once, at the grain elevator in town, and was surprised he remembered me.

"How's that golf links coming?"

I shook my head as we shook hands. "A ways from looking much like a golf course. But we're making progress."

"Ain't on somebody else's timetable, are you? What I've found, best when you're onto something on the land like that, you let it come to you. Project like that takes more than the right soil, seed, and sweat. Weather's going to have its way, no matter what. You can fight the weather and you can fight the land, fight 'em 'til you drop from exhaustion, you can't never beat 'em, neither one."

I motioned toward the roller and we walked that way, along a stand of ripening wheat. John stopped and plucked a few heads of grain, shucked them, and cut into a grain with his thumbnail.

"Looks like you're in for a good crop there, John."

He tossed the kernels down and snorted.

"Depends on what you call good. Used to call wheat 'farmer's gold.' Now they oughta call it farmer's fool's gold. Less'n a dollar thirty the bushel. Can you believe that? Say I pull forty bushel the acre. Hell, cost me more'n that for fertilizer, diesel for the tractor, chemicals for the weeds. Know what that makes my time worth?" He held up his thumb and forefinger to make a big zero.

"Better had plowed it under as a green manure crop, take the government's fallow acreage allotment, and hope for next year. That's what the damn feds got us doing, you know. Hoping for next year."

"Like when your baseball team's out of it by the Fourth of July."

"You got it. Wait 'til next year. And you know what we hope for? Hope for once to get the breaks—good weather, rains at just the right time, dry when it's harvest time. No insects. And that everybody else in the county has lousy luck, gets flooded out, or the rains just miss 'em when they need it. Or a blight hits their fields and not mine. Now, ain't that a hell of a note? Wishing bad on your neighbors and friends, just so you can catch the high dollar in a good year for you, a down year for the rest of 'em."

We reached the roller and stood there silently, looking at it, as John cooled down. He took out a red bandanna and mopped his shining forehead and balding pate. I looked at the roller and while it looked pretty sad from the road, it looked a lot worse close up. It was six feet long, with a thirty-inch diameter. It did have a good long towing tongue that seemed solid enough. There was a bung hole on the side of the tank with a threaded plug where you could fill the tank with the water needed for the weight that would crush dirt clods. A roller this big could smooth out a green or a tee after you had gone over it with hand rakes twenty to thirty times. But this roller had a wound in the side of the tank that would spew the water out as fast as you hosed it in, so instead of water for weight someone long ago had wired a dozen cement blocks to the top frame to add ballast.

"Hank Dubois says you just gotta have this here roller or your whole golf course goes down the drain."

John had just set a floor price for the roller. Now I had to figure out what that might be.

"John, our good friend Hank would have been overstating it. But I could maybe use it. How much you have to have for it?"

He thrust out a big boot and kicked at a clod of dirt that had dried on the roller's rim.

"Don't make 'em like that any more, you know. Built that roller before they knew there was any such thing as 'built-in ob-so-les-ence.' My pa laid out a pretty penny for that roller. What I oughta do, sell you that new one I bought, piece of junk that it is, and put this one here back in service. Knew how to make 'em right back in those days."

Then he looked at me over his shoulder, squinting one eye, and said sharply, "So, Mr. Golf Course Builder, what be your top dollar?"

"Well, John, I'm not here to poormouth your roller. That is one terrific antique roller, all right. And it'll do the job just fine, after I pay Norman Brown twenty dollars to weld that broken frame arm, and patch a metal plate over that big hole there on the side of the tank where it's rusted out. Then I can load it with water like it was designed for and take off those cement blocks that weigh about a tenth of what's needed to do even a half-ass job on a golf green." I bent over and took a closer look. "And you're right, it'll run fine once I put a new bearing in this left side. Yeah, when I'm done, if I'm lucky I'll only be into it for twice the cost of a new roller."

John laughed a couple of short barks and looked away. He fished a packet of Mail Pouch out of his bib overalls, dug out a big pinch of tobacco, and wedged it in his check.

"That's what they teach you over to the university, eh? Come out here and do a feller out of his equipment, 'cause you figure he don't know its true value? That it? Well, I'll let it sit right there before I'll give it away for less'n it's worth. Give me a number, Mr. Future Rich Golf Course Owner."

"I was thinking—and I'm not here to insult you or your fine heirloom roller, John, and I hope you believe that—I was thinking, how's fifteen dollars sound?"

John coughed and spat out a stream of brown juice, almost hitting my foot.

"Fifteen dollars? For that rusted piece of junk sat there since I rode on those cement blocks when my pa rolled out the mole hills in the front yard? Too much, city boy. I'd have settled for ten. But I'll take your fifteen, thank you very much."

We started back toward the house. John looked at me and shook his head.

"Now why the hell didn't you bring a trailer? Never mind, give me a hand and we'll load it on my flatbed, follow you over to your place. Been curious to have a look at what you're doing there."

"You know that land?"

"I guess I do. Wondered when somebody would get the place who would figure out it couldn't be worse for row-cropping."

"But do you think I can I grow a decent stand of grass there?"

"Try and stop it. Grass is about all you'd want to grow there. Reckon you're aware nobody's ever made a nickel off that place since old Nate Fish got that fool idea to grow popcorn on that blow sand he mistook for topsoil. But then, I suppose you know everything there is to know about old Nate by now."

I doubted that anyone ever knew everything there was to know about old Nate Fish. But I was learning.

TAKING OUT THE DOGS for the night was not a chore to be avoided, it was a ritual to be savored. Whatever the time of year, whatever the weather, unless you were totally wiped out from the day's work, it was refreshing to walk into a silence that was almost palpable, to walk beneath a canopy of stars, to see the Milky Way in the summer and the northern lights in the winter.

On winter nights the glow of the mercury vapor light would float a blue-white blanket over a bed of snow. On truly frigid nights, the still air would crackle as temperatures plummeted and fissures split the ice sheets on the Willow Pond. Even when the icy winds pierced your coat and stung your face, you knew that in less than five minutes the dogs would be bedded for the night and you would be toasting your feet over the kitchen register, sipping hot cocoa, feeling warm and dry against the taste of winter you had just savored.

As much as I enjoyed that take-out-the-dogs break, Marcy relished those moments even more. At first she had protested that it was too cold for the dogs, or they would be lonely out there. But soon she agreed that they were happier and healthier sleeping in their own snug doghouse in the pole barn. The pole barn was closed on three sides and open on the east side, facing the house, so we could look out the west windows in the kitchen or mudroom and see light reflected in the dogs' amber eyes.

The mercury vapor light on the pole at the curve of the U-shaped driveway was controlled by a photocell. At dawn, the sun's rays would trigger it off and soon after sunset, the absence of light would bring it flickering to life. It would sputter and blink for a few moments, then glow steadily brighter until soon the entire area was bathed in cool blue-tinged light. For a while after we moved in the girls had grumbled about the light spilling through their window at night, but they soon got used to it.

The kids marveled that a single lamp mounted on a twenty-foot pole cast so much light. One 60-watt bulb and it illuminated the back porch of the house and the driveway and flooded across the grass of the old paddock area and into the open pole barn. The dogs could keep an eye on anything stirring in the area and would sound the alarm if they sensed trouble.

One night, Marcy walked Rusty and Blazer out onto that blanket of light. She had long since gotten used to the solitude of the country after years living in suburbia. Any concerns for safety had long since evaporated.

After hooking the dogs to their chains, Marcy walked back toward the house, crossing the healthy stand of grass in the area that had been Pokey's paddock. As Marcy got to the concrete slab that had been the foundation for Nate Fish's wind-driven corn sheller she sensed it. Right there, behind her. So close, she said, if she were to reach her hand back over her shoulder, it would touch something . . . or someone. But she didn't reach back, didn't dare even look back, did not want to see what may or may not be there. She felt gooseflesh on her arms, and her heart began to race. Instantly, she was aware that there was no sound. The dogs were silent. If someone or something was looming up behind her, surely the dogs would have been in a frenzy, barking and growling long before this.

She hurried across the driveway and up the back porch stairs, her heart pounding as she slammed the door behind her, locked and bolted it. Only then did she look out the window. The glow from the mercury-vapor lamp washed over the driveway, the yard, the old paddock area, and into the pole barn where the dogs lay peacefully. There was nothing else to be seen. But there had been something to be felt, of that she was certain.

"I never before had the slightest concern," Marcy said, "about taking the dogs out late at night. It never occurred to me to worry about someone grabbing me. If there had been a person there, the dogs would have kicked up a ruckus. But there wasn't anybody there. And before that moment I never for a second had the slightest thought about anything like a . . . a presence. But there was something. Of that I am absolutely positive. I never felt anything like that in my life. And then I thought, Nate Fish. I don't know why. I don't know what it was. But something happened there, of that I am certain."

Marcy took the dogs out countless times after that. It was always a nice break from the hustle-bustle of the house, and always without incident.

"BILL, CAN YOU GET OVER HERE right away?"

"Well, Henry, in a couple minutes. What's up?"

"Soon as you can get here. Bring a rifle."

"A rifle? What for?"

"I need for you to shoot— just come over."

And he hung up.

What was happening at Henry's place? Why did he need me and a loaded gun? I tried calling him back but he didn't answer.

As I reached under the bed to pull out the gun cases, I tried to imagine what could be going on at Breezy Acres. Which of the half dozen rifles or shotguns to take?

For years, I had kept all the guns out of sight. I respected the craftsmanship and felt a bond to my father and grandfather whenever I looked at them and would not consider disposing of them, even though Marcy had urged me often to do that. I would no longer use them for hunting. I didn't think of them in terms of self-defense. And I didn't want the kids exposed to them and start thinking that guns were a normal and desirable part of any house. But I did know that, despite my pacifist leanings, if a truly desperate situation developed, I would be able to reach for a gun in defense of my family.

Now, something was going on at Henry's place and he wanted me there right away and with a loaded gun, ready to fire at something. But what?

Unable to decide from what little he had said, I loaded the ancient Enfield .303 and the Winchester .22, jumped in the pickup truck, and was at his place in two minutes. As I pulled into the driveway, I was relieved to see Henry standing alone, alongside his truck. At least he hadn't called me to help fight off a lawless band. Then I saw what he was looking at, lying there in the gravel. And I knew that for Henry it was something much worse.

"Only time he ever did that," Henry said, and he bent down and gently stroked one of Boots' paws. "Riding shotgun with me, down to Maumee, like he always did. The second I opened the door, he bolted out. God, before I could catch him, he was out there in the middle of the road. Can't figure what the hell he was after. Must have smelled something. Always had a hell of nose, that Boots."

I had walked up beside Henry, still carrying the deer rifle.

"You can put that away," Henry said. "He must have slipped away while I was on the phone talking to you. All the way back from Maumee, the old fella laid there, head on my lap. So busted up I knew a vet would put him down right away. I kept thinking he'd go any minute, but damned if he didn't make it to home. Figure he knew? Wanted to be buried here?"

"Henry, why don't I bury him? Is there a place that would be best? Maybe we put a bush or a tree over him."

"Naw, I'll do it. Shouldn't have called you, hell of a thing to do. But I couldn't bear to see him suffer and the idea of doing it myself . . . See those paws? That's why I called him Boots—that black coat of his and then it looks like he went and dipped his paws into a pan of white paint. Wasn't any other name would have been right, really."

Twenty-One

Mary Joseph, our baby sitter and a candidate to be our pro shop attendant, told us that her boyfriend, Danny Campbell, would like to talk with us about a job on the course. Danny came with the only requisite qualification: he was Mary's boyfriend. With that attribute, we probably would have hired him if he had been the town ne'er-do-well.

We assumed that any teenager in this farm community would know about equipment and would be used to physical labor. I recalled my days at Sylvan Glen, when I started as a greens mowerman and was embarrassed when I was exposed in front of the rest of the crew as a kid who didn't even know there were two-cycle gasoline engines and there were four-cycle models and that if you pour regular gasoline into the tank of a two-cycle engine without mixing in the proper amount of two-cycle oil, that's not a good idea.

We were also spoiled in our early days building The Boondocks by our good fortune in hiring Larry Lape, a six-foot five-inch gentle giant who grew up in a large family headed by a father who was not only a consummate welder but who also imparted to his large brood some of his knowledge about what makes things work. And Larry also brought another valuable trait—he wasn't afraid of work.

That was an uncommon quality. When Larry left for much higher pay than our $1.50 an hour, we looked for other candidates with the same work ethic. And we learned how rare it was. Just as difficult to find, we learned to our surprise, were kids in this farm community who knew much about farm equipment. The ones who did were already fully engaged at their family's farm.

Mary's boyfriend Danny was certainly eager enough and said he knew his way around tools and equipment. Greens mowers are trickier than an ordinary lawn mower, so I was not surprised when it took some explaining and demonstration, but soon Danny got the hang of it.

One day I heard at a distance the engine on the E-3 Co-op tractor running unevenly out at number six pond, where it drove the PTO pump that irrigated greens three, five, and seven and their adjacent tees. I asked Danny to listen carefully, to try to hear whether the engine was running irregularly, which probably would be caused by a spark plug misfiring.

Danny listened intently. He nodded his head emphatically and said he agreed. I told him the engine was not hitting on all four cylinders, so would he go out and check the plugs to see which one was missing.

"Danny, do you know how to do that?"

"Sure do, Mr. Haney. I'll check 'em and let you know. Be right back."

And Danny jogged out toward number six pond.

Fifteen minutes later he came back into the maintenance shop.

"It's okay, Mr. Haney."

That was a relief. I walked outside and listened. The engine was still running just as roughly as before.

"Danny, listen. Hear that? Hear how it's misfiring? That plug is still missing."

"No it isn't, Mr. Haney. I hear it and I agree it doesn't sound right. But I checked the plugs, just like you said. They were all right there in their sockets. All four of them. Not a one of them was missing."

"I'M TAKING THE KIDS SHOPPING," Marcy said. "Promise me you won't do anything dangerous while I'm gone."

"Me? Do something risky? If there's anybody more cautious, more conservative, more safety-conscious—"

"Yeah, right. There's food in the fridge. We'll probably swing by a drive-in while we're out and bring home what's left. Remember, do no dumb."

What was Marcy's problem, anyhow? There was plenty for me to do without getting into trouble. There was the barn roof to repair, for example. On second thought, that could wait for Hank Dubois, who welcomed any excuse to get way up in a tree or on a roof.

Well, there was other repair work on the barn, then.

The siding of the big barn was one-by-ten unplaned barn boards, running vertically all the way from ground to peak. The boards had shrunk over the years to become one-by-eights or less, so when the rain came almost horizontally, which it often did, the wind whipped through those gaps, soaking the flooring and everything on it. I had stocked up with several hundred feet of one-by-two's to cover those gaps. I could get started at ground level but could reach only so far without using a ladder. To get to the highest sections involved getting up more than twenty-two feet on a ladder. Not a good idea, considering the rickety ladder, the uneven ground for the ladder's feet, and no one around to pick up the pieces. The barn boards could also wait until Hank was available.

There was equipment to work on, but then, there was always equipment to work on. After the big wind and rainstorm two days ago, a high pressure front had moved in and the sky was cloudless, the air shiny clean, the temperature cool. Too perfect to work inside.

There were always fairways to mow, but that was a job better done when the grass was drier. We were nearly ready to plant four of the remaining six greens, but the soil would be too wet to work for another day or two.

Lots of tree damage from the storm, mostly small limbs and branches to be picked up. For that kind of job, the kids were as good as I was, so that could wait until they were available.

One thing I could do was clean up the big black willow by number eight pond that had been fractured and blown over in the storm. The huge old tree had split about twenty feet up its massive trunk and most of the tree had come crashing down. Now it lay directly across number eight land bridge. Next spring—in less than nine months—golfers would use that crossover bridge to come back to the high ground on the south ridge of the marsh.

The primary tee boxes for number eight already had a good stand of Windsor bluegrass. They were set in a 60-yard-long slender rectangle starting back at the edge of a copse of young oak trees and ending just short of the marsh. Good golfers—or overly bold not-so-good golfers—could play from the tips of the blue tees, demanding a 180-yard carry across the watery trouble and a total of nearly 200 yards to the middle of the green. Or they could play the red tees from 160 yards, or the yellows from 130.

Because many beginning golfers get jittery having to fly a ball over water, we had built a set of white tees on the crossover bridge, just 80 yards from the green. And that is precisely where the willow tree had fractured and fallen. Its big trunk now totally blocked the crossover and its thick, gnarled arms were either submerged in the pond or reaching futilely toward the sky.

It was going to take the tractor and many lengths of logging chain to clean up the debris. But first, I would have to cut the limbs and trunk into manageable lengths. The trunk was almost four feet in diameter, so I wouldn't be able to drag out very long sections. The problem, though, was that a good quarter of the trunk had not fully separated from the rest of the main trunk. Up about fifteen feet, the tree was still connected with so much solid wood there would be no pulling the broken upper trunk loose from its lower part with a chain—it would have to be sawed.

I sized it up, thinking, How would Hank Dubois do this? He'd find it pretty simple. Heck, he wouldn't even need a ladder. The fallen trunk lay at a gentle angle and there were big branches jutting out in every direction. It would be a simple matter to cut a few branches to open up a pathway to the trunk, then take the chain saw and walk right up the trunk. Once up there, step over onto the still-upright portion to get good footing, then start up the saw. In a couple minutes I could cut it apart and drop the severed trunk down onto the crossover, where I could cord it up. I would lower the saw to the ground with a rope, then pick my way down the main trunk a branch at a time. Nothing to it. Hank would be proud of me.

I easily cut my way through the small branches and scrambled up the trunk. When I got to where the trunk was still connected, I was surprised how high up it was. I must have been twenty feet above the water level and fifteen feet above the land bridge itself. The view was nice, but one I hoped to never see again. I took the coil of rope I would use later to let down the saw and hung it on a shard of the shattered trunk.

As I primed the saw engine and set the choke, I hoped I would get lucky and the damn thing would start before I had to yank the rope a couple dozen times as usual. I had regretted buying this saw since the first day I owned it. I bought it for one reason only: it was the cheapest big saw to be had. With all the trees that would need pruning and thinning, I needed a strong and big saw. But as I learned quickly, there are different kinds of big when it comes to chain saws. A big blade is good. A big engine is good. But big as in heavy, that is not good. This was a Sears saw and its twenty-four-inch blade and powerful two-cycle engine were strengths. But at nearly twenty pounds, it was more than twice as heavy as a user-friendly saw should be.

Worse than the weight, though, was the frustration of trying to start it. If you missed it on the first pull, you would wear out both shoulders getting it running. I could see myself balanced fifteen feet above earth, yanking that starter rope while trying to keep from falling out of my precarious perch. But miracle of miracles! It fired up on the first pull. I warmed it up until it settled into a nice throaty purr.

I squeezed the throttle trigger and set the throttle lock button so the saw would race at maximum speed. I wanted to make this cut quickly and get down. I knew there was a great buildup of stress right where I was cutting, at the hingelike junction where the split trunk and the shattered upper half were still connected.

I had learned from earlier mishaps not to let the chain get pinched as the wood splintered. If the saw blade seized up, it would take a wedge and hammer, if not another chain saw, to get the stuck saw free. To avoid that, I reached as far as I could to make an undercut, figuring that would both relieve the pent-up tension and also separate the hinged bark, which would keep the trunk from hanging up once I made the cut from above. That went fine.

As I started the final cut from up top, the saw melted through the soft willow wood as if it were butter. Too fast in fact. The blade was within two inches of cutting completely through the hinge when something suddenly exploded, tearing the saw out of my hands. There was a second sharp crack as the remaining stress burst the hinge and the shattered trunk was free. And so was I.

One moment I saw the sky above me, then the chain saw swirling, roaring in front of my face. Then the blue of the pond, the greens and browns of the berm and marsh, then the sky again.

There was an instant of absolute silence as my back slammed against the spongy side of the berm. There was a flash of intense white light, then suddenly a loud roar and a whomp as something slammed to the ground two feet from my right ear. Still dizzy and unsure what had happened, I turned my head to see what was causing the roar. Not six inches from my throat the chain whirred around the blade, the trigger still locked, the engine still racing at full throttle, the saw teetering on an uneven patch of ground.

I swallowed hard and endured a couple more seconds of the noise before I rolled clear. I shut off the engine and the silence pulsated in my throbbing ears. I lay there, flat on my back, taking inventory of my body parts, all of which had remained connected, intact, and apparently fully functional. Except my feet were cold. I moved them and heard a splash. My feet were in the pond up past the tops of my boots. I lifted my feet out of the water and decided it would be a good idea to just sit still a while.

I turned and looked toward the south, at the knoll on which we planned to build number eight green in a few weeks. I wondered if I would be alive to see someone putt on that green. I knew that if Marcy appeared right now, the odds were against it.

AUGUST MELTED INTO SEPTEMBER and by Labor Day we were mowing eight of the ten greens. The older four greens had a full year's growth and were looking splendid. The second batch—numbers three, four, five, and seven, planted this year—were well up and filling out. Every week, I lowered the cut on the four newer greens one sixty-fourth of an inch toward a goal of five-sixteenths of an inch in height by winter.

Although those eight greens looked good, we were still racing to ready greens six and eight. The weather was hot and muggy, unpleasant for living and working but just right for quick germination. Still, there was no telling how long the high temperatures would hold. We had to get these last two greens in and sprouted right away; otherwise, they wouldn't establish well enough to survive the winter.

I already regretted saving greens six and eight for last. Each presented its own special problems and as the last days of our final growing season before opening the course dwindled away and as we continued to pour our time and energies into greens three, four, five, and seven, I feared I had made a serious strategic mistake. I should have started on the two problem greens first. Instead I had planted the easy ones, like number seven, on Gladys's knoll. That green was a snap—great angle for the sun, perfect airflow, ideal percolation. Anybody could grow great grass on number seven.

The green for hole number six was tucked into the mixed woods at the base of Smedley's hill, twenty yards from Kent's sassafras tree. This testing par four hole was the very heart of the course—the heart in location and also the heart in regard to aesthetics because from the tee it commanded a splendid view. The vista below featured the shimmering deep blue of number six pond, a ribbon of green fairway bending to the left and out of sight into a mixed woods aflame with crimson and gold in autumn, and the pale blue crescent pond beyond the elbow of the dogleg. All this was framed against golden sunbaked Smedley Hill.

As handsome as the hole was shaping up to be, we still remembered it as the bloodiest battlefield in the great thornapple war. This par four

hole would play tough, but to us it looked tranquil since we had con-
quered the last of the vicious thornapple bushes, ripping it out by the
roots with unapologetic delight. That final thornapple had occupied
precisely the spot where a low-handicap golfer would like to position
his tee shot.

Number six green was also the strategic heart of the course, the
climax of the course's toughest hole. To reach it in two shots demanded
skill, good judgment, and the right measures of restraint and courage.
To avoid disaster, the golfer playing from the back tees must carry a
drive nearly 200 yards from a highly elevated tee on the south ridge. A
well-struck shot would soar over the pond and draw into the elbow of a
narrow fairway doglegging sharply left. But too bold of a drive pushed
slightly off line to the right would run through the fairway and bounce
into the crescent pond all but hidden in the rough beyond, at the very
base of the Smedley Hill. The golfer who survived this gauntlet and
landed safely in the fairway had an inviting approach to a small, tricky
green nestled snugly in an arc of aspen, hickory, and oak with the sassafras standing sentinel on the golfer's right.

This would have been a fine hole anywhere on the course, but it
was especially dramatic because it came at a crucial spot in the round.
If a golfer found himself down by, say, two holes as he stood on number six tee, with only four holes to play, this was where he would try to
turn the match. If his opponent played first and knocked one wildly
into the spaghetti—as the kids called the marsh—the golfer could play
a safe shot into the fairway and try to win the hole with a par. But if the
opponent hit a decent shot, then the golfer could "let the big dog bark";
he would pull out his driver and try to blast one across the entire sea
of trouble and within a chip shot of the green. And that is where Kent
Smedley's sassafras tree came in.

Stationed just to the right of the green, the sassafras tree was like
a beacon. Early in fall it turned a fiery red, except for the top leaves,
which were tinged with gold. Other times, its lobed leaves were a
brighter, shinier green than the surrounding oaks and hickories on the
slope above and the quaking aspen and ironwood alongside. If you
aimed at the sassafras tree and caught every bit of the ball as flush as you
could strike it, you could fly the pond, the marsh, and the intervening

trees and land safely in the fairway, and the ball would come to rest safely short of the sassafras tree, a mere twenty yards from the green.

A shot like that could break the opponent's spirit.

The problem with number six green that had stymied me and made me tackle the planting of it so late was airflow. The green was so protected by Smedley Hill on the north and the woods on three sides that it was rare for a breeze to reach it. And the green opened to the east, the least likely direction for any wind.

We were conflicted about what to do to correct this. From a cold, objective golf course operator's point of view, we should have torn into the trees behind the green and above it on the slope to the right. That would have let the wind flow across the green, moderating its moisture and keeping it from stagnating and developing fungus infections. But we couldn't bring ourselves to cut down so many healthy trees, including the sassafras. We compromised, pruning lower branches and thinning a few scrubby or lightning-damaged trees, perhaps committing ourselves to forever nursing a problem-child green.

Number eight was almost the opposite problem. It too was a very important hole and second only to number six as the most picturesque. There the golfer also played over a pond carved out of the marsh, this time in the opposite direction, heading south. Just to clear the hazard, the ball must carry 140 to 180 yards, depending on the tee box chosen. But in total contrast to number six, there was not a tree in sight near number eight green, except for a stately conical juniper growing naturally on the slope at the green's left front.

Lynn Negus had used the small bulldozer to shape the green more than a year ago. He bladed down the crest of a natural sandy knoll that thrust up onto dry ground 20 yards from the edge of the marsh. Now the sparkling water of the pond was the ultimate guardian at the hole's front door.

The sandy base beneath number eight green would have been ideal for a course with a fixed underground water system that could be actuated on demand. But at the low-budget Boondocks, keeping the seedbed moist even during the critical germination phase was a serious challenge. On this site we had an additional problem—at the same time that we were racing to plant the green itself, we also had to seed the collars, approach, and slopes around the green with a mixture of red fescue and bluegrasses.

It would do us no good to have a healthy green resting atop barren, sandy slopes; we also needed a solid catch of blues and fescues on the slopes all the way around.

As Mark and I hurried to get seed, fertilizer, and oat straw mulch down on eight green, storm clouds boiled far off, toward Leoni. Lightning flashed and we heard low rumbles of distant thunder. Mark, his nine-year-old hands flying, hurried alongside me to spread seed and fertilizer, lay seven bales of oat straw, and then wet it all down before the winds blew everything away. On number six green, several hundred yards to the west, Marcy and our other three kids were, I hoped, doing the same.

Angry black clouds boiled overhead. I was conflicted. I wanted the rain, wanted it badly. But I didn't want the winds that were rushing before the storm. In another few minutes, these thirty-mile-an-hour gusts could blow away precious seed and fertilizer. Just as costly would be the precious time we would lose driving to Maumee for replacement seed, and doing a second seeding.

Mark finished mulching while I got the pump going and trained its puny spray onto the straw. The winds grew stronger and I doubted I could get the entire green and its slopes wet down in time. Some of the straw was already blowing away. Many of the tiny bent-grass seeds would have already nestled safely between sand particles, where they could germinate, but countless thousands were sure to blow away if the wind increased. Even then, once the storm began, if we got a real gully-washer before germination, much of what we were doing would be carried away in torrents right down into the pond. As if punctuating that thought, the sky above us split in a sharp crackle of lightning, followed instantly by a boom of thunder.

And then I remembered something that made all this seem trivial. I got a sudden image of those trees behind six green where Marcy and the kids were working, those trees that in previous storms had been frequently struck by lightning.

I was just about to run up the slope to the top of south ridge to try to see Marcy at six green when I heard the pickup truck behind me, coming across number eight land bridge.

Marcy parked the truck alongside the green and as Jen, Pat, and

Becky tumbled out, the winds slackened, then completely died down. The sky to the east darkened as the storm rushed away from us and toward Chelsea and Ann Arbor. The temperature had dropped at least fifteen degrees in a matter of minutes behind the departing low-pressure front. To the west, fluffy white clouds dotted a pale blue sky.

"We got ours in, how are you guys doing?" Marcy said.

"Almost there. How's number six look?"

"Kids did a great job. Sprinkler's going. Even with all that wind, the mulch didn't stir. The tops of the trees were whipping but you could hardly feel it down there on the green."

"I know. That's going to be a problem there forever. No airflow."

"Not like here, right Dad?" Mark said.

"That's right, Mark. Just the opposite, really. Marcy, how about if you guys go back up to the house? Mark can toss the spreader and those empty bags into the truck and ride in the back. I'll come in on the tractor as soon as I get this wetted down."

Off to the east, thunder rumbled and you could see gray sheets of rain against the dark sky.

I looked straight overhead and shook my fist, probably much like old Nate Fish and others had done on this land for generations, and I shouted, "Rain, damn it, rain! Just this one time—a nice steady rain."

"I don't think that's going to help any," Marcy said.

"Don't be too sure. I feel better already."

WITH TEMPERATURES WELL INTO THE EIGHTIES, and the mulch kept moist by hand sprinkling, the bent-grass seed on six and eight greens exploded like popcorn. Each afternoon, after Mark got home from school, he would tramp the half mile to number six green, get down on his hands and knees, gently brush some straw aside, and look for signs of life. It didn't take long. On the fourth day after seeding, he came back excited.

"We've got germination on both of them! It just came up today on number six and when I looked again under the mulch on eight I found spots that have probably been up since yesterday."

Mark was right. He had said we needed some breaks on the weather more now than ever before. And finally we got them. Or at least the warm temperatures we needed.

In the next three weeks we had only one decent shower; the rest of the time we still had to gently water the greens by hand every day. Once the new seedlings had rooted deeply enough, we set out sprinklers without fearing that their waterfall would be so heavy as to dislodge the shallow roots.

Temperatures stayed high, reaching sometimes into the eighties during the last days of September. We peeled off the straw mulch tenderly with our fingers this time, not even risking gentle raking, so as not to dislodge a single grass plant. That took a long time but when we had finished, both greens had a lustrous pale green sheen totally covering the putting surface, except for two worrisome patches on eight green. We had saved out a half pound of Penncross bent-grass seed for just such an eventuality and carefully sowed those spots by hand and re-mulched them. At eight million seeds to the pound, we needed only an ounce to cover both spots thickly. It was a long shot that the reseeded patches would catch but we had no choice but to try.

ON OCTOBER 1, 1969, with the temperature at a near-record eighty-four, we mowed numbers six and eight for the first time. We were now mowing not only every green at The Boondocks, but also every fairway, tee, and rough. It had taken us more than three years but we were mowing the entire sixty-eight acres of turf grasses on our golf course.

ON OCTOBER 13, I CALLED to wish my brother Dick a happy forty-eighth birthday. I had been giving him regular updates on our progress and was delighted to be able to report that the temperature was near an all-time high of seventy-six degrees on that day and the final two trouble spots on the last green had germinated. Brother Dick had contributed importantly to our efforts by arranging for the dump truck, G-5 tractor, and Wisconsin engine with its Marlowe pump, all of which had been used almost daily, it seemed, during work seasons for two years. Because of those contributions and countless others by scores of people, we would be opening The Boondocks to the public next spring.

Weather permitting.

Twenty-Two

W alt Bauer looked at our newly sprouted bent grass and said we should thank the Lord we had gotten such a good catch but we still had work to do. We needed to get as much growth as possible going into the winter if the newest greens were to be puttable by the spring. To do that, we had to keep fertilizing, mowing, and watering right up to the first hard frost.

After several modest showers and one good rainstorm in mid-October, the fall turned warm and dry. Every night when I came home from work I filled the fuel tanks and got the pumps going. The tanks held enough fuel to keep the engines going until about two a.m., when I would get up and refill them and move the sprinklers.

I had been bone-tired when I got to bed about midnight and even though I had slept only two hours, I got up feeling so refreshed in the crisp autumn air I thought I might stay up and write for a couple hours before going in to my job.

As I walked to the pole barn I looked out onto the course, where the full moon cast a soft gray glow on the fairways. It was almost bright enough to play golf. It was easily bright enough to see the ball well enough to hit it. Finding it might be more difficult.

I backed out the pickup truck and set two five-gallon cans of gasoline and a quart of oil in the rear deck. I put in the spare Wayne pump just in case one of the others had pulled up lame in the last three hours. All the tools I might need were in the toolbox—box-end wrenches, an adjustable wrench, screwdrivers, rubber washers, knife. A can of dry gas to prevent vapor lock in case a drop of water got into the fuel line. A can of Nox-em to add into the gasoline tanks of the small engines to keep the hot pistons from seizing up in the cooler night air the instant they ran out of gas. A small coil of wire to poke through the sprinkler nozzles to clear bits of wood or tiny pebbles that may have gotten sucked in past the intake screen.

That reminded me that I still needed to buy a pair of chest waders so I could get down into the ponds. I needed to set the intake screens into buckets to reduce the debris that more and more frequently was being drawn in and jamming up the sprinkler heads. So, until I improved the setups for the intake pipe screens, I'd have to take a few extra minutes at every pump site to unscrew the nozzles in the sprinkler heads and clean them out.

I let Rusty and Blazer off their chains and they hopped up into the deck of the truck. As I backed out of the pole barn, I glanced in the rearview mirror and was startled to see someone standing in the driveway, looking toward me. He was backlit by the glow from the mercury vapor lamp and I couldn't make out who it was. When I stopped the truck, he came toward me.

"Thought I might catch you on the night watering detail about now."

Now I knew why the dogs hadn't barked. It was Hank Dubois. Hank reached over and stroked Rusty with one hand and Blazer with the other, then got into the cab and sat down in the passenger seat.

"Hank, why aren't you home in bed?"

"Gave that up for a lost cause. Mary Jane finally booted me out, said my flopping around kept her awake. Figured I might as well get up and play with my telescope. Got it all set up but then the moon's too bright for stargazing. So now I'm wide awake. Figured why not come over here, see if there's anything needs breaking."

"Always got plenty of that."

The Willow Pond setup was running fine so Hank moved the sprinklers on the practice green and number two green while I changed the settings on number one green, number two tee, and number nine green.

When we got out near the system in the channel serving number four green and five tees, I parked the truck on the plateau, leaving the lights on so we could see where to move the sprinklers. But none of the sprinklers were putting out water. When I shut off the truck engine, the only sounds were frogs and crickets. The Wisconsin engine had quit. That was the loudest engine on the place, and at night it was reassuring to hear it throbbing away, even from more than a half mile if there was no wind.

We carried the gasoline and tools down the hill to the channel we had Larry Briggs gouge out two years ago for the sole purpose of bringing water from Willow Creek as close as possible to number four green. We had graded a level area to serve as a foundation for the Wisconsin engine and its Marlowe pump. Every time we mowed the fairway and the sandy slope, a cloud of dust would drift toward that setup and I could visualize it sifting into the air cleaner to be sucked in every time we started the engine.

"It's that carburetor float again," Hank said.

Hank and I had field-dressed that engine so many times we could almost do it in the dark. Almost. Hank held the flashlight while I took the carburetor off and rinsed it with clean gasoline. While I reattached it, we listened for the other engines. Just before we fired up the Wisconsin, we heard the Wayne pump—off in the distance at number eight pond—sputter, cough, and die.

"Might be just out of gas but it sounded a little strange," Hank said. "Wonder if something choked up the pump impellers," Hank said.

We got the Wisconsin going and soon it was running smoothly, driving a strong stream through the sprinklers on the front of four green and on number five's tees.

We bypassed the big setup at six pond. There the E-3 Co-op tractor was easily powering the PTO pump that pushed water to greens three, five, and seven, and their companion tees. We went straight to number eight pond to see what had happened there.

Hank started to fill the fuel tank, then shook his head.

"Wasn't out of gas. I'll top it off but that isn't why it quit."

He yanked on the starter rope, or rather tried to. It wouldn't budge.

"Something's frozen up. That rope won't give an inch. We'll have to break it open. You got a socket set in the truck?"

"Before we do that, I was going to tell you sometimes those intake screens work loose. Before we go digging into the pump, let's disconnect the intake, see if something got drawn into the impellers."

Hank gave me a look like, You really want to waste our time doing that? But he indulged me and said, "Sure, could be. Start with the easiest thing first." And as we talked he loosened the four bolts fastening the intake pipe to the pump.

As he pulled the pipe away, he said, "What the heck is this? Bill, does that look like blood to you?"

I shined the flashlight and looked over Hank's shoulder.

"Yeah," Hank said, "it's blood and this is—fish scales?"

Now he had the pipe clear of the pump, lifted the pipe out of the water and turned it upside down, shaking it. Something fell out of the pipe elbow and onto the ground at my feet. It was two-thirds of a fish.

"Can't tell with its head gone," Hank said. "Maybe it's a sucker. They're bottom feeders. The intake screen must have come off and he got too close."

I looked at the fish, then at Hank. I couldn't tell if he really didn't know it was a brook trout in his hand. I guess it shouldn't have made any difference whether it was a sucker or a brook trout anyway.

We flashed a light down into the pond and saw the intake screen lying loose, separated from the intake pipe. Somehow it had gotten disconnected.

"Yeah, sucked that sucker right in," Hank said. "Bet when you check that sprinkler, the nozzle will be chock-full of whatever parts of that fish aren't still stuck in these impeller blades."

A half hour later we had the spare pump installed and running. As we headed back to the barns, the eastern horizon began to lighten.

Hank came into the kitchen with me and I made a pot of coffee. We took the steaming mugs out and stood by the practice green, drinking coffee, saying nothing of consequence, watching the sunrise. I was thinking that despite the hassle of having to water greens in October, we were fortunate to have good growing weather. Hank's mind was probably working on a way to shield the Wisconsin engine so that carburetor wouldn't suck in grit and plug up. And I was silently chastising myself because I hadn't made sure the intake screen was secure and because there was one less curious trout in number eight pond.

Twenty-Three

Miz Johnson was right. When, just a year ago, we transplanted the sugar maple trees bare-root they had not been hurt at all. We had gotten them into the ground within hours after digging them up at her place that cool November day. We kept the roots moist and were lucky that a soaking rain began to fall just as we were setting the last one in. We had moved nearly a hundred maples from her volunteer nursery and nearly all of them caught.

We had not been so lucky with trees we transplanted from our own land. We moved young oaks, walnuts, hickories, quaking aspen, and blue beech. We tried to relocate them into conditions similar to what they had sprouted in. Our success rate with those was far below 50 percent. Water, and water at critical times, was the key determinant. The trees located near tees or greens got water regularly from the nearby sprinklers. But we had no water system for the fairways and roughs and only rarely were we able to take time and water away from greens to run water to those trees. We hated to lose even one tree and we were determined that eventually we would have groups of trees throughout the course, wherever they were needed and would thrive.

We already had a nice crescent of fir and spruce behind number two green. Some of these trees were Christmas presents from son Mark or gifts from the Boyers for our letting them put up a sign in our front yard during December to help steer passersby to their Christmas Tree Lane Farm. Those evergreens would grow into a backdrop to number two green, shielding it from the practice green and the house beyond. To the west of two green, the two rows of Miz Johnson's maples flourished.

Beyond nine green stretched an open expanse of grass extending more than 150 yards to the barns and pro shop. That area was interrupted only a bit by the pink boulder that the kids still called, for whatever reason, the "blue rock." Something more was needed there to mute the starkness of the barns looming up beyond the green and make a more inviting backdrop for the golfer's approach shot to the home hole.

We didn't want only maples everywhere and I didn't like our success rate on transplanting our native trees, so I ordered twenty green ash saplings. When the trees arrived, I soaked the roots and Mark and I went out to get them in the ground right away. The moment we opened the back door, Rusty and Blazer bolted out ahead of us, took their great tour through the woods, along the crest of the ridge, and circled back to meet up with us by the blue rock.

While I dug the holes and Mark planted the trees and tamped down the soil around the trunks, the spaniels lay nearby in the cool moist grass, where they could oversee the project. The dogs didn't seem to notice when a flock of Canada geese flew not twenty feet over our heads, coming from the Coppernoll fields where they had gorged so heavily on grain that their normally sleek bellies were swollen. These corn-fed honkers would go more than twenty pounds. You could hear the air whistling through their wing feathers. Usually this flock would fly from Coppernoll's fields directly to Walker's Lake less than a mile to the southwest. But this time they made a pit stop not a hundred yards from us, in the lush grass in the field that would become our practice range, west of the parking lot.

Mark and I watched them land, always fascinated by how they twisted their bodies and changed the angle of their wings to spill air to slow themselves down. Then we went back to our work.

A few minutes later the geese began to honk as if angry or in peril. One after another they ran as fast as they could, flapping their wings frantically, trying to lift their heavy bodies into the air. Several geese, though, weren't flying off; they were squawking and running in little circles, darting in, scuttling back, attacking something. Mark and I started over and suddenly realized what was going on. Rusty and Blazer were in the midst of them, growling, yapping, attacking, and being attacked.

I was afraid for the geese and just as worried for the dogs. I had heard that a goose could break a man's leg or an attacking dog's neck by running into it with its powerful wings. Mark and I raced toward the melee, shouting at the dogs as we ran. Hearing our shouts, the dogs retreated toward us. The geese turned the other direction, racing along the ground, making several false takeoff jumps until they gained enough lift to get airborne. All but one. Rusty had one goose by the neck and was dragging it toward us. Springer spaniels are not retrievers and these dogs had never been field-trained to bird hunt, but obviously there was an ancient genetic imprint at work here.

Rusty dropped the goose at my feet and looked up for praise, a scratch of the head, a doggie treat, something. All I could think was that he had apparently broken the neck of this beautiful wild bird. But the goose stirred slightly. Maybe there was a chance it could still be saved. Blazer had heeded Mark's yells and went to him. When the goose stirred again, Rusty growled, bared his teeth, and started toward it. I took off my jacket and snapped it at Rusty and he backed off.

Maybe if Rusty didn't see the goose, I thought, he would leave it alone. I tossed the jacket on top of the woozy bird, took off my belt, looped it through Rusty's collar, and made a leash of it. I dragged him away from the goose and decided that the best exit strategy was for Mark to take Blazer up to the house while I took Rusty. Then we could come back for the goose, while Marcy called local veterinarian Doc Chappel. The doc would tell us whether to take the goose to him or some animal rescue shelter.

It was a good plan but Blazer had other ideas. We were halfway to the house when he broke free. He headed straight for the fallen goose. The goose woozily got up, shaking a neck that clearly was not broken, flapping its wings and honking loudly if somewhat hoarsely. It waddled a few feet before wriggling out from under my jacket.

The big bird moved slowly at first, dragging its shadow as if it were a hundred-pound ball and chain. Then, hearing Blazer bark and seeing the dog racing toward it, the goose began to run. Twice it made feeble efforts to get airborne and failed, but it kept running, picking up speed. Just before it got to the road, with Blazer now only a few yards behind and closing fast, the goose jumped into the air. Beating its wings madly, it somehow cleared the fence and then the road with inches to spare.

Well across the road now, the goose disappeared for several seconds and I wondered if it had crashed. Then it appeared again, having taken the easy flight path, dipping into the long, deep drainage ditch running through Henry Samyn's land before the stream turned west and emptied into Walker's Lake. In the far distance we heard honks we assumed to be greetings and congratulations from the rest of the flock for the laggard goose's return.

Blazer padded back up to us, just as his sire Rusty had moments before, looking for his reward. Mark beamed as we went up the back steps to the mudroom. He was anxious to get into the house so he could tell his mother and the kids all about it.

THE FALL RAINS—such as they were—came late in 1969. In the first three weeks of November, temperatures hovered in the fifties and with the warm rains the grass continued to grow and we continued to mow. The heavy seeding, fertilizing, and mulching of the slopes around number eight green had paid off and we had a solid catch.

We used the bonus warm weather to arrange and rearrange, locate and relocate, configure and reconfigure our pump setups. When the time came to break down the irrigation systems, we were pleased that we would go into our first open season with enough capacity to handle all our greens and tees, with two small pumps in reserve.

We were relieved when finally, Thanksgiving week, temperatures plummeted and we woke up to a blanket of snow.

Now that cold weather was upon us, it was a pleasure to start up all the mowers and small engines—we had more than twenty—one last time, drain the pumps, run the engines dry, and winterize them. By the time I was done, the storage room in the maintenance shop was wall-to-wall with mowers, pumps, and utility machines I wouldn't have to fire up again for five months. I rolled the sliding door shut on that room and hoped not to open it until March.

I already knew how we would spend the winter. There were signs to make, hundreds of them, for the course and to post along the area roads. That we would do in the warm basement of the house. There was a lot of promotional activity facing us too—contacts with the press and media covering towns and cities nearby; visits to local schools, clubs, and other organizations; meeting community leaders and businesses to encourage formation of golf leagues. Winter would be just as busy as the previous three years of construction and house remodeling, but in different ways.

Even with the good progress and fortunate weather since Labor Day, we were behind an ideal schedule for an early spring opening in 1970. And maybe that wasn't all bad. April weather in Michigan is so fickle that many golfers don't trust it enough to get their clubs out. Every winter when I ran the Bendix golf leagues, a few members would get overcome with cabin fever along about February and start pressing for an early April start. And every year, I would give in and we'd try to tee it up the first week of April. Almost invariably, two or three April dates would be weathered out, either by rain that left the courses unplayable or by a freak snowstorm.

If April turned out to be as warm and dry in 1970 as it was one or two years out of ten, there would be golf to be played and income to be made on hundreds of Michigan's golf courses. But on our new course the risk of severe damage to tender young greens was too great.

So, we decided against an April opening. In November and December, as we checked the greens daily, we wondered: are we even safe for a May grand opening of The Boondocks?

ALTHOUGH WE SAW OUR NEIGHBORS during the day, we seldom had people over or visited them in the evenings. Gladys Smedley was hardly a social creature, but once she learned that Marcy and I played bridge, she was determined to have us over for an evening of cards at the Smedleys. It took only three years to make that happen.

The kids were delighted when I brought back their favorite baby sitter, Mary Joseph—that meant an evening of games, popcorn, and hot cocoa. They scarcely noticed when Marcy and I left. We had fed the kids, but weren't sure whether Gladys's invitation meant just an evening of cards or if she intended to feed us. I had long since learned that it was impossible to visit the Smedleys without Gladys putting food in front of you, so Marcy and I nibbled something light before we left, just to tide us over.

Gladys looked a little tired when she opened the door to us, but she perked up quickly and pronounced herself eager for combat.

As Kent dealt the first hand we learned that the Smedleys' brand of bridge was different than we were used to. We had always played contract bridge; they played auction. But bridge was bridge and we figured we'd spend most of the time talking anyhow. I was the only one who didn't smoke, the kids having succeeded in getting me to quit for good again. Before we played two hands we were engulfed in a blue cloud in the cozy kitchen of Smedley's tight little house. Gladys got up to open a door for some fresh air and, as she sat down, suddenly barked, "Kent Smedley, I give you one job and you botch it."

"What might that be, my little chickadee," Kent said in a very pathetic W.C. Fields imitation that Gladys had to identify and disparage for those who missed it. We had long since observed that Kent's defense against Gladys's harangues and browbeating was to act naively innocent and shower her with transparently saccharine terms of endearment.

"Cut the horse crap," Gladys said, "and get that plate of cold cuts and cheese out of the fridge. That was your one and only assignment and you blew it. Person have to be deaf not to hear these people's stomachs growling."

Kent went to the refrigerator and took out a platter. He lifted the wax paper covering the platter and began to laugh.

"What's so funny?" Gladys demanded.

Kent peeled a soggy Ritz cracker from the platter and held it up. It went limp between his fingers. Then, trying hard not to, he started to laugh and so did Marcy and I.

"You know, Kent, I could make a crack about things going limp around here but I wouldn't want to embarrass anyone," Gladys said. "Sometimes you can be a right horse's ass. Anybody ever tell you that?

"Yes, dear. You. Generally several times a day. If I may ask, was there a particular reason you put Ritz crackers in the fridge?"

"Well, damn it, it seemed like a good idea at the time. Have the whole blamed platter ready at once that way. Now scrape off those soggy crackers and pile on some fresh ones from that box up in the cupboard. Do I have to do everything?"

When Kent came back to the table, I suggested we change partners, men against the women. It seemed safer that way. If any mistakes were made by Gladys's partner, better that partner be Marcy than Kent or me. Somewhere along the line Marcy had learned how to cope with would-be intimidators.

1·9·7·0

Twenty-Four

Mark got the toboggan out, Dad," Jen shouted. "And the long ropes. And we've all got our stuff on."

I finished lacing my boots, pulled on a sweatshirt, and grabbed a light jacket and a scarf. I would be moving around a lot and unless the wind came up, that would be plenty warm enough. I put on the Russian Cossack hat with the flaps that kept my ears warm and looked stupid enough that it made the kids laugh and Marcy roll her eyes and shake her head.

It was that perfect winter day that kids in the upper Midwest see in their mind's eye when they think of the Christmas holidays. A high-pressure system dominated, plunging temperatures until the ice froze so solid you could hear big fissures split across it at night. During the days between Christmas and New Year's Day the sun shone brilliantly in a cobalt-blue sky. There was a foot-and-a-half blanket of powdery snow, ideal for what the kids had looked forward to since the first snowflake of November, four weeks ago.

Mark handed me the long toboggan rope and I tied it to the tractor drawbar. The kids got into their places, squeezing their legs around the kid in front of them, tucking their feet inside, grabbing tight onto the hand ropes alongside the cushion on which they sat.

"Ready!" shouted Jen.

"Aim! Fire!" shouted the other three.

I found a station on the tractor radio playing lively Christmas music and turned it up full blast. I revved up the engine and eased out onto the course. The kids yelled "Faster, faster!" Until the ground was solidly frozen, though, I didn't want to tear up turf where the snow cover was shallower. I needn't have been concerned—the snow was even deeper once I was out onto the fairways.

I stayed well away from tees and greens but there was plenty of room to swoop across the roughs, along ridges and down into valleys, the snow churned up by the tractor tires stinging the faces of the kids and giving them something else to scream about. We'd stop every few minutes so the kids could empty snow out of their mittens and boots and reposition themselves. On the flats I'd get the tractor up to its maximum speed of sixteen miles an hour, but in the biting air and the whipped-up snow it must have felt like sixty to the kids.

We stopped at the Crossroads and parked on the crest between three green and six tee.

"Dad," Pat pleaded, "Can we slide down three hill? Down to the marsh? That would be so fun."

"Yeah, Dad," Mark said. "Can we?"

In December 1966, the year we moved in, we had used the slope behind three green as a sliding hill. My brother Bob and his teenaged children had come from California to Michigan for my mother's funeral and we had a family gathering at our place. We built a fire at a windbreak near the Smedley property line and the kids used sleds, skis, flying saucers, and the toboggan, flying down the slope, trudging back up, until the sun set. Bob's son Matt, an avid skateboarder, thrilled the kids by going down standing up on the toboggan.

I remembered that day from four years ago as I trooped down the hill to see how firm the marsh was. With all the springs being charged up by rain and snow falling on the sandy ridges, there was always standing water in pockets of the marsh, no matter the temperature. But in this area, where the toboggan might run out, the foliage was dense, and a heavy layer of snow made footing safe.

As I climbed back up the hill I could see the kids untying the toboggan, assuming they would get the all-clear. I nodded that it would be okay and they cheered and scrambled for their places on the toboggan. Usually I would give them a big push to get them started, sending them off with a shout of "So long, suckers!" that always made them scream in mock dread. Five, ten, fifteen times they shot down the hill, most times going farther than the previous run. Every time they did, they proclaimed a "new world record."

They weren't running out of energy, but we were running out of daylight. It was time to head back to the house and I started up the tractor.

"One last time," the kids begged.

Okay, but this time it would be different. I jockeyed the toboggan to the most favorable track, one that had been packed down slick and hard. I started the run farther back, building up speed as I pushed against Mark's back. But instead of letting go, I hopped on behind, thrusting my boots up in the air because there was no place else to put them.

Down the hill we shot, far faster than I had expected. We hit the ledge near the bottom of the hill and for a split second were airborne. We landed with a thud but still plenty of momentum. We flew well past the old "world's record" and knifed through fresh snow. For a moment I wondered if our momentum would carry us straight across the marsh and into Willow Creek and I lowered my legs, ready to dig in my boots. The prow of the toboggan began to strike clusters of protruding marsh grasses and slowed us gently, fifteen feet short of the open water and many, many yards farther than any toboggan run down number three hill had ever gone before. We tumbled off the toboggan, shook off the snow and looked back up the hill. I had never been that far into the marsh before, had never seen three green from that perspective. The tractor seemed so tiny, sitting up there, and I could barely hear the engine chugging.

"Hooray!" the kids shouted. "New all-time world's record!"

April brought decent weather. We needed it for the grass to further establish in the problem spots on greens six and eight.

Our prime-the-pump ads were appearing in the *Grass Lake News* and I had done several interviews with other newspapers for articles before our May 2 opening. Bob Mather was ready to distribute, tucked into his tabloid newspaper, green-and-white bumper stickers he produced for us as a bonus, proclaiming I'VE BEEN TO THE BOONDOCKS. And of course the grapevine had been working overtime for months.

I was mowing the still-tender grass on number eight when a thought came to me. A title for the short story that had been fermenting in my head for weeks. "Super Shank," I'd call it. And now I knew just how to end it.

It was a short fiction I had dreamed up one night while Marcy and I took turns sitting up with son Mark's high fever. But for weeks the perfect ending had eluded me.

I finished the green and hurried back to the house, washed my hands, and typed out the first draft while it was hot and fresh.

There would be this golfer—call him Max the Slax—an amalgam of half a dozen characters I had known on golf courses. He dressed like a Paris pimp—chartreuse shirts speckled with amber flecks, flare-cuff pants the colors of a dying Hawaiian sunset. His tam-o'-shanter was in the plaid of the day from St. Andrews, Carnoustie, or Turnberry. To complete the ensemble, tangerine FootJoy shoes.

Max would have everything after which a totally addicted, fully obsessed golfer could lust. Everything but talent.

Actually Max had a fair swing. But a fair swing in golf is like second-best cards in poker—just good enough to be expensive—because Max was infected with two fatal conditions. First, he had a terminal case of best-game-itis. He would make wagers as if he regularly could shoot as well as his one long-ago best round. Second, he was the lowest link on the golf food chain, for Max was (one trembles even to utter the dreaded word) a shanker.

From there it was obvious where the story would go. The problem would be how to craft an ending that was at the same time unexpected and right. Of course Max would one day have that magical round in which everything falls into place. Every tee shot hit flush and into the fairway. Every iron struck crisply and onto the green. Every putt rolled true and if not into the hole, mere inches away for a tap-in. That part was easy. But how to end it so that it was true and satisfying? And more than that, so that the ending was an expression of the relevant unexpected.

Once I had nailed the ending, I sent the story to Carlton Wells, not only my old English professor and merciless critic but also himself a champion golfer. It was the shortest critique that any of my writing had ever received from him: "Bravo. As I read, I loved every line but feared for you, wondering how you could possibly end it. You found the only way."

So I sent it to my agent, Knox Burger, who had previously warned me that he stood behind no one in his detestation of golf. But he read the story and reacted the same way as Professor Wells. He got a quick, effusive, but reluctant turndown from *Sports Illustrated*, then made a quick sale to *Golf Magazine*. That $300 check arrived just in time to buy a replacement for a Jacobsen mower that had shaved its last green.

Hank Dubois drove with me to Royal Oak to pick up the reconditioned mower I had bought with proceeds from the sale of the short story. I told him where the money came from.

"Well, don't keep me in suspense," he said.

"What?"

"How does it end? What happens to old Max the Slax?"

"Oh, that. Well, he's coming up to the last green and he's got the round of his life going. Seven birdies, ten pars. He's on the eighteenth green putting for a birdie that would give him a sixty-four, a fabulous round by anyone's standards. And then it hits him, the thought that he has not dared entertain: He has played the entire round without hitting a shank. Not a single one. He has never, ever played a shankless round before.

"He's overcome with dread. He knows that he has been cursed by the golf gods and that it is impossible for him to play a full round without a shank. Yet, he's already safely on the green. So could this be the one magic day?

"He lines up the putt, begins to draw back the putter. Stops. Steps away. Addresses the putt again, but this time he lines up facing forty-five degrees to the left. The crowd that has gathered around the green is baffled. What can Max be doing? He draws back his putter, strokes, and shanks the ball! But, finally knowing and accepting his fatal weakness, he has actually played for it. The ball is shanked, all right, but it is a shot no one has ever before dared to play—an intentional shank. The ball bounces, then rolls straight and true directly into the cup.

"He marches off the green, takes his clubs and tosses them into the river behind the green. Then flings his shoes and tam-o'-shanter in behind them. He strides barefoot over the bridge, off to his car, never again to touch a club."

Hank thought about it a while.

"Can a guy actually do that?" he asked. "Intentionally play a shank? And with a putter?"

"I doubt it. But it seemed like the only way to end it."

Hank nodded.

"Works for me," he said.

MARCY CLOSED the *Huron Valley Advisor*, pushed the tabloid newspaper away, looked at me and said, "Where's the pain?"

"What pain?"

"Well, let's see. There's the agonizing over money. The doing without because the golf course has first claim to every dime. The fears, like those I felt the time you got the tractor stuck on number nine tee and I had to pull you loose in the truck, every second waiting for it to tip over and crush me. The kids' skinned knuckles from picking up a million rocks. That pain. Where the hell is the blood, sweat, and tears?"

She stared at me. My coffee had gotten cold and I wanted to get up and warm it but I knew it wouldn't be good to move just yet.

"For that matter, where are the kids and me in this story? It's just like the other articles, Bill. Bob Mather's gushy piece about you in the *Grass Lake News*, 'One Golfer's Dream Comes True.' Isn't that special. And Al Cotton's tribute to you in the *Cit-Pat* as if you're a lone hero fighting the odds, Mother Nature, and cruel fate to build a golf course single-handed."

"Now that's not fair, Marcy—"

"You bet it's not fair. Single-handed. It's like the kids and I, and Hank Dubois, and Walt Bauer, and Henry Samyn are invisible. And my sisters Bevie and Kathy and her kids and your own brother and nephews and the others who have helped, it's like we never existed. Is that the way you think of this? That you did this all by yourself? That the rest of us were just in the back seat, along for the ride?"

"You know that's not what I think. I never could have done this alone."

"Then tell me, why is it there have been three glowing articles about this place and there's nobody but you in any of them?"

"That's not what I told them, Marcy. Maybe the writers turned in copy about you and the kids and everyone else—because I sure as hell did tell them a lot more people than me had their hands in this—and the editors didn't use it."

"Now why would an editor do that?"

"Because an editor might decide it's a better story to emphasize this 'lifelong dream' angle. This 'one guy against the odds' slant."

Marcy lit a cigarette and sat there quietly, puffing. The smoke drifted toward me and I got up from the table and poured another cup of coffee. She knew that since I had quit smoking I wished she would do the same. This didn't seem like a good time to bring that up.

"No, Bill, not one guy. One superman."

"I never told them that. Never once tried to give that impression."

"Then what a coincidence they all latched onto the same things. Here's this incredible guy. Works full-time as an editor at the prestigious Institute for Social Research. Formerly involved in exotic NASA space programs. Publishes books. Writes articles and short stories for national magazines. And in his spare time single-handedly builds a golf course."

She opened the *Advisor* and tapped a finger on the last paragraph.

"Oh, I almost forgot. Here we are. 'Haney lives at the soon-to-open Boondocks Golf Course with his wife and four children.' Not important enough to have names, of course, that wife, those kids. Just five additional responsibilities for the Man of the Hour."

It was pointless to protest further. Marcy just didn't understand about these things. These three articles were terrific advance publicity. They would ensure a strong opening next weekend, on May 2. No, they hadn't been written as I would have written them myself. But it was great publicity. And that was what mattered. Wasn't it? And I really hadn't botched those interviews—all three of them—so badly that the reporters each went away thinking the same thing, that this was a Herculean effort by a single individual. Had I?

Twenty-Five

It was time.

I was thirty-three years old and had been looking forward to this day for fully two-thirds of those years. For the last three years and nine months, Marcy and the kids and I had been building toward this day. In just three days, the golf course would be open to the public and I had somehow forgotten to do something I had promised myself for more years than I could remember.

I had not yet played a real round of golf on my own course.

Countless times I had played each hole or sequences of holes. I had played straight through from the first tee to the last green many times, but always playing several balls to get as many shots from as many angles as possible. But never had I played a single ball in a fully regulation round of golf.

Traditionally, the owner, designer, architect, and construction chief are the first foursome to play a legitimate round on a new course. The owner putts out first on the last green and so, however briefly, he can claim to hold a course record.

Because I wore all four hats, I would be a foursome of one.

It was the Wednesday before our opening on Saturday, May 2, and I had taken off the entire week as vacation time to make final preparations. With the kids in school, Marcy shopping, and the workers not coming until later in the day, the course was totally mine.

It surprised me that I felt nothing special about that first tee shot, nor the pitching wedge that nestled eight feet from the pin. But when the birdie putt dropped into the cup, it hit me that it was real. The course was no longer a dream—it was something real in nature.

As I hoisted the bag onto my shoulder and headed for the second tee, I wondered how long it would be before my brothers Dick and Bob would play this course with me. Dick, who had gotten me the dump truck and Worthington tractor that had been so important in the construction. Bob, who had taken me onto a golf course for the first time, just weeks after he got out of a military hospital and was still recovering from forty-four months in Japanese prisoner-of-war camps.

Bob had left home when I was six months old and had spent four years in China before being captured in the fall of Corregidor, so I was almost ten years old when he came home after months in military hospitals to stay at our house. Most of the time he was off by himself and Mother said not to bother him, he had issues to work out. Then, one day he brought home a brand-new set of golf clubs.

Come on with me, Billy, he says. We're going golfing at Sylvan Glen and you're going to be my caddie.

On the first hole, in the left-hand rough, I find a Spalding Kro-Flite. When I show it to Bob, he tells me it's a lost ball. Should I take it back to

the pro shop and turn it in, I say, so when the golfer asks about it, they'll give it to him?

Bob smiles. "Golf balls are still scarce because they stopped making them during the war. But they're not that valuable. Put it in your pocket. That ball is now yours."

As I lug Bob's bag I check that pocket every few steps to make sure my Kro-Flite is still there. Every tee box has a ball washer, a shiny white metal box with scrubbers inside. It's filled with water, and there's this red wooden handle with a slot where you put the ball and then you work the handle up and down real fast. But not when someone's teeing off or they'll back way and give you a dirty look.

"You're going to wear the paint off that ball, Billy," Bob says, but not in a mean way like Dad would. And the ball is as shiny as new so I stop washing it and just leave it in my dungarees pocket but I'll keep checking it, just in case.

Bob swings real hard, so I back away another step. Sometimes when he tees off with the big-headed driver, the ball goes rocketing down the fairway in a line drive that would knock over any centerfielder. Other times, when he hits the ball from the fairway or the rough, it soars real high—that's when he uses the wooden-headed club with a number three on it, except that he calls it a spoon, and that's a silly name for a golf club, but I don't say so.

I hurry to keep up with him. He takes long fast steps and I have to almost run sometimes, and the clubs rattle in the bag. That makes him look over his shoulder at me. He doesn't say anything but I know what that look means—That's valuable sports equipment there, Billy, not toys, and it must be treated carefully.

We come to a creek, and I dip in the little towel that hangs in a hook from the bag and while we hurry down the fairway, I wipe the dirt and grass stains off the faces of the clubs. "Good job, Billy," Bob says, "Can't hit clean shots with dirty clubs."

We catch up to the group ahead—Bob calls it a threesome—and they invite us to play along with them. I'm glad because that will give me a chance to look at their clubs and watch their swings. But Bob says "Thanks, no. I play alone." One man kind of snorts and says, "Suit yourself." And they go on without us.

While we wait for the threesome to get out of range, I go around the front of the tee box and find a bunch of broken wooden tees and some that aren't *even broken or chipped. "A lot of rich people must play this course," I say to Bob, and I show him a big handful of perfect tees. I sit down on the green wooden bench next to Bob and count my tees. I see hundreds of little holes poked in the wood of the bench and I run my finger over them.*

"Golf spikes," Bob says, and he shakes his head. "People stand on this bench to see if the group in front is out of the hollow yet."

A bell rings.

"Hear that, Billy? They have a bell on a post up the fairway. When the group is out of range they ring that bell. No point in standing on this bench and poking it full of spike holes. What's the matter with people?"

People. For sure when I get my first pair of golf shoes, I'm not going to stand on any bench. I just take one of my broken tees and use the sharp point to scrape the dirt out of the grooves on the irons.

"That's the idea, Billy."

I say, "Can't hit clean shots with dirty clubs."

That evening, Hank Dubois showed up to see if I needed a hand. I did, I told him. I needed someone to play my second round of golf on The Boondocks with me. Hank asked what the first round was like. I told him it was like your first kiss. Maybe the first kiss isn't the best one you'll ever have, but it will always be the first.

Twenty-Six

It was ten p.m., May 1, 1970, and in a few hours it would be Opening Day for The Boondocks Golf Course.

The Three M's—Marcy, Mary Jane Dubois, and Mary Joseph— were still working on the pro shop when Hank Dubois and I went out in the pickup truck to put the final touches on the golf course. We filled the ball washers and put out fresh tee towels. We made sure there were trash barrels at every tee and that the tee markers were in place. We positioned the dozens of directional signs we had cut, sanded, lettered, and lacquered so they would be easy for golfers to follow. We took a last look at the greens sporting their latest checkerboard cut.

When we drove back in the rough between numbers three and nine fairways, we saw that every light was on in the barns and we could see through the big picture windows of the pro shop how much Marcy and her crew had done. It looked like a real pro shop. Marcy had laid out items in the ancient showcase we had bought for thirty dollars and spiffed it up as it hadn't been in fifty years. She had it neatly arranged with golf paraphernalia including golf shirts, socks, tam-o'-shanters, baseball-style golf caps, and visors, and had fanned a spray of golf gloves of every size, color, and style.

We didn't have rack after rack of sets of woods and irons or expensive golf slacks on hangers. But we did have, as a tribute to tradition in this age of stepped-down metal shafts, a nice collection of handmade Otey Crissman putters. The Oteys were painstakingly fashioned in Selma, Alabama, with seasoned hickory shafts and shaved leather grips. We had bought an overstock of closed-out golf bag models from Spalding for what amounted to 70 percent discount. So, leaning up against the walls were two dozen golf bags from the old standby white canvas Sunday stick bag to multipocket, garish monsters that would make their owner a standout at any club.

There were golf balls: three kinds of Acushnets—Club Specials at three for two dollars for the entry-level player, Pinnacles for the medium handicappers, and the top-of-the-line Titleists, used by the very best golfers as well as by many who never would hit a single shot well enough to justify playing the world's finest golf ball. In my days in the pro shop at Sylvan Glen, I marveled at how many golfers bought Titleists not because they were the best for their swing, but simply because that was the ball the pros used.

As a kid, I grimaced when I would find a shiny Titleist in the woods or fish one out of a pond and it would have a huge gash in the cover (ironically called a "smile"), put there by a golfer who would have been much better off playing a lower-compression, tough-covered ball. Many golfers never understood that unless you could generate the clubhead speed to fully compress a golf ball, you could actually hit a lower-compression or "soft" cover ball farther than a high-compression "hard" ball like the pros use. Next to the Titleists were our own "club balls"—the mid-range Acushnet stamped simply "The Boondocks."

On the wide shelf behind the counter, we had the small oven to heat the sandwiches I would bring home twice a week from Krazy Jim's Blimpee Burger in Ann Arbor. Next to the oven was the intercom we used to communicate back and forth with the house. We had it set now to monitor the kids sleeping in the house.

Resting on the display-case front counter was a big white plastic tub full of the golf balls Carlton Wells had brought out in bushel baskets. This was the donated bounty from Carlton's forty years of daily dawn bird-watching walks along the railroad tracks bordering Huron Hills Golf Course. His pockets were often bulging when he returned home—one pocket full of scrap paper and litter he found along the way and the others chock-full of golf balls.

Some of these used balls were showcase new; others were of types that hadn't been manufactured for decades. Some were duds yellowed with age. But nearly all were serviceable to some golfer or other, so in they went, into the tub to which Marcy had affixed a hand-lettered sign, "Previously Owned Balls – Choice, 50 cents, Five for Two Dollars."

Mary Jane Dubois put the third coat of white masonry paint on the fieldstone wall and turned her brush to the molding around the doors and windows. Hank and I adjusted the door we had just hung between the pro shop and the maintenance area. There was an ugly but efficient twenty-five-year-old Frigidaire we shoved around the corner into the storage area so it couldn't be seen if you

were standing in the pro shop, but the regulars would soon learn they could open the door, reach in for a cold one, and put a donation in the can. Besides the beer—which of course was not legally available for sale—the fridge was full of soda pop, meltable candy bars, and the sandwiches from Krazy Jim's.

At one a.m., Hank and Mary Jane left, dropping Mary Joseph off on the way. An hour later, Marcy and I finished cleaning up the paint drips, wiped the floor, and cleaned the display-case glass yet another one last time. We decided to leave the windows open for the rest of the night to air out the paint fumes. Then, for the first time all day for both of us, we sat down.

Marcy lit her usual morning Winston. I had quit smoking for good a year earlier, something I had done several times over the past ten years. But this time I was determined to stick with it, for all the usual reasons, and one special one. A year ago, Mark, Jenni, and Pat had come up to me solemnly as I sat sipping a cup of coffee and smoking a Pall Mall.

"Daddy, we don't want you to smoke any more," Mark said, and his brother and sister, eyes wide and lips pursed, nodded vigorously.

"We don't want you to die," Jenni said.

"That would make us sad," Pat said.

And so, just a year ago, after twenty years of on and off smoking any tobacco that burned, I snubbed out that cigarette and had not inhaled a firsthand puff of tobacco smoke since.

But on an impulse, I decided that this special opening day called for a special moment, a symbolic punctuation mark to all that had gone before, a salute to all that would be. So knowing that in four hours the sun would rise on a newly opened Boondocks Golf Course, I poured a fresh cup of coffee and—without having planned to do it—reached into the display case and took the first Dutch Master Dart from a cigar box. Marcy gave me a look as I peeled the wrapper, licked the cigar, and bit off the tip.

"What?" I asked.

I snapped a kitchen match to flame with my thumbnail and fired it up. Just like old times.

We sat at the small table by the east picture window and luxuriated for what I fully expected to be the last time in a good long while. Marcy filled her glass from a Pepsi bottle and puffed her Winston. I was about to urge her yet again to quit smoking herself, but with a smoldering cigar clenched in my lips, that seemed somehow untimely.

"When do you think they'll start showing up?" Marcy asked.

I took a deep drag and inhaled the blue smoke to the very bottom of my lungs. Funny, after a year off tobacco, I half expected to explode into a fit of coughing. I held the smoke a couple seconds and then blew a series of perfect smoke rings, one inside the last inside the last. Just like riding a bike—the kid hadn't lost the touch. The blue-gray rings drifted to the ceiling, melded, and dissolved.

"Could be as early as 6:30. That story in the *Citizen-Patriot* is bound to stir some interest. We already know Bob Mather's article in the *Grass Lake News* has people around the village talking. Those 'I've Been to The Boondocks' bumper stickers are already all over town. I don't know if the piece in the *Huron Valley Advisor* will draw many from Ann Arbor and Ypsilanti, but there should be a few. We'll see where they're coming from when we check the signup sheet."

Marcy looked at me closely. "How's it feel? This is something you've wanted to do since long before I met you."

We had been so busy for so many days, and up all night last night, that I really hadn't had a chance to think about it until then. And when I did, I heard myself answering, "It feels . . . I feel . . . lousy. My chest. It's—"

"What's the matter? Your face is all red."

"Hurts to breathe. Marcy, I think I'm having a heart attack."

She leaned across the table and looked closely at me. "Your arms. Do you feel any numbness, tingling?"

"Arms fine. My chest. Heart. It's my heart. Dammit, finally ready to open course . . . always wanted—"

"Just relax. It'll pass."

"—and I'll be dead . . . heart attack . . . before first ball is struck."

"No you won't. It's probably just nerves. And lack of sleep. And . . . that cigar. When's the last time you smoked?"

"It's a heart attack, dammit. Only took two drags, maybe three. I don't know . . . a year ago. Around last Easter, maybe. Pat's birthday, I think. April 17, last year."

Marcy put out her cigarette and my cigar.

"Then that's what caused it. I didn't know you intended to inhale."

"Neither did I. Just happened."

"Well, just sit there and rest for a few minutes. You'll see. It'll pass."

I shook my head. "Only thing going to pass is me. Right the hell on out of this world."

"Just relax. Sit there perfectly still. And then we'll go in and get a couple hours' sleep. You'll feel better then. And don't worry about the golfers—we're ready for them."

Marcy was good at silence. She knew the best thing was not to do or say anything for a few minutes. That whatever this was—and she was certain it was nothing more than those couple of inhaled puffs of a cigar—would pass.

What Marcy didn't know was that this time she was wrong. Dead wrong. Okay, so I was feeling just a little bit better. But I knew it was just temporary relief. A second wave would hit any minute now. Stronger than the first. These heart attacks can be sneaky. I thought about going into the maintenance area, finding a comfortable place to die. Thinking about it, there really wasn't any convenient place. The pallets were stacked to the ceiling with sacks of fertilizer, seed, and supplies. Moving a couple of those heavy sacks to make a comfortable spot to lie down, that would be all it would take and I'd be dead on the cold concrete floor. The golfers come in, say, Bill around? Marcy says, Sure. He's on the other side of that door, stone cold dead on the maintenance room floor. That'll put a damper on your opening day.

"Marcy, I haven't been as good a person as I had hoped, but not as bad a person as I had feared."

"Work on it, Bill. A little long for a tombstone. Come on. We're going in to get some sleep."

Then again, maybe she had a point. Just sitting here quietly for a few minutes, I was starting to feel a little better. Actually, a lot better. The cool, fresh breeze was nice.

Marcy didn't have to say "I told you so." We both knew she was right. And I knew something else: at that moment I went from being a smoker who wasn't smoking and metamorphosed into a nonsmoker, even a fierce anti-smoker. I knew that was the last tobacco I would ever have. Yes, and I would inspire the rest of the world to quit, too.

Okay, maybe for just this once, Marcy was right. Maybe with a couple hours' sleep when the sun came up on opening day, I'd still be alive. Maybe.

WHEN THE ALARM WENT OFF, the sun was just rising over the fence line to the east of number one fairway. Saturday. May 2, 1970. Opening Day.

I heard the popping of a two-cycle engine and looked out the north window. Our newest greensmowerman and another high school friend of Mary Joseph's, Kenny Younkin, had finished mowing the practice green and was starting on number two green. Danny Campbell had finished number one and far off I could see his tiny figure starting on number three. I had gone over the sequence with them, stressing the importance of getting the early holes finished first, saving numbers eight and nine for last. Once you had a steady stream of golfers on the course, it was impossible to mow greens.

We got out to the pro shop quickly, started the coffee, and turned on the electric heater.

In another hour, all the greens would be mowed out. The tees, fairways, and collars had been finished the day before. I heard the distant muffled sound of a car door slamming in the parking lot to the west of the pole barn. Customers.

As the first golfers came into the pro shop to buy their greens fees tickets, something struck me that I hadn't thought about. The last time I was behind a pro shop counter was twelve years before, when I was a college sophomore at the University of Michigan. While that had been an important job, it was just that—a job. I felt pride in Sylvan Glen Golf Course because I had worked there in so many different capacities and I didn't like to hear any criticism of it. But if I heard a disparaging comment about the layout, I didn't take it personally because the course had been designed many years ago by someone else. But The Boondocks was my creation. It was my statement about character in a golf course. It reflected my judgment of the best destiny for this piece of land.

I could understand if someone didn't like it. In golf, as in everything else, there is no accounting for differences in personal taste. So I expected that some people would simply not like our golf course, for whatever reasons. I just didn't want to hear about it.

I decided that the best place for me to be was any place but the pro shop. Marcy, aware of my unease, took over as I fled to the comfort

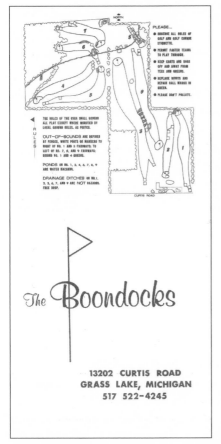

The Boondocks

13202 CURTIS ROAD
GRASS LAKE, MICHIGAN
517 522-4245

MEN'S COURSE

BLUE TEES					Hole			RED TEES		
YARDS	PAR	HDCP						YARDS	PAR	HDCP
355	4	(9)			1			340	4	(9)
225	3	(2)			2			180	3	(8)
545	5	(1)			3			480	5	(1)
415	4	(4)			4			350	4	(6)
410	4	(5)			5			350	4	(5)
405	4	(3)			6			330	4	(4)
390	4	(7)			7			380	4	(3)
200	3	(8)			8			160	3	(7)
470	5	(6)			9			390	4	(2)
3415	36				TOTAL			3060	35	

WOMEN'S COURSE

YELLOW TEES					Hole			WHITE TEES		
280	4	(8)			1			270	4	(7)
150	3	(9)			2			140	3	(8)
465	5	(1)			3			410	5	(1)
340	4	(3)			4			330	4	(3)
340	4	(7)			5			300	4	(5)
290	4	(5)			6			250	4	(6)
330	4	(6)			7			320	4	(4)
145	3	(4)			8			80	3	(9)
380	4	(2)			9			360	4	(2)
2720	35				TOTAL			2460	35	

of my tractor seat. And there was grass to mow—not on the playable golf course, but the practice range and the meadow beyond the oak woods, far to the left of number three fairway. Away from the action but where I could see the cars entering the parking lot from Curtis Road and watch the golfers moving along the fairways.

All morning long they continued to stream in. By nine a.m., the first foursome putted out on the last hole and headed for the pro shop. We would soon have our first reactions to our four years of work.

When I couldn't avoid it any longer I parked the tractor well away from the barns, walked around the pole barn, and came into the underside of the big barn through the maintenance shop sliding door. From there I walked to the inside door into the pro shop, steeled myself, and went in to face whatever the music might be. The first thing I wanted to hear was that golfers liked the course and the last thing I wanted to hear was anything else.

That first group to finish was a foursome from Vandercook Lake, a suburb of Jackson, and they said the course lived up to what they had read in the *Citizen-Patriot*. Sporty. Demanding. Old-style. A second foursome came in, and a third, and soon the little pro shop was jammed with golfers sharing their reactions. A couple of comments were especially good to hear: "Looks like one of those old Scottish courses . . . darned nice greens for a new course." And my personal favorite: "Must have been easy enough to build, Mother Nature designed it for you."

So far, so good.

Then, coming through the door, unexpected, a familiar face. Jim Owens, a friend from the past.

I knew Jim when we caddied at Red Run, and a few years later he showed up while I was working the pro shop at Sylvan Glen. He told me he was going to the University of Michigan on an Evans Scholarship from the Western Golf Association. He teamed up with the captain of U of M's golf team, Bob McMasters, to goad me into applying for the Evans, even though I already was content with the two other scholarships I had to U of M.

Three years later, a roommate in the Evans House introduced me to Marcy, something that otherwise never would have happened. If not for Jim, no Marcy, no four great kids. Everything different.

During my junior year at Michigan, in the fall of 1956, I took a job as a cook in a restaurant seven miles outside Ann Arbor. Because I worked at the student newspaper, I was granted one of only four permits to own, drive, and park a car on campus. I talked the restaurant owner into letting me experiment with some abandoned pizza ovens and letting Jim Owens drive my 1950 Plymouth to deliver pizzas into Ann Arbor and the U of M campus.

We named the place Pizza from the Prop because somehow a propeller from a passing airplane impaled itself in the parking lot—a sign from the heavens, we decided, because no plane crash was ever reported. Our most effective promotion was with a series of upside-down cheap ads in the student newspaper, the *Michigan Daily*. That worked so well we distributed funky fliers and bridge score pads with our menu on one side, including prominent phone numbers and the words that seemed so natural but had never been used before in the pizza business: FREE DELIVERY. And we could do that because we had gotten a handyman to build heated, insulated boxes that kept the pizza hot. They were big, cumbersome, boxy things—and they worked. The concept was simple and obvious: If the customer can't come to the pizza . . .

Along about ten p.m., when student stomachs started growling, the phone orders would start pouring in. In less than a year Pizza from the Prop was the hottest thing in town. In two years, there were three outlets, all thriving. And five years after the first free pizza delivery business in the United States was started with Jim Owens driving my 1950 Plymouth to deliver pizza that I had cooked in a brick oven in a restaurant seven miles outside Ann Arbor, the business was sold and renamed. The new name was Domino's.

In the years since those college days, Jim and I had laughed about our pioneering pizza efforts, about hearing the Domino's CEO, Tom Monaghan, call me "the real father of free pizza delivery." For that billion-dollar brainstorm, Jim Owens and I each earned $1.50 an hour. I reminded Jim there was a difference—he got tips. He reminded me that while he was out in the cold weather driving on icy roads, I was in front of a warm pizza oven with Marcy, my date, nearby taking phone orders and cutting and boxing pizza.

With that shared history I shouldn't have been surprised that Jim showed up on opening day. And not to play golf, but to help out.

Help out he did. By mid-morning Marcy and I felt the effects of very little sleep for three days. While we took a break and a refreshing nap, Jim minded the pro shop.

JUST AFTER NOON, I walked back down to the pro shop to see how Jim was doing.

It had quieted down so we sat and talked. I told Jim there was only one thing missing in the inauguration of this course which owed so much, as did all golf courses everywhere, to Scotland, the cradle of golf. That was a true Scot to baptize it.

As a boy working at Sylvan Glen and Red Run, I had learned very early that the Scots are not only passionate about golf, they are proprietary about the game. They had good reason to feel that way, several centuries of it.

Bill Catto, my boss at Sylvan Glen, was one of a legion of Scots who built or maintained golf courses in Michigan and were themselves the distilled essence of the game. By the time they were done transplanting the Scottish national pastime, they had made the state of Michigan—despite its short season—one of the world's golf meccas. I lamented to Jim that the Scots dearest to me were gone now, would never see the course Marcy, the kids, and I had built, would never see in it the extension of their influence.

Then, as if on cue, I saw a familiar angular figure coming around the pole barn from the parking lot. Angus Campbell, my boss at the institute, my mentor, and my friend. Now I had at least one pure Scot to christen the course. I had hoped Angus would come eventually but I knew how busy he was so I had not counted on his presence on opening day.

Angus rested his clubs against the bag rail, then looked around at the place. I went out to say hello to him and his three guests.

"Well, you actually did, didn't you?" Angus said.

Over those last four years, Angus had quizzed me often on our progress in building the course. It was clear from his tour guide's description to his guests that he remembered what I had told him. It felt strange to hear someone else describing, and more eloquently than I could have, what we were trying to do here.

I watched as he teed off on the first hole with a classical fluid swing that sent his drive well down number one fairway. Clearly Angus had not spent all his youth in the classroom.

It was late afternoon when Angus and his group putted out on number nine for the second time. They had played their first round from the red tees, as I suggested. The second time around, they moved back to the blues, which brought several of the ponds into play. I had missed seeing them at the turn so I was anxious to hear Angus's reaction.

"I never took you for a sadist," Angus said, but with a smile. He went on to tell me he had come a cropper of number four, one of the easier holes, on his second turn around the links. He had parred the hole in his first round, then got careless with his tee shot the next time and sliced his drive far into the marsh. The seven on his scorecard was the only blemish on a good round, but he went on to say that it took away none of the enjoyment and admiration for what we had fashioned from the old farm.

Angus's critique was much the same as we had been hearing all day. Low-handicap golfers playing from the back tees found the layout challenging but fair. Less capable players said they appreciated the options offered of playing to a safe landing area instead of having to hit shots beyond their abilities and were able to avoid most of the hazards. Many complimented the greens. Almost everyone said the course reminded them of Scottish courses they had seen in photographs or on television—which we took as high praise.

Jim Owens, Marcy, and I looked out the big picture window and watched the last golfers hole out their putts on the ninth green.

If some were dissatisfied, we had yet to hear that. Still, we were sure some would have ignored our admonition to play from the front tees the first time around to reduce the threat posed by the six ponds. Those who were in over their heads would surely have found it too difficult and would probably spread their criticisms. The course was not that tough but golfers are a brash lot and most have an inflated opinion of their own abilities. Most of the area golf courses had no water hazards at all and so regulars from those courses were used to being able to hit a "worm-burner" and still have it remain on safe ground.

While some customers who are unhappy with a department store or restaurant simply leave in silence and never come back, that often is not the case with the typical golfer. He came out for enjoyment, for a pleasant break from the pressures of his job—and what does he get? His ball came to rest in an unrepaired divot. He had to hit out of an unraked sand trap. As if that wasn't bad enough, just as he was stroking a testy four-foot putt a bird sang and unnerved him. If a putt hits a spike mark and veers away from the cup, that's not the fault of some golfer ahead of them, it's that goddamn lazy greenskeeper or that cheapskate who owns the place.

I had seen this on the golf courses of my youth. I had been chastised while on duty at the pro shop at Sylvan Glen because the fairway on the number twelve was burned out or the cup on number six had a ragged edge and a putt spun out.

We expected some grumbling because The Boondocks, like any new course, had its birthmarks. The grass had not filled in completely on the approach to number four green. Number eight green—the last one we had seeded—was sparse in a couple small spots. And there were visible areas that needed work that weren't part of the course.

I could imagine each golfer somehow hitting his ball into these bad patches and going away grousing about what a cow pasture the place was. If some felt that way, not a single one expressed it to us. To the contrary, they loved it.

At dusk, the course was still. The sky was clear and the temperature was falling. It would be a crisp night and another sunny day tomorrow. We were halfway through our opening weekend. So far it was a success.

By ten o'clock, Marcy was already sound asleep. She certainly had earned it. With all the final preparations over the last couple days, she had only a couple hours' sleep, then there was the long, hectic opening day. I was tired too, but I was wired and wide awake. I laid there in bed, going over it all again, our first day open to the public.

Just hours ago, but it already seemed so long ago that I had sat there in the pro shop in the dark of night with Marcy, truly believing I was having a heart attack and would never live to see the first golfer play the course I had wanted all my life to build.

Then to have Angus Campbell show up and bring a foursome. Jim Owens coming to pitch in. And then more than 150 golfers, some from many miles away.

All those thoughts—I couldn't sleep. I got up and went downstairs, made coffee, and thought about it. About those countless thousands of days working on golf courses. At Sylvan Glen, I had mowed greens, built tees, and planted trees. I had raked sand traps, baled hay, learned to drive tractors and trucks. I had done a trick as night watering man, run the pro shop, sold clubs, and given golf lessons. Earlier in the day, Jim Owens and I had reminisced how at age eleven I had shagged balls for Gene Sarazen on the Red Run practice range, graduated to caddying, caddied for Sam Snead, and got my first "management position" as assistant to the caddie master.

The first couple of years I caddied at Red Run, I stayed to myself. I still remembered how it felt sitting for hours on the log rail that was set up for the long line of Trainee or "C" caddies. There were more than a hundred of us who went there day after day after day without hearing our names called.

Jim Owens is a year older than me. He knows Ty Damon, the assistant caddie master, and the older boys who clean clubs and shine shoes and do stuff around the pro shop. That means his card gets put in a smaller stack with the old caddies and he gets out a lot. Today it rained so much that all but two caddies gave up and went home. I waited around, trying to decide whether to run for the Martin bus when I saw it make the turn at Twelve Mile Road and head north toward Big Beaver. But now the sun is coming out and some golfers are coming from the men's grille.

"Haney! You gonna just sit there all day or you gonna loop."

Ty Damon says he just called my name three times and now I have to tell him if I'm deaf or just stupid. He's a lot older, at least eighteen, and he wears the flashiest clothes of any of the pro shop helpers. The older pro shop men—the real assistant pros—pick on him and so he picks on the caddies and they pick on the trainee caddies and they didn't have anyone to pick on.

"Well, Haney, which is it?"

"Is what, Mr. Damon?"

"Deaf or stupid? Remember, I know you can hear me, so that leaves only one. Even a kid from Big Beaver should be able to figure that out. Which is it? Deaf? Stupid?"

I know I'll never get a bag again if I give the wrong answer.

"Stupid, Mr. Damon."

"Did you just call me Stupid Mr. Damon?"

"No sir, I—"

"Ty," Tom Talkington says, "just give the kid his bag."

"Yes sir, Mr. Talkington," Ty Damon says, and scowls at me. I'm always getting someone in trouble.

Mr. Damon makes us call him Mister or we'll get a demerit and if you get three demerits for fighting or sassing or whatever, you're out of here. Mr. Damon has a favorite name for young caddies. Every young caddie is "punchy loopy." Punchy loopy Owens. Punchy loopy Haney. Mr. Damon doesn't dare call Bob McMasters punchy loopy because Bob is taller, tougher, and the best caddie golfer anywhere.

Anyhow, Mr. Damon gives caddie lessons first thing Mondays, which is caddie day. You have to attend five sessions in a row before you earn your red and yellow caddie badge with a printed number and your own name printed on a little card. But you could print your name on the card or have your mother do it on a typewriter if you want people to read it. Then you slip the card into a little window from the back of the badge, next to the pin you use to hook the badge onto your tee shirt or your baseball cap.

The regular caddie badge is neat because then you can hand in your dumb "Trainee" badge, but you still have to attend four more "Coach the Caddie" sessions before you can play on Caddies Day. If you start in April, it's June before you can play on Caddies Day. Lots of kids stop coming back by then. Besides the money you can earn, the biggest reason for being a caddie is playing for free on your country club course on Mondays.

After Mr. Talkington spoke to him, Mr. Damon slid a bag to me over the counter of the bag storage room. I know that bag. That big, yellow, cracked leather thing is the ugliest bag anybody has ever seen. I know whose bag it is.

Still, I look at the bag tag, hoping I'm wrong.

"That's right, punchy loopy. You win the prize." Mr. Damon leans forward and whispers to me, "You've got yourself a loop with the legendary Flat-Rate Flood." The only good thing, there's Jim Owens coming from the men's locker room, carrying a bag. Maybe we'll be in the foursome together.

Aubrey Flood is the loop caddies run away and hide from. He always has a scowl on his face, and that scary thick mustache and that ratty tam o'shanter he pulls down over his bushy eyebrows. Every caddie at Red Run knows that before you get down the first fairway, he'll be complaining about you to the other players in his foursome. He'll gripe about the weather, the slow group ahead, someone honking a car horn a half mile away. He'll grouse about his ball landing in a divot and about unfixed ball marks on the green. But most of all he'll grumble about how lousy caddies are these days, not like when he was a kid, carrying at the Detroit city courses for a quarter a round, and no soft drink treat at the turn either, not like these lazy kids today all take for granted.

Nobody wants to caddie for Mr. Aubrey Flood. Nobody wants to play with him. He doesn't have a regular foursome. He always shows up alone, looking for an opening. But Aubrey Flood is a very successful businessman in Royal Oak and a member of long standing at Red Run Golf Club, so the starter has no choice but to fit him into a group if a player doesn't show. He must be at least fifty-five, way older than the good players he sometimes gets paired with. With his eighteen handicap he plays a different game than the others in the foursome. On the long holes, he will be hitting his fourth shot when everyone else is on the green in two or three, waiting to putt.

Mr. Flood's golf bag may be ugly but it sure is heavy. When we get to the second hole, the players take their drivers and walk back a hundred yards to the tee leaving us caddies to fore-caddie. We sit down behind a bunker and I unzip the big side bags to see just what all this weight is I'm lugging around. There are two dozen Spalding Dots, still in their pre-war boxes, six-year old balls. I know that soon after World War II broke out, manufacturers stopped producing golf balls because the rubber was needed for the War. Golfers hoarded all the balls they could find. The war's been over for three years but I guess some people like cheapskate Flood can't bear not using up the old balls. These balls are so dead that when you hit them, instead of a sharp click you get a sick thunk.

In another compartment, there's an extra pair of golf spikes with those heavy wooden shoe trees still in them. And a nearly full bottle of Jamison Irish Whiskey.

"What a pack rat old man Flood is," Jim Owens says.

Big Jack Hoxie, the other caddie in our foursome, snorts at me and says, "After toting that crap around four and a half hours in this steam bath, you'll get a buck fifty and a 'below average' check on your caddie card. Just right for a punch loopy like you."

I'll bet Big Jack is at least twenty. He's carrying double, one bag on each shoulder. He scowls if you even talk to him, so Jim and I stay out of his way.

I watch Mr. Flood the first few holes and by the fourth hole I've got a good idea how he hits the ball and which club he should use. So I hand him a club before he has to ask for it. He looks at me, surprised, the first time, but after that, it's like he expects I'll know.

On the fifth hole, he gets behind a tree and is going to try a shot I know could hurt him. I point out the root under his ball and tell him he might sprain his wrist or bend his club shaft if he hits down on it. He nods and changes his mind and carefully chips the ball back out into the fairway.

On the next tee, we're waiting for the group ahead to get out of range and Mr. Flood walks over to me. "Where do you go to school, son?"

It's the first thing he has said to me except for, "Here, boy, wash this ball."

Then he asks my name and where I live and who is my favorite Detroit Tiger. He asks if I know that Dizzy Trout, the Tigers pitcher, can hit the ball farther with a four iron than these other fellows can with a driver.

When Mr. Flood goes over to tee off, Jim Owens gives me a strange look. "Someone must have put a spell on that man."

By the time we get to the back nine, the other golfers in our foursome are kidding with Mr. Flood. They tell him he's playing so well they're going to have his handicap investigated. He smiles.

Coming off the eighteenth green, Mr. Flood hands me his putter and golf glove and stands there adding up his score.

"Eighty-three. That's the lowest score I've had on this course in fifteen years." And he smiles and squeezes my shoulder.

I wait with the other caddies by the window where the caddie master gets the pay cards and the rating cards from the golfers. The caddie master has gone for the day, so Bob Gajda, an assistant pro, is doing the cards.

"Mr. Flood," he says. "I want to be sure I have this right." And Mr. Gajda shows the card to Mr. Flood. Mr. Flood checks the card, nods his head, then waves to me and goes into

282

the men's grille.

"All right, boys," Mr. Gajda says. "Come and get it. But not so fast. No pay until you've read your rating cards."

"I don't believe it," Jim Owens says, looking over my shoulder at the rating Mr. Flood gave me. "He even wrote a comment."

I read the words again and again. Next to the Outstanding box, there's a big checkmark and some writing. "Great job," it says. "Knows how to club his player. Polite. This young man deserves promotion to captain caddie."

Jim comes back with his pay and I go up for mine. I hand my card to Mr. Gajda and he counts out two quarters, then one dollar, two dollars, three dollars. I stare at it.

"You gotta be kidding," Jack Hoxie says. "I get four bucks for lugging two bags and this squirt gets three-fifty from Flat-Rate Flood. And captain caddie? That's a laugh. Owens, how much you get? Two-fifty? That's more like it, but I still got hosed. Three-fifty this shrimp gets from Flat-Rate Flood."

"Kid," Jim Owens says, "I think you might have a future."

Twenty-Seven

Mr. Haney, there's something wrong with the greens," Kenny Younkin shouted through the pro shop window. The sun had just risen on the second day that we were open but overnight the temperature had plummeted. I went out with Kenny toward the practice green to see what was wrong. The air was perfectly still and the rising sun glinted off sheets of light frost rather than dewdrops.

The routine was that the boys would make one quick round with cane poles to whip the dew off the greens before golfers showed up and before the sun rose high enough to be magnified through dewdrops and burn the roots of the tender bent grass. Cane-pole whipping also broke up worm casts and raised the grass blades to give a more uniform cut. And it was the traditional way to do golf greens.

"See, I started to whip the green and wherever I stepped, look what happened."

Kenny pointed at the green but didn't have to. Wherever he had taken a step, there was his black footprint.

"I didn't do anything, Mr. Haney. I just started to whip the grass and when I looked down that's what I saw. Is the green ruined?"

"No, Kenny. It looks a lot worse than it is. It's the frost. Don't do any more until I get back. I have to get out there and stop Danny from walking on his greens."

I couldn't drive the tractor or truck on frost-coated fairways and leave black tracks, so I jogged out in the rough between numbers three and nine fairways, following Danny's path, easy enough to see. The mower wheel tracks and his black footprints were not as prominent in the long grass compared with the practice green, but I had to reach Danny before he started whipping number three, his first green. He was running his mower up the slope to park it alongside the green and with the noise of the engine didn't hear me coming up behind him. I waited until he put the mower up on its kickstand and shut off the engine. He was startled when he turned around and saw me there.

I told Danny that bent grass could withstand frost or even being completely frozen. But what the tender blades could not take was being stepped on or lashed with the cane pole while they were still frost-covered and brittle. The root and crown of grass plants wouldn't be permanently damaged, only the exposed blade. There were already black footprints on the part of the green where Kenny had stepped and they would be there for a few days until new blade grew out from the crown.

"Danny, just wait a few more minutes until the sun melts the frost, then go ahead with whipping before you circle back and mow."

As I walked back toward the pro shop, I remembered the weather forecast from the night before. I should have told Danny and Kenny to stay off the greens until the frost melted.

I looked at number nine green as I passed it on the way to the pro shop. Because it faced north, it would be the last to melt, but it could still be whipped and mowed long before a golfer reached it. I angled over to number one and found it already mostly melted, as was the top level of number two green. Kenny was standing guard by the practice green, explaining to a couple of foursomes why they had to wait to stroke a few putts.

Our first weekend open and already we were being ambushed by freakish weather. But the golfers understood and were patient. They had heard about the place from friends, had read about it in various newspapers, and decided it was worth waiting another half hour or so to venture into The Boondocks.

I WAS IN MY OFFICE at the Institute for Social Research building in Ann Arbor, looking up Carlton Wells's number in the faculty directory when the phone rang. It was Carlton.

"Professor Wells, I was just going to call you to tell you how our opening weekend—"

"May I come see you, William?"

"Certainly, I want to tell you about—"

"I would like to come right now, please." His tone was cold, his voice hollow.

"Well, sure. Of course. Is there something the matter?"

But he had already hung up.

Five minutes later, Professor Wells came into my office, closed the door, and slumped into a chair. Just two weeks ago Carlton and his wife, Cecily, visited us to deliver two bushel baskets of golf balls. That day this short, wiry man with rimless glasses and a wispy shock of white hair had looked much younger than his seventy-three years. Now, as his body shook and his lower lip quivered, he looked ancient.

Obviously something serious had happened. I waited for him to gather himself.

"They're right, you know," he said finally, barely audibly. "When they say the most horrible tragedy that can befall a parent is to lose a child."

I knew little of Carlton's family life, except that Cecily was a dear lady who drove him everywhere because Carlton had never learned to drive. He told me he attributed his good health to never getting a driver's license; because of that he walked five to ten miles every day. He had his daily dawn bird walks, his three-mile daily walk to and from his campus office in Haven Hall, treks around campus over lunch hour to pick up litter that offended him, strolls around neighborhood parks every evening, and an occasional round on a golf course.

I knew he had children but could not recall that he ever spoke of them to me.

"He was over-tired," Carlton said, "and had been fighting a severe cold for weeks. It just drew his resistance down. When his report was rejected, it was more than he could take."

Carlton put his arms on my desk, and his head on his arms, and began to moan. His shoulders heaved with each sob and I came around the desk, stood by him, and put a hand on his shoulder. I could think of nothing to say.

In a few minutes, Carlton regained his composure. He sat up, wiped his eyes, and cleaned his glasses. I poured a glass of water from a carafe and handed it to him. To my surprise, he drank it entirely.

"Cecily and I had serious doubts when he told us of his plans to join the Navy. We discussed it with him at some length. Truly, no parent wants to see their son in a situation where he might be called into harm's way. But he was an adult and the decision was his."

Carlton was now completely composed, telling his account almost dispassionately.

"He had been passed over for promotion once previously. And somewhat unfairly, it seemed to us, although to his credit, he never complained that had been the case. But this time, his advancement seemed a certainty. He invested so very much . . . too much into his quest for that promotion. He had written a truly fine paper and when it was published that seemed to clinch it.

"But then, with his weakened physical condition, and a debilitating insomnia associated with it, he apparently did not produce a report of sufficient quality and that doomed his chances. If his service revolver hadn't been so near at hand . . . if he had just a few moments to get ahold of himself after opening the rejection letter, I just know . . ."

And Professor Wells stood up abruptly and grabbed my hand.

"I had no place else to go, William. Still, it was not fair to come to you."

"Professor, I'm honored that you did, as much as I am anguished over this. I know there's nothing I can do or say, but please know that Marcy and I—"

"I know, William, I know. And you're right, there is nothing. Until this happened, I myself could not comprehend the depth of despair into which one plummets when hearing their child has died. Not only died, but has taken his own life. May you never know that feeling."

Then he was gone.

I looked at the photographs on my desk. Mark, Jennifer, Patrick, and Rebecca. And I tried to imagine how it was for Carlton. And then I tried with all my might to think about anything but that.

THE COURSE HAD BEEN OPEN two months and some patterns were emerging. We were getting the expected play from the immediate area and more than we anticipated from communities twenty, thirty and more miles away. Our few promotions played on the theme, "Lose Yourself in The Boondocks," with an enticing photograph by our friend Doug Truax of a lone golfer in the valley of a spacious, hilly fairway. And it worked. The problem was we couldn't afford expensive display ads in the larger newspapers. So even though our concept of a quiet, natural, old-fashioned golf course in the country struck a resonant chord, it was not a chord we could sound loudly and frequently enough to build on that good start.

We hadn't been able to add new leagues beyond the three we had since our opening. The economy in the area was so depressed that many people remained out of work. As a result, we were on track in terms of our original conservative financial projections but hadn't gotten any hoped-for surprises that would produce revenue for an underground sprinkler system, or more fertilizer, or an improved, expanded clubhouse.

One expense I knew we would have to incur eventually was new fencing between our land and Ed Harrison's. I didn't want trouble from him because golfers went onto his land to look for an errant shot on holes number eight and nine. I hadn't thought about problems coming from his side until one day when Danny Adams, one of our authorized golf ball scavengers, raced in, breathless.

"They're on the shoulders of number eight green, Mr. Haney! I chased them away but they might be back by now."

"Hold on, Danny. Who's on the green?"

"Harrison's cows. I was fishing balls at number eight pond and heard them mooing. I climbed up the bank and there they were. They broke through those rusted old wire strands he had up. Had eyes for that nice green grass, I guess."

Danny jumped in the truck alongside me and we were there in two minutes.

None of the cows had gotten onto the putting surface, although the east slope, which was moist from the runoff from watering the green, showed damage from their hooves. We rounded up the cows and herded them back onto Harrison's land, then began to repair the broken fence with a large coil of wire I always carried in the truck, along with sidecutters and some Day-Glo tape I thought might keep the cattle away.

I hadn't noticed Harrison come up and it startled me when I heard his voice right behind me.

"Well, if you didn't have your golf links right up against my pasture, then my cattle wouldn't be running on your green lands when they got out, now would they?"

There was no arguing with that. And I couldn't have if I wanted to because Harrison stalked off and left me to mend the fence.

As I watched him walk away, I remembered once asking Kent how Gladys came up with the nickname Ol' Flannelmouth for Ed Harrison.

Kent had taken a long drag off his Pall Mall, drummed his fingers on the table, and said, "I'm tempted to say it's because it fits him."

"But what does flannelmouth mean? I never heard that word before. Where does that come from?"

"God only knows. Actually, He probably doesn't even know. But don't ask Gladys or she'll probably start wondering about you."

Marcy stirred in bed as I jabbed her with my elbow.

"Marcy. Listen. What's that sound?"

I was already on my feet, ear to the intercom.

"I didn't hear anything." Marcy's voice, sleep-fogged. "Get back in bed."

"No, there's somebody out there."

"Out where?"

"In the pro shop. Listen."

The rustling had stopped and for a moment I thought maybe Marcy was right, that there was no intruder in the pro shop. Then it started again.

"See? There it is. There's somebody out there. Did Mary leave the cash box there? I'll bet that's what he's searching for. Hear it? That rustling, like he's got a sack and he's filling it with stuff."

"What kind of stuff? A burglar breaks into the pro shop at what—God, Bill, it's 3:30 in the morning—to steal golf tees and unpaid invoices? The dogs haven't made a sound. They'd be going wild if there was anyone there. Go back to sleep."

Back to sleep? She had no idea. I had to deal with this.

"Bill. What are you doing? Put that gun away. You're not going out there with a gun. Even if it is a burglar, it's not worth somebody getting shot. Probably you with your own gun."

"I know how to handle a gun, thanks."

Now the sounds were louder, much more aggressive. Like he was making off with everything in the pro shop. Probably already had stashed the golf bags and clubs in a pickup truck he left running on the other side of the barn where we couldn't see it, and so quiet it must be outfitted with a super-silent muffler. And the Otey Crissman putters, handmade with hickory shafts, each a collector's item. Any cat burglar worthy of the name would go for the Oteys first thing. I carefully laid the pistol on the bed, pulled on a pair of pants, and laced up my quietest shoes. I was ready.

I crept down the hall to look out the girls' window, keeping lights off so as not to be seen. The driveway was bathed in the glow of the mercury vapor lamp and the pro shop was plainly in view. There was no sign of anybody in there, no flashlight moving about. But then, he would be too smart for that. He would have broken in through the back door to the maintenance shop, then come through the underside of the barn and through the back door into the pro shop. Sure. Then once his eyes were well adjusted to the darkness he could easily see in the light of the mercury vapor lamp streaming through the east pro shop window what was there for the taking. See well enough to know what were the quality goods. He was no amateur, this cat burglar.

I felt my way back down the hall, into the bedroom, picked up the pistol, and headed down the stairs.

"Bill, there could be more than one of them, you know."

"Oh, so now you agree there is someone out there."

"No, but I did hear more noises on the intercom. If anyone's going to investigate, it should be the sheriff's department. That's what they do. They don't want homeowners rushing around with pistols, shooting at anything that moves. Now put that gun down, pick up the phone and call the police."

"By then he'll be gone."

"Who'll be gone?"

"The cat burglar."

"Bill! You're going to wake the kids. Now call the sheriff so I can get some sleep. I mean it."

"By the time a deputy gets here, they'll be gone."

"It's not worth risking a life over. Go call the sheriff. Now."

It had been five minutes and still no sign of a police car. Soon the burglars would have the place cleaned out and have vanished into the night. I eased open the front door and sidled out to the porch, back against the wall, in the shadows, out of sight. Through the downstairs intercom, I heard more rustling, a sharp crash, then silence. He's tipped his hand now. Got careless and knocked something over. Good. He'll either crouch there, knowing I'm onto him, or he'll bolt and I'll race out and get his license number as he drives away. Either way, that's one dead-meat cat burglar.

Headlights distantly on Curtis Road, approaching. No siren. No flashing lights. Good. This deputy had moxie. He wasn't about to drive into an ambush. He flicked off his headlights as he eased into the driveway.

I slipped the pistol back inside the door and laid it on the floor. I stayed to the shadows as I made my way to the deputy's car.

"You Mr. Haney, the property owner who called this in?" he rolled down his window and looked out at me.

"Shhh. He's still in there. Did you see his vehicle on the other side of the barn as you drove up?"

"Sir, there was no vehicle on the other side of the barn."

"Ahh. So they're on foot."

"They? How do you know there's more than one intruder in there?"

"We have to assume there is, don't we? With no vehicle, it would take more than one man to carry everything off."

The deputy studied me a long moment.

"Sir, now just what is it this gang is stealing?"

"Golf bags and clubs. Maybe money. We might have left the cash box in there overnight."

"And how much money might there be in cash?"

"Could be twenty, thirty dollars. Plus the change. And then there's my shop tools. All kinds of stuff they could fence."

The deputy set down his clipboard, clicked a button on a two-way radio, and got out of the car. No interior dome light came on. This cop was one sharp cookie, not letting himself be backlighted so a perp could get off an easy shot.

"Gotta put a new bulb in my overhead," he said, and headed toward the pro shop.

"I've got your back," I whispered.

He turned and looked at me.

"Mr. Haney, you just stay right there. You're not carrying a gun, are you?"

"Me? A gun? No sir, I'm not carrying any gun. Not me."

"How about a key? You wouldn't happen to have a key to that pro shop, would you?"

"It's right above the storm door. Just reach up and it's on a little ledge up there."

"Well, that's convenient, isn't it?"

As he walked straight through the light spill from the mercury vapor lamp, his boots crunching loudly in the gravel, Rusty growled, and Blazer began to bark.

"You have dogs and this is the first time they've barked?"

"Yes. The intruder must have been very quiet."

The deputy looked back at me, shook his head, and continued toward the pro shop. He flicked on his big flashlight and shined it through the large pro shop picture window, shrugged his shoulders, then got the key and opened the door.

Silence. Then the pro shop overhead fluorescents flickered on. Through the window I saw the deputy moving through the room, then around the counter. He was looking at something on the counter, then raised an arm and motioned for me to come in.

Apparently he had found evidence. Even though the burglar had eluded him, making his escape while the deputy and I talked, he had left behind valuable evidence, evidence the police would use to track him down and prosecute him to the fullest extent of the law. We might not recover the stolen property, but our swift action would result in bringing a felon to justice and so—

"See this, Mr. Haney?"

"Yes."

"And what is this, sir?"

"That? That's a bag of cheese corn."

"That's right, Mr. Haney. And do you notice anything about this bag of cheese corn?"

"Well, it's been torn open. So obviously the intruder decided to have himself a little snack while he went about his business."

"And do you notice anything missing or disturbed anywhere in this office?"

"It's not an office; it's a pro shop. And no, now that you mention it, it doesn't appear that anything has been disturbed."

"And, sir, what is this?" He tapped a box on the rear shelf behind the counter. I noticed that there were kernels and fragments of cheese corn all around it. A clue?

"Oh, that's the intercom. We use it to communicate back and forth between the pro shop and the house. And we push that little button there on the left and that locks the intercom on so any sound coming from the pro shop at night we—"

"So you could hear something as harmless as, oh, let's say, a mouse chewing open a bag of your cheese corn and sitting on your intercom having a late-night snack."

It was plausible.

"So what happens if I push this little button here, Mr. Haney?"

"Well, now you've shut the lock off so someone inside the house—"

"Bill, what is going on out there?" It was Marcy's voice, over the intercom. She had heard the entire conversation between the deputy and me. Good. She would be relieved that what she had feared was a burglar was only a harmless little rodent scurrying about, gnawing open a bag, eating cheese corn.

"Bill, will you please come into the house and let that man go back to work? Officer, would you like a cup of coffee? We're sorry to put you through this trouble."

"No trouble at all, ma'am. That's what we're here for. Can't be too careful these days. We don't want some agitated homeowner getting out a gun, taking matters into his own hands."

"Or heaven forbid," Marcy said, "shooting an intruding mouse."

"That sort of thing, right, ma'am."

Marcy had a way of quickly establishing rapport with people.

I turned out the lights, locked the door, returned the key to its secret location, and walked the deputy back to his car.

"Well, officer, I think we've solved our little mystery. Thanks for your excellent response to this situation."

"Right, Mr. Haney. As I told your missus, better that than property owners playing around with guns. That can be a recipe for disaster."

"No doubt about it, officer. Leave that to the professionals, I always say."

"Glad to hear that, Mr. Haney."

I was going to go up and tell Marcy what had happened out there in the pro shop, but then, she had heard most of it over the intercom and knew everything was back to normal. So instead I fixed a cup of coffee. By the time I got back upstairs, she was sound asleep. I looked in on the kids. None of them had stirred. It felt good to crawl back under the covers. I could get at least another two hours sleep before sunrise. Unless, of course, something happened. If it did, I would be ready for it.

THREE HOURS LATER I was up and the events in the middle of the night seemed like a distant dream.

I went into Ann Arbor to my office and spent the day immersed in monographs, book manuscripts, and newsletter articles reporting the results of research studies by the institute. By the time I returned home I had all but forgotten the intruder in the night.

Marcy and the kids were in the pro shop. I could hear them laughing in there with Mary Joseph.

"What's so funny?" I said.

"Hi, Daddy," Jen said. "Mary was telling us about the mouse who stole the cheese corn."

"Oh?" I said and gave Marcy a sharp look. "And how did Mary get the news?"

"The first foursome this morning told me about it," Mary said. "One of them has a police band on his radio and he heard the report. Some others mentioned it later, too."

"Oh, that's delightful," I said.

"Yeah," Pat said. "Tell us about the policeman, Daddy. Did he use his big gun to scare away the bad mouse?"

Everyone had a big laugh at that. It was nice to see my little family so happy.

THAT EVENING, AFTER I FINISHED setting out the sprinklers at the Crossroads, I sat on the old church pew we used as a resting bench at the back tee boxes for numbers three and five. I could hear all the pump engines running smoothly as the last rays of a glorious sunset danced in the domes of spray above the sprinklers.

I thought about the deputy and the mouse and smiled. Then laughed out loud.

When I was a kid, I was in awe of men in uniforms. Maybe it began with my three older brothers, all of them in the military during World War II. My first memories of them were of Dick in his jaunty Air Force pilot's cap with the captain's bars on it, and Ray and Bob in their Marine Corps uniforms, much like the framed portrait of my father in his World War I Marine uniform, that tinted photograph hanging on the living room wall. But there was another memory, even earlier, of an encounter with a man in a uniform. A policeman with a big gun.

Someone is in trouble. I know that when I see Sheriff Don Menzies drive up and park in front of our house. I better go find out what the sheriff wants.

"Hi, Sheriff Menzies," I say.

He picks me up, and in Sheriff Don Menzies's arms up is a long way because he must be the tallest man in all of Big Beaver. I let my hand brush against the shiny pistol with the checkered walnut grip that he keeps strapped in a holster on his hip, so later I can tell Ronnie Steinke I touched Sheriff Menzies's gun, and he won't want to believe it he'll be so jealous, but he'll know it's true because he knows I don't lie for that would be a sin, even if only a venal one but that's only after you've made your First Holy Communion but I haven't done that yet and anyhow that just gets you three Our Fathers and three Hail Marys and a good Act of Contrition so you're not in peril of eternal damnation if you die with only a venal sin on your soul instead of a mortal sin which is all she wrote, brother, Dad says, hell fire and damnation for eternity and that's a very long time, but if there's a line to heaven and a line to hell and the line to hell is shorter, I'll see you around because you won't catch Red Haney standing in line for anybody nor anything, Dad says.

"Dad home, Billy?" the sheriff says.

Mother opens the door and Sheriff Don Menzies carries me in. He takes off his special hat with all the gold braid and the big badge pinned right in the middle and the shiny black leather beak. He sits down on the piano bench, me on his knee because he's too big for our chairs, and then Dad comes in from the kitchen where it smells like he's cooking one of the two things he cooks better than anybody, which is oyster patties; the other is Red Haney's special pineapple upside-down cake.

"Madeline, will you finish up those patties? The Sheriff and Billy and I have to have a little man-to-man talk."

I have never been included in a man-to-man talk before with Sheriff Don Menzies. Or anybody else. But now I'm five so maybe I'll be included in man things.

"Sheriff Menzies came here to talk to you, Billy. Seems there's a report that got to the Sheriff about a little boy who's been using bad words. Now, they don't like to lock up little boys in that cold, dark prison they've got in Pontiac for the worst criminals in Oakland County. So maybe if we can get this straightened out that won't have to happen."

I wouldn't want to be in that little boy's shoes.

"Billy," Sheriff Don says, "I hear you've been using some powerful blue language. Is that true?"

I don't know what blue language is. I didn't know that language came in different colors. If it did, then red language would be mean. And yellow language, that would be for cowards, and—

"Billy, pay attention," Dad says. "The Sheriff asked you a question. Have you been using swear words?"

Oh, that's what they meant. I know there's such a thing as swearing like when my father says "damn" or "hell" or "get that stupid bastard off the road," and my mother says, "Ray, not in front of the boy." But I'm not always sure what is swearing and what isn't. I know that it's a sin to take the name of our Lord in vain and I sure haven't done that and never would because I'm going to keep my soul pure so that when I made my first Holy Communion, I—

"William Valentine Haney," my mother calls from the kitchen. "Pay attention and answer Sheriff Menzies. Ray, Billy's confused and worried. Take it easy on the boy."

"The boy is old enough to cuss, he's old enough to stand up for it," my father says. "Junior and Chucky Gardner told their mother, old busybody that she is, and she told me Billy was using language would make a sailor blush. Billy, come over here."

I slip down off the sheriff's knee and go over to my father. He smells of Old Gold cigarettes, motor oil, Old Spice, and oyster patties. He pulls my head toward him and whispers some words in my ear.

"Now, Billy, I know you promised to always tell the truth. Tell me, were those the words you used when the Gardner boys played keep-away and wouldn't give you back your ball?"

I nod. There are a couple others he forgot to include, but he didn't ask me about them so I don't say anything.

"Billy," the sheriff says. "Wherever did you pick up those words?"

"They were just laying there."

"What was laying there?" Dad says. "The words? Madeline, he's not making sense. Billy, who said those things?"

"It was when the big slide fell off."

Mother came in and all three of them looked at each other and then stared at me.

"What big slide, Billy?" Mom says.

"That the truck backs up by the basement window and they hook the big slide on and then the coal goes sliding down and into the bin except they were talking to each other and not paying attention but I was. I saw the slide fall to the ground and the coal kept coming out of the truck and it made a nice pile there outside the window but I guess they wanted the coal to go down the slide and right into the bin because when they saw the big pile they weren't happy about it and blamed each other that the slide wasn't hooked on right and so they had to get out shovels and put all the coal in through the window that way and while they were doing it they said these things about each other and the coal slide and the lousy, shitty pay they got for a fuckin' dirty job that cocksucker of a boss—"

"Billy!" And my mother clamps a hand over my mouth and my dad grabs me by the arm and jerks me over and swats me hard twice on my hinder and it stings right away but I'm not going to cry right here in front of Sheriff Don Menzies and his big gun. So I just stand in the middle of the room and watch them all watching me not cry even though my lip is quivering and I can't swallow down that hot fuzzy tennis ball in my throat.

"Now, son," Sheriff Don Menzies says, even though I'm not his son and he knows that because he knows I'm the son of Raymond (call me Red) Haney who just spanked me twice, hard. "You know why your father did that, don't you?"

I fold my arms across my chest so they won't see my fingers shaking and I look straight at Sheriff Don Menzies and say, "Sure, you fat son-of-a-bitch, because he's bigger than I am."

And I run out of the room and down the porch steps and hide behind the bush with the yellow flowers and wait for my father to come after me and spank me again but he doesn't come and something else must have happened because all three of them are in there laughing and I'm glad they already forgot all about me, the way grownups do when you're just a little kid.

Twenty-Eight

Having fun is serious business on Fourth of July in Grass Lake, Michigan.

As we were preparing for a big turnout of golfers at The Boondocks on the long holiday weekend, we got rumbles that something other than patriotic celebrations and golf might be on peoples' minds. We had been to Independence Day celebrations in the village the previous three years and knew that it was big stuff in Grass Lake.

The oldest club of its kind in the state puts on an all-you-can-eat pancake and sausage breakfast and no one quarrels with the culinary talents of the Grass Lake Rifle Club members. Queues sometimes wind for hundreds of feet to get into the Cakewalk. There is the annual turn-of-the-century parade with vintage tractors ("one-lung-ers," some of them are affectionately called) and Norman Brown, dressed as a clown, rides a unicycle.

Celebrating the Fourth in 1970, though, would be different from any of the hundred previous Fourths since the Village was established. While old-timers and parents were busy readying the tried-and-true events and festivities , their teenaged children had their minds else-where. There was a buzz around the Village and the neighboring townships. Soon it was the talk of Jackson County. And within days, the word had spread throughout the state and into Ohio, Indiana, Illinois, New York, Pennsylvania, and nearby Ontario, Canada. The subject was not upcoming holiday celebrations but rather a date one month hence. The date August 7 was circled on the calendars of count-less tens of thousands of young people in places far away from Grass Lake, Michigan. The kids called it simply "The Festival."

In sheer numbers as well as notoriety, it promised to be the biggest thing to happen in Grass Lake—indeed in Jackson County—in more than a hundred years. National attention would be focused on this area as it had not been since Governor William Seward of New York State came to Michigan in 1851 to lead the defense of county farm-ers and businessmen arrested in the aftermath of the Great Railroad

Conspiracy War and Trial of the 1850s. The violence and long trial had produced international headlines for months.

Grass Lake Village became a popular health resort in 1880 but when the healing springs petered out, the spa was closed, and the town slipped once again into quiet obscurity.

Now all that was about to change.

The young people of Grass Lake went to the Fourth of July events in the Village in 1970 just as they had in years past. They drew together in little knots and talked about The Festival, sharing the latest about who among them were going as workers and who as paying customers. Whichever way, they would say, you better believe it, one way or another, they were spending that first weekend in August at The Festival—and as many days after that as the music and the juices were flowing.

This was to be Woodstock all over again, baby, but Grass Lake-style.

The boys and young men who worked for us at the golf course—as well as their parents and girlfriends—were swept up in the controversy, along with everyone else in the township. If "The Great Goose Lake Rock Concert and Festival" became more than a huge outdoor hard-rock music concert and spiraled into the drug-laced orgy of sex and violence that many expected, it would rip apart tight families and youthful romances.

"You go to that depraved place," a girlfriend or a parent would say, "and you can just keep right on going."

Lifelong residents were dazed it had come to this. Why here? they asked.

There are hundreds of lakes in Jackson County and scores of them in the adjacent townships of Grass Lake and Leoni. Less than two miles northwest of Grass Lake Village, surprisingly secluded despite a location convenient to Jackson, Ann Arbor, and the I-94 expressway, is Goose Lake, one of the largest lakes in the area. On the shores of Goose Lake, a developer named Richard Songer had purchased 350 acres and created what his advance publicists termed "a family campground." More like "Gomorrah comes to Grass Lake," the nearby residents spat. The location offered quick access from hundreds of cities throughout the Midwest and Canada, and scores of college campuses. The developer's target audience ran to tens of millions of prospective customers.

"The full range of summer recreational activities for the whole family," the promotional literature said.

"A magnet to attract troublemakers and drug users into our town to get high, get naked, and wallow in carnality," the Goose Lake Property Owners Association warned.

In May, when the developer's plans were presented to the township board, a figure in the low thousands of attendees was projected. In July, the estimate was "30,000 persons are expected to remain overnight." Later that month, developer Songer ran an ad in the *Michigan Daily*, the University of Michigan student newspaper. All lowercase and written as if from one cool dude to another, it began: "dear brothers and sisters" and closed with ". . . let's all come together . . . at goose lake park, peace, dick songer." And in between was a reference that brought smiles to the youngsters even as it raised the eyebrows of the older set: ". . . fresh air, rolling meadows, and unlimited grass" with the word "grass" in boldface.

Golfers visiting The Boondocks from other towns would ask, "Now where exactly is it they're holding that big rock concert?"

As the word spread from college campuses to high-schoolers' haunts, it was clear that those estimating the crowd size had misplaced a digit. In spring, the talk had been 30,000 attendees. Six days before the concert, 70,000 tickets had already been sold. The upside number was now 300,000 and climbing.

As the momentum and the tension built those last weeks of July and the first week of August, Mary Joseph asked how I felt about it.

"Curious, like everybody else," I said. "I'll let you know after I've seen it for myself."

"You're going?" Mary looked shocked.

"Well, granted I'm thirty-three but I'm not ready for a rocking chair yet. And it is the biggest thing to happen around here since who knows what."

"But what about all that . . . you know . . . stuff that they say will be going on?"

"Remember, I work at the University of Michigan. Sit-ins, anti–Vietnam War demonstrations, people dressing however they want, doing whatever they feel whenever and wherever they feel it. And there's a rumor some students there have actually smoked pot. Whatever I might see at Goose Lake would not be exactly new to me."

"But still . . ."

"Maybe it's the reporter instinct in me. I don't know. One way or another this is going to be big news around here and maybe even nationally. How can I be less than five miles away from the scene and not be there?"

"You need to get away from here for a while," Marcy said. "You don't know how cranky you've been. Yes, we need rain. Yes, we've got a lot to do to get ready for the Leoni Tool Shop's summer outing tomorrow. But snapping at everybody won't help that. Mike and Danny have something they want to invite you to. Go ask them about it and then go do it. Mary can help get the pro shop straightened up and I've got lunch to prepare for thirty-two golfers tomorrow. We'll get more done with you gone for a while and if we're all lucky you'll be in a better mood after the break."

Well, if you want to be that way about it.

What the Campbell brothers, Danny and Mike, had in mind was a baseball game. And not just any baseball game, but Grass Lake's annual fundraiser father-son genuine fast-pitch no-quarter-given hardball game. I had written articles in the *Grass Lake News* about the success of this year's Warriors team—they were the best Class C team in the entire state.

"We've got the whole school team but we're short on fathers," Danny said. "We figured that you're kind of a father to the guys on the team working here and the others from writing sports stories for the *News*. So we asked around and everyone agrees, so will you?"

"When is this game?"

"Seven o'clock."

"Seven o'clock today? Man, with no practice and I haven't played hardball in . . . must be fifteen years. Yeah, my senior year in high school and even then I broke my wrist at the start of the season and couldn't play all year."

"Yeah, Mr. Haney," Mike said. "But you play catch with Mark and Pat and hit fungoes to them."

"And I've played catch with you," Danny said, "and you've still got a pretty good slider."

"Yeah, right, but I've seen Mike pitch," I said. "I know better than to stand up there against the stuff he throws."

They looked at each other and beamed.

"Then there's no problem," Danny said. "Mike's not pitching. He's playing outfield. It'll be Brian Sturgill."

I had never seen Brian pitch but Mike had a great heater and a killer curve so anything had to be better than that.

"All right, but you guys better promise you're not coming at me with sharpened spikes."

"Hey, great," Danny said. "This'll be fun. And your kids can get in free because you're playing."

"You'll be glad you did this," Mike said. "You'll have a great time and it'll help us raise money for new uniforms."

We got to the baseball field at quarter after six, plenty of time to get a few swings in batting practice. I was in good condition but timing was another matter. When you haven't seen fast pitching in ten or fifteen years, no way are your reflexes hair-trigger sharp. But I knew I'd be all right once I stepped into the batter's box and got a few practice rips against real pitching.

The temperature and humidity were both near ninety but Marcy was right, it was good to get away. I was looking forward to the game. There were only a couple dozen spectators, so Mark, Jennifer, and Pat got good seats on the little four-tier wooden plank stands. The stands were in foul territory along the third-base line between home plate and third base; those seats seemed awfully close to the action. I asked one of the coaches if little kids were in danger of getting hit by a foul ball. He agreed and said they would have older kids sit nearby and intercept any balls hit that way.

One of my teammates tipped open an equipment bag and a half dozen Louisville Sluggers spilled out, clattering with that sound only a seasoned ash baseball bat can make. I picked up a couple and swung them around to loosen up, just as though I did this every day.

I made my way to the plate for my batting practice swings and started digging in a stance. Just as I was ready to get my first cuts, one of the coaches walked to the pitcher's mound and held up his arms.

"Listen up, guys and fathers, I've got an announcement," coach said. "We were going to start at seven p.m., right? Well, couple things. One, if the game runs long, we've got no lights. Two, since we've got everybody here and hot as it is, we'll skip B.P. and get this show on the road right now. Dads, you get first bats. Where's your lineup?"

So much for batting practice. At least I wasn't batting leadoff. Our captain wasn't one to interrogate his players about their high-school batting averages before setting his lineup. He just wrote down names and positions as people said them. As if any batting order would matter against these young studs. I looked over his shoulder at the lineup card and saw I was playing second base, hitting fifth. Somehow he knew that at five-foot-ten and 160 pounds I was a power hitter.

By the time Brian Sturgill polished off our leadoff hitter on strikes, I was wondering why I assumed he would be easier on us than Mike Campbell would have been. Oh, I could see the differences. Mike was a true pitcher with good speed, deceptive off-speed stuff, fine control, and he knew how to mix his pitches. He could set a batter up with a fast one on the inside corner, then snap off a wicked curve low and away that had the batter waving in the breeze, two feet from the ball. Brian was taller and stronger than Mike, a good six-foot-four and 200-plus pounds, it appeared. And he could hum the seed, as major league scouts liked to say, a heater that looked to be clocking better than ninety. What was worse, it was a heavy fastball. Before striking out, our second batter fouled one off the handle, broke the bat, and his hands are still stinging.

What Brian had in raw speed, he gave up in control. But that often makes a pitcher even more effective—batters are afraid to dig in for fear of getting hit. Our batters were so aware of Brian's speed and wildness, they just stood as far away as they could in the box and still reach the plate with the bat. If Brian had been able to harness that speed, he could have struck out the entire team by simply pumping strikes over the outside corner. But he couldn't find the plate. What he did do was walk the next three batters. That brought me to the plate with the bases loaded.

As I stepped into the batter's box and scratched out a good footing, I squinted my eyes against the setting sun slanting in from left field.

"Hit a good one, Dad," one of the kids yelled.

"Yeah, pitcher's got a weenie arm. You can do it, Dad," shouted

Pat, who was showing signs of becoming a decent pitcher himself and already knew the classic baseball taunts.

With what I had seen thus far from Brian, I wasn't about to cut at the first pitch. Good thing. Brian had started me off with a breaking pitch and it did break wickedly, but outside and in the dirt. Ball one. The second was a hot one, high and inside and I could hear the seams whiz as it burned past. Ball two. Another off-speed pitch, way outside. Ball three.

So there I stood, 3 and 0, and one pitch away from taking a base on balls and forcing in the first run of the game. But also—it dawned on me in a flash of great clarity—just one swing from immortality. No one would expect me to swing at the 3-0 pitch, right? Not after the pitcher has walked the bases loaded. Okay, so I hadn't hit a fastball, or even swung at one since before I went to college. Still, with Brian providing all that velocity, all I had to do was make good contact.

I moved closer to the plate and up a good couple of feet in the box. Crowding the plate, I dug in. I took a couple of menacing practice swings and fixed steely eyes on Brian Sturgill. And it never occurred to me that Brian might have an idea of what I was thinking.

I thought I had picked up breaking-ball spin as the ball left his hand. There was that fraction-of-a-second guessing whether Brian had gone to the curve ball, so I hung in there, waiting for the ball to break away from my head and toward the plate. I wasn't going to bail out only to see the ball break belt-high across the plate and hear the umpire shout "Strike one!" No. Once it broke, this might be the most hittable pitch I would see. If only it would break.

How many thoughts can race through a mind as a ball travels that sixty feet, six inches at eighty to ninety miles an hour? Batting coaches will tell you there should be none. The batter's box is a place for instinct and conditioned response, not reflective thought. As Yogi Berra said to Casey Stengel, "I can think and I can hit, boss, but I can't do both at the same time."

I was doing too much of one and none of the other. Because that ball never broke. I had misread the spin and what was coming straight at my head was not Brian Sturgill's breaking pitch but his high heat. And all I had to do was get out of the way and it would be ball four.

Now, there was a time that baseball players didn't wear batting helmets. If helmets were available or optional or compulsory that day, I was not aware. Whatever, I did not have one on.

Some spectators said it appeared that I never saw the pitch at all because I seemed to make no effort to get out of the way. Maybe I thought it was going to sail over or behind my head and at the last instant it broke slightly and became the irresistible force against the not-quite immovable object—my face. When the ball clips the batter and caroms away, it stings and raises a smart bruise, but doesn't do serious damage. However, when instead it goes "thwop" and falls directly to the ground, alongside the fallen player, then you know the batter has taken the entire force of the pitch.

Thwop is not a good sound, especially when heard from the inside. And this was a major-league thwop. There was an instant of blinding light and a searing flash of pain through the left side of my face. I do not remember going down. I do remember being down, there in the dust beside home plate, seeing my bent glasses in the dirt, a few inches from the ball. Beyond and out of focus, coming in from the pitcher's mound, Brian Sturgill looked down at me, grimaced, then shook his head and turned away.

I felt something cold against my cheek. Whatever it was made things move around inside that part of my face, things that hadn't moved that way ever before. There was a dull buzzing in my left ear. I couldn't see much out of the left eye, but given my extreme nearsightedness I hadn't been able to see much without glasses before I intercepted the pitch with my face.

"Does that help any?" The angel-of-mercy woman must have started out of the stands just as I hit the ground—otherwise how could she have gotten there so quickly, have wrapped those ice cubes in a towel, pressed them against my face. It could only have been seconds ago. I tried to answer but I found my jaw didn't work. Mumbled something. She pulled the towel away slightly.

"Oh my goodness," she said, looking at the towel.

"Never saw anything quite like that," the umpire said.

I turned my head to look at the towel to see if perhaps my ear had come off.

No, the ear was intact, but there on the towel was the imprint of the baseball's stitches, in blood. If this is what mortality is like, I thought, I'll take Option B, thank you very much.

"What happened to Daddy?" It was Jenni's voice.

"He hit the ball with his face," Pat said.

"Did it break his glasses?" Jenni said.

Mark, his voice closer now, "No, only his face."

"Mr. Haney, we better get you to a doctor." It was the umpire or a coach or some other adult who had come to have a look.

"He's got a big dent there in his face," said another voice. "See it? There where his cheek was. Doesn't look natural, does it?"

Here I am, one good crack of the bat from being a hero and instead I've become a spectator sport, lying in the dirt with my glasses bent and an unnatural canyon in my face where my left cheek used to be. No doctor, damn it. I took one for the team and got the game's first RBI. I paid my way onto first and I was damned well going there. And so I got up, brushed myself off like a Prime Time Player would do in the Big Show, and started toward first base.

Hey, listen to that. Five or six people clapped. Given the size of the crowd, that was a good percentage. Bet the angel-of-mercy woman was saying to the ump and the coaches right now, "What a guy. What a guy."

The runner from third base had long since crossed home plate, and the other two runners moved up, forced along by my getting hit by the pitch. One to nothing. We had drawn first blood.

"Mr. Haney," Jim Allshouse, the first baseman, asked, "you sure you're okay? You look . . . kinda . . . a little green."

I searched for words I could say through my teeth, and finally settled on "Just a flesh wound."

That got a laugh from my first-base coach—I think he worked at the veterinarian's office and I wondered if he had formed a professional opinion about what was left of my face. But first baseman Allshouse, who towered above me anyhow, just looked down at me strangely. Brian Sturgill glanced over my way a couple times but there was no way I was leading off that bag to draw a throw. I had seen enough stuff from Mr. Sturgill for a while, thank you very much.

306

Somehow the next batter was retired and our half inning was over, so I had to move only a few feet over to my second-base position while someone brought my glove. That was good because I really didn't want to go to my team's side of the diamond because that would put me too close to the spectators and my kids. I wasn't entirely sure how I would deal with any clever or even sympathetic comments.

The next two innings passed in a very slow blur. If I talked to or even noticed the kids or other people, I do not remember. Then someone was saying, "You're up, Mr. Haney. Or you want me to put in a pinch hitter?"

Hey, no one pinch hits for the Kid, I thought but did not say. I just shook my head, picked up some Louisville lumber and headed to the plate.

I didn't care what that first pitch was or where it was, I was by God swinging at it and hitting it somewhere. And I did. Brian must have thrown me something soft—maybe he floated it in underhand—because I made decent contact and sent a sharp bouncer between second and third. The shortstop backhanded it deep in the hole as I took off for first base. Every footfall sent electrical shocks through the left side of my face and lightning bolts shot from the top of my head with each stride. It seemed to take about three hours to get there but somehow I crossed first base a half-step before first baseman Allshouse snared the shortstop's toss. "Safe!" yelled the umpire.

Safe, indeed. I was not going to take one more hard, jolting step, let alone run and feel those stabs of pain again. I waved my arm to our manager and he sent in a pinch runner.

I gestured to the kids to come to me as I stayed well away from the stands and circled behind home plate and the backstop screen on the way to the parking lot. I waved to the iced towel lady and she may have smiled a blurry smile.

When I pulled the car into the driveway, Marcy was coming out of the pro shop. She smiled and looked up.

"Game's over already? I guess you didn't break a leg. Now aren't you glad you—Your face! What happened to you?"

Pat had the answer. "Daddy hit the ball with his face."

The first stop was at Chelsea Medical Center. The doctor on duty looked me over and made a face I would have preferred not to see.

"Um-hmm. If the incisions were made right over the wound, you'd have substantial scarring, all right." He studied the x-rays, looked at me again.

"No. Un-uhh. We don't have the capabilities to do this." He made a phone call, then said, "They'll see you right away at St. Joseph's Hospital in Ann Arbor. They handle a lot more of these than we do. You're better off there."

It was our great good fortune, the examining doctor at St. Joe's said, that Dr. Reed Dingman, who literally wrote the definitive book on the reconstruction of the human face, was on call and had agreed to come in and have a look.

Dr. Dingman talked briefly with the examining doctor, barely glanced at the x-rays and my face and said, "What was it? Two and oh, three and one count?"

"Three and oh," I said between clenched teeth.

"Huh. Digging in to rip one and he comes up and in and you freeze."

"Something like that."

"Well, take a look at what you've done."

He showed me a plate in the textbook he had authored and then put my x-ray next to it. The two images matched almost perfectly. Break for break, and there were several of them.

"Seven breaks in the left zygomatic process. Or if you prefer, fractured left cheekbone, upper jaw. Do you have any idea how lucky you are?"

"Lucky?"

"You are indeed. An inch lower, you lose several teeth and still break your upper jaw and perhaps the lower one as well. An inch higher and over a tad, you lose your left eye. An inch back toward the ear, it gets the temple and, well, you'd probably have a tag on your big toe by now. All right, let's get you some rest. We'll fix this thing tomorrow."

"Got golf tournament."

"Stop trying to talk. You've got an operation is what you've got."

"Through roof of mouth?"

"Oh no. Nothing like that. And there won't be any visible scar from the incision. These stitch marks in your skin from the ball? Nice pattern, but they're just superficial, no scarring there either."

He held up a mirror to show me while he drew a line with his finger in my hairline.

"No, what I do is make the incision up here above your ear, say about there. In the hair where you'll never see it, at least until you're eighty years old and slick bald, that is. Then I reach down with this special tool I've invented specifically for people who misread the spin on a fastball, and click, click, click, just like the tumblers of a safe falling into place, your zygomatic process is back the way it was designed. Oh, it will be tender for a while but if you stay out of barroom brawls, in four, maybe five weeks, good as new."

"When do?"

"The operation? Let's say ten a.m. You need a good night's sleep. And so do I. See you then."

By the time Marcy filled out the admitting papers and I was placed in a room, it was past nine o'clock and whatever painkillers they gave me hadn't yet kicked in.

"Kids. Outing tomorrow," I mumbled.

"Don't worry about those things. I called Mary Joseph and she's taking the kids to her folks' place for the night. She fed the dogs and chained them up. I already had the lunch spread prepared. The weather forecast is for clear. Everything will be fine."

"Where's the car?"

Marcy told me she had parked the car in the big lot two long, dark blocks away. I had visions of hooded muggers ambushing her from the darkness. She agreed to call Doug Truax, who lived in town. Doug and his wife, Grace, arrived quickly and talked Marcy not only into letting them walk her to the car but also into getting a few hours' sleep at their apartment.

I remembered very little that happened after that until long after the operation was over and the anesthetic had worn off. Marcy told me later and it was not a pretty story.

The operation was routine and completely successful. Dr. Dingman's reputation was well-earned.

Perhaps five or six hours after the surgery, there was this moment in the late afternoon when I could see three toy figures far, far away, at the end of this very long tunnel that somehow terminated just at the foot of my hospital bed. They said they were Marcy, Doug, and Grace, but I didn't believe it and didn't care. A figure in white came up beside them and someone said, "He's totally out of it."

And the nurse said, "He shouldn't be. The anesthetic should have worn off long ago."

"Not with Bill," Marcy said. And for a moment everything was so sharp and distinct and those figures I thought were dolls were really Doug, Grace, and Marcy, but that was just for an instant and I wanted to ask them why they were floating backwards again, getting smaller and smaller but I knew I couldn't talk and even if I could, I was just too tired to try. "Medication really hits him," Marcy was saying, far, far away, "stays . . . in . . . his . . . system . . . for . . ."

ON THE RIDE HOME FROM THE HOSPITAL after I was discharged Sunday morning, Marcy brought me up to date. The kids were fine—Mary Joseph and her sister had been very helpful. Marcy had gotten back to the course by five-thirty in the morning to make final arrangements for the Tool Shop outing. The man who had organized the event was quite understanding and handled several things Marcy normally would have. Kenny, Danny, and Mike had the course in good shape. There was nothing to worry about. And Marcy made me take one of the pain pills she had already picked up at the hospital pharmacy.

Nothing to worry about? I knew better.

When we got home, Marcy tried to find something I could eat. She was also aware that the codeine had now taken over and that all I saw before me was a dismal tableau of failure, gloom, and despair. Marcy had long known that when I hadn't eaten for a few hours, I was not the easiest person to get along with. Here I hadn't had anything to eat in two days. Marcy hoped that if I ate something, it might counteract the effects of the drugs. Soup. Juices. A milk shake. She gave me lots of options but I was well past being hungry and so far gone with worry that nothing sounded good. I went out of the house to try to clear my head. That didn't work. I went into the pro shop where Mary Joseph was on duty.

Mary asked how I felt, but I didn't want to talk. All I could think of was that there were ashtrays heaped with cigarettes. Why hadn't someone emptied them? And food wrappers and empty pop bottles on the tables. A mess, that's what it was. I don't get out of the way of a pitch and everything falls apart. Nobody does anything.

This accident was just the first domino to fall. One by one, every piece of equipment—every mower, every pump, every motor—would break down and there would be no fixing it. The greens would be infected with a fatal fungus. It would never rain again and the course would turn to cinders. The leagues would move elsewhere. There would be no income, no money to pay the boys and they would all quit. The bank and the Smedleys would call in their notes. We'd lose the place. I would be away from my job at the institute too long and they would find that everything went better without me. Out of work the first time in my life. And all this was Marcy's fault. She had done nothing to help in my hour of need. Here I was with a broken face and racked with pain and she didn't understand—worse, didn't care.

And that is just what I ranted to Marcy as soon as I got back into the house. Right there in front of the four kids, berating her for letting everything go to hell, for everybody not caring, for them being lazy, for her being lazy.

Perhaps I don't remember anything of that tirade because it was just too hideous. Too shameful. Perhaps at that moment I thought the codeine-induced despair gave me license. Whatever, I had no memory of that outburst or its aftermath until Marcy told me later, mercifully much later.

Horrible as it was, my crazy explosion triggered a defining moment in our relationship. I had stepped far over the line and Marcy was taking no more. Get ahold of yourself or I will leave you, she said. There is no justification for this behavior. Everyone has stepped up and done a wonderful job to hold things together, Marcy said, including me, and I simply will not take this kind of treatment any more. And in front of the children, too.

Then, I'm told, I lost it. Her ultimatum must have pierced the drug haze that had enveloped me in a gray cloud of desolation. For though I have not the slightest recollection of it, Marcy assures me and I believe it, I wept, I pleaded, I apologized, I promised this would never happen again.

I do remember that she fixed me something soft to eat and soon after I swallowed it, the world did not look so very bad after all. And never again would I allow codeine into my system.

Twenty-Nine

My face was healing rapidly and within a week I was back to work. A few days later I could handle most things around the course. I had taken no pain medication since codeine plunged me into that black pit the day after the surgery. And I would not—pain was infinitely preferable to that ineffable certainty that the world was coming to an end and it couldn't happen soon enough to suit me. I didn't want to look in the mirror and see that monster who had been so surly to Marcy.

I had had many encounters with pain in many different body parts, but there was always something new to learn about it. For one thing, I had discovered with gratitude that pain usually is not forever. Bad as it is, after a while you learn that one day the pain will be gone.

Another thing I learned about pain: if you are hurting, you know you are alive. When that insight occurred to me, I realized how indelible were the impressions made on me by my Roman Catholic childhood. I recalled impaling the middle finger of my left hand with a big three-pronged meat-fork tine when I was drying dishes. I had shoved the silverware drawer shut with too much gusto and the big fork was sticking up at the wrong angle. It went deep into the first knuckle in the middle finger of my left hand. The wound bled very little but the fork was still sticking far in there when I raced into the living room to show my mother, who was crocheting yet another doily. She dropped her needles, gasped, then took control and started to pull the fork out.

"Mom, that hurts."

"I know, Billy. But once we get the fork out we'll put iodine on your finger and a nice bandage. There's nothing broken. It will be fine."

"But it hurts."

"Yes, but it will hurt less if you offer it up for the poor souls in purgatory. Now hold very still."

"Offer up my finger?"

"No, Billy. Offer up the pain."

"How can that help the pouring souls?"

"Poor souls, Billy. Because they have to endure a certain amount of pain. That's what purgatory is. Pain from the absence of the face of God. So any pain that we on earth suffer and offer up to the benefit of the poor souls, why, God counts that as just that much less pain for them to endure. There. You were a very brave little boy."

"How do I do that? Where do I go to offer it up to the pouring souls? To church?"

"No, Billy. Just do it in your heart. And you'll see. Soon it won't hurt at all."

While I might have tried to be philosophical about the pain that had almost entirely ebbed away from the fractured cheekbone, I was not eager for a new dose. That meant I could not personally view history in the making at the upcoming Great Goose Lake Rock Concert and Festival.

Dr. Dingman had been emphatic in my follow-up visit. Healing perfectly but still very fragile, he said. Think Humpty-Dumpty. Be grateful for how you're going to come out of this, he told me. Could have been far worse. And will be if you take another blow there before it is completely healed.

That meant no Goose Lake. Too many people. Too many opportunities to get bumped, accidentally or otherwise. And that meant I would have to find other ways to cover the event because clearly it was shaping up as a major story for the publication I had agreed to write and produce as a fundraiser for next year's Centennial Celebration. And I could see a chapter or two on this in the historiography on the region I had already well under way.

But there was time enough later for those projects. If The Boondocks was going to be a vital proposition in 1971 and beyond, our golf course had to have top priority for the rest of 1970.

IN THE FOUR MONTHS SINCE WE OPENED on May 2, 1970, we slowly had built up a decent foundation. We had three leagues and possibilities for more in 1971. The course had gotten good word-of-mouth for our special outings and events. And we had a small base of members, some of whom had season playing privileges they either purchased or got in barter from us. So far we had exchanged memberships for a year or longer for goods or services including newspaper advertising and printing jobs (Bob Mather and the *Grass Lake News*); on-call mechanical genius (Hank Dubois); surveying (Chuck Wilson); mini-bike trade-in (Stub Willis); flagpole construction and installation (Jim Gallas); scorecard and logo design (Bob Lister); promotional photography (Doug Truax); house siding installation (Mel Clark); and financing (Gladys and Kent Smedley).

That may seem like a lot of golf to barter away, but we felt we came out ahead. If we had paid going rates it would have cost us much more than the value of the golf, and we knew that many of these people would have played far less if they were on a pay-as-you-go basis. Moreover, they often brought paying customers with them which meant not only more income but also helped us cast an ever-wider net for new players.

IT WAS A GEM of a Michigan autumn day. That meant the course would be almost empty. Most golfers had long since packed away their clubs and were either hunting, sitting in a college football stadium, or raking leaves. It was a great day for golf but I was glad that only a few groups had come out.

That gave me an opportunity to finish some overdue maintenance around the pro shop without inconveniencing customers. I was troweling concrete on a small new slab at the front of the pro shop when I heard footsteps crunch in the gravel behind me and a shadow came up over me. I turned and looked up at Gladys Smedley.

"Now what are you making," Gladys asked, "besides a mess?"

"Gladys. You finally came to play some golf."

"That'll be the day, Mr. Smarty Pants. You gonna show me around or I have to do that myself, like everything else?"

I made one last swipe with the trowel, rinsed it off, and stood up, still getting over my surprise at Gladys's first visit to the golf course. As I looked at her, I realized this was the first time I had seen her when she wasn't wearing her apron with her special drink glass in one pocket and a pack of Pall Malls in the other. And it was the first time I had seen her anyplace except her own home.

She didn't look very perky and I couldn't believe she really intended to tramp around on foot to look the place over. I offered to drive her around in the pickup but she said she'd save the full tour for another time but did want "the ten-cent version."

What that meant was that Gladys was content to walk with me less than a hundred yards from the pro shop and lean against the blue rock. There, in silence, she looked the place over. After a few minutes we walked to the practice green, where she stared down at the closely mown grass. We stood there quietly for a time.

"Well, how was your first year?" she asked.

"At the risk of boring you with things I've already moaned enough about to you and Kent, I'd guess it was about what we expected. Built a fair base of regulars and leagues. Plant closings and a bad economy didn't help. The course itself came along well, considering the weather. Had to spend a lot more time just keeping the greens alive and that cut into other things that needed doing. Equipment is wearing out faster than I'd like. A few surprises we could have done without. But Marcy and the kids were terrific or it never would have happened. And the golfers liked it, so over-all a pretty good start."

Gladys nodded and looked at me closely.

"Well, you and your family ought to be pleased. Never thought I'd see it looking like this, the old Fish place and the land you bought from Kent and me. Yes, a right pleasant place. Not your fault if the economy and the weather don't cooperate." She paused, cleared her throat, and looked off toward Marcy's woods. "Kent and I have talked. We want you to know if you folks find yourselves a little short of cash somewhere along the line, we hope you know where to come for it."

Then she looked up at me with mischievous eyes. "Any law against me doing something I've been wanting to do?"

"Gladys, whatever it is I promise not to call the cops."

She kicked off her sandals and took a tentative step onto the green with her bare feet. She scrunched up her toes, squinted her eyes in pleasure and giggled like a little girl, walking around the green, feeling the cool smooth grass on her feet.

"Damned if that isn't just about the best thing since sex. If I'm remembering right."

WE HAD A GOAL OF BUILDING UP the local golfing population by encouraging kids to play. We provided free golf to the area high-school teams and their opponents, and The Boondocks became their home course. I gave free golf lessons to school kids and in the winter took a projector and films of the Masters golf tournament to local schools and talked with the kids about golf. All that brought in zero income, but it introduced the game to young people and, we assumed, created goodwill.

There was one other category of golfers, a very important one: the regular daily fee players. These were golfers from near and far, golfers who weren't in leagues and didn't play in special events or tournaments. They might come out every once in a while at various times or they might show up every Saturday, week after week, at the same time.

We would check the sign-in book to see where our play was coming from. We were pleasantly surprised to see how many came from long distances to play regularly at The Boondocks. There were golfers from Jackson, Ann Arbor, Chelsea, Manchester, and other cities and towns within a twenty-mile radius. But there were also some coming from Plymouth, Northville, Belleville, Romulus, Dearborn, and other Detroit suburbs forty and fifty miles distant.

One of our favorite regular groups was a threesome of two young men in their early twenties and their father. At least one day every week they drove seventy miles each way from the east side of Detroit to play all day long. When I met up with them once on the course, they told me it was the most pleasant golf setting they had found. They liked it for a challenging test, and because it was clean, quiet, and natural.

After seeing them week after week, we wondered if something had happened when, in August, they stopped showing up. Then in early September, the two boys came out alone. I was working on the course when I noticed them on number eight green and walked over to say hello.

"We've missed you. I hope everything's okay."

I looked for their father and when it was obvious it was just the two of them, I was almost afraid to ask.

"Your father . . .?"

"Oh, he's recovering well, thanks," Jeff, the oldest one said. "He said to say hello."

"He's been ill?"

"No, his leg is still healing. It was a pretty bad break."

"He broke his leg? How?"

The two boys looked at each other and finally Rod, the younger one, said, "Jeff, he told us not to say anything."

"I know," Jeff said, "but I think we should. Mr. Haney, Dad didn't want you to worry about a lawsuit so he said we shouldn't even tell you. But last time we were out—maybe six weeks ago—Dad's tee shot landed right down there at the edge of the pond." He pointed down the slope in front of eight green, near the pump setup. "He chipped a real nice shot onto the green and ran up the hill to see if maybe the ball went in the hole."

"He wasn't watching where he was going," Rod said. "And he stepped on that irrigation pipe and turned his leg real crazy. It was pretty obvious it was broken."

I couldn't believe this.

"What did you do? Who helped you?"

"Nobody had to help," Jeff said. "We carried him back up, laid him in the back seat and took him to the hospital. I stayed with him and got him settled in and Rod came back and picked up the clubs.

"He made us promise we wouldn't say anything to you folks. He was concerned you might worry he'd sue. He was embarrassed and said it was entirely his fault. It wouldn't be fair to make you worry about it."

That night Marcy and I talked about the accident. She agreed the boys were right. I would have been concerned, but not only about the prospect of a lawsuit. I was going to have to take a look at our entire place from a safety point of view. We were relieved that the man was recovering well from an accident we had never known had occurred on our place. And we realized how vulnerable we were to accidents that could happen on these hundred acres.

OUR FIRST SEASON ALMOST OVER and many lessons learned, we thought less and less of distant futures. We would be content making it through the next season just a little bit better off than the last.

In October 1970 we had our final special event of the year. Earlier, we had launched a very popular format for tournaments. It was called The Boondocks Scramble. The key ingredient to its success was that it conferred forgiveness for sins. In a scramble, instead of a golfer playing his ball through to completion on each hole and competing against the other three players in his foursome, the golfer was a teammate of those other players. If the golfer hit a bad shot, he simply picked up his ball and played his next shot from the position where the best shot of his three playing partners had come to rest. Each time, only the best shot counted. So, instead of four scores on a hole, there would be only one, with the best shot being selected all the way around the course and each golfer hitting from that preferred spot. If a golfer hit a ball into a pond or out of bounds, no problem.

As a result, even poor golfers had the rare experience of putting for many birdies, of hitting shots from positions they never could reach on their own. And of course scores were very low, and that fed the most voracious appetite known—a golfer's ego.

The regulars at The Boondocks enjoyed this format so much they asked us to have one final scramble event in the fall. Two teams finished with the same score and in the gathering dusk and misty rain, embarked on a playoff. So great was the interest that instead of staying in the warm, dry pro shop, all the other teams trooped along behind to see which team would win. The playoff went on and on, hole after hole, beer after beer, until finally in the gathering darkness, a putt was missed, a putt was made, and we had a champion.

And we had closed out our first season on a high note.

In November, we buttoned down the course for the winter. Our primary concern was for the greens. The older four greens had wintered beautifully while the course was under construction. For the six newer greens, this would be only their second winter. A typical winter would see snow by Thanksgiving and a blanket of it by mid-December. And "blanket" was a fitting term because a protective cover for the greens was precisely what was needed. Bent grass can withstand brutal temperature extremes, so Michigan's sub-zero readings in January and February are not, in themselves, a problem. And it can endure dry stretches of a week or two. What it cannot handle is a winter drought with no protective snow cover and an Alberta Clipper with its dry sub-zero air ripping through at forty miles per hour, day after chilling, killing day.

I talked with Walt Bauer about my concerns and asked him if there was any such thing as a manufactured synthetic sheeting to protect greens in the winter and get them warmed up earlier in the spring. He said there had long been talk of that and some products were being developed, but there were none on the market and when they arrived, they would surely be very expensive.

So, for the winter of 1970–71, we would do what several hundred other greenskeepers in Michigan do—hope for decent weather. Even though the previous four winters had brought more snow and spring flooding than we would have liked, we would be content with more of the same.

Thirty

Every time I went into the basement—to fuss with the furnace, to re-prime the water pump, to paint tee signs—I looked at the pool table. It hadn't moved an inch since we lugged it down there, a slab of slate and a section of rail at a time, four years ago, in 1966. Once in a while I checked to see that the slate wasn't delaminating, that mice or insects hadn't gotten into the bag holding the green felt cloth and nylon mesh pockets.

Whenever I thought about it as I walked by the pool table, I would rub the brass Brunswick plate on the oiled walnut railing, character burned into the smooth wood by decades of cigarette scorches. The plate had raised lettering and after a while your fingertips could make out the words as if reading Braille.

The table was already more than forty years old when I bought it at a north Detroit tavern but to me it was a symbol of a brighter future. It held the prospect that one day we would have the money to turn the top level of the barn into a rustic clubhouse. The entire north wall would be picture windows looking out onto the course. We'd have a country restaurant there and at one end, there would be a jukebox with 45's from the Fabulous Fifties and a place for the pool table. Maybe we'd bring in a Blodgett brick pizza oven like the one at the Prop and I'd start slinging dough again. A spacious clubhouse in the barn's topside was a vision that hadn't changed since July 1966, the first moment we looked at the place.

Other things, however, had changed. And greatly. For almost four years prior to opening in 1970 we had a very active cash flow. The problem was that the flow was almost entirely outward bound. That was supposed to change once we opened. And for a time it did. We never got close to recovering a meaningful fraction of our initial investment, but we made it through our first season slightly exceeding our income projection, producing enough income to meet current expenses.

But it had been a struggle and the expenses trend line was not good. Our aged equipment was often out of commission. The Ford 2000 tractor was solid but most of our mowers, pumps, and other equipment wouldn't make it through the upcoming 1971 season without major work. And even doing the work myself with lots of help from Hank Dubois and Walt Bauer, there would be expensive repair parts and replacements needed.

Even though in 1970 we had spent only a fraction of the budget of an average course on supplies and maintenance, we went well over our projections. "When you buy a used tractor, you buy somebody else's ulcers," the farmers say. And they're right. Except for the Ford 2000, we had not only used tractors, but also used everything else. There may not have been a day in 1970 that a piece of equipment was not sulking or moribund somewhere, or disassembled on the work bench. With three ancient Jacobsens and one Toro we had four greens mowers, and seldom were more than two running properly. The irrigation pumps throbbed away eight to twelve hours a day much of the time spring to fall—breakdowns and catastrophic failures were frequent.

When all those extraordinary expenses cascaded to the bottom line, we had spent well more than planned. That meant unplanned trips to the Grass Lake Bank for fiscal transfusions that kept us current on other accounts but increased our monthly payments enough that Marcy would remind me about it as we sat at the kitchen table with a fat stack of bills and a slim checkbook balance. The golf course was already worth much more than we had spent in actual cash or incurred in debt so it had been a good investment. Our credit rating remained solid but what weighed especially heavily on Marcy was that we had so little breathing room.

At the same time, the economy in the area and especially in Grass Lake was dismal. Car buyers were not pleased with the offerings from Detroit's Big Three. The effects dominoed throughout the state. Several major employers in or near Grass Lake had moved or gone out of business just in our brief time here. The unemployment rate continued to climb to all-time highs; it seemed to worsen daily. Out-of-work people had the time to play golf—they just didn't have the money, even at $1.50 a round.

Employment was better to the east, in Ann Arbor, Chelsea, Manchester, and Ypsilanti, from where we had drawn many golfers. But concerns about the nation's fuel supplies and rising prices were causing people to reduce their driving.

And then there was the greatest threat of all—the weather. Farmers feel they are hostages to the weather, and they are. But not to the extent that a golf course operator is, especially one without an underground sprinkler system, or the money and manpower to run a portable above-ground system effectively.

Our first season now fully behind us, we could look back on a successful launch if measured by the way the course had been received by our golfers. But in terms of cash flow and short-term expenses coming up, we were finishing the season in a more testing financial position than we had started it.

I looked at the Brunswick pool table, rubbed the brass plate, and wondered if we would ever see it set up in a clubhouse at The Boondocks.

"Dad, come on up," Pat called down the stairs. "Let's go to the barn and play basketball. Mark's pumping up the balls."

An offer I couldn't refuse. On the way out to the barn, Mark bounced me the ball, which felt like a brick; Mark obviously had pumped it up harder than the manufacturer recommended. But he knew that even though we'd be in the barn and out of the wind, the air and wooden floor were so cold the ball had to be overinflated to bounce well.

So, dressed in sweatshirts and light jackets, we jogged up the barn hill in the crisp November air and rolled back the big sliding door. I turned on the floodlights I had installed way up in the rafters and the makeshift court was bathed in light. I looked up at the backboard, remembering the lucky coincidence that its brackets were just the right length to fasten to a beam where I could adjust the rim to its proper ten-foot height or lower it for the little guys.

It would be a while before seven-year-old Pat could hoist a full-size basketball up to the regulation-height rim with ease, but he could already dribble around like a miniature Globetrotter. While the boys went one-on-one, I looked at the great old barn. With enough money, one day it would indeed make a terrific rustic pro shop and clubhouse.

With enough money. That day now seemed so far off it would take a time warp to get there.

There was a very long list of more immediate and urgent needs than this, I knew. Sure, it would be fun to have a go at this level of the barn, re-shingle the roof or maybe put on a new one, preserve those hundred-year-old hand-hewn timbers, install big windows the full length of the north wall. While you're at it, beef up the floor on the west end. That's where you can put the pool table, yeah, and one of those cool old Wurlitzer jukeboxes. Right. Just as soon as we discover that buried treasure chest.

Even so, say you do that, then what have you got? Without a healthy, functioning, revenue-producing golf course, what have you got? You've got a lot of time on your hands to shoot pool and admire those hand-hewn timbers and listen to Elvis and the Four Lads, that's what you've got.

Refurbishing the barn would have to wait. It would have to remain far down the Fantasy To-Do List. There were prior demands on any money we might find. And before we spent the next dollar, we had to get that dollar to spend. Well, the pool table sure wasn't doing anybody any good sitting there in pieces in the basement. I had paid $300 for it; surely it was worth at least that much now. Might as well sell that set of special Belgian pool balls and sticks with it. And the racks and that heavy-duty table cover I got to keep the cats from jumping up and tearing the cloth. Throwing all that in, the package had to be worth $375 easy. That would buy a lot of fertilizer. Even a used greens mower shouldn't cost that much if I bought it in the off-season.

Right now, though, there was something I should be doing that didn't cost a cent.

"Pat, if you stop dribbling and toss that ball here, I'll show you guys how to play 'round the world.'"

Who needs a pool table anyhow, when you've got a backboard in your barn and two little guys who make you feel seven feet tall?

IF THE POOL TABLE COULD GO, how could I justify keeping the sitar? Herb David's Guitar Studio in Ann Arbor was the logical place to sell it. Two days after Herb put it out on display, it sold for $375. After his commission, we cleared about $300. The price of heating oil and gasoline was rising and we were expecting another big increase in fertilizer costs. I would never draw a raga from the sitar with my plectrum, but the proceeds from its sales would play at least a little music on our ever-growing stack of golf course bills.

The first caller responding to our ad in the *Cit-Pat* took the pool table and all the accessories. Three hundred seventy-five dollars. Exactly the same as the sitar had fetched. Only this time there was no commission, just the $12 cost of the *Cit-Pat* newspaper ad. The proceeds from both sales went from my hands immediately into Marcy's, en route to the creditors on the top of the stack.

I felt only a little pang but mostly relief when they lugged the table out. I hadn't enjoyed seeing that fine table sitting there in pieces year after year, especially now that there was no immediate prospect that it would be put back in service at The Boondocks clubhouse. Psychologically, for me and for Marcy, it was good to convert the pool table and sitar into cash. But to be ready for the 1971 season, we needed a far more substantial infusion of cash.

One thing I had never aspired to get adept at was borrowing money. But, like most everything else, you practice it enough, you get better. In the three years since launching The Boondocks project I had gotten quite proficient at refinancing our home.

And that meant showing bank president Dave Findlay that we had converted the last cash advance into an even greater increase in the value of the place. Which we had, so it was actually not that tough a case to make. I had done a preliminary workup of our Federal income tax; as far as the IRS was concerned, we had made a profit for our first year. Easy for them to say. And easy enough to figure when you took into account the thousands of unpaid hours that Marcy and I—and assorted friends and relatives—had contributed. And how much the kids had accomplished at 25¢ an hour.

Our controllable operating expenses were ridiculously low by any standard. We had paid wages to no fewer than eight young people during the year but at $1.50 an hour that was still undoubtedly less for hired help than any course around. Every other expense category—supplies, fuel, maintenance and repair, marketing—was already laughably low against area standards.

As for income, the raw numbers showed a solid base established and decent prospects for building on it.

Beleaguered though Marcy and I felt, the balance sheet for The Boondocks didn't look all that bad. As I headed into town for another refinancing negotiation session with Dave Findlay, my spirits were higher than they had been since before the gray, gloomy days of November.

I sat down in Dave's dowdy office in the old building in the center of what had been "The Block" a century earlier, when Grass Lake was a thriving town drawing thousands of visitors from around the Midwest to its mineral baths. There was still an occasional whiff in the air of that rotten-egg aroma that suggested the sulfur still lingered in the town's water supply.

Dave took maybe two minutes to scan the numbers I had spent hours assembling.

"Well, looking at the record," he said, "when you took out your first mortgage here and paid off Daryle Heselschwerdt's land contract, your mortgage was—let's see here—$29,000. That left you with $6,000 cash, which you promptly sank into seed and fertilizer."

I knew all this by heart, but Dave seemed to need to recite the history before telling me the decision on our refinancing application.

"Okay, Mr. Haney, then in September of 1968 we rewrote you again, taking it up to $31,500 but now at 6.5 percent. That let you upgrade your water system, certainly another necessity, and acquire gang mowers, greens mowers, and some miscellaneous equipment. Lot of equipment on this list, must all have been used, I presume?"

"Right, Dave. Well used, but the price was right."

"I'm sure it must have been or you wouldn't have bought it. All right, then, a couple small allotments, and here we have a draw early this year, February of '70, actually, and that brought us to $34,000 even, still at the 6.5. You used that to stock your pro shop, another shipment of fertilizer, pay wages for half dozen of our local teenagers. Sound about right to you so far?"

I nodded.

"And on your application here, this would bring you to an even $40,000. The bad news is, interest rates have gone up to 8 percent. And over a longer term, fifteen years, your payment would be $382.28 a month, plus taxes and insurance. Now are you sure, $40,000 is going to be enough?"

I stared at him a while, then said, "We're sure going to try to make it do. But are you comfortable that the place justifies that big a mortgage?"

"Let me put it this way—I'd sure like to have that place for what you've got in it, let alone what its potential is."

"To be forthright with you, Dave, we don't expect any significant money coming in for a couple years. With the soft economy and high unemployment in the area, Marcy and I are looking at break-even in '71. We're figuring we'll still be making off-season payments out of my salary."

"I see here your last raise at the university was a real nice one. Brought you up to $24,300 per year. That shows they value you highly. You'll probably get another good bump again this fall. And as frugal as you and Marcy are, the higher payment won't be a problem."

Easy enough for him to say.

ONE OF THE LESSONS LEARNED in our first season: building a golf course is a lot more satisfying than owning one.

In fact, fantasizing about building a golf course is more fun than owning one, which may be why more people entertain such notions than act on them. Only once you're in it do you learn one of the most distasteful parts of the business: it is a business. The complaints of businesspeople over the years are justified. There is too much red tape. There is too much paperwork. There is too much aggravation getting information, service, or often even a response from government officials. And there are people who treat you differently when you are on the other side of the counter from them.

We were more fortunate than many businesspeople because nearly everybody is in a good mood when they come to a golf course. And why not? They are getting away from the pressures and frustrations of everyday life for an interlude in the outdoors with some light exercise. They are usually with people they like. They are in a setting where a lot of money and effort has been expended to create an experience they can enjoy for a time, then leave for others to maintain and worry about.

But over the course of a season, thousands of different people play even a small country golf course and the law of averages says that a few of them will be disagreeable to deal with. We had very, very few of these and not a single one that was unbearable. Marcy and Mary Joseph bore the brunt of it, smiling through the occasional expectations of pampering that would be customary only at the most elite country club, listening to discourses on shot after shot of round after round, hearing excuses from delivery men who didn't arrive when promised or had the order wrong. The typical aggravations of any person behind any counter anywhere.

As trivial as that might seem, we occasionally chafed under the feeling that some people felt that when they paid $1.50 for a nine-hole round of golf along with it went a right to treat you or your workers as a slightly lower form of life. It certainly made all of us more sensitive to waitresses, salespeople, and service people.

Perhaps the sorest point with me was the way a very few people treated the land. We knew that we weren't being singled out. A look at almost any roadside in the United States shows that we were not alone. Littering has long been a national disgrace. The accumulation along Curtis Road was much the same as in the drainage ditches bordering any country road. It ranged from beer cans and fast-food bags to entire sacks of garbage and trash to discarded furniture. And house pets dropped off, dead or alive.

We did the same thing that Henry Samyn, the Walkers, and anyone with frontage on a country road did—we cleaned up other people's messes, took it to the dump, buried the dead, and shook our heads while muttering "what kind of people do such things."

But on the golf course itself, littering was especially noxious. Fortunately, we had little of that. We had printed on our scorecards: Please Don't Litter. And while I doubt that helped much, it may have sensitized a few minds. We had trash barrels at every tee box, so there was plenty of opportunity for people to correctly deposit their disposals. Still, we would sometimes find an empty bottle or can floating in one of the ponds, a golf ball package on the ground. Once in a while we'd have a minor repair to a green when someone left a cigarette or cigar butt burning and it would leave an ugly scorch as it turned to ash. Compared with other places, these were minor annoyances.

Still, they irritated me. And three or four times that first year, the much more rare littering offense would really set me off. We had a decent parking lot west of the barns. It was simple—closely mowed grass with railroad ties flat on the ground, arranged to identify rows for parking. Why someone would choose such a place to empty an entire dashboard ashtray of filter-tip cigarette butts, I could not imagine, and I would swear out loud as I cleaned them up.

One day as I swept past number nine green on the tractor, I saw something lying on the ground and hopped off to pick it up. It was a scorecard, and it had been torn into a dozen or so pieces. I looked at the piece that had the final scores of the three players and I could see why someone had wanted to get rid of the evidence. All three scores were ugly and each of the players had obviously encountered the ponds on numbers six, eight, and nine, posting the number that golfers call the Abominable Snowman, an eight, or worse.

I picked up all the pieces and later laid them out on the pro shop counter, arranging them as if constructing a jigsaw puzzle. Then I checked the three names against the sign-in book. The culprits were the superintendent, principal, and a teacher at one of the high schools for which we allowed the golf team, their opponents, and coaches to play free.

I taped the card back together and sat down at the typewriter. I wrote a note to the superintendent advising that I knew he would be pleased to learn that his scorecard wasn't lost after all, that I had discovered it just before my mowers would have cut it further into micro-pieces. I had reassembled it for him and was pleased to return it to his care.

From a business and local public relations standpoint, that was not prudent. By now I knew better, but I did it anyhow. I felt that those who were entrusted with the education of our young people could use a lesson themselves. And, believing that the customer is always right except when he is wrong, it felt good.

As Marcy and I thought about that first year, about the things that we liked and didn't like about dealing with the public, we agreed that that kind of stuff really bugged us. And that was something we needed to think seriously about as we looked toward the future. Yes, we could endure that kind of behavior from a very tiny minority of our customers. But did we really want to?

I COULDN'T GET OUT OF MY MIND the image of going after a mosquito with an elephant gun. Professor George Katona had given sage economic counsel to cabinet officers, heads of state, and the world's largest corporations. And now, at his invitation, and with the first season of The Boondocks behind me, he asked me to lunch so that—I presumed—we could without interruption discuss the financial development of our small-potatoes country golf course.

My father—and countless other fathers—used to say free advice was worth what you paid for it. That was glib enough that I probably said it a few times myself but if I did, I regret it. First of all, I don't actually remember paying for advice very often. So most of the best advice I ever got necessarily came to me without cost. Without cost to me, that is; it undoubtedly cost the adviser a great deal in the learning. But clichés are clichés for a good reason: they often carry a lot of truth.

My problem was not that Dr. Katona would give me bad advice. I was concerned that I would be unable to follow it. And that was the problem with free advice: if people give it to you and you know it is good and they know it is good and you still don't heed it, then where do you go in that relationship?

"Now, Beeel, now look here," Dr. Katona said, pointing his salad fork at me as if he would stab me on the forehead with it if he thought I wasn't looking here. "It isn't news unless it's new. People will grumble about an increase in the price of gasoline. They will complain for a week, maybe two or three. Then what? They will get used to it and quiet down as that price becomes the new reality. Then in a few months when the price goes up again, they will grumble once again. The cycle repeats."

He dug into his salad as I wondered how this applied to my golf course. Perhaps it didn't.

"Beef. Interest rates. Taxes. Bread. Cigarettes. Coffee. It makes no difference." With a flick of his wrist he waved them all away. "Prices go up, in a few weeks what was alarming, outrageous, unacceptable, now Poof! and you have the new norm."

"Professor Katona, are you suggesting that I should increase greens fees?"

"Ha! I suggest nothing of the kind. Every merchant must determine the value he places on his product or service. That is for you alone to decide. Let me qualify that. That is for you to set the price. But the decision of whether that price is fair, ah, that will be made by the catalytic element in this formula—the consumer. Now, look here, Beeel. The consumer is all-powerful. The corporations, governments, small businessmen—they propose but finally and forever the consumer will dispose."

I thought about it as we finished our lunch in thoughtful silence. The professor was allowing the student to digest what he had served up.

"The good man who mows my lawn," Dr. Katona said, "told me that he had just paid one dollar for a sandwich he used to buy for twenty-five cents. He wanted to know what I thought about that. I told him, the difference is that today he has the dollar."

Dr. Katona looked at me intently, as if his stare would burn the thought into my memory.

"Now if any of that is of use to you in your enterprise, there you have it. And you also have my personal hopes that however your golf course venture proceeds from a business standpoint that it rewards your spirit and that of your good wife and children. After all, at the end of the day, that is the greatest asset you possess and the one on which the richest dividends may be earned."

I reached for the check, but Dr. Katona brushed my hand away.

"Now for the real purpose I invited you to dine with me." Dr. Katona smiled that almost-scary smile. "Last year I promised myself a round of golf at your course but was never able to arrange for that. The coming season will be different. Therefore, I have gone to an indoor driving range in an effort to scrape a decade-old layer of rust off my swing. Now, will you please explain in terms I can understand, why all my shots take a sharp left turn and dive into the ground. Look here, Beeel, I have a theory about this."

DURING THE WINTER, I thought about what Professor Katona had said. I was sure his points were valid in the abstract, but I couldn't see how they applied to our situation. The course would be more mature in 1971, but how could we ask more money for essentially the same product?

We were just coming off a first year of operation that had been moderately successful in terms of the goals we had set. Then again, we had set what most people might consider to be very modest goals.

When we put aside the business aspect and looked at what we had done with the land, we felt good. We had halted the wind and water erosion inflicted by so many years of agricultural misuse. The maintained roughs blended almost seamlessly into the marshes, meadows, and woodlands. Ducks and herons nested in the ponds. The skittish sandhill cranes had not deserted us. Bountiful apples hung from the rescued tree behind five green. After teeing off on number seven, with its majestic view, golfers could pause on the Smedley Hill slope for a handful of juicy blackberries. Willow Creek still held frisky brook trout, and northern pike cruised upstream from Little Wolf Lake. The Willow Pond and crescent pond teemed with largemouth bass and lunker bluegills, just as little Pat had asked for.

Marcy's oak woods was now clean, natural, and serene. These things counted to us.

A manager of a suburban country club ringed by elegant homes would have been horrified at the amount of natural Michigan meadow grasses and plants we not only tolerated but encouraged. But ours was a rustic course in a rural setting—primping not practiced.

I wouldn't be happy with the fairways until we had money enough for regular fertilizing and someday for a fairway sprinkling system. The turf on the main tees was satisfactory, but they also deserved much more fertilizer than we could afford, as well as more water, and we needed to expand surfaces on the secondary tee boxes. But the heart of the course, the bent-grass greens, had completely filled out and as cold weather arrived the greens were well prepared for a normal winter.

After only one year of play we had achieved a main objective: a course that fit so comfortably into the land it looked as if it had been there all along.

If in 1971 and beyond we could build steadily on our decent startup year, we would be okay. There had once been this dream, always indistinct, and this hope, always unspoken, that in fifteen or so years the course would be a solid business producing strong profits; that we would have long since expanded to eighteen holes; that our property and that of our friends bordering the course would have appreciated greatly in value; and, most desirable to me, that Mark and Pat could take over the course if they wished—and that they might wish to.

Lately that dream and those hopes seemed more distant than ever and receding into the mist.

THAT WAS OUR FRAME OF MIND as we closed the books and our minds on 1970.

Then, in the winter of 1970–71, we were hit with the blow that is the fear of farmers and others who depend on the land for their living. The weather turned even more bitterly against us.

1·9·7·1

Thirty-One

No snow cover. Early February in Michigan and no snow cover. This was not the way it was supposed to be.

I leaned into the needles of sand grains driven by the stiff north wind and headed toward number one green, kicking up dust with each step—dust in Michigan fields in February. Our year-old golf course into which so many thousands of hours had been poured to make it green was now gray, arid, and seemingly lifeless.

I walked up barren number one fairway and stood on the apron of frozen number one green. There was not a single ball mark to be seen. Mark and I had fixed them all one nice early November day a couple weeks after we had closed the course for the season.

That was three months ago and while there were no unrepaired dents on number one's putting surface, there were few signs of life in a green that had taken so much time and effort to build three years before.

If the crowns of these countless millions of bent-grass plants were as dead as they looked, we were in for tough times come spring. Still, as Walt Bauer reassured me, even if the crowns were dead there could still be a spark of life in the roots, though the greens might not show it until late May when the ground is warm. Not all the greens were as distressed as number one and the higher and more exposed ones that had been blasted by frigid, dry winds. But if several greens were not playable, we surely couldn't open the course to the public in spring of 1971.

We were not alone. Throughout southern Michigan in the winter of 1970–71, other golf course operators and farmers were shaking first their heads and then their fists at the skies that refused to deliver moisture. I felt their pain, and then some.

In Michigan, virtually every year since records were kept, there has been a January thaw. Usually in mid or late January, the winds will shift and funnel warmer air up from the Gulf of Mexico, enough to raise temperatures well into the forties and sometimes into the fifties. After four or five days of almost balmy weather, the jet stream will again dominate and predictably an Alberta Clipper will roar down from the northwest with sub-zero temperatures, then another system will move in with a heavy coat of snow. That is, in a typical year. In 1971, the January thaw came on February 5 and lasted six hours. On this day, the thermometer read forty-two degrees at The Boondocks, scarcely torrid enough to melt snow and ice, but then, there was no snow and ice to melt.

I looked up at the clear, pale blue sky, at that waxing gibbous moon.

It was February 5, 1971, and on that moon 280,000 miles away from The Boondocks Golf Course, three men were at that moment setting out scientific experiments on the lunar surface in fulfillment of a program I had worked on several years. But I had left Bendix Aerospace long before Apollo 14 lifted off. So I missed out on the exhilaration of shared success that many of my friends at Bendix, at the Manned Spaceflight Center in Houston, and at Cape Kennedy were now enjoying. I had kept in touch, though, and after the near-disaster of Apollo 13, I was relieved that Apollo 14 and the deploying of the Apollo Lunar Surface Experiments Package was proceeding with textbook precision. And I was grateful to have had even a small part in that program.

I stood on the rear collar of number one green and looked back toward the house and barns. Everywhere in between was a landscape that to me was as hostile as the lunar surface. For five days, raw winds had torn out of the northwest; now a cloud of fine dust stung my face. It had warmed from fifteen-below-zero temperatures and wind-chill factors of fifty and sixty below. This day, with its few hours of above-freezing temperatures, was merely a taunting too-brief interlude in a seemingly endless string of bitingly cold days. But what was truly bizarre was the spectacle I now watched: mini-sandstorms whipping up here and there on my golf course.

Not a drop of water in sight, save for the deeply frozen ponds, and even that ice seemed dry and brittle. There was water locked in those ponds, under maybe a foot of ice. And with a chain saw I could cut a hole and get at that water. Then what? Pump it onto the greens, where it would freeze into a sheet that would extinguish any flickering life in the grass beneath it. And the pump would have to be drained immediately after every use, otherwise the expanding ice would crack the housing. Of course that was assuming I could get the engine started in the first place. And that would have to be done for each of the nine greens.

Water, water in the ponds and not a drop for greens.

What the hell was I, an English major and a writer, doing standing here on this desolate landscape, chained to this brutal mistress of a golf course? But then, I had been just as much out of my element at Bendix working with engineers and scientists who were devising and fabricating those sophisticated experiments and lunar vehicles. Because I could organize and communicate, I had become Configuration Manager for the Apollo Lunar Surface Experiments Package. In that role I was responsible for seeing that each element in the experiments package was the right size and shape and drew only its allotted power from the radioisotope thermal-electric generator and could be stowed in the Apollo 14 spacecraft. These experiments—the suprathermal ion detector, the passive seismometer, the solar wind detector, and five others—would unlock secrets of not only the moon but also of our solar system, and perhaps shed light on the origin of the universe.

I had taken a strange and circuitous route to get into that role, and even into the military-space industry.

In 1956, while an undergraduate, I was hired for a summer job as a technical editor at Rocketdyne, a division of North American Aviation, in Canoga Park, California. I had a sharp eye for typos and was a stickler for consistency in style, habits that had been drummed into me as a reporter on the *Michigan Daily*, U of M's student newspaper. My brother Bob got me the interview for the job and then told me, "Whether you get it and how you perform is up to you."

The summer at Rocketdyne was a life-changing experience. For one thing, I witnessed the testing of booster rockets at Santa Susana Proving Grounds. We stood there on a ledge across the canyon from the test site and felt the ground vibrate and saw the canyon boil with fire and smoke as clusters of Redstone and Jupiter rocket engines roared. You couldn't hear, see, or think of anything except the awesome thundering explosion before you. I wondered for several anxious moments if those scientists and engineers knew what they were doing or if perhaps things might get out of hand and they would trigger the apocalypse.

That job also required that I have secret clearance and that fact was to change my life for years to come. NASA did not yet exist in the summer of 1956 when I worked at Rocketdyne. The infant space industry, cloaked in secrecy, was presumed by most people to be a socially acceptable cover for clandestine work to perform engineering and science for military use in space.

When I took that job, my motives were simply to make some money and have a tiny role in man's exploration of space. I had no idea that the secret clearance would open the door for a succession of jobs and travel around the country with Chrysler Missile Division, Lockheed Aircraft, and finally Bendix Aerospace.

Now, I was out of that world. And into a much different one that I was equally untrained for, the world of social science. And, at the same time, inhabiting the disparate worlds of business and golf course management.

From my arid and seemingly lifeless golf course, I stared at the moon and thought about what the astronauts might be doing. I knew that when they lifted off from the lunar surface the next day, leaving those scientific experiments behind, they would leave the moon 65.1 pounds heavier and the Earth 65.1 pounds lighter because of the efforts of thousands of earthlings to build and deliver those scientific experiments. And I was one.

Somehow that put into a tolerable perspective the efforts of Marcy, the kids, and me to transform these hundred acres. We hadn't unlocked any vital secrets to share with mankind. But we had labored long and mightily and had given birth to something on this land that was more right than what had come before.

We knew when we began it could not be forever. Someday we would have to walk away from it, turn it over to others who would have their way with it. We could not control the destiny of this place, any more than Nate Fish had been able to, or than the farmers who came before and after him. We could not control the weather, the economy, or the other forces that would mold our fates on this place.

We were doing here what the astronauts were doing at that moment more than a quarter million miles away: taking the risk to make the dream come true, giving the challenge the best we had, preparing ourselves for whatever lies ahead.

THE TALK AT GRASS LAKE FEED & GRAIN, at the Napoleon Livestock Auction House, in every farmer's kitchen, and every rural coffee shop in the county was the weather. And that was not unusual. What was unusual was that for once everyone agreed: there had never been weather here quite like this. Were we really going to have back-to-back drought years?

More than two months into the year, when there should have been a snowpack still building up for a spring melt, the fields were brown and gray and bone dry.

What traces of precipitation did fall in March, whether snow or rain, evaporated in a puff.

Maybe April will make up for it, the farmers said, and went uneasily about their business, readying equipment for spring chores.

And that was all we could do at The Boondocks. But the difference was we weren't facing just the loss of a season's crop, which was plenty serious; we were looking at the destruction of our entire enterprise. If the greens were indeed stone dead, there was no way we could go on. We would lose the entire season and its revenue. We would have to tear out the dead bent grass and start over virtually from scratch. If our greens had died, we would lose not just this season but also at least the next one too. There was no way we could sustain the financial loss. And I doubted that we had the stomach or the energy to go through all that again.

Walt Bauer came out, took one look, and shook his head.

"It's the same all over," he said. "Mine at Loch Alpine don't look much better."

He took out a pocketknife and sliced into the turf at half a dozen spots on number one green.

"Desiccation, they call it. Fancy name for dried out. Roots haven't withered, though. That's a good sign. But until you see some green, there isn't anything you can do but wait and . . ."

Walt's voice trailed off and he gave me a sad smile and shook his head. He reached in his pocket and held something out to me. It was a *Watchtower* publication.

"Pray. That's what I'm doing, Bill, and my family and I have included you in ours. Door's always open to you, ever you want to walk through it."

It came so slowly it was almost imperceptible.

The first signs, here and there on number seven green, pale olive flecks among the dead brown blades, a shade of green so faint and weak you weren't sure if it was seen or imagined. And this was the first week of April when, in a normal year—if there was such a thing—we would have already mowed several times.

But number seven was built on Gladys's knoll, the richest soil on the place and a location shielded from the worst winter winds. If any green was alive, we would expect it to be number seven. But what of the others? Still only the faintest traces of weak life.

So we kept up what we were doing, pouring on water, nitrogen, and hope. And at last we got a break in the weather. Still no rain of consequence, but the temperatures warmed, to seventy, then seventy-five, and amazingly to a balmy eighty degrees on April 12. The warm sun in combination with our constant watering and heavy fertilizing finally stirred the countless millions of traumatized bent-grass plants from their deep survival hibernation.

Once the temperatures rose and held well overnight to warm the soil, it was as though a galaxy of switches were turned on and within days, one after another, the greens came back to life.

Jack Welch, the representative from O.M. Scott Seed Company, came by to see if his dire forecast of a month ago had come true. He had said in March we should resign ourselves to closing for the 1971 season and prepare to reseed all the greens in August.

"I'd like to say it's a tribute to the endurance of our grass strain," Welch said. "But it's more a commentary on how healthy you had the greens going in that they have come back this well. In fact, that they have even survived."

Walt Bauer had a different theory. He looked at the resurgent greens, smiled, and handed me another Jehovah's Witnesses publication.

The secretaries of our last year's golf leagues understood when I told them we had to push back schedules a couple weeks to let the greens establish fully. Our members and regulars had been prepared for worse news and were relieved to hear we'd be open for business in May, not as early as we had hoped, but at least there would be golf again at The Boondocks in 1971.

It was a telephone call I had been dreading, but expecting.

"Bill?"

"Is that you, Kent?"

Before Kent answered, I knew it was him and I was afraid I knew why he was calling. I looked out the kitchen window and to the northwest, although I knew I couldn't see the Smedley house from there. But at least I could see the Smedley Hill where Gladys had stood so many times and looked down at the marsh and the woods beyond.

"She's gone."

"Kent, I'll be right over."

A long silence.

"No. I'm not home. I'm calling from Foote Hospital in Jackson. I've got arrangements to take care of here. I don't know when I'll be home."

I didn't want to think about Kent alone the first night in that little house he had shared all these years with Gladys.

"Kent, will you call me when you get there? I'd like to come over."

"Well, I'll be all right. I'm going to have to face it sometime. Might as well be tonight. You don't have to come over for my sake."

"Maybe not. But I do for mine."

The Smedleys' house was even quieter, emptier than I had dreaded. Kent sat there at the kitchen table, staring into space, occasionally glancing at me, moving his lips without saying anything, barely shaking his head. Then he laughed, one short, mirthless bark.

"Everyone thought she was so tough. If only they knew. And if they did know, that really would have gotten her goat." He finally took a sip of his coffee, which must have been cold by now. I noticed he had lit just one cigarette—and that one more than a half hour ago—and then let it burn down to nothing in the ashtray without having taken a puff. "She was an orphan, did you know that?"

"No. She never told me."

"Not surprised. I don't believe she was embarrassed about it. I always guessed it was more that it hurt her to talk about it. Even with me. The idea that she had been abandoned. Or maybe worse than abandoned. Rejected. That her parents took a look at her and decided they just didn't want her. I'm not one for amateurs trying to psychoanalyze people but if I were . . . Ever notice how people say something like that, then go right ahead and do it. Everything that comes after the 'but' ought to be totally ignored. Anyhow, I'm rambling. If I were to offer my theory, I'd say that was why Glad put on the face to the world that she did. Didn't want to be rejected. If a relationship was going to end, Glad would damn well be the one to terminate it."

Kent was no professional psychoanalyst and neither was I but it made sense to me.

"She'd push people, intimidate them. If they let her, she'd dominate them. But if they just took it, she wouldn't have a thing to do with them. Even Ed Harrison—she sure didn't like Ol' Flannelmouth but I'd guess she had a little respect for the crazy coot. She respected people who would come right back at her. Give as good as they got. I think that's part of the reason she took to you."

I couldn't help but laugh.

"Kent, I have to tell you, I don't recall ever once standing up to Gladys toe-to-toe, not one time. She had my number from the start."

"Well, she had mine, too. From the first time I saw that little gal, anything she wanted, I'd do it. And she damn well knew it, too."

It was quiet again for a while. I looked past Kent's shoulder into the sitting room where Gladys's favorite chair sat facing the fireplace. There was no fire in the fireplace. The room was cold.

"Thanks for coming over, Bill. I think I'd like to be alone now. I'm going to have to get used to that, I guess. But I'm not entirely sure I want to or that I'll be able to."

Thirty-Two

For decades, change had been slow to come to Grass Lake. But as in many communities, teenagers chafed under policies and rules that were too restrictive to suit them. Increasingly they found grownups on their side in opposition to the school board and township board against policies enforced so harshly that they were actually driving kids out of school instead of keeping them in.

For years, the board was adamant that their codes for suitable attire and facial hair restrictions "will be enforced to the letter." On the few occasions that those policies were timidly challenged, board members pontificated on the damage that could be done to community morals if boys were allowed to grow sideburns lower than the notch in the ear. Beards and mustaches? Out of the question. No exceptions. Girls were expected to wear "appropriate attire," which meant certainly no miniskirts or revealing blouses, and dresses were to be of "conventional length."

Those policies were, to the board, an impenetrable brick wall that shielded the community from the pernicious influences of nearby liberal hotbeds such as the Ann Arbor campus of the University of Michigan.

Ironically, it was a celebration of old-time community values that dislodged the first brick in the edifice.

Grass Lake Village was about to celebrate its centennial. The village actually had been in existence far longer than a hundred years—at least some forty-five years longer. But it had become incorporated only in 1871. A hundred years later the merchants of the area, not immune to the country's economic slowdown, saw an opportunity to energize business. The Grass Lake Centennial Celebration was born.

Among the first revenue sources was the Old-Time Grass Lake Jail, with construction on the vintage building already underway in January, six months before the festivities would be in full swing. The idea was to ensure completion in plenty of time to arrest "outlaws" who would be incarcerated until they had paid their fine. They might do their time in a few minutes or an hour or two, depending on whether Bob Mather had film in his camera, or whether the lawbreaker was carrying a spare dollar in wallet or purse.

There were a number of illegal acts for which Sheriff Roy Damaron or one of his many deputies might make an arrest. High on the list was, for females, failure to wear a full-length dress; and for males, not having sufficient facial hair.

Spirits were high around the village as the mayor, council members, school officials, business owners, and other community leaders were hauled off to the pokey in the genuine antique "Paddy Wagon," which often had to be pushed by the Keystone Kops and prisoners alike to get it to the jail. A key design feature of the lockup was a large, barred window, which permitted easy viewing of the hardened criminals by throngs of passersby. And, not least, the coffers grew as fines were paid, and the cash registers were set to jingling at the Spartan Grocery and Braun's Pharmacy and Wolfinger's Hardware and the town's half-dozen other retail establishments.

Then there arose the dilemma.

A clean-shaven high-school junior was arrested. He had come into town to buy groceries and was spied by a deputy who took him into custody for a clear violation of the facial hair law.

Not only that, he was arrested by some of the very citizens who were instrumental in implementing the facial hair policy at Grass Lake High School.

Wait a minute, the young man protested. I wanted to let my sideburns grow, maybe start a beard or mustache, and the school officials said that would violate the school board's facial hair policy. So then I get arrested by the very same people, but now they're talking as Centennial Committee members and saying I have to pay a fine because I'm in violation of a different facial hair policy.

This required an emergency meeting of the various boards.

Certainly it was not feasible, one man suggested, for high-school boys to be clean shaven at school, then sprout the required facial hair the minute they stepped into the village.

True enough, another said, but if we exempt these kids and let them go hairless, think of how that will look. You'll have clean-shaven young men walking around alongside their bearded older brothers and fathers—ruins the whole ambiance.

Then too, someone ventured, think of the revenue we'd forgo.

And what if one of these big farm bucks didn't want to be hauled off to jail? Wouldn't that be a nice scene?

Someone asked, If we let these school kids grow beards and what all, couldn't we be accused of being inconsistent?

How'd you figure that? another asked.

Well, here we're saying it's inappropriate on school grounds because it makes our young people look just like those peaceniks over to Ann Arbor. At the same time, not only are all us adults doing it, now we'd be saying it's okay for the kids, too. How is it that if kids protesting the establishment wear beards and long hair it shows they're rebels and here we are, the establishment, and we're sprouting face hair, so—

When the talking was done, the decision was supported all around, including school officials and members of the school board. Henceforth, facial hair for all young men capable of growing it was hereby required within the village limits. Therefore, for the rest of the spring and summer, until the Centennial Days festivities were officially concluded, high-school boys were permitted to have facial hair and long hair. But as soon as the celebration was over and school resumed in the fall, the school board ban would again be in force.

Without realizing it, the Centennial committee had just clarified the hair issue so neatly that only the most reactionary refused to see how preposterous the school board's ban had been. In the coffee shops and gas stations, in the Three Sons Tavern and Big Al's Gun Shop, people began to chuckle over the school board's flip-flop. Beards are bad, except for sometimes when they're good, but after that, they're bad again.

That brick down, the much more harsh school board policies came under challenge. Opponents of the board's haughtiness and callousness toward kids under its charge saw a glimmer of hope. It might take a while and it would be too late for the kids already hurt by unfair and long-outmoded policies, but the day was coming when the policies—and the politicians—that drove kids out of school or made it miserable for them would be discarded.

SLOWLY SOME THINGS were returning to normal at The Boondocks. The Thursday Men's League was back and that meant I could expect some barb or other from Al Cooper. It wasn't long in coming.

"They pay you in yen at the university?" Al asked me.

"Al, I don't know what you're talking about but I'll bet I'm about to learn."

"Japanese money for Japanese iron. Anybody paying for their greens fees here in Asian currency?" and he jerked his thumb toward the shiny new maroon 1971 Datsun 510 sitting in my driveway.

The little hatchback station wagon was the first new car we had bought in seven years and the second new one we had ever owned. The first had been a sleek 1964 Plymouth Fury convertible, white with blue upholstery, which was a gorgeous vehicle and an ugly mistake, in that we then had four children, the oldest not yet five, and I somehow had neglected to involve Marcy in the purchase decision.

I loved the Fury and was amazed at Marcy's reaction when I brought her out to see what I had come back with on what started as a scouting expedition for a good, sensible station wagon. There it sat in the driveway in all its showroom gleam, our first new car, still emitting its seductive new-car aroma.

I could tell that Marcy had mixed emotions about it when she said, "Are you nuts? We have four little kids and you bought a convertible? Just what the hell were you thinking?" And she went back into the house without so much as a spin around the block.

After two years, when Marcy's attitude about the Fury convertible hadn't changed noticeably, it seemed prudent to dispose of it, although swapping it for the sporty Austin-Healy didn't prove to be the final solution either. When I told good friend Pryor McGinnis about my dilemma, he said he always wanted a little sports car and promptly took the Healy off my hands for enough money that we could buy a vehicle of consummate utility for the aspiring golf course builder. It was a sensible and simple 1965 Ford F-100 pickup truck. Marcy agreed that a pickup truck was a necessity on the golf course, as long as I drove it and promised to do nothing impetuous with her Olds wagon.

The Haneys had a lot of history with products of Detroit's Big Three about which Al Cooper was obviously unaware. But I had known Al for a while and he knew very well that I had been buying used made-in-America cars since the day we moved to Grass Lake. We had, in fact, become an equal opportunity used-car graveyard, going through half a dozen Valiants, Chevvies, Oldsmobiles, Dodges, and miscellaneous brands in the next four years.

Eventually we realized cheap cars were just too expensive. We were spending more money on acquiring and repairing junkers than we would in payments on an inexpensive new car. Since no American car manufactureres were building a sensible, fuel-efficient, compact station wagon, the only decision was whether to buy a Toyota, Honda, or Datsun.

There were months-long waiting lists for Toyota and Honda, so that further reduced the choice. There was, however, a brand-new Datsun dealership in Jackson. They had exactly one Datsun 510 station wagon and I could have it in any color I wanted as long as I wanted maroon. The price was $2,557, which seemed, pound for pound, a bit excessive but since we had no cash and none coming in that wasn't already encumbered to reduce the growing pile of golf course bills, any amount was substantial. So we did the American thing with the Japanese vehicle: we financed it.

And two days later, there it sat, under Al Cooper's disdainful glare.

"Lots of people around here fought the Japs not that long ago," he said. "Men like that, they might wonder why a man taking their money on an American golf course isn't buying Detroit iron."

Cooper was an influential man and his views probably reflected a typical viewpoint. I truly hadn't thought about such ramifications; I was just buying the most sensible low-priced car I could find. I was already known in this conservative community as "that feller who doesn't think we oughta be kicking ass in Vietnam." Marcy and I were the radicals who challenged the school board's married students policy and now I was violating some code of conduct by buying a Datsun.

"Al, nothing would delight me more than being able to buy an American car. In fact, I've bought quite a number of them and hope to buy more."

"Then what's with this, whatever it is, Datsun? What've you got against, Ford, or GM, or Chrysler?"

"Just that they don't make a sensible car, at least one that makes sense to me."

"Meaning what? What do you consider a sensible car?"

"One that gets more than twelve miles a gallon. One that doesn't weigh half again what it has to and then has an engine three times too big because it has to carry all that weight. One that doesn't have an inflated price just to pay for sheet metal changes every year that're strictly for appearance and have nothing to do with function. One that—"

"Okay, okay. But how do you justify shipping American gold to Japan, hurting our own automobile manufacturers? And right here in Michigan where we're dead in the water without healthy car companies, for God's sake."

"Al, I didn't buy this car to make a statement on patriotism, but when you think about it, it's probably more patriotic right now to buy a foreign car than a domestic."

Cooper looked at me like he thought I was smoking a controlled substance.

"Now, Mr. Haney, that's going to take some fancy explaining."

"All right. Do you agree that the buyer has the right to determine what it is he wants in a car? That, as with golf clubs and balls in that pro shop, the buyer gets to choose and not have the manufacturer dictate what he must buy?"

"Well, of course. Nobody going to tell me what I have to buy with my own money. Even so, how do you get around the question of patriotism?"

"Al, what incentive is there for Detroit's Big Three to start making more fuel-efficient, smaller, safer, less expensive cars if people just swallow hard and keep buying whatever Detroit churns out, just because they feel obligated? As long as you buy it, they'll keep cranking it out. It won't be until American manufacturers see their market share dwindling that they'll wake up and see that if Detroit won't make it, people will buy it elsewhere. VW, Volvo, Fiat from Europe. Or the Japanese stuff. You want to talk about patriotism? A case can be made that buying foreign right now is far and away more patriotic in the long run."

"Now, Haney, that's pushing it pretty far."

By now I had myself convinced, if not Al Cooper. I really hadn't thought about it before, but as I listened to myself, it seemed plausible, even reasonable. But while the debate techniques I had learned at Troy High School may have helped me build a case that was sensible, I could tell from the expression on Al Cooper's face that there was more at work than logic. I may have scored a technical point and prevailed in a skirmish, but once again I hadn't won any points in the battle for men's minds in Grass Lake Township.

Thirty-Three

The phone had been ringing for some time before it registered with me that it was two longs and a short, our ring. That also meant phones up and down Curtis Road were ringing and many of my neighbors would be looking up from their pillows, as I was, wondering who the hell was calling at two-thirty in the dead of night. One thing I knew, it couldn't be good news.

"Bill." It was Kent Smedley's voice, a million miles away. "I had no idea it was this late until it was already ringing. Then I had to let it ring until you answered because—"

"Kent, it's all right. Don't worry about it. What is it?"

There was a long pause and I could hear a couple of clicks as neighbors hung up, curiosity satisfied though perhaps disappointed that it wasn't something exciting or juicy.

"It's a lot to ask, Bill, but is there any chance that you could come over here?"

I almost said, Now? but it was obvious Kent wouldn't be calling me at this time of night to ask me to come over later the next day.

"Well, sure. I'll be there in ten minutes. Want me to make a pot of coffee?"

"Just made one. See you then."

I pulled into Kent's driveway and parked alongside Gladys's lifeless fire pit. Kent had kept the place up just as tidy as ever since the funeral. But looking at the empty chair by the fire pit, then at the little house, I felt a very big emptiness, just knowing that Gladys would not be sitting at the kitchen table, sipping whatever from her glass, one Pall Mall dangling from her lips and another one she had forgotten about smoldering in the ashtray near the sink.

Kent came out and stood on the back porch steps, probably wondering why I was sitting there.

"I suppose it's too late to tell you to go back to bed and accept the apologies of a silly old man," he said.

"Just pour me that cup of coffee you promised."

I finished one cup of coffee and was starting on a second and still Kent hadn't said another word. Two or three times he opened his mouth to speak, then just shook his head, saying nothing. I knew how he felt because I didn't know what to say either.

Finally, "Kent, we all miss her. I really can't imagine how it must be for you. I only knew Gladys a little over four years and since she's gone, there's this damn big hole in my life."

"Yes. A good way of putting it. But that's not why I wanted to talk with you. I mean, that's part of it, sure. But there's something else. Actually, two things."

He got up and went into the bedroom. When he came back he was carrying a very old book that he set down carefully on the table in front of me. The book was perhaps ten by thirteen inches, with a cover of thick binder's boards overlaid with cloth and a mottled tortoise-shell paper, long since dried and flaked. It appeared to be not a manufactured book but rather a handmade artist's portfolio.

"Go ahead," he said, motioning for me to open it.

I did that, and very tenderly because the glue on the spine was dried and cracked and it looked as if it might easily come apart. I looked at a few pages at random. Each page was a pencil or charcoal sketch of a long-ago scene, a figure, a face, or an animal. It was indeed an artist's sketchbook. I turned back to look at the first page. At the top right-hand corner was written:

Mary Warren
French Street
Dublin
1799

This was the sketchbook of a young artist who lived in Ireland when Dublin was a rural village. It covered two years of her life, showing the progress of her skill and her changing interests. Toward the back of the book was a haunting self-portrait.

"Gladys wanted you to have this book. It was her most cherished possession."

"Was this Mary Warren an ancestor of Gladys's?"

"Hardly. Remember, Glad was an orphan. And I have no idea how she came by that book. But I do know that every once in a while she would sit there in her chair by the fireplace and look at those drawings, never saying a word. It was very special to her, for whatever reason. Maybe she did know something about her parents after all. I don't know. Anyhow, the last hour of Glad's life she gave me a few orders, as you might expect, and one of them was that I give you this book. 'Bill will know,' she said. That's all. A few minutes later, she was gone."

I sat there for a long while, looking at the book, wondering about it. Finally Kent coughed and that reminded me he had said there were two things he wanted to talk with me about. It hit me then that Kent was going to tell me he had just learned that he too was fatally ill. Here were two of the most delightful characters and dear friends a person could ask for and now if I was about to hear that not only had I lost one—

"Bill, you remember that story people tell about the boy sitting behind the pretty girl with a ponytail? And the boy dunked that ponytail in his inkwell?"

"Well, I've heard that, yes. But inkwells were a bit before my time. And it always sounded like an apocryphal story to me. I doubt that except in a Mark Twain story someone actually ever did that."

"Oh, yes. Someone did. At the time, it just seemed like something I had to do. No way was I going to tell sweet little Junie I had this schoolboy crush on her. But doggone it, I was a schoolboy. Fifth grade."

Kent got up quickly and went into the bedroom. When he came back, he was puffing on a Pall Mall.

"I know. I quit for good six months ago. But Gladys was alive then. Things are different now. I didn't go in there looking for smokes. I was trying to find a picture of my fifth-grade class at Addison. If you saw June's smiling face you'd understand." He looked in old yellowed folders and through some books stacked on a shelf. "Would you believe it? This house is less than a thousand square feet and I can't find anything in it. Except Gladys's Pall Malls. Every drawer I look in, another pack of her smokes. Ought to just throw the damn things out, what I ought to do."

He poured us each coffee, angrily crushed out the cigarette, and sat down at the table.

"The next summer, right after school let out, she moved away. Junie, that is. She moved just over to Hudson, only fifteen miles away but it might as well have been to an island in the South Pacific. I remember being so heartsick it ruined my whole summer. When school started back up in September, there was another girl at that desk in front of me. The new girl had flaming red hair and it was all frizzy and done up and not a ponytail in sight. I just put my head down on my arms right there on my desk in front of all those kids and I cried like a newborn baby."

I wondered where this was going. Kent's wife of more than thirty years had been dead less than two months and he was talking about a sixty-year-old memory of a girl whom he hadn't even known well enough to call her his grade-school sweetheart.

"Eventually I got control of myself," Kent said, "and crawled up out of my pool of self-pity. To keep my mind off it, I concentrated on my studies to where it made me a better student than my folks ever thought possible. Time passes. I hear June has married a fellow down in Morenci, right above the Ohio border, about thirty miles away. Sells insurance. Elks, Rotary, Optimist's Club, secretary of the Men's Bowling League. You name a club, he's in it, making contacts, selling contracts."

"So what did you do, Kent?"

"College was out of the question. Farm kids didn't even dare think like that. Felt lucky to get hired at the *Cit-Pat* as a type chaser. That's how I met Gladys. Bunch of us went bowling, then to this ballroom with a real live band and the next thing I know, I'm out there dancing with Glad. And pretty fair at it, she's telling me."

"You could have done worse."

"You're good and well told I could have. Even when she was in her thirties, Glad was a crotchety scold to most folks, but when there was nobody else around to see her being kind and think she was weak, she was gentle and as playful even, as a kitten. And loyal. She had been married once before, you know."

It was hard to imagine Gladys with some man other than Kent Smedley.

"Oh, yes," Kent said. "But she never talked about it and I never pressed her."

"Kent, did Gladys know about this girl? About June?"

"Heavens, no. I have now spoken of that to exactly one person in my life. Figured anyone I told would have laughed right in my face."

"I didn't laugh, did I?"

"No. No, you did not. So I'll ask you this. Do you think I would be a total fool to get in touch with her? I mean, here Glad's gone not yet two months and—"

"Let me stop you right there. Turn it around. Say you had checked out first. Would you have wanted Gladys to go into mourning for years? To not have a relationship with another person who could make her happy, just for the sake of what is considered conventional and proper?"

"No, but—"

"No buts, then. Fair is fair. How long since you've seen June?"

Kent looked up at me, surprise in his face.

"I told you. Fifth grade."

"But since then?"

"Not since school let out that year and she moved to Hudson. But I've kept tabs on her over the years. Kind of easy what with that Charlie being a pillar of the community and all. And I've still got friends down by Addison, where they since moved to and they keep me—"

"Wait a minute. How's Charlie going to feel about this? You're not planning to see him about insurance are you, just so you can get back in touch with her through him?"

"Charlie won't be selling any more policies. They paid off on his six months ago. June's a widow."

"But you haven't seen her for what—more than fifty years?"

"Well more than fifty. But we had a real good rapport."

"Kent, you said you couldn't even work it up to talk with her. The closest you ever came to communicating with her was when you had your hand on her ponytail, dunking it in your inkwell. Do you think that's enough foundation for a relationship? Do you have any reason to believe she'll remember you?"

"I don't see why not. After all, it was a one-room school. Everyone knew everyone else. And I didn't tell you that even though we never really

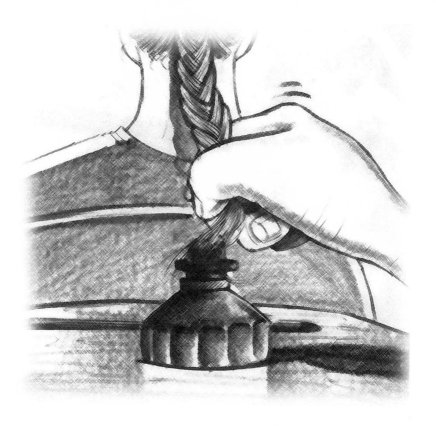

talked, I could tell by the look in her eyes when she cussed me out at recess for dunking her ponytail that she felt the same way about me. It's just something you know. Might not sound rational, but it's one of those things you just know."

He sounded more animated, more excited than I had seen him since Gladys's health starting failing. Then, just as suddenly, he sagged and shook his head.

"Hearing myself talk like this," he said, "it sounds so stupid, so childish. I was right to never mention it to anyone else before. I should just forget it, right?"

"No, Kent. Not right. If June is half the person she sounds to be, she'd be very fortunate to have a shot at a charmer like you. I think you should get yourself a good night's sleep, then tomorrow get yourself spiffied up and take a nice little drive in the country down to Addison.

It's a small town—never know who you might run into."

"I've never been the one for just dropping in. Besides, might give June a heart attack if she answered the doorbell and I'm standing there with an inkwell in my hand."

Kent reached across the table with his big paw and squeezed my hand. Then he did something I hadn't seen him do in months—he smiled.

I WAS ACTUALLY RELIEVED when the Federal Government turned down my offer. It had been both a joke and an attempt to make a point about national priorities as interpreted by Congress.

The government had just announced it was discontinuing funding of the controversial Supersonic Transport aircraft and pundits speculated about what would be done with the work and prototype hardware that had already been produced at a cost reckoned in the hundreds of millions of dollars. So I made an offer to the government of the United States to buy the SST and set up what I could promote as The Boondoggle at The Boondocks. If the government sold the SST on a first-come, first-served basis, I had a chance. If, instead, they were going to be biased in favor of highest bid, my chances were somewhat slimmer. I had offered one dollar. But cash, not terms.

Hank Dubois came over while I was typing out the final words of the letter on the old Royal typewriter. He read over my shoulder, as usual, and said he had never seen a letter to a president before. He urged me to get it published, and not just in the *Grass Lake News*, circulation 1,100, but big-time, in the *Jackson Citizen-Patriot*.

"I don't see how that can do me any good with the golf course, Hank. Enough people around here already think I'm a malcontent."

"Two things: First, you know what they say about not caring what kind of publicity you get, good or bad, long as they spell your name right. Two, you're always going on about the country's priorities being out of whack. Well, here's your chance to make your point."

He had me there. So I mailed the original to President Richard Nixon and sent a carbon copy to the *Cit-Pat*. Two days later a reporter and photographer showed up. The photographer had me hold one of the signs we had posted on area roads, showing an arrow pointing to The

Boondocks. The next day my bearded face was plastered on the front page of the March 30, 1971, *Cit-Pat* in the pose daughter Jennifer called the "sleepy Chinaman" picture. And in that photograph with my speckled goatee, droopy mustache, and half-shut eyes, I did look more like Charlie Chan than any of my German–Irish–Dutch–Native American ancestors. Under the photograph and the headline "He'd Like SST Gear" and a photo caption, the letter went:

> Dear President Nixon:
>
> This is to advise you of my interest in entering into negotiations for the purchase of the rights to the mockups, tools, blueprints, prototypes, and construction rights of the Supersonic Transport (SST) which, as you may recall, recently failed to obtain financial support from Congress.
>
> I am proud to say that for many years I have subscribed to the "Buy American" policy. Now that the U.S. will be disposing of its interests in the SST market, it seems only fair that we "Sell American" and give preference to American citizens rather than traffic with those "fat Japs" that your Mr. Agnew has cautioned us about.
>
> I don't mean to bring unfair pressure to bear, but I must remind you that we in Jackson County, Michigan, already have made a sizable investment in this publicly financed venture. We don't mind paying taxes—no, sir—for after all that's the very life blood of democracy; it's just that, well, after spending all that money we'd kind of like something to touch. Then too, as you are aware, again and again it has been suggested that there could be no more appropriate place to locate the SST than at our place . . . The Boondocks.
>
> Please advise when would be the best time for us to get together to wrap up the details. Oh, one other thing . . . do you deliver or will we have to send a man to pick the stuff up.
>
> Cordially,
>
> Bill Haney

We thought this was just some innocent fun, with maybe a pin-prick at the pomposity of the current Washington administration, which just happened to be headed by my least-favorite politician of all time. In fact, I had once said that if Dick Nixon was elected president I was going to New Zealand. I didn't know at the time that it would take me another thirty years to get there—and then only for a vacation.

That little jab aside, we didn't think that making an offer to buy the dinosauric SST would position the proprietors of The Boondocks as mavericks, which, by comparison to virtually all our neighbors we were. Or as liberals, which, in a conservative village in a conservative township in a conservative county we most definitely had already been labeled. Or even as social gadflies nipping at the flanks of the establishment, which we were surprised but delighted to be so considered. All told, by offering the Feds one dollar for the rights to the SST, I demonstrated yet again that we did not reflect the conventional demographics expected of members of the local business community.

Thirty-Four

Marcy and I had tramped our land hundreds of times and thought we knew it well. Then one day, I chanced onto a strange and intriguing place we had no idea existed. As reliable an authority as Kent Smedley had told me he had trod every square foot of the forty-five acres he had sold us. If he had ever set foot on this special place he surely would have told me about it. But perhaps Kent did know about it and wanted me to discover it for myself.

Before we came to know the secret place, each of us had our favorite spot. For Marcy, it had always been her oak woods, idyllic and serene, a place where she always found peace and solitude. One very preliminary course layout I had sketched showed a tee tucked into the north edge of the woods. The idea was that golfers would play the previous hole to a green ending at the south or east border of the woods, then could walk through the majestic trees to the next tee.

Marcy took one look at the sketch and said, "I hope you're not seriously thinking of disturbing the woods."

I said I could do it in a way that we wouldn't have to cut a single tree, but still give the golfers a brief interlude in the cool shade and a few moments to experience the beauty of the woods.

"I'm sure there are other ways to lay out the course that we don't have to invade the woods," Marcy said.

So, except for pruning and cleaning up debris, we left the oak woods untouched. Over time, though all of us enjoyed it and though we would walk visitors through it, the woods became and would always be Marcy's place. In any kind of weather, but especially on a quiet winter evening with soft fluffy snowflakes spiraling gently to the ground, Marcy would go there with her advance scouts, Rusty and Blazer, ranging out ahead of her. Certain of the destination, they would race past the blue rock, disappear a few brief moments into the valley by the Willow Pond, then pop into view far up on the ridge. There they would look back to be sure she was following, then pad into the dark shadows of the oaks and wait for her there.

The children had their special places, too.

Pat, always looking for excitement, was captivated by the sheets of ice that would form in the hollows after a winter rainstorm was followed by a sudden drop in temperature. Especially in front of number three and five greens, the water underneath the ice would quickly percolate into the sandy soil, leaving an ice shelf an inch or so thick, suspended above only air. Pat learned quickly that if a rapid fall in temperature was followed by snow, then he could sled down the hill onto the ice sheet to see if he could slide fast enough for it to shatter just inches behind him as he zoomed past. Then he and Mark discovered, heck, when the ice is smooth as glass you don't even need a sled. So, wearing their boots, they would race down the hill and onto the ice to see how far they could glide before the crack racing open behind them finally caught up with their boots and brought them through the splintering sheet.

Mark was intrigued by the south ridge, somehow drawn there even before he learned how very special that place was not only to him but in the geography of the state of Michigan. From that high ridge, a little boy commanded a sweeping view of the expanse across Willow Creek marsh to Smedley Hill, the highest point on the golf course. And when Mark turned and looked to the south, his eyes would trace back along number three fairway, past Marcy's oak woods, and spy the big red barn and our white frame house some six hundred and more yards away. This was a panorama of which he never tired.

His curiosity whetted, Mark investigated enough books until he discovered that this very ridge was smack on the peninsular divide. One way to think of it, he explained to me, was that a drop of rain falling at the crown of that peak could, in theory, split in half. One half of the drop could run north, into the marsh, into Willow Creek, then west into Little Wolf Lake, on to the Grand River, and into Lake Michigan. From there it could go into the Chicago River, to the Mississippi, and into the Gulf of Mexico. The other half of the drop could run south through a similar series of waterways, then east into the Raisin River, Lakes Erie and Ontario, thence through the St. Lawrence Seaway, and into the Atlantic Ocean. One raindrop, two destinations, thousands of miles apart.

Jen had a succession of favorites, not all of them on the land itself. When we moved in, a stout steel wire mesh corn crib stood on a concrete slab under an oak tree in front of the barn and just fifteen feet from the road. The corn crib soon became a playhouse for the girls, a fact of which I was completely oblivious until after I gave the crib to Henry Samyn. One day Henry came down with his tractor towing a skid. We shinnied the crib onto the skid and off it went down Curtis Road to Henry's Breezy Acres. Only then did the faces of the kids, especially Jen, show me how oblivious I was.

Fortunately, Jenni took only moments to discover the old granary in the upper level of the barn, an even better sanctuary. It was a cozy ten-by-twelve room with a single small window on the north wall that had been the hole for a boom or conveyor to shoot in grain for storage. And there was a hole in the floor that had been the passageway for the funnel that carried oats and cracked corn to feed the livestock housed in the ground-floor level. That granary served as clubhouse, retreat, sanctuary, Halloween spook house, and as a dozen other special sets in the theater of imagination for Jen, young sister Rebecca, their friends, and their brothers.

I shared feelings for each of these places but somehow the sassafras tree alongside number six green had a special pull on me. I liked standing in the middle of six fairway, looking toward the green, bordered on the right by the sassafras tree Kent had showed me.

This was the arena of the great thornapple battles, with more set-backs than victories.

One blistering summer afternoon, all able-bodied hands had been deployed on the rocky, bumpy, dusty rectangle of 40 yards by 170 yards from the marsh edge to the future site of number six green. We were trying to shape this unyielding battlefield into number six fairway, and as the dust rose and the roots refused to budge and two new rocks popped up for every one removed, something said, No way. This is not going to happen. At least not today.

I stopped the tractor and looked at the beleaguered crew. There was Marcy and our four kids. And there was Marcy's sister and brother-in-law, Kathy and Don Schoenhals, and their two little kids. Every one of them too tired to speak, yet each of them still slogging one tor-tured, slow-motion step at a time, loading rocks and rubble into the stoneboat, pulling out thornapple tree roots. The whole volunteer crew was coated in dust caked in layers on their sweating skin.

I shut off the tractor and said, "Whoa. This looks like the Bataan Death March. We're getting out of this oven and going back to the house. This can wait until it's cooler."

It was the only time anyone could remember that I had called a halt while there was still daylight and bodies were still standing.

I would look at that tree, the only sassafras tree I had found on the property, and wonder how it got there. Perhaps many years ago a mal-lard or a blue-winged teal had flown into the marsh from a place where sassafras trees grew in abundance. And it waddled out of the marsh to poke around for food or material for a nest and on that spot a sassafras drupe—a seed pod—slipped off the duck's webbed foot and there grew the tree. Or perhaps there had been many sassafras trees there centu-ries ago when only Ottawa lived here and Chippewa and Potawatami wandered through. And those Native Americans might have harvested the sassafras roots and bark to make tea until this lone tree was the last seedling left when the last Native American departed the area a century ago.

And then I wondered, is this tree really the only one? Have we really covered every inch of these 110 acres? These were questions I had asked myself many times and the answer was always yes, yes we had tramped the entire property. But had we, really?

Yes, every place. Except one.

When I had placed the stakes to mark the pond perimeters for Larry Briggs and his crane, that was the only time any of us had ventured more than a few feet into the great marsh on either side of Willow Creek. You couldn't walk safely in the marsh, even with chest waders, because the muck would seize your boots and glue you to the spot. And if not that, with one misstep you could drop like a shot into one of the countless hidden springs and be chest deep in an instant.

Still, I had often looked at a small island of mixed woods in the middle of the marsh to the south of number six green and wondered how scrub oaks and hickories as well as the expected blue beech and aspen could live there. Oak and hickory could tolerate moisture but unlike willows and aspens were not permanent wetfoot species.

I circled behind number six green and instead of turning right and climbing the steep slope up to the north ridge and number seven tee, I went left, to the south and toward the marsh. I had tried this a couple times before when the water table was higher and in a few yards I had to turn back. But this time, after two drought years, the footing was much drier. In a few steps I was surprised to be across and out of what had been a very narrow band of spongy marsh and onto a ribbon of solid ground.

I looked more closely and could see that, when looked down upon from the higher ridges from which we had always viewed this spot, it had been only an optical illusion that the entire area was one flat surface. The ground I now stood on was several inches above the general marsh level. Not only that, it continued to rise, gently but distinctly, into the stand of trees.

The way was not straight—it took some maneuvering around hawthorn, aspen clusters, great spreading yews, and thorny Russian olive bushes. But in a hundred yards or less, I had snaked through a small patch of blue beech and in a few steps was on the island, standing in its little copse of mixed growth.

I could now see that this was a hill at least six feet above the marsh level. The soil was different than the peat and marl and muck of the marsh, and unlike the loamy sand of the ridges. It seemed to be a mixture of clay and loamy-sandy soils. As I got to the crest, I saw there was a clearing at the top, a grassy plateau in the shape of an oval of about thirty by sixty feet. This grassy knoll was clear of trees except for an irregular ring of healthy oak and hickory trees at the perimeter. The trees were gnarled and old, though healthy, but none was taller than thirty feet.

The top branches waved gently in the wind, but where I stood the air was still. I sat in the grass and took it all in. Then I laid back and looked up, past the enclosing circle of green leaves and at the white clouds drifting slowly against the blue sky. The only sound was the faint rustling of leaves. The maintained areas of the golf course—number four fairway to the south and number six green to the north, where I had just come from—were at most two hundred yards away. I should have been able to hear a mower engine, a tractor motor, a chain saw, some sort of equipment somewhere. Total silence.

We had walked this land for five years and had not the slightest idea this place existed. This grassy knoll rising out of the marsh was the most surprising, serene, and special spot I had ever stood on on this property.

I knew somehow that I was in a place where no man had set foot since a Native American moccasin had padded here. Of course, those people would have known this place. Perhaps they had even made it like this, had cleared the brush, had opened up the cap of the knoll into this oval shape. Maybe they allowed the trees to encircle it to shield it from notice from the ridges. I imagined what might have happened here, the rituals that might have been performed. If I were to scrape into the earth beneath the grass, I might find pottery shards, arrowheads, bits of ancient metals or tools. But to do that would be to disturb what had lain tranquil for untold years.

Finally I forced myself to head back. I wanted to bring Marcy here to see this for herself. I felt sure it would become a special sanctuary for her and Mark as well as me. I made a full circle around the tiny island to look for another pathway of firm ground but found that I had chanced upon the only way in.

When I was back on the firm ground near number six green, I turned and looked again in the direction of the island. Even though I had just been there moments before, there was no sign there was anything in that direction but simply more marsh and a few scrub trees. And unless you knew exactly where you were going, you would never know what was to be found there.

Thirty-Five

One day the same Marcy who was always scolding me for taking on too much, the same Marcy with the four kids and a golf course to manage, came home to tell me she had agreed to serve as president of the Get-Acquainted League.

Several regulars at The Boondocks were members in the League; a few of them were Marcy's kindred spirits. The purpose of the league was not only to greet newcomers but also to let old-timers get to know others in the community better. And it worked. They would call on new arrivals and welcome them with an abundance of congeniality. But it wasn't entirely focused on new arrivals because a surprising number of women who had been in the area for years had never gotten to know each other.

Over the previous months, as if Marcy wasn't busy enough, she had put in many hours with her friends on league projects. They staged a big rummage sale and other fundraising programs and gathered community support for a major event. It not only would be Marcy's first as head of the organization; it also was to be the league's most ambitious undertaking—a Fourth of July fireworks show at nearby Little Wolf Lake. The club members had worked for months to accumulate the funds to buy enough fireworks to wow the hundreds of expected spectators. The league hoped this inaugural show would start with such a bang that it would become an annual event.

A friend of a friend of a league member donated a raft from which the fireworks could be launched a hundred yards offshore. The throngs would assemble at sunset on the beaches of Little Wolf Lake and have an unimpeded view of the spectacular show.

There had been concern about the weather, but as usual, the rain never came. The raft was anchored in position out in the lake and as darkness gathered the signal was given—let the show begin. The rocket launchers were in place and loaded. In moments the opening salute would be touched off. A murmur of anticipation ran through the crowd as the lighting torch was ignited and the fireworks chief moved forward to set off the rockets' fuses. Silence. Then the crowd was stunned by a brilliant flash and a deafening explosion.

The league's first major event had indeed been launched with a bang.

Through the cloud of smoke and flames rising from the raft, men could be heard shouting for help. In seconds, the smoke cleared enough that spectators could see that this was not a part of the show. The raft was in trouble. Another boat quickly came alongside to help. In minutes, the rescue was completed and the fireworks crew brought safely ashore. No one was seriously injured, the crew chief told the crowd, but there was bad news. The explosion had blown a hole in the bottom of the raft. All the fireworks had exploded or sunk into the lake without a single rocket streaking airborne.

The next day, Marcy and the other leaders of the Get Acquainted League met with the owner of the severely damaged raft. He accepted their offer of full compensation for all expenses to repair or replace his raft. The league, under new President Marcy, was now committing itself to a year of the most intense fundraising they had ever undertaken. Marcy's already-full plate had just been served another king-sized portion.

IN MIDSUMMER, those of us in Grass Lake Township who lived on the land and off of the land ran out of ways to curse the weather. The cold, dry, and windy winter had been followed by a warm spring with few rains, and those at the wrong times. Then, although nearby farms got some showers, there was no measurable rain on The Boondocks after Memorial Day.

There was little grass to mow on the fairways and because running over the turf in the blistering temperatures stressed the weakened turf further, we drove on the course as little as possible. That meant we had to walk, constantly it seemed, to get from one pump setup to the next, to rotate the sprinklers on the still-recovering greens, and to get water to the parched transplanted trees.

One day as I was tramping on the baked brown fairways, carrying buckets of water to Miz Johnson's maples, I heard someone shout at me. I looked up to see Ed Harrison in the shade of the shattered walnut tree on the fence line dividing our properties. I walked over to him.

"See that sick heifer?" He pointed at a scrawny cow that looked about the same to me as his cattle had for five years.

"Well, I see the cow you're pointing at. But I'm no veterinarian, so—"

"See this here?" He was holding up a golf ball. "You know what this is, don't you?"

"Yes, I do, Mr. Harrison, that's a golf ball. A Titleist 3."

"Maybe to you and your golfer fellers it is. But not to me. You know what that is to me? Poison, is what it is."

"How do you figure that, Mr. Harrison?"

He was sputtering so he could hardly speak.

"That green mound yonder with the flagstick on it and the flag has a big number 8? Right aside my property where I'm grazing my prize dairy cattle and your golfers broke down my fence and let my cattle out that time? Well, what happens if one of those cows takes and eats one of those . . . those Tit-ly threes or whatever? I'll tell you what happens because I cut up one of those balls and I know what's inside 'em. Lookit here."

And he reached into his jacket pocket and came out with a great fistful of rubber strands of which each golf ball supposedly has one mile, very tautly wound.

"Rubber bands," he said, spittle flying. "Miles of 'em. And that's all from just one of your Tit-ly threes. Cow eats that ball and there you go. Binds up her insides something awful. Milk runs dry. Maybe kills her."

"Well, Mr. Harrison, do you really think—"

"Makes no nevermind. Could happen. Or worse, say one of those careless golfers of yours hits one off-line and POW! hits a heifer between the eyes. That's the way we slaughter 'em you know, a blow between the eyes. That cow dies and it's on you. Don't say I never told you. Next cow of mine dies from one your Tit-ly threes and it's on you."

As he stalked away, it occurred to me that almost every conversation I had with Mr. Ed Harrison ended with me staring at his receding back.

AUGUST 1971 WAS THE FIFTH ANNIVERSARY of our buying the old Nate Fish farm and moving to Grass Lake Township. Just as I was wondering if we should commemorate that in some way, Kent Smedley phoned and gave us another excuse for celebrating.

Kent invited Marcy and me to dinner at his favorite country restaurant in Jackson to meet June of the braided ponytail and the fifth-grade crush. Kent had indeed taken the bold step and the two became reacquainted after sixty years. Even before I met June, I knew I would like her if for no other reason than she had put the light back in Kent's eyes.

June was surely a fine and pleasant lady, and took it well when I said I was a bit disappointed she no longer wore a ponytail. Over dessert, Kent and June said they had a special favor to ask of us: Would we do them the honor of serving as their witnesses in their wedding ceremony at June's church in Addison in October? In a year so marked by loss, frustration, and disappointment, that gave Marcy and me something nice to look forward to.

"THAT'S ALL THE BALLS they found?"

I looked at the small bucket, a piddling fifteen balls, all of them with the covers cut through, most of them discolored from lying in the muck on the floor of the pond. Not a usable one in the lot, even for the practice range.

Mary Joseph had a serious look on her face, too serious I thought, for the circumstances. So it had been a washout, letting the Adams boys don their scuba gear and dive the ponds for lost balls. They were good kids. Too bad they had gone to all that trouble lugging their equipment over, spending who knows how much time walking in the goop at the bottom of the Willow Pond, and they had found a measly fifteen balls? We had thought it would be a win-win deal—we would get all the balls they found and pay them ten cents apiece regardless of condition. They would make a few dollars and so would we, as well as giving golfers an inexpensive alternative to new balls costing up to a dollar and a quarter each. But fifteen balls in all that time? Another bright idea that fizzled out.

"Well, that's hard to believe," I said. "After all that complaining from golfers who lost a match by dunking a couple in the pond on the last hole. And these ones the Adams boys found are no good. Mary, just throw these clunkers out, no one would buy them. But a deal's a deal, so give the boys their dollar and a half."

"I already paid them. Here's the receipt."

She handed it to me and I glanced at it. Then looked again.

"Thirty-four dollars! They found fifteen useless balls and you gave them thirty-four dollars? Why?"

Mary pointed down at the floor behind the counter. I went around to take a look. A bushel basket, brimming with golf balls, and from the looks of it, many of them shiny and easily resalable for fifty cents each or five for two dollars.

"You're not mad, are you, Bill? The Adams boys were so excited, but they made me promise I'd do it that way. They thought it would be fun to pull your leg a little."

"All those from the Willow Pond?"

"They said that in some of the low spots they weren't walking on the bottom, it was just solid golf balls down there. They really combed it over carefully. I went out and watched for a few minutes and they'd be underwater, then an arm would pop up above the surface, tossing a handful of balls onto the bank. I gave them a couple of brushes and they hosed them down and cleaned them up real good."

"They sure did. Well, fill up the Previously Owned tub on the counter and put them back in service."

The Manchester High School golf team had a match that night and I knew they bought lots of used balls. Actually, though, the kids didn't buy as many balls from our recycled tub as did several of the coaches and teachers, especially a certain athletic director who was already a local legend. We were pleased to provide free golf not only to the golf teams but also their coaches. Occasionally they would bring along a teacher or a school official and that was fine with us. It may have been Marcy who pointed out that our complimentary roster had grown about as long as the paying-customer list.

One day the Manchester coaches invited their A.D. to join them. They knew he had taken up golf only recently and urged him to play the front men's tees because that greatly minimized the threat posed by three of the ponds. But high-school athletic directors often come equipped with an excess of testosterone and there was no way he was going to tee it up from the "sissy tees."

He made it through the first five holes without much trouble and wondered what was all that talk about this being a tough course. Then he marched up to the sixth tee and saw nearly two hundred yards of water and marsh between him and the next firm ground. Undaunted, he teed up, took a swat, and watched the concentric rings expand on the pond as his ball fell fifty yards short. Another swing, another goner. His playing partners told him local rules permitted him to hit a shot from a drop area on the land-bridge crossover. He declined. After he plunked his tenth and final ball into what the locals now called "the dreaded spaghetti patch of The Boondocks," the rest of the foursome thought he would surrender, that he had to give up because he was out of golf balls.

Undeterred, the A.D. strode over to the golf coach's bag, unzipped the ball pocket, and announced, "I'm not leaving this tee until I get across that pond. And if that means I lose every ball in every bag in this foursome, then that's what it means."

The eighteenth ball found the fairway.

In the fall of that year, the A.D. came into the pro shop and selected five balls from the counter tub. He paid his two dollars, held up one of the balls, and said, "This is the fourth time this year I have bought this same ball."

I WALKED OUT TO THE WILLOW POND, trying to imagine the bottom of that pond covered with the balls the Adams boys had found. The pond had steep sides so once a ball trickled in it quickly rolled out of sight into deep and often cloudy water.

When I was a kid hunting for balls at Sylvan Glen, I hated it when the water was muddy and you couldn't spot balls and fish them out with a long stick on which you had coiled coat-hanger wire as a scoop. If you couldn't see the bottom, then you'd have to take off your shoes, roll up your pants and wade in, probing for balls with your toes. Even with your pants rolled up, you couldn't resist going deeper and soon you were up to your chest. And there would be that anxious moment when you got out, soaked all over, and looked for leeches on your legs.

If you had forgotten your shaker of salt to pour on them, you had to light a cigarette or cigar and touch them with the glowing tip. The bloodsuckers would sizzle like frying bacon and drop off but it made the tobacco taste awful.

The greatest fear at Sylvan Glen was being caught out on the course by one of the workers or by Bill Catto himself. I would sit under the big bridge, just off the golf course property, with the older golf ball scavengers and listen wide-eyed to their stories of torture inflicted on kids caught looking for balls on the course.

Two years later, I was applying for a job at the course, having gotten an interview with none other than the same Bill Catto, set up by his daughter Barbara, a classmate in school. I hoped Mr. Catto had never gotten a good look at me while I was trespassing on his course. If he did, he gave no indication during our interview and hired me for $1.25 an hour. I would be a greens mowerman Mondays through Fridays and a pro shop attendant on weekends and holidays. And since that was the year my father was dying of leukemia and we could use the money, Mr. Catto would also let me do the night watering trick when the regular man didn't show up and for that he paid me time and a half.

My first week on the job, following Mr. Catto's instructions, I reported to him that I had seen the notorious Corey boys hunting for balls in the creek behind number five green. Mr. Catto got up from the mower he was adjusting, loomed over me, and appeared on the verge of beating me about the head and shoulders with his crescent wrench.

"For the great Chrissake, Haney," Mr. Catto bellowed in his Scottish brogue, "you'd have me chasing after schoolkids when the damned brown fungus is chewing at the heart of my work."

Except for an old British movie, I had never heard anyone talk like that. There didn't seem to be any good response to make to Mr. Catto and, remembering the long-ago horror stories about his flaming Scottish temper, I quickly got out of his sight. My mistake. I had thought he'd want to know the Corey kids were wading the creek for balls again, after he himself had chased them off just days before. He had said then that the Coreys were pestering golfers, trying to sell balls to them, and that cut into pro shop sales.

Not only that, he said, there was the question of liability. He said the insurance company considered a golf course to be an "attractive nuisance," that it would naturally appeal to kids to wander onto it, and if you didn't try to keep them off and one of them got hurt somehow, their parents could sue you and maybe get a settlement that would bankrupt the place. So, he told the greens crew, "Chase those damn kids off or tell me about it and I'll put the fear of the Lord into them."

Well, I told him and the only one feeling the wrath of the Lord was me.

Since I started building The Boondocks, I thought often about Bill Catto and those days at Sylvan Glen. The workers there used to grumble, "That Catto, obsessed is what he is. You'd think it was his course, way he goes on about it. Got insomnia, did you know that? Lays there at night, listening to the sprinklers and one of 'em gets plugged, he's up and in that pickup truck, tearing across the fairway to chew ass on poor old Renshaw for not watering right."

"Yeah," somebody else would say, "and pity the poor mowerman who forgets to wipe off his grease fittings. Damn thing is, that banker that owns the place knows we need the money. Taking advantage of us, is what they do. Everybody knows a golf course is the next best thing to having a gold mine."

I looked out at my gold mine and wondered what Bill Catto would think of it.

THERE ARE MANY LAKES in Jackson County, quite a few of them in Grass Lake Township. While Marcy and her friends were blowing up rafts and sinking their budget on Little Wolf Lake, I was in Grass Lake Village signing copies of my new book, *From Spirit Lake to Goose Lake: A Bridge Over Time.* The lakes had been important to Native Americans for centuries and for the more recent immigrants for the last century and a half.

When I found Indian arrowheads, fragments of pioneer wagons, and horseshoes from the first farmers, I got curious about the history of the land we had turned into a golf course. When I did research to write a commemorative brochure as a fundraiser for the centennial, I became fascinated, and finally something like obsessed to learn the history of the place.

After hundreds of hours of interviews with old-timers, digging in attics, poring through hundred-year-old letters, jailhouse journals, yellowed diaries, logbooks, newspaper accounts, and trial records, I was amazed that no one had told the rich and important story of this area.

The Detroit-Leoni War episode, also called the Great Railroad Conspiracy War and Trial, was itself an event of major historical significance. But so much else had happened here. And so often it seemed to reduce down to a fundamental struggle between the established residents and the newcomers. That was true centuries ago when it was the crop-raising Ottawas fighting off the transient hunting tribes of Potawatamis and Chippewas. It was true from 1830 to 1855 when the local farmers battled the railroad that at first improved, then disrupted, and finally destroyed their way of living and more than a few lives. And it was as true in 1970, the year we opened the golf course, as more than a quarter million young people descended on the tiny village of Grass Lake for the Great Goose Lake Rock Festival just two miles to the northwest.

And in between those upheavals, there had been many events that could never have been predicted, events that changed the history of this place and its people.

I thought about these things as we worked to do something on this land that would last. We now suspected that we would not be in this place for the rest of our days, maybe not even long enough for the kids to finish grade school here. But we did hope that while we were here we would enhance the land for which we felt more custodians than owners. At the least, we were committed to leave it better than we found it. At the most, we hoped to leave behind us a golf course that would preserve the land, the marsh, the stream, and the resident wildlife while providing pleasure to those who visited the place.

As I signed books at the Sesquicentennial in Grass Lake, in Jackson, and around southeastern Michigan, interviewers often asked how I came to write the book. And that in turn led to conversation about the golf course itself. I had not thought that a regional historiography would afford opportunities to promote the golf course. But in a small way, that is what happened. And as the economy went from cool to frigid and the weather from warm to hot and the rainfall from sparse to nonexistent, we needed all the help we could get.

In August 1971, the time finally came when the recession, the weather, the parched fairways combined to dry up play.

Golf greens need an inch of water a week, and more in the hottest, driest months. From the first of June to Labor Day, we got less than one inch total. The good news was that week after week there was little mowing to do. And that was also the bad news. We saved money on labor and supplies only to pay it out in increased fuel and maintenance costs for irrigation pumps that we seemed to run almost around the clock just to keep greens and tees barely alive. And the revenue stream slowed to a trickle. We kept current with bill payments but hopes of setting aside funds for a fairway watering system evaporated. Transforming the red barn into a rustic clubhouse and restaurant was unthinkable.

More than the grass curled up and died in that drought. It also sapped my enthusiasm for our future there. I had never before known that feeling of futility that countless farmers felt when facing relentless elements. Weather has no agenda, no conscience. It offers no negotiation. It inflicts. You cope. Or you are destroyed.

Thousands of successful golf courses have been built and flourished in the presence of that reality. So too, could The Boondocks—in years of normal weather. Or even in years of foul, despicable, diabolically vicious weather—if one has a fixed underground irrigation system and a reasonable budget for equipment and supplies.

We had been here now exactly five years, the first three of which had been more normal than we realized at the time. Some heavy snows, yes. Some torrential rains, fine. Some hot and drier spells, we can live with that. Unpredictability was, well, predictable. Frequent, rapid, and extreme change was typical weather for southern Michigan. But now we were just finishing back-to-back brutal, arid summers. And no meteorologist and no *Farmer's Almanac* could reassure us that the next year or two or five would be any different.

Thirty-Six

Finally the weather, the depressed economy, and a litany of accumulated frustrations grabbed me by the throat and shook any remaining good sense out of me.

When you have no idea that something you do or say will offend someone and get bad gossip circulating in a small town, that is unfortunate. But ignorance or naiveté is excusable. When you take an action you are absolutely certain is going to offend someone and get the gossip mill churning in a small town, that is just plain stupid. For a businessperson, it can be suicidal.

Larry Willis was one of our very favorite regular customers at The Boondocks. He was aptly nicknamed Stub because his short, powerful frame packed considerable muscle per square inch. He had that unusual combination of strength coupled with suppleness and an apparently innate sense of timing. He flowed into a shot with an explosion of power made graceful by a perfectly controlled tempo. Put that together, and you had a fellow who, as the high-school players said as they watched him, "hits the snot out of the ball."

Larry played regularly in the Men's Thursday Evening League, on weekends, and in every tournament and outing. In fact, in the Men's Scramble, he and his foursome would play two, three, or more rounds, as long as there was daylight. Larry was a fine golfer, a pleasant person to be around, and displayed a ton of that rare commodity, loyalty.

If I had any sense when I heard The Rumor, I would have remembered those things about Larry.

A couple months earlier, Larry had proposed a barter deal which I quickly accepted as a win-win proposition. Larry swapped us a minibike for a season's playing privileges. That was fine with us because we figured once you have the course maintained, it makes little difference whether 120 people or 121 play it on a given day. And the more Larry played, the more likely he would be to introduce new golfers to The Boondocks, the more equipment he would buy, the more sandwiches and soft drinks he would consume, and so on.

I was happy with the transaction, especially after I got the bike running and we tooled it around the practice range for fun and used it a few times to make the rounds rotating sprinklers.

It would have been prudent to keep in mind the nice relationship we had with Larry, to remember all the good stuff when we started hearing "the buzz around town."

The buzz went something like this: The Boondocks is going under. They're not getting enough play to keep the place open. Probably belly-up by the end of the season.

Before we asked around, we suspected that the rumor had been started by the owners of one of the two other area courses whose play had been cut into by our presence. Earlier a grandson of the owner of one of those courses bragged at school that he had vandalized a few of our road signs. This time, though, we were surprised at how easy it was to trace the buzz back to a different origin. Everybody could have been wrong, but they all said the same thing. It was unanimous—the person quoted as saying these things to several people on several occasions was one of the leading citizens of the village: Larry Willis's mother.

I felt many emotions racing through me at that moment. I was angry. Angry that anyone would presume to make such remarks. Particularly angry that someone who had never been to the course would voice an opinion. Doubly angry that even if our condition had been that perilous, a mature adult would make such comments knowing what the consequences might be. I was saddened. I knew this would not be good for us and I regretted the emotional cost we would be paying just knowing this had happened. As Marcy had said often and rightly, I could never be accused of under-reacting.

So, I was angry and I was sad and I was embarrassed. Regardless of the merits or lack of merits of the remark, every time I saw someone in the village or the township, I would wonder if they had heard this, what they thought about it. There were people in town with well-deserved reputations as rumor-mongers, pot-stirrers. Folks discounted anything these people might say. These people weren't malicious, necessarily, they just liked to hear the sound of their own voice and wanted to be seen as in the know, the first with the juicy tidbit. But from what I knew of the Willises, they were not like that.

I wondered if Larry Willis, someone whose friendship we so

valued, had said something to his mother that triggered this incident we now had to deal with. Or was there an agenda here we simply knew nothing about?

What I should have done immediately, of course, was see Larry and talk with him about it. No, what I really, really should have done was keep my mouth shut and try to forget about it.

I did something other than that.

Years earlier I had written a humorous piece called "How to Write the Gripe Letter for Fun and Profit." Now, as I faced this down-the-tubes rumor, I figured my gripe letter article made me an expert on writing just the right letter to handle any testy situation. After all, I'd had great success getting satisfaction from any number of companies when I had a legitimate beef. We got a new Dishmaster kitchen appliance when the brand-new one we had just installed would squirt you in the chest, just for the hell of it, especially if you were a lady guest wearing a new party dress and just wanted a drop of water for your Scotch. We got boxes of cashews from the Kar-Nut company when our package of mixed nuts contained not a single cashew. Then there was the box of baked goods from the Farm Crest folks. Write a letter, get goodies. All this in response to light, good-natured letters describing unsatisfactory purchases.

This letter, though, this squelch-the-rumor letter had to be different. I didn't want to let Mrs. Willis know just how much this had stung us, how gratuitous it was, how harmful to any business to say such things, even if one had the facts straight. I would not deny that we would like to have more play on the course, to have, please God, just a nice little cloudburst once in a while instead of the longest drought in the recorded history of the township. I would not deny that the course, like every other course in the area, was not in prime condition. Although the greens of The Boondocks had come back to be surprisingly good, clearly it was not desirable to have a puff of dust arise after an iron shot from a fairway instead of a clean, green divot.

All that to the side, it was a crappy thing to whisper it around that a guy's business was on the brink. Even if it was. Which it wasn't. Quite.

In such situations, old friend Milt Coulson would say simply, "It's a hit duck that flutters." I wasn't about to admit just how wounded I was, but it would be clear that some feathers were ruffled.

So my letter inflicted its damage with its very first clever and not entirely original sentence. I don't remember what came after that. Perhaps Mrs. Willis didn't read past that first sentence. She didn't need to go beyond the lead paragraph to get the thrust. For with that one sentence, without wanting to, and stupidly without fully realizing what would inevitably flow from what I had penned, I ruptured a relationship with Larry Willis, a relationship I cared about. I offended a leading citizen of the town. I jumped to a conclusion that was suggested by the testimony but which was certainly not a proved fact. And, given the vitality of the rumor mill that had brought us to this pass, I had tried to put out a smoldering ember by pouring gasoline on it. How could I not know that now those so inclined would really have something to buzz about? My letter opened:

"Dear Mrs. Willis:

I thought that for your sake I should tell you that some ignorant busybody gossip using your name has been spreading unfounded rumors about our golf course . . . "

I have no memory, nor want it, of the florid text that must have followed.

From that day on, no one ever mentioned the subject in my presence. I had never met Mrs. Willis and I was never to make her acquaintance. If a new spate of rumors had circulated about my intemperate letter, they were never passed along to me. I did hear that not long afterwards, Larry Willis gave up golf and turned his attention back to water-skiing, at which he had previously been a champion. That he went on a health food regimen, slimmed down, and "you'd never recognize him." But I never had that opportunity because I never saw him again.

But I have thought of that letter often. Many times since then I found myself advising corporate executives or just regular folks on how to handle situations in which they feel themselves mistreated. For a CEO, it's often the press that is the perpetrator; with less exalted folks it's a bill collector, a nasty neighbor, or an in-law. When they ask for my counsel, I give it to them, forcefully.

Sit down right now, I say, and write that letter. Vent your spleen totally. Get it all out. Next, edit your letter until you're content it will reduce the bastard to a seething pulp. Read it aloud, savoring how well you have expressed your contempt, outrage, and disgust and while you're at it, toss in all the other negative feelings you have lying about, unused. Don't stop editing until it has captured your sentiments perfectly.

Satisfied? Good. Now tear up that letter. Throw the pieces in the wastebasket and get on with your business and your life.

Thirty-Seven

As I pulled into our horseshoe driveway, I thought I saw a familiar figure shuffling toward the ninth green. Instead of going in and changing from the casual clothes I wore to work at the institute, I walked onto the course to see if I was right.

It was Kent Smedley, playing in a twosome with his step-grand-daughter's husband, Mel Clark. It was Kent's first time out to play golf since Gladys's death. Kent had a special routine for playing his round at The Boondocks. Instead of driving a car over and starting on number one, he simply went out his back door with his golf cart, walked two hundred yards, and started his round on number seven. Then he played the holes in order, finishing with number six, which left him just a stiff walk up Smedley Hill to his backyard. Mel lived next door to Kent and sometimes joined him. Since both had full-season playing privileges, they could play any time they wanted to without bothering to check in at the pro shop.

Kent came over and told me he was such a lousy golfer his game had actually improved from the layoff. Then he said he had been meaning to tell me something Gladys had told him just before she died.

"She was concerned about how you're doing financially. She said she hoped you knew that if you needed additional cash, you'd come to us and we'd add it to the contract and have the money for you the next day. She told me I had to make you promise you'd do that. We both knew you're good for it, and at six percent, we're doing better with you by twice than we'd get at the bank."

"Kent, that's really thoughtful of you but—"

"Bill, I'm not blind and neither was Glad. With this lousy economy and even worse weather, it's no surprise there's not much play. I want you to come over this evening and pick up a $1,500 check I've got made out for you. And an addendum to the contract you can sign. If that's not enough, you just tell me what you need. Now, that's the last word on it."

Before I could say anything, he grabbed the handle of his golf cart and headed toward number one tee, picking up Mel along the way.

IT WAS POURING when I left Ann Arbor and the western sky was so dark I knew it had to be raining nineteen miles to the west. But it had seemed that way before and by the time I got to the Grass Lake exits, a downpour would become a light shower and by the time I got home, The Boondocks would be dry as dust.

This time, however, it was still a deluge as I pulled into the Village to stop at Wolfinger's Hardware for some parts before heading home. Leon Lockwood saw me and knew what I would be thinking. I had grumbled to him often about the long dry spell.

"Well, Haney, it's got to be raining at your place. Just came from brother Lew's and it's coming down there like a cow pissing off a flat rock. He's just four miles from you so I don't see how this one can miss you."

As I headed home, I was encouraged by Leon's weather forecast. I had no idea if he knew anything more about weather than I did but if he was selling rain, I was buying. When I turned off Norvell Road, it was still raining steadily. I looked longingly again at the fast-flowing artesian well at Frank Smith's place, coveting for the thousandth time my neighbor's eternal source of pure, fresh water. Frank, who had nine of these artesian wells on his 360 acres, had little need for that water as he kept the entire spread in pasture for his herd of Shetland ponies. But there it was, not three-quarters of a mile from my golf course, precious water spewing forth without the slightest assistance from mankind, tens of thousands of gallons of sparkling clear water day after day, year after year, and mankind not having to do a damn thing to get it.

Less than a half mile to go now. The rain is letting up. Another two hundred yards and as I pass Walker's place the pavement is dry. If a single drop fell it would sizzle on the concrete and go poof.

I pull into the driveway, get out of the car and look at the sky. To the east, black clouds billow. Behind me to the west and as far as I can see to the north and south, lightning flashes, distant thunder rumbles, the sky boils, and sheets of rain paint the horizon gray. Yet directly above The Boondocks, the sun shines gaily against a pale blue sky. It defies belief. It is as though the old Nate Fish place has been conferred status as the permanent eye of the storm.

I LOOKED AROUND THE PLACE as I walked to the car. It was seven a.m. of an early September day and the only golfers were two groups of regulars. Many players had put their clubs away for the season as early as Labor Day, missing the finest time of the year to play golf in the Midwest. An occasional shotgun blast echoing from the cornfields by Walker's Lake meant some were afield, firing over their bird dogs, getting them steeled for pheasant season. Some were already sighting in their rifles for deer-hunting season. Still others held religiously to the Easter–Labor Day schedule, golf in the warm months and bowling in the cold. Those who stuck it out on the links until the snow flew saw The Boondocks at its best.

Almost predictably, as the golf season wound down, the weather improved and the grass recovered. The entire course was now a healthy emerald green.

A liquid morning sunlight flowed west across the fairways, bathing the oaks of Marcy's woods in burnished copper and drenching hickory leaves with an almost electric gold. A lightning storm two days earlier had released so much nitrogen that the fairways were the richest blue-green they had been all season. The Willow Pond was a clear steel blue again, the cool nights having driven the algae to hibernation. Out on number three green, more than 500 yards away, Mike Campbell whipped away the blanket of morning dew with a cane pole.

Everything seemed normal. Almost everything. But something didn't belong. I scanned the horizon again. The woods . . . the Willow Pond . . . numbers three and nine fairways, across to numbers two and one fairways . . . closer now, to number two green . . . the horse on the practice green. A horse on the practice green?

Unwilling to believe what I was seeing, I walked slowly toward the practice green. The roan gelding paid no attention, preoccupied as he was with trying to get a mouthful of this delicious-looking but very, very short grass. He worked his lips furiously and flecks of foam drizzled onto the bent grass, which had been mowed to 9/64 of an inch the day before and offered no blade into which he might sink his teeth. The big gelding—I couldn't guess how many hands high—moved a few feet and with each step, his sharp hooves knifed a half inch or more into the green.

There was a rope hanging from his bridle and if I could grab that rope, I could lead him off the green without spooking him.

But it was too late. He heard me and jumped, pawing his front hooves in the air and bouncing on his rears, gouging out half a dozen chunks of soft turf.

I moved away and he quieted. I took the long way around and went into the mudroom. When I came out, I had a pocket full of apples. This time I approached the horse from the front, where he could keep an eye on me. When I got within ten yards of the green, I rolled an apple toward him. He snapped it up before it stopped rolling. Then another, rolled shorter this time, so he had to walk toward me to reach it. Three more apples and he was off the green and I grabbed the rope.

I tied the horse to the fence corner post and went to survey the damage. I was kneeling on the green, trying to figure out the best way to make repairs, when Mike Campbell walked up, cane pole over his shoulder.

"Well, that doesn't look too good," Mike said.

"Forget about the mowing for now, Mike. First thing is we have to fix this green. Then I have to find out whose horse that is."

In one way the timing was good because the season was almost over. Also, it was cool and the green was moist so it could be repaired more easily than if it were hot, dry, and hard. But there was little growing weather left for the green to heal. Any seed we planted now would have little time to germinate and that meant that next spring those hoof marks would stand out for weeks.

I remembered how Bill Catto had us greens mowermen fix number six green at Sylvan Glen when someone drove a car right across it and made two big deep slits. We got edgers and turf cutters and cut the turf all along the edge of the slits and then lifted up the sod that had been dented in and laid it back in a long fold. Then we poured enough sharp sand in the trench so that when we put the damaged flap back in place it would be flush with the rest of the green. The green was playable again in a week, but it took a year to get that wound perfectly smooth. Two years later if you looked very closely you could still see the scar.

Mike and I put the dislodged patches back in place and tamped them down. Then we pried up the indented sod from each hoofprint, cut it as neatly as possible, and laid the flap back. We poured a handful or two of sharp sand mixed with fertilizer into the wound, eyeballed the flap to gauge how well it would fit, then sealed it up. Then I sprinkled on bent-grass seed, which I always kept on hand for such emergencies. As soon as we had finished a few feet, we watered in the repaired area to keep the bared roots from drying out.

By midmorning three foursomes had come and they all stopped by to see what was going on. The horse was still tied to the post because we didn't know to whom it belonged or what else to do with it. Fortunately, the gelding had confined most of his prancing to an arc across the upper level of the green, so there was ample room for the golfers to roll a few practice putts on undamaged grass before starting their rounds. By noon we had heard every horse-on-the-green joke imaginable and some of them twice. But it wasn't until one p.m., when we were almost done with repairs, that Leon Lockwood told me who owned the horse. It belonged to Joe Smith, the man who ran the township landfill and to whom, four years earlier, we had given a springer spaniel pup. I had seen Joe's horse Toby in the pasture beside his barn. That horse had traveled three miles without getting hit or causing an accident—at least as far as we knew. Joe didn't have a telephone, so I drove over to the landfill and found him sitting on a discarded hot water heater, staring into the distance.

He probably had told his story several times that day, lamenting how someone had stolen Toby. I cut him off right away and gave him the good news. His eyes filled with tears and he vowed to pay for any damage. I told him there had been none and that it gave our golfers another good story about the weird things you see when you spend a day in The Boondocks.

"SON-OF-A-BITCHING piece of junk." I slammed the socket wrench down on the workbench and stared at the mower.

It was the third time I had taken the gearbox cover off the Toro greens mower, gotten into its innards, and calibrated every possible adjustment. I had installed new seals and gaskets and it should have been as good as new. I started it up, confident I had done it right this time, but increasingly apprehensive. The instant I shifted it into gear, it stalled out.

"What's the matter, Daddy? Did you break something?"

Pat must have come in while I was fooling with the mower. I wondered how long he had been standing there, tossing the ball up, catching it with his new glove.

"Yeah, my heart. My bank account. This greens mower. Whatever I touched, it broke."

Pat threw the ball to me and when I caught it I got grease on his brand-new official league baseball. I took a clean shop rag and wiped it off, then wiped my hands. When I tossed the ball back to him, he looked at it.

"See? Can't even tell. You didn't ruin my ball, did you, Daddy?"

He came up and stood by the greens mower, studying it carefully.

"It looks okay to me, Daddy. Why are you mad at it?"

"It's not the mower's fault, Pat. It's me. Equipment hates me. Nobody likes me because I'm old, fat, and dirty, and my feet stink."

Pat hugged my leg. "You're not fat, Daddy. And I like you anyhow. That's something, right?"

MARCY WAS QUIET AT DINNER and I had a feeling about what was coming after the kids were in bed.

"We're low on money again," she said.

"Goddamn it, how can that be? There was that $1,500 loan from Kent and it seems like just last week I was signing papers refinancing the place."

"I hope you're not goddamn-ing me. It was two months ago, actually. And it went the same place it always goes."

"I wasn't goddamn-ing you, Marce. It's just that we worked up a budget and projected expenses and figured that would hold us until the first of the year. Then I should get a good raise at the institute and—"

"And we're going to need that. And more income from the course or somewhere before the season's over."

We sat at the table under our shared cloud of doom and gloom.

"What I don't get," I said, "is where it went. I mean, despite the weather, play has actually been not that far below what we projected and—"

"You really want to know? Okay, here it is in living black and white and red."

Marcy got out the checkbook and the thick manila folder with all the receipts for bills paid and all the invoices for bills yet to pay. Every dime that had been spent and the many dimes still owed for absolutely essential items. Wages for Mary Joseph, Mike, Danny, Kenny and the other part-timers. Standard Oil for fuel. Grass Lake Bank for mortgage payments. O.M. Scott for fertilizer and seed. Kids' orthodontist and dental bills. Ford tractor payments. The Smedley land contract. Spalding, Wilson, Acushnet, and MacGregor for golf supplies. And more.

"How far behind are we on payments?" I asked. "Has it hurt our credit rating? Are we overdue with major creditors—the bank, Scott's, the tractor payment?"

"No, I'm still operating from your long-standing edict. Remember? We shalt not get into the threatening letter stage or damage our standing with major creditors? Well, we're okay as far as that goes. But we're so tight on finances it's taking its toll in other ways."

I knew what she meant, and while there was no way we could increase our revenue significantly in this depressed economy, maybe we could cut expenses somewhere. Let's see.

We couldn't save a cent on wages. These young people were already making less than they were worth. A dollar and a half an hour. Hell, I was making a dollar and a half an hour at Sylvan Glen fifteen years earlier when you got back a few cents in change from a quarter when you bought a loaf of bread or a hamburger or hot fudge sundae or pack of cigarettes or a gallon of gas. Now most of those things cost two or three times more and these kids were still making a measly dollar and a half.

Fuel? Yes, that was way over budget, even though we were already nursing every ounce. Until we started getting some decent rains the fairways had been dormant and we didn't have to expend fuel and spend man hours mowing them. But we still had to run the pump engines to get water to the greens.

Fertilizer? We were so far below what we should be putting on the fairways they looked sparse long before the drought. The greens were getting less than the needed nutrients already. No way to save on fertilizer.

The marketing budget is always a good target—except we didn't have a marketing budget. In fact it hurt us that we spent so little promoting the place. We had lots of good, free publicity in articles done on the place. Every time an article appeared, we got a spurt of new business. The free ads I got from the *Grass Lake News* in exchange for my sports articles and photographs helped. But we couldn't afford ads where a continuing campaign could really make a difference, in the *Ann Arbor News*, the *Jackson Citizen-Patriot*, and the weeklies in Manchester and Chelsea.

Our marketing strategy, such as it was, was to draw golfers from the crowded courses in Ann Arbor and Jackson while introducing the game to new clientele in the country. Our problem was that we couldn't follow through on it because we didn't have the money to advertise or promote. And once a newspaper has done a story on the place, that's it until there is some new news.

Item after budget item, the story was the same. In our first two seasons of operation, we had spent less—and usually ridiculously less—than we should have to launch and sustain, let alone build up, a new business.

Marcy sat there, just watching me as I went through the files. She tapped a stack of invoices.

"Those are the ones yet to be paid. Every month I go through this—which do I pay, which can I set aside for a week, a couple weeks maybe without hurting our credit rating. I hate this, Bill. I hate it, hate it, hate it." She looked at me and there was nothing I could say. "I know what you say about not being overdue on a bill. About keeping our credit rating perfect. I agree with you that's important and we've done it. But at what cost? I don't want to juggle money like this forever."

For the first time, it hit me what the problem was. What the real problem was. This wasn't working because it couldn't work. It was doomed from the start and I never realized it. Pouring every cent you had, going in debt for lots of cents you had yet to earn. Working full-time in a position most people would consider a great gig. Get a good raise, pour it into the golf course. Sell an article or short story, put the check into the golf course account.

The litany had no end. The peanuts raised from selling the pool table, the sitar. Driving fifteen-year-old cars bought for $80. The kids going five years now without a true family vacation trip. Pumping your own blood, sweat, and tears and those of your wife and four little kids into the place every waking hour away from the job, from school. And there were the others who had contributed without taking a penny. Hank Dubois, Henry Samyn, Marcy's father and sisters—anyone who chanced by. It wasn't enough. And it would never be enough.

When was it that this stopped being the realization of a dream and became a masochistic obsession? When was it that we started re-enacting the Myth of Sisyphus, rolling that boulder up the hill, almost to the peak, only to have it roll back down—again and again and again.

"Undercapitalized," I said. "Everything we've all put into it is not enough. What they say about it being impossible to build your own golf course is dead solid right on. Oh, you can build one, all right. And we did. But you can't build the kind of course we wanted to and live to tell about it. A course that doesn't tear up the existing land and impose some formula design on it. An ecologically defensible course that doesn't pour on chemicals and destroy wildlife habitat. You can't build a modest course in the country and generate enough revenue to ride out an economic downturn like this county has seen since we opened."

"Or a drought" Marcy said, "that bakes your fairways. It's not as though you could have foreseen a recession and a drought hitting at the very time we opened the course. And then continuing for two years."

"We didn't have grandiose expectations," I said. "But you can't even make it into a break-even business without adequate money to ride out the down times. You need money to buy time, and you need time to build a base."

Several times earlier that summer, incensed by the drought, I had blustered about closing the place. Marcy had said simply, "You just can't shut down in the middle of the season. That's not fair to anyone. Including yourself."

We sat there a while, each of us going over it for the nth time in our minds, saying nothing. It was quiet in the house. Down the road, the Walkers' German shepherds started up over something and Rusty and Blazer perked up.

"My mistake," I said, "one of many, I admit, was that I thought we'd be different. I thought we could build up enough play fast enough to meet expenses the first year. And we did. As far as the IRS is concerned, bizarrely we actually made a profit. But in this economy, no way could we make enough to fund up an underground water system. And anymore that's what golfers expect, even on a public course in the country."

"I had hoped we could consider eventually building a nice clubhouse in the barn, or better yet out on the Smedley Hill." I thought about it. "You know, that hill is really the prime spot for a clubhouse. We have the access lane coming in from Phal Road. Yeah, all you'd have to do is renumber the holes, make number seven the first hole and—"

"God, Bill, listen to yourself."

"What?"

"You're still doing it. For a minute there I thought you finally got it into focus, that you saw the reality. Now, here you go again, envisioning a future that's never going to happen. Not unless you have some magic you haven't told me about."

She was right, of course.

The reality was that stack of unpaid invoices. The reality was the two-season track record. My friend Jack McGrath once told me as we stood in line at the two-dollar window, "Don't ever bet that a horse will do something it's never done before. If a trotter you're liking has to run 2:02 to win and the best it's ever done is 2:04, find another horse."

The reality was the stagnant local economy. Before we moved to Grass Lake, there were several major manufacturing plants in the area employing hundreds. One by one, they cut back shifts, then closed down or moved to southern states.

The reality was the worst drought in this part of Jackson County since records were kept. The reality was that the longer the drought continued, the more the course suffered, the more the play fell off, the more the bills piled up, the greater the refinanced mortgage balance grew. If there was a miracle out there somewhere to change that reality, it could manifest itself anytime now.

There was nothing new to say and no new way to say the old things.

"One thing I've wondered about for a long time," Marcy said. "You haven't been satisfied since we opened this place. I mean, not like I thought you would be. And you looked forward to this for, how long?"

I didn't have to think long about it. "Since I caddied for my brother Bob that first time at Sylvan Glen when I was ten years old."

"I remember the first day we met," Marcy said, "on that coffee date in Ypsilanti. I hadn't known you an hour and you were telling me you were going to build a golf course. Now you've done it. But even last year, when play was better and the money concerns weren't as bad, even then you didn't really enjoy it, did you? And yet you said you always wanted to have a golf course."

"No, I didn't say I wanted to have a golf course. I said I wanted to build a golf course. This was about building The Boondocks, not owning a golf course."

Marcy stared at me.

"Oh, that's clever. The old debater parsing words again. I sure wish I had known about that fine distinction before I signed on for this. Here I am, up to my eyebrows in paperwork. Listening to golfers telling me their entire round, shot after boring shot. Like I give a damn they finally broke fifty? And in the meantime, the rest of it doesn't go away. The kids. The house. All of it. And now you're telling me you never really wanted to have a golf course in the first place? Excuse me, but just what would you have done with the golf course once you had built it?"

I tried hard not to be a smart aleck, but the truth was just what I said: "In the best of all possible worlds, we would have built it, just like we did. Then when it was done, I would have played a round on it, just one round. Then walked away."

We sat there a while, both stunned by what I had said.

"I guess I knew going in that for me there's no romance to running a golf course," I said. "After a while, it's no more fun than running a pizza parlor or a dry cleaners."

"Tell me about it," Marcy said.

Thirty-Eight

O ctober 15, 1971, was a jewel of a Michigan autumn day, the kind that makes you want to jump into a pile of crinkly leaves and then take a big bite of a cinnamon doughnut and wash it down with a swig of just-pressed apple cider.

Marcy and I escorted Kent and June Smedley out of the tiny church and into the brilliant sunshine. As they kissed one more time for the camera, they did not look in the least like a pair of septuagenarians; they looked like a couple of school kids, ignoring the final bell warning that recess is over. They'd take their chances, lingering after the others were gone, holding hands where nobody else could see them.

GEORGE WOLFE, THE AREA'S OLDEST old-timer, said if it was all the same with me, he would rather come over to our place. He had agreed to let me interview him for an article that would run in the *Grass Lake News* to promote sales of the centennial commemorative brochure. My book had triggered a flurry of letters to the editor asking for more articles on the colorful history of Grass Lake and Jackson County, so Bob Mather asked me to write an article featuring George Wolfe's recollections.

George was over ninety but his mind and memory were sharp. He had been helpful to me the previous year in providing information and opening doors to further sources. We talked for a while in the house, then George asked if I minded if we walked around outside for a while. He was wiry and spry for his years and he strode quickly to the opening in the fence that led from the backyard to the practice green. He bent down and stroked the closely mown grass.

"How short you mow this?"

"We had it down to seven sixty-fourths through September. Now that we're almost into November we're letting them go a bit longer. Another mowing or two and that's it for the winter. These greens have had a rough two years. It took until June before they got vigorous again."

"Never thought I'd see grass like that on this place," George said. He stood up and pointed toward the barn. "See right there, where you've got your pro shop in the underside of the barn and that wall butts up against the milk house? Well right on that big round cement slab you've got the picnic table on, that was the foundation for the great silo Nate Fish built. Built it out of glazed tiles and it was about the best-looking silo anywhere around these parts."

I recalled that when we moved in and were cleaning up around the barn, I had found a few broken pieces of shiny tile, the color of burnished copper. I described the tiles I had found to George.

"They would have come off that silo, all right. Worked fine for old Nate for years. When he wasn't wasting his time on popcorn, he was partial to green manure silage. Had that silo packed right on up to the peak, and it was a tall one, higher than your barn peak."

"What happened to the silo, George?"

"Well, this place has always been known as a strong magnet for bad luck. So, no surprise when up comes a big lightning storm and flash, bam! Big bolt of lightning hits the silo's lightning rod but either it isn't grounded right or it's the fumes from that silage or maybe both and BOOM! That silo blows and there's tiles raining down all over and green silage pasted all over the west side of your house, and the barn, and the milk house. By God, it was everywhere."

George looked around and shook his head. "Folks far away as Sharon Valley Road claimed they heard the explosion. More than likely if they heard anything it was just another thunderclap from that storm, but once they heard about the exploded silo, it made a better story every time they told it. Those things, it gets to where even if it didn't happen, it should have."

He walked a ways away, to a spot

perhaps fifty feet from the pro shop door and seventy or so feet from the back porch of the house. He leaned up against the railing of the bag rack and looked down at the concrete slab that we had been told was, more than fifty years ago, the foundation for Nate Fish's wind-driven corn sheller. George looked down at it a long while.

He looked up at me, nodding his head, and said, "This is where it happened."

"Where what happened?"

"Nate's accident. This very spot. I know because I came out and had a look for myself when the word got around town. Still got the newspaper stories at home in a trunk somewhere. I'm guessing it was 1916, maybe 1917, when it happened."

"George, you know what happened to Nate?"

"Ought to. Everybody did back then. Like I say, it was big news, Nate and the corn sheller." He walked around the slab, showing with his arms how the rig was set up. "Used to be a steel-frame windmill

tower right here, right smack over this foundation slab. Now, if you scraped an inch or two of that gravel away to expose the whole slab, you'd see the four holes at each corner where it was bolted down with steel eyebolts into lead concrete anchors. Yep, that's where the sheller stood. And that's where Nate Fish bought the farm, as they say. You must have heard all this before."

"Well, we heard that Nate died after a strange illness or an accident but no one ever seemed to know the real story."

"You know, people back when it happened, they said it was his own temper cost him his life."

"How would that be?"

"Well, if he hadn't been railing on his wife that day maybe she wouldn't have picked up and left. And even after he had got himself trapped like that, if she'd been in the house, she'd have heard his yelling for help. She could have shut down the rig and got him out before he lost all that blood. See, there was a lever to shift the rig out of gear so the big windmill vanes up there would run free, instead of turning the gears hour after hour and him with his hands caught up in there."

George walked round and round the slab, shaking his head.

"He still would have had him a pair of mangled hands, might've lost 'em both, and that would have only made him meaner, but he'd have still been alive. Least that's how the reasoning went then. I recall it was your neighbor down the road, Loyall Walker, found him. Passing by and he sees Nate's legs sticking out, pointing straight up in the air, still kicking after his arms been seized up in those gears Lord knows how long. Hours, anyhow. Loyall's tough as cowhide, but it shook him up real bad. Kept saying, Oh, the blood, the blood. That's all he would say, over and over. Wouldn't say another word about it then. Or since."

George and I looked at the spot for a while.

"Didn't die right away, you know," George said. "No sir. They got him into your house there, white as a sheet he was, but still breathing. Doc patched up what was left of his arms and they right away had phoned down to his brother in Ohio, get up here right away. Took him a few hours, but Nate was still alive when he got here."

"They called the brother so he'd be here at the end?"

"No, no. Doc had heard about a new operation, never been done in Michigan before. They figured it was Nate's only chance, so they gave it a try. Put Nate on a mattress on the floor and his brother they laid on a makeshift pallet higher up. Tapped into the brother's arm and ran a hose right down into Nate's arm."

"A blood transfusion? Directly from brother to brother?"

"That's right. Never been done before in the state of Michigan. Well, Nate's color came back, he opened his eyes and mumbled something. For a few hours they thought he was going to make it. Then he took a turn and they lost him. See, they didn't know much about different types of blood in those days. Blood is blood, they figured. Especially among kin. 'Course it could have been the shock or some other complication did him in. Or maybe he didn't want to live with no hands."

George turned and looked at the house for a while. He nodded

slowly, remembering.

"Right there in your front room, it was. First blood transfusion and Nate Fish's last breath. Guess his wife was wrong, after all."

"Wrong how? For leaving him that day?"

"Nope. Wrong for always saying Nate Fish was too mean to die."

Thirty-Nine

Overnight several inches of soft granular snow fell. With the white dusting on the evergreens, with the house and red barn standing out against a clear blue sky, the place looked more like a Christmas card scene than a golf course in winter.

Mark reported right away that the snow was the kind that scraped easily off the ice on the ponds. That meant the hockey game was on. This was our sixth winter since moving to the Nate Fish farm in 1966, and the kids measured time by weather milestones, among which solid ice for skating was one of the most anticipated. That meant much more than just the first skate of the season. It also meant a big bonfire built from an immense pile of prunings and brush alongside number one pond. It meant sloppy joes and hot cocoa. And it meant the Haneys against the Duboises in a family hockey game.

This would be an ideal day for it. Best of all, there was not a breath of wind and the temperature hovered just below freezing, cold enough to keep the ice firm and fast but warm enough that you could skate with just a light jacket, as long as you kept moving.

After breakfast and the search for skates, hockey sticks, and a puck, there was the long ordeal of getting everyone dressed. Marcy got the food ready while I got the toboggan hooked up behind the tractor and started the shuttle service out to number one pond.

The kids complained at first that it was too cold but after chugging up and down the makeshift rink with snow shovels a few times to clear the ice for the hockey game they had been promised, they began peeling off layers—first the heavy winter coat, a few minutes later a sweatshirt, finally one of the two sweaters. In a few minutes the kids were generating their own heat and had noses and cheeks like strawberries.

While the kids scraped the ice, defining the rink with ridges of piled snow, I got the fire going. Over the months we had built an impressive pyramid of brush and prunings.

I made a separate small burn pile, separating the wood so the entire pyre wouldn't be consumed at once. A few feet away I set up a propane grill for the big kettle of Marcy's special-recipe sloppy joes and a huge pot of hot cocoa dragged out on the toboggan, Mark in charge of keeping the lids tight and the pots from tipping over.

The kids cleared off the ice so well it was a glistening smooth blue sheet. Never sure when Hank and his kids would show up, we took a break and sat around the fire. The kids were well into the hot cocoa when we heard the Dubois family shouting to us as they approached along our path in the snow.

There weren't enough skates and hockey sticks to go around but that made little difference. Rummaging through the woodpile, we found three stout limbs that looked as if they had been grown for the sole purpose of serving as hockey sticks. As for skates, even wearing big clunky boots, Hank and the bigger Dubois boys could move faster than the smaller kids on skates. Some of the skates had double runners and others were long overdue for sharpening. Easy to tell which kids didn't have ankle supports in their skates. Their feet would splay outward and instead of being up on the blades, they would slide along on the inside of the skate shoe. I remembered that frustrating feeling.

We outfitted each goalkeeper with a snow shovel in place of a goalie's stick and because there were no goalie pads, it was strictly against the rules to raise the puck off the ice when shooting—to do so would mean instant banishment, and the threat of a whack upside the head with a goalie's stick. There was no net, just a log on either side of the goal. Jen was one of the quickest-thinking goaltenders. Whenever a big kid had a break-away and was skating in on Jen for an easy shot, she would reach out a boot and hook a log and instantly shrink the size of the goal mouth. With her big snow shovel centered, there would be only two or three inches on either side as a target.

When one game was done, we shuffled players to give the los-ers an advantage and kept swapping bodies until everyone scored and played on a winner. We played until our calf muscles cramped up when we took breaks to sit by the fire.

As the sun sank in the west, the temperature plummeted. Hank and his kids trudged back to their van parked by the barns. I gave my kids a toboggan ride back to the house, but only after a long detour to the Crossroads at south ridge plateau, where I swooped down the slopes to make the kids shriek with fake panic. I left them in the mud-room, peeling out of their snow-caked togs, then went back alone to the hockey pond to bring in the pots, pans, and hockey gear.

As evening fell the wind died back and the fire glowed invitingly. I sat on a nearby log and watched the blood-red sunset. A new front was moving in and the temperature was dropping quickly. The ice was solid and clear now, smooth as glass.

I got my skates and long socks from the toboggan and put them close enough to the fire to warm. As I laced up, I could see a nearly full moon rising; its light and the glow from the fire would be enough to see by for a couple last circuits around the ice sheet. No telling when a guy might get another chance for skating this good.

1·9·7·2

Forty

As usual, it took longer to sink in with me than it did for Marcy—life was not as enjoyable as it should be and something had to change.

I couldn't keep working at the university, publishing other people's books on the side, pursuing my own writing, and continue to work on the golf course and try to develop it as a viable business. Marcy had made a decision and it was a firm one—she would not manage the pro shop another year. She would get a job if necessary and she would keep up the paperwork, record-keeping, and bill-paying. But she had to cut the all-day tie to the pro shop to be the kind of mother to four young kids that she demanded of herself.

So, it seemed that there were four options.

Option One. I could give up my job at the university. Not feasible. Not remotely feasible. Our primary concern was the well-being of the family. That meant we had to have an income to handle all the customary expenses of a family of six, plus the financial obligations already incurred for the golf course. Throughout these five and a half years, the kids had never done without anything important. They were well fed and had not only plenty of intellectual and physical stimulation, but also whatever medical and dental care was needed. They liked their home and the land. We didn't take typical vacations but their lives were full of books and music, fresh vegetables from our gardens, sports and pets, and they probably spent more time with their parents than did most kids. And they knew they were helping to create something worthwhile. To have all that, we had to have a secure, steady income from my employment.

So Option One was a nonstarter.

Option Two. I could give up developing and publishing books for others. Okay, I could do that and it would free up a few hours here and there. It would have very little financial impact because the modest fees I might forgo were never predictable and never factored into our budgeting. So I would stop those activities. But Option Two by itself wouldn't do it.

Option Three. I could quit writing. Marcy and I both knew that wasn't going to happen, ever. She said, in effect, You may be tough to live with now, but I don't want to be around you if you even tried to stop writing.

Option Four. Sell the golf course. Unthinkable. Yes, we built the golf course to build it, as a creative venture, but we didn't have in mind selling it after nearly four years of construction and only two years of operation. Unthinkable. The buildings would have to go with the property and we certainly wouldn't want to live in this house with daily reminders right outside our door of all we had poured into the place. It would be dreadful to be spectators to changes a new owner would inevitably make, so to sell the course would mean we would have to move. Unthinkable.

And yet.

And yet, because we had built the course primarily for what we would gain from the experience itself, for the process and not the results, maybe it wasn't totally unthinkable.

Maybe there was more to that flip answer I gave Marcy a while back than I realized at the time. As I blurted out then, it was true that what I really cared about was just the building of a course, not owning one. It took us close to four years to build The Boondocks. We had launched it successfully, run it two years as well as anyone with our resources might in the face of the depressed economy and brutal weather. As far as the Internal Revenue Service was concerned, the venture had been profitable for two years and if the place sold for, say, $150,000 we would have capital gains tax to pay once a sale was completed. We had grown the place to enough maturity that it was a respectable golf course with good potential as a business. Was it really important to us that we be the ones to realize that potential? Did we really want to run the place as a proper business?

We had cleaned up 110 acres that had long been abused. We healed its wounds and patched its scars. We planted hundreds of trees and established turf that secured fragile soil from further erosion. We had cleansed Marcy's woods. Without harming a delicate wetlands, we built ponds that attracted birds and fish and animals. We had done all that and no one and nothing could take that away.

And, in the process, we learned some secrets about the place and some things about ourselves.

When we finally looked at the issues and options in those lights, considered each alternative—even the unthinkable ones—I was no longer amazed at the conclusion we reached: The course would stay. We would leave.

We would sell The Boondocks, but we would take the essence of the place with us. The friendships were eternal, the memories indelible. That is what each of us would carry away and keep for the rest of our days.

Mark would remember the most of the four kids and his memories would be the sharpest. From then on, every time he picked up a rock, his fingers if not his mind would recall the countless thousands of stones, pebbles, boulders he handled on this place. He would remember the first fossil. The first tractor ride. A sprint back to the barn to fetch a socket set. The time his boot got mired, trapping him in the quicksand-like mud and he had to be lifted free, the boot extracted separately. One day he might return to see a Colorado blue spruce he planted as a seedling now thirty feet tall and Miz Johnson's maple trees grown to a shady copse. He might sit on the big pink boulder by two green and wonder why in the world he had named it the blue rock.

Jen would remember playing in the corn crib and hiding in the granary and the other secret spaces in the barn. She would remember hockey games on number one pond, warming by the bonfire with hot cocoa and sloppy joes. Some future cool morning might trigger thoughts of trudging out at dawn to the pro shop, making a pot of coffee for the first foursomes, selling previously owned balls from the tub on the counter. She would remember those mornings when she was in charge, the one responsible, at age nine, for the pro shop at The Boondocks.

Pat would someday be a terrific athlete and a fine golfer but would never have a thrill in sports bigger than his first par. He would remember that as a six-year-old he laced a tee shot 80 yards on the par three number two, hit a perfect five iron onto the front edge of the green, then knocked in a 30-foot putt. He would remember racing around those acres with a ball, any kind of ball, playing anything with anybody he could talk into a game. He would smile secretly at how the adult golfers marveled that this little tyke would play, on a hot summer afternoon, two, three, four rounds and never tire.

Beck would take away mostly secondhand memories, stories told by her brothers and sisters of the days she toddled about the place, playing with the litters of Siamese kittens and springer spaniel puppies. She might not remember but would hear about the time, as a four-year-old, she wandered away from the baby sitter. She walked the half mile from the house to number seven green where we were working, her arrival signaled by a deer she scared up along the way, her mother gasping to see this toddler stumbling down the hill and across the land bridge, marsh on the one side, deep pond on the other.

Marcy could fill a book with her memories. And should. They would not all be happy, but many would be priceless. Doing whatever was necessary to turn a hundred-year-old house into a pleasant home, whether that meant painting, wallpapering, carpeting, or stuffing a new shear pin in a coal-stoker worm gear. Learning to drive not only a clutch shift, but also tractors and trucks. Feeling that weird sensation on the nape of her neck at the spot of Nate Fish's last accident.

Long after the pressures and pains of the place had ebbed away, Marcy would savor the memories of solitary walks under a soft snowfall into her oak woods with the dogs, as spiritual an experience as any she had known. And her visits to the secret place, the hidden knoll in the marsh where she could feel in her bones the Indian rituals of centuries ago.

Perhaps for Marcy, the proudest takeaway would be the simple fact that she had prevailed, had overcome being a stranger in a strange land. When she walked onto the old Nate Fish's place, she opened a door that time would never close. She had discovered how the outdoors fed her spirit, how she felt most at home in the country. Her most cherished memories of this place would have nothing to do with the golf course and everything to do with the place, the land itself, and the person she had become there.

What I would take away was something for which I hadn't bargained. It was all those things Marcy and the kids had done with me, had done for me. It was something emerging in me now that I recognized as a sense of relief. It was the growing awareness that with this change, some future day I would have the time and the juice to do other things. And there was one thing more I would carry with me. It was a lesson learned: a dream fulfilled is a dream vanished.

THE KIDS TOOK IT WELL, with varying mixtures of sadness, apprehension, regret, relief, and indifference. They had learned about loss. Since we had moved to the country, they had seen a grandmother die and their ponies given away. They had seen their first dog, Yukon, leave to make their home safer. They had watched the birth of one litter of puppies and three of kittens, had played with the cuddly, furry things, then seen them off, one by one, to new owners. They had seen me bury too many strays and a few of our own pets. They knew now that nothing is forever and if you plant trees and seeds, they might grow into something.

Marcy and I also had gotten better at handling loss than we would have preferred. Hank Dubois learned that Mary Jane had multiple sclerosis and other complications and abruptly moved the family to Casa Grande, Arizona, in the hope that the warmer weather would ease her discomfort. Marcy and I helped Hank fix up their house with new carpet and paint to make it salable. It was a wrench to see them go but a pleasure to do something for a man who had done so much for us. We lost Gladys Smedley, a person much more to us than one of life's great characters, a fiercely loyal friend and mentor, without whom there was no Smedley Hill for us, no forty-five acres, and without that land there may never have been The Boondocks Golf Course.

And we had lost any shred of innocence that might have remained about what it is to run a small business.

We knew we had yet to learn how time would deal with the loss of this place we had transformed with nearly six years of our lives, even as it transformed us.

We had long since lost the romance of the dream, the fuel that had stoked us the four years while we were building the course. When we were on the quest, we had no trouble sloughing off or dealing with setbacks, accidents, bad weather. But once the place was open, once we were running a business, things changed. Perhaps our resilience, stamina, and determination just got consumed by the act of creation and there was not enough left to make tolerable the prospect of continuing indefinitely the obsession that must dominate everything else. We had lost the thrill of the chase.

And when that happens, when you have run your course, there is only one thing to do—find another quest.

Forty-One

Gladys Smedley once told me that Grass Lake Township had not changed very much in her lifetime—and that meant since the turn of the twentieth century. When the big interstate highway from Detroit to Chicago was built in the 1950s, it was routed well north of the Village, so the little town shrank even smaller, and the township remained a quiet farming locale, literally off the beaten path.

"But as far as changes that made any real difference," she said, "to my mind, the biggest single thing that happened hereabouts is you folks building a golf course on our land and the old Nate Fish place. And as far as that goes, for the land and the wildlife and such, that was a change for the better."

Many of the kids who had worked on the course helped us move from the place. Mary Joseph, our baby sitter and pro shop girl, and her boyfriend Danny Campbell. The gentle giant Larry Lape, our first course maintenance employee who spoiled us for everyone who came after. And Lonny, Butch, Mike, Carol, Barbara, and all the others who had put their hands in at The Boondocks. They were so good-natured throughout the move that the trek from Grass Lake was enjoyable, if poignant.

Nearly all of the golf course equipment went with the sale, so nothing big had to be moved. But it still took two trips with the big rented moving truck and a convoy of tightly packed cars to convey the household goods eighteen miles from Grass Lake to our new place in the countryside nearer Ann Arbor.

If we thought our involvement with The Boondocks was over, we were quickly proved wrong. We had turned over the keys but retained a hefty land contract. And it took the new owners less than six hours to call me on my promise to give them a hand if they ran into problems. The day we moved the last of our goods, I stayed until well after dark showing one of the two new co-owners how to coax a balky greens mower engine to life and gave him another in an ongoing series of lessons on the idiosyncrasies of the several irrigation systems. We retained a lifetime membership in The Boondocks—and they loved the name and would never change it—so the umbilical would not soon be severed.

We had been so busy getting the new house ready, packing and moving, then making the old Nate Fish house clean and tidy for its new occupants, that it was not until a week after the move that I had a chance to do something that needed doing. So, one morning after showing the new operators of The Boondocks something or other about a piece of equipment, I took a drive.

I retraced the same route, as best I could remember it, that we had used that July day six years before when we first saw the Nate Fish farm and gave Daryle Heselschwerdt a $500 earnest-money check.

THERE IS BREEZY ACRES, with Henry Samyn heading out to his fields on his big John Deere, still missing Boots, I'm sure. Fishville Road and Christmas Tree Lane Farm, unchanged. I roll down the windows and hear the German shepherds barking loudly as Loyall and Edna Walker stand near the dog kennels, talking to a man leaning against a black sedan.

At the old Dubois house, the new residents haven't changed things much since we helped Hank and Mary Jane pack up for their move to Arizona. Little change too along Norvell Road, all the way into the Village. The ancient headquarters of the *Grass Lake News* looks just as it did more than a hundred years ago when it was the depot for the Michigan Central Railroad. The newspaper is still coming out weekly, but with Hank Dubois gone, the big roll-fed letterpress is long since silent and the paper is printed on a small, quiet, and efficient offset press.

I drive past the Dairy Freeze, where we had our first meal in Grass Lake. Then, before heading home, there are two more places to see and and one last swing past the golf course.

In the tiny cemetery, Nate's weathered headstone tilts to the west, but still stands amidst his parents, uncles, aunts, cousins, and children. Fishville Road running past still bears his family name and until the Walkers and the other old-timers pass on, The Boondocks will be referred to by them if no one else as the old Nate Fish place.

Turning off Fishville Road and onto Phal Road, I pass Horace Coppernoll's big spread, marveling as always at how much a loyal John

Deere owner must spend every year just in green and gold touchup paint. Then, a half mile along, I coast slowly past the bare clapboards of Ed Harrison's place. It doesn't appear that Mr. Harrison has erected an amusement park or a skyscraper in the week since we moved.

I know I won't see Kent; he has already moved to Addison and into the home of his bride Junie. He told me some time ago he had turned the Phal Road place over to relatives so it would be cared for decently until he decides what to do with it. And although it may be occupied, and although the grass is mowed and there's a car in the garage, the little house looks forlorn. Glad's garden is still neat from last year's cleanup. Kent committed no seeds this season, so no danger from the Day of the Rot.

I pull over onto the gravel shoulder and shut off the engine. From my recollection of Gladys's description, I'm parked at the very scene of her showdown with Ed Harrison in the Great Phal Road Barricade Incident. I look up the driveway. There's an empty chair beside Gladys's fire pit. No persnickety smoke and no fire.

I look as far as I can see past their backyard, beyond their pasture field to the crest of Smedley Hill, to the ridge where the newlyweds Gladys and Kent took their evening strolls. From there they would look down past the blackberry patch and sassafras tree, searching Willow Creek and its marsh for a pair of patrolling sandhill cranes. From that spot they would take in the whole of the south ridge and its sandy plateau, shaking their heads at the thought of Nate Fish trying to grow a stand of popcorn in that blow sand. And from that overlook on Smedley Hill, at the far extremity of their vision, they would see the old Nate Fish place, its house and barns, and at night the bluish glow of its mercury vapor light.

But from where I sit, The Boondocks Golf Course is over the hill and out of sight.

2·0·0·4

Forty-Two

A thousand times since the days of The Boondocks, when Marcy and I drive in the country, I look off to the distance. And there will be a long gentle sweep up a hill to a graceful crown, more than large enough for a kidney-shaped green with a sand trap nestled in the elbow guarding the approach. And there, off to the left by those twin oaks, the perfect spot for the next tee. Yes, and the next hole would be a majestic downhill par three that—

"Don't even think about it," Marcy will say.

"What?"

"You know what."

We are silent for a while.

"Doesn't hurt to look," I mutter.

"Look all you want, but just remember: one golf course per husband."

Acknowledgments

I thought we moved to the Michigan countryside to build a golf course.

And we did. But as it turned out, we built a lot of other things as well. Like friendships and memories. And not ours alone, for The Boondocks became a magnet that drew together people who might never have met otherwise. Farmers and rural handymen became pals with distinguished scholars and city folk. Strangers became friends. There were weddings and christenings; graduations and funerals. Lives were changed—we hope for the better—because there was The Boondocks Golf Course.

The building of that golf course was possible only because of the kind and helpful people mentioned in these pages—they volunteered or allowed themselves to be swept up in someone else's quest. To each of them, my thanks for breathing your life into another guy's dream. Truly, we drained a lot of blood, sweat, and tears of many people into that land, first to restore it to the way the glacier left it, and then to nestle a golf course within it.

Building the golf course was one thing. Doing a book to tell that story was itself an undertaking with a long gestation period. I knew that some years after we sold the course, the wounds would heal, time would afford a decent perspective on those events, and one day I could tell the story. What I didn't know was that thirty years would whisk by before I could do it. Then, in 2001, Beth Wareham and Rica Allanic at Simon & Schuster encouraged me to get on with it. I read a chapter aloud to author Jody Delzell and he insisted that I get out of my own way and get the rest of the story down. Once I had a manuscript in hand, Tom Wolfe was helpful at a critical moment.

Tom Ferguson read an early draft; surprisingly, he didn't wield his trademark editor's machete as vigorously as usual. David Rompf offered invaluable insights, suggestions, and encouragement.

The easiest decision was the choice of a publisher. I was pleased that two distinguished New York houses were interested in publishing this book. But as a long-time Midwestern book publisher myself, I have strong feelings about the importance of small regional presses. These presses are doing books that are worthwhile, and they limit themselves to a few carefully chosen titles. They do books out of an intense passion for the story told, and with profound respect for their authors and their readers.

To work with Doug Truax at Crofton Creek Press is to work with a publisher who helps create books the old-fashioned way: with collegiality, camaraderie, and an attitude of being a partner with an author on a worthy quest. He brings a wealth of experience as a publisher and devotes his many other talents to every book he undertakes.

Kate Petrella worked her editorial magic on the manuscript and cleansed it greatly. Kristen Milligan pitched in with a final proofreading. Joe Simko not only turned his fine artist's hand to the cover drawing, his drawings also captured eerily accurate images of scenes and incidents treated in these pages.

All of these people and others not mentioned here made contributions to this book for which my thanks are inadequate but heartfelt. As with The Boondocks Golf Course itself, any mistakes in the way I have told the story here is my fault and mine alone.